IN BANGKOK
Siam's Capital through Foreign Eyes, 1895-1935

IN BANGKOK

Siam's Capital through Foreign Eyes, 1895-1935

Edited by **Graham Jefcoate**

First published and distributed in 2024 by
River Books Press Co., Ltd
396/1 Maharaj Road, Phraborommaharajawang,
Bangkok 10200 Thailand
Tel: (66) 2 225-0139, 2 225-9574
Email: order@riverbooksbk.com
www.riverbooksbk.com

@riverbooks   riverbooksbk   Riverbooksbk

Copyright collective work © River Books, 2024
Copyright introductory texts © Graham Jefcoate
Copyright photographs © Graham Jefcoate,
except where otherwise indicated.

All rights reserved. No part of this book may be reproduced or transmitted in any form or by any means, electronic or including photocopy, recording or any other information storage and retrieval system, without prior permission in writing from the publisher.

Editor: Narisa Chakrabongse
Production supervision: Suparat Sudcharoen
Design: Ruetairat Nanta

ISBN 978 616 451 090 6

Cover illustrations: Rachel Wheatcroft, 'Wat Phra Keo Enclosure from the Outer Precincts', from *Siam and Cambodia* (1928), facing p. 94; 'An Austin Twenty at Bangkok, Siam' (1920). Mary Evans Picture Library.

Printed and bound in Thailand by Parbpim Co., Ltd

Dedicated to the memory of
Rongrucha Sihasurakrai who encouraged
my first visits to Bangkok
over thirty years ago.

Contents

Preface	8
Introduction: Bangkok in the Early Twentieth Century	13
Bound for Bangkok	23
First Impressions	43
Ice	53
The Sudden Death of an Engineer	56
Palaces and Royalty	58
Doing the Wats	66
Built Upon the Waters	72
The City of Magnificent Distances	76
Post and Telecommunications	92
Along New Road	95
An Up-to-Date Building for Business	98
Almost a Danish Colony?	101
Germans and the Great War	105
The People of Bangkok	114
One of the Truly Great Men of the World	136
Dinner at the Room of the Moon	139
Food Production	145
Ceremonies and Festivals	148
The Foreign Colony	154
Legations and Consulates	163
At Home	170
Shopping	181
Chummeries	190
Beer	194
X'mas	197
Language	201
Mias	206
Servants	209
Flora and Fauna	214
The Snake Farm	223
Night Life	227
Vice	253
Crime and Punishment	266
Missions	275
In School	283
Health and Hygiene	296
Sports and Games	313
Wongkit's Dream	320
The Press	324
Scholarly Pursuits	330
The Visual Arts	339
Tourists	345
The Aerodrome	365
What Price Progress?	369
The Protestant Cemetery	373
Going Home	377
Sources	382
Further Reading and Visits	387
Index	389

In Bangkok, by Berton Braley

In Bangkok, in Siam,
Twelve thousand miles from home,
The palms are waving gently
Beneath the blue sky's dome;
And brown-skinned smiling natives
In groups or lazy throngs
Slip by in boats and slim canoes
Upon the crowded klongs.

In Bangkok, in Siam,
The priests in yellow decked,
Go forth upon the city streets
For alms they may collect.
The little gharry-horses trot
Along the paced New Road
Where rickshas, cars and tiny trams,
Each bear their human load.

In Bangkok, in Siam,
They have a pleasant knack
Of chewing scarlet betel nut until their teeth are black -
But though their ways are different,
Their manners strange and queer,
At heart they're just about the same
As you and me, my dear;
In Bangkok, in Siam,
Twelve thousand miles from here.

The Popular Magazine, 7 September 1924, pp. 174-175

Preface

Verses from the poem *Bangkok* by the American writer Berton Braley (1882-1966) stand as epigraph to this book. Braley called himself a "modern minstrel", but he is probably best described as a popular versifier. He seems to have spent a very short time in the city during a world tour, mentioning in his autobiography only that he "went to Bangkok and didn't have any fun".[1] His poem, however, suggests the city made a stronger impression on Braley than he later cared to admit. It certainly recalls some of the topics that will become familiar in the following pages, including Bangkok's klongs, yellow-decked monks, betel-chewing people, and New Road with its "rickshas, cars and tiny trams".

In Bangkok is a collection of texts which, like Braley's, reflect the foreign experience of Bangkok, the foreigners in question including both long-term residents and short-term visitors. The focus is on the period from 1895 to 1935, in other words the final years of King Chulalongkorn (Rama V, who died in 1910), and the reigns of his successors King Vajiravudh (Rama VI, 1910-1925) and King Prajadhipok (Rama VII, 1925-1935).[2] This period might plausibly be called the heyday of western influence, ending as it does shortly before the historical break of the Second World War.[3]

The book can be seen as a companion to *Enchanted Land* (2023), an anthology reflecting the foreign experience of Chiang Mai and the north of Siam (as the country was officially known until 1939) in broadly the same period. Like *Enchanted Land*, it draws on a wide range of documentary sources in a variety of genres. In *In Bangkok*, they include official

---

1 Braley, *Pegasus Pulls a Hack*, p. 281.
2 Among the earliest texts are those of Henry Norman (1895) and Maxwell Sommerville (1897). The latest were published after the Second World War, although they recall earlier decades. Dates of publication are cited at the foot of texts, though these may of course be later (or much later) than the impressions recorded in the texts.
3 In 1941-1942, many westerners (including long-term residents) were interned or expelled in the wake of the Japanese invasion.

publications, directories, travel books and memoirs, novels and short stories, verses and inscriptions, and periodical articles. The book draws heavily on reports and advertisements from contemporary newspapers published both in Bangkok (especially *The Bangkok Times*, the English-language "newspaper of record") and in Singapore.

As many visitors remarked, Bangkok was not an ancient city: the young Chakri dynasty had only established a new capital there in 1782, some fifteen years after the fall of Ayutthaya to Burmese invaders. Foreign missionaries, diplomats and merchants took up residence, as they had at the old capital, notable dates being 1828 (when the American Presbyterian Mission was established) and 1856 (when the first British consul was appointed under the so-called Bowring Treaty). By the early twentieth century, Bangkok's status was assured: according to A. Cecil Carter, it had become "the chief city of Siam in every sense":

> It is the chief port, the chief commercial centre, the centre of the Government, and principal residence of the king and royal family".[4]

If diplomats, missionaries and "teak-wallahs" are the groups most strongly represented in *Enchanted Land*, then Bangkok's resident westerners were engaged in a much wider range of businesses and professions. By the end of the nineteenth century, they had established their own religious, medical, social and recreational institutions and had started a flourishing English-language press. A majority were Anglophone, though many European nations were represented.[5] Bangkok's improving accessibility by sea and rail encouraged international travellers to visit the city. In 1904, Carter observed their numbers were increasing "year by year". As it

---

4 Carter, *The Kingdom of Siam*, p. 106. Brief biographical information about many of the writers can be found in the text, often at their first appearance (for which see the index).

5 One French visitor described Bangkok as "an Anglo-Saxon tourist fief", regretting that so few French travellers ventured there (*The Bangkok Times*, 20 November 1926, p. 6).

happens, it was in 1904 that the first printed "traveller's guide" appeared.[6] After the Great War (as the First World War is called here), the number of visitors increased further. In 1928, *The Bangkok Times* reported that there was "no end to the visitors to Bangkok who feel impelled to write and subsequently print their impressions of the 'jewel city of Asia'".[7]

One of those early post-war visitors was the young American "tramp" Harry L. Foster. In his *A Beachcomber in the Orient*, published in 1923, Foster gave his chapter on Bangkok the title "The City of the Great White Angels". He explained:

> The Siamese, with their love of pomp, are very fond of grandiloquent titles. The river's full name is the Menam Chow Phya, meaning "The Grand Duke of Waterways." Bangkok's complete name signifies "The City of the Great White Angels".

In fact, neither Bangkok's "complete name" nor its short form in Thai (*Krung Thep Maha Nakhon*) precisely signify "The City of the Great White Angels", but that is the point of mentioning Foster's mistranslation here. The present book is not a history of Bangkok in the early twentieth century, but rather a mosaic of impressions, memories and observations about the city and its "foreign colony" by foreigners. It reflects their experience, their insights and perceptions, but also their misperceptions, as in the case of Foster's "great white angels". The coverage is not comprehensive, and some imbalances and omissions will be apparent to anyone familiar with the history of Bangkok and its foreign communities.

Bangkok was a creation of all its communities, both Siamese and non-Siamese. The great majority of the non-Siamese residents of Bangkok during the period were not westerners but migrants from elsewhere in Asia, and particularly from China. I have tried, however inadequately, to acknowledge their role in the book. I have also included a few texts written by Asians themselves (Chinese, Japanese, Indians and Siamese) but only

---

6 According to the titlepage, J. Antonio's 1904 *Guide* was "revised" by the Bangkok journalist William W. ("Bill") Fegen (d. 1940). This might suggest a previous, unrecorded edition but probably indicates Fegen revised Antonio's English text.

7 *The Bangkok Times*, 11 August 1928, pp. 9-10.

if they were published in English (or in one instance French) for a largely foreign readership. People of mixed race ("Eurasians") were frequently the subject of prejudice and condescension. I have included texts which reflect this, but also some which take a more enlightened view.

In Bangkok is intended (like *Enchanted Land*) to be read and enjoyed; it is not a scholarly edition to be studied. The texts are sometimes introduced and briefly annotated but, as far as possible, I have allowed the writers to speak for themselves. Many of the texts have been silently abridged and edited so that they can stand alone. Otherwise, no attempt has been made to standardise the spelling of Thai-language names and words; letter-casing and punctuation are generally as found in the sources; and differences between British and American spelling have been respected. I have not attempted an analysis of the collection as a whole beyond the remarks in the Introduction. Some suggestions for further reading and visits can be found as an appendix.

I would like to thank Ajarn Pam Akarapisan, who has transcribed a number of the texts. Most derive from my own collection or from digital copies of books and periodicals made available by libraries around the world.[8] I am grateful to the Siam Society for providing access to their copies of *The Bangkok Times* and *Siam from Ancient to Present Times*, and to the Landon Trust for permission to include excerpts from published works by Margaret and Kenneth Perry Landon.[9] Thanks are likewise due to the Mary Evans Picture Library, Martyn Gregory Gallery (London), Maryanne Stanislaw, and the descendants of C. B. Ainslie for permission to include a number of photographs from the family's albums.[10] In my

---

8 The author and publishers would be grateful for any corrections with regard to copyright that should be incorporated in future reprints or editions of this book.

9 *Siam from Ancient to Present Times* had been compiled to accompany the Siamese Kingdom Exhibition which was to be held in Lumpini Park in early 1926. Although the exhibition was cancelled by King Prajadhipok's government as an economy measure after the death of his predecessor, the souvenir volume was published as intended. Illustrations from the book (as also from *The Bangkok Times*) are reproduced by courtesy of the Siam Society.

10 G. R. Ainslie worked for the Borneo Company Limited in Bangkok, 1893-1898; his brother, C. B. Ainslie, worked for the company as a forest assistant in the north, 1900-1914.

research, I have used the collections of the Church of Christ in Thailand Archives at Payap University Library; the library of the École française d'Extrême Orient at Chiang Mai; the Damrong Rajanubhab Memorial Library (National Library of Thailand); the British Library; and the London Metropolitan Archives. I would like to acknowledge the help of the staff at all these institutions.

I am extremely grateful to Ronald Milne and Carol Biederstadt for reading, correcting and commenting on the texts in draft. Thanks are also due to many other friends and colleagues, but I should like to make special mention of Rebecca Weldon (for a new translation from the French), Malcolm Ward and David Lawitts (for their help in obtaining material from Britain and the United States), and Lucy Leonowens (who drew my attention to "Zulu" Fyshe's letter about Christmas in Bangkok in 1908). Translations from the German are by me. Janet Andrew has kindly supplied the index. As ever, Komson Teeraparbwong has supported my research and accompanied me on "field trips" to Bangkok. Finally, I would also like to thank my publisher, Narisa Chakrabongse, for suggesting the book and for her wise counsel, and also the team at River Books in Bangkok and London. Any editorial or interpretative errors are of course solely the responsibility of the author.

Chiang Mai, 2024

"An Austin Twenty at Bangkok, Siam", from *Illustrated London News*, 3 July 1920. The car is parked in front of the Throne Hall and the equestrian statue of the late King Chulalongkorn. This may be the same Austin Twenty pictured in *The Tatler* in the following year, when the owner was identified as C. G. Cranmer, Assistant Manager, Steel Brothers & Co., "sometimes known as the rice kings of the East". Mary Evans Picture Library.

Introduction:
Bangkok in the Early Twentieth Century

"What is Bangkok like?" asked an unidentified American missionary early in the century. As we shall find, he or she tried to answer the question by listing impressions (sights, sounds and smells, both pleasant and unpleasant) and by describing the city's "atmosphere". Travel writers (and writers of travel brochures) frequently used epithets to characterise the city. Apart from Foster's "City of the Great White Angels", those we shall encounter in the book include:

City of Wild Fruit Trees
Venice of the East
City of Klongs
Jewel City of Asia
City of Brilliant Diamonds
City of Palaces and Temples
City of Magnificent Distances, and
Heavenly-Royal City.

Some of these became established clichés, but few seem especially helpful in characterising early twentieth-century Bangkok. Other writers described the city – or were obliged to describe it – in less impressionistic terms.

Walter Armstrong Graham (1868-1949) was not untypical of his day, being a British civil servant who spent his entire career in the service not of the British but of the Siamese government. His systematic mind clearly made him the ideal author of the entries on Siam and Bangkok in the celebrated eleventh edition of the *Encyclopædia Britannica*, published in 1910-1911.[1] In the following year, his own, long-awaited *Siam: A Handbook of Practical, Commercial, and Political Information* appeared

---

1 Graham, 'Bangkok', in: *Encyclopædia Britannica*, 11th edition, vol. 3 (Cambridge and New York 1910-1911), p. 316 (signed: "W. A. G.").

in London, with "90 illustrations and a map".[2] In November 1912, the Bangkok store Harry A. Badman & Co. printed advertisements for the book in *The Bangkok Times*, praising it as "without doubt, the most comprehensive work on Siam yet published". As a Siamese government employee, Graham could be seen as an official spokesman, but there is no reason to believe that his accounts of Bangkok do not reflect his own views.[3] Certainly, anyone seeking information in English about Bangkok in the years after 1912 is likely to have started with one or both of Graham's accounts.

As one might expect, Graham's two accounts differ somewhat. His entry for Bangkok in the *Britannica* is conceived in typical encyclopedia style. Avoiding the various clichés about the city, he begins by emphasising its modernity:

> The whole town covers an area of over 10 sq. m. Two companies provide Bangkok with a complete system of electric tramways, and the streets are lined with shade-trees and lit by electricity.[4] All over the town are scattered beautiful Buddhist temples, which with their coloured tile roofs and gilded spires give it a peculiar and notable appearance. Many fine buildings are to be seen – the various public offices, the arsenal, the mint, the palaces of various princes and, in addition to these, schools, hospitals, markets and Christian churches of many denominations, chiefly Roman Catholic. There are four railway stations in Bangkok, the termini of the lines which connect the provinces with the capital.

Rather unexpectedly, he adds a paragraph about climate change: recently, the city had become "hotter and less humid".

---

2 A second edition followed in the same year, and a third in 1924, by which time more than sixty further illustrations had been added. An American edition had been published in Chicago in 1913.

3 Indeed, his views about the supposed physical characteristics of the Siamese ("not very prepossessing") cannot have endeared him to the people amongst whom he lived. Nevertheless, they were carried over into the 1924 edition.

4 Gerini claimed that Bangkok "already boasts of 120 kilometres of carriage roads [and] of 40 kilometres of electric tramway line, besides being entirely lighted by electricity" (*Siam*, 1912, p. xxiv).

Graham's *Britannica* entry continues with a description of Bangkok's port and its trade, in which he notes the importance of trade with the British Empire ("75%" of imports and exports). He briefly summarises the system of government, emphasising the role of "expert European assistance" (such as his own) in modernising the administration. He also mentions the so-called "extra-territorial rights" acquired by western powers after the Bowring Treaty, rights which Britain, for example, had only begun to relinquish with the new Anglo-Siamese Treaty of 1909. Graham next describes the multi-ethnic population of Bangkok ("estimated at 450,000") and the poor but "improving" sanitary conditions in the early years of the century. Finally, he provides a brief historical overview, emphasising the city's relative youth.

In his account of Bangkok in *Siam: A Handbook*, Graham makes a number of interesting additional observations.[5] Rather oddly, he begins by giving a much larger estimate of the city's population ("about 630,000" or "nearly one ninth part of the people of Siam"), perhaps in order to emphasise its significance for Siam as a whole. The relative size of the capital was a problem for the country, a theme that would later be taken up by others:

> Bangkok overshadows the rest of the country to an extraordinary extent and both Siamese and foreign residents and visitors are still too apt to think that to all intents and purposes the capital is the only part of the country which counts.

Graham continues with a brief historical account, including a description of the construction of the city to explain its present urban fabric, the city being "built very largely upon, or close beside, the river and the innumerable creeks and canals which were excavated with some degree of system at varying distances surrounding the Royal Palace". In recent decades, however, transport was no longer exclusively "by water": now there were "some eighty miles of well-laid out streets, crossing the old canals at a thousand points and lined with neat brick-built houses in which the erstwhile riparian

---

5 Graham, *Siam* (1912), pp. 21-26.

population now resides". Graham defends the aesthetic value of Bangkok's urban improvements, ending his account with a description that almost anticipates some of the tourist brochures of future decades:

> Before long Bangkok will be a city of bricks but it will be also a city of trees, the verdure of which, together with the graceful spires and bright-coloured roofs of its religious and public buildings, will always redeem it from the monotony of appearance which characterises many cities of the west.

Some contemporary writers found Bangkok "difficult to grasp" as an urban space. Somerset Maugham, for example, found it "strange, flat, confused". By European standards, its built heritage was hardly ancient. A number of writers referred to the city's "dual personality". For Noel Wynyard, for example, it was both "crude and disgusting" by day and a "fairyland" by night. Leigh Williams described what he called "inverse progress": Bangkok might boast electric trams and an aerodrome but these existed in a country which still had few viable roads.[6] "We have got a bridge across the Menam now", observed a Siamese resident in 1933, "but behind it the world ends for us again". As for its population, some asked where the Siamese were to be found in their own capital city in view of the fact that its streets were thronged by Chinese and migrants from elsewhere in Asia. Others reflected on the changes in Bangkok's urban fabric during the period and on the impact of the west on Siamese culture and society generally. Frank Carpenter described Bangkok simply as a "city of contrasts". Allister Macmillan concluded that its inherent contrasts and contradictions rendered any attempt to describe it convincingly all but impossible.

In describing Bangkok's urban lay-out in the early twentieth century, writers generally identified several distinct districts, all on the left bank of the river. If Carter had insisted in 1904 that, "unlike most other Eastern cities, there is no foreign quarter but the European houses are dotted about the city, the suburbs, the banks of the river, and the busiest part of the town", then the city map printed in Leipzig in 1914 clearly marks

---

[6] He might well have added the electric car (complete with charging-point) that was exhibited in Bangkok as early as 1911.

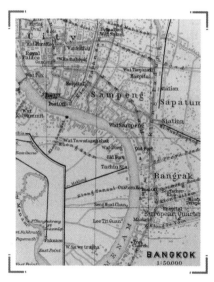

Bangkok map, Leipzig 1914 (detail).

the district south of Silom Road as the "European Quarter". In his entry for Bangkok in the directory *Glimpses of the East*, Tomoyuki Kawata attempted to explain its lay-out during the 1930s in a way that might usefully supplement Graham's:

> The city spreads south and east, following mainly the course of the river. The roads of the city have been much improved in recent years. In the northeast there are many magnificent boulevards, shaded by trees, royal palaces, princely residences in which is disclosed the landscape-gardener's art. It is also the seat of all the Ministers, all the big administrations and the centre of the intellectual, commercial and industrial life of the country. Here are to be found, close by the Menam Chao Phya, the Royal Palaces and Government offices, the chief places of worship, and a few big business houses. Sampeng (China town) is located to the south and then Bangrak, where banks and large European commercial firms are situated. In the north-east of the city, the Samsen and Dusit quarters contain palaces, princely residences and barracks. The private residences of Europeans, formerly grouped at Bangrak and Sapatum, now tend to spread towards the east and south-east. The right bank of the river is mostly occupied by Siamese, Chinese, and Mohammedan residents.[7]

---

7   Kawata, 'Siam' in: *Glimpses of the East* (1939), p. 5.

Introduction 17

To summarise: the Bangkok early twentieth-century residents and visitors knew extended along the left bank of the river towards the south and south-east, encompassing the central government area (with its palaces, ministries and *wats*), the Sampeng (where many Chinese people lived), Bangrak (where many European businesses were located), and the area of Suriwongse and Silom Roads (which some at least called the "European Quarter"). These districts were linked by the New Road, Bangkok's first paved road (constructed in the early 1860s for the convenience of western merchants), and later by the electrified tram service.

As Kawata pointed out, by the 1930s the residential areas were spreading farther to the south and south-east. Nevertheless, many of the areas of Bangkok most familiar to residents and tourists today lay beyond the boundary of the city proper in 1935. When for example, the Siam Society's new building opened in 1933, it was located among rice fields on the edge of the city. Reginald Le May had predicted that its members would be cooled there by "invigorating breezes". Today, the building is overshadowed by skyscrapers and stands near Asok, one of Bangkok's busiest intersections. Happily, the area along New Road/Charoen Krung Road (with its surviving built heritage) retains something of the atmosphere of a century ago and is currently enjoying a renaissance as one of Bangkok's "creative districts".

According to a character in Harry Hervey's novel *The Black Parrot* (1923), those in search of the "real Siam" (in effect, Bangkok) would not find it "in guidebooks" but rather in the city's floating underworld. In truth, the "real Bangkok" may not have been found in any single location. As Macmillan would have agreed, Bangkok was better understood through its inherent contradictions, bringing together, as it did, the "orient" with the "occident", beauty with squalor, the "Siamese" with the non-Siamese, tradition with modernity. These contrasts and contradictions, as experienced by the city's foreign residents and visitors, are the theme of the following pages.

Timeline, 1782-1942

1782	Foundation of Bangkok[1]
1828	American Presbyterian Mission established
1852	Mission's Boys' High School founded
1853	Protestant Cemetery opens
1855	Anglo-Siamese Treaty ("Bowring Treaty")
1856	First British and American consuls posted to Bangkok
	Borneo Company Limited opens Bangkok office
1864	First paved road (Charoen Krung/New Road) completed
1868	Accession of King Chulalongkorn (Rama V)
1869	Ladies' Library founded
1871	H. Swee Ho founded
1873	Windsor & Co. founded
1878	National Museum, B. Grimm & Co., and Falck & Beidek founded
1879	Kiam Hoa Heng & Co. founded
1882	Suan Kularb school founded
1884	Harry A. Badman & Co. founded
1886	First telephone exchange
1887	*The Bangkok Times* and the Oriental Bakery founded
	The Oriental Hotel opens in new premises
1888	S. S. Marican's firm founded
1889	Siam Electricity Company founded
1891	George McFarland opens "the first American dental office"
1892	British Dispensary founded
1893	Paknam Railway opens

---

[1] Some of the dates are derived from the contemporary sources cited in the text and have not been verified from other sources.

1894	Electric tram service starts
1896	German Club and R. Omoda's "International Toilet Saloon" open
1897	East Asiatic Company founded
	George McFarland opens the Smith Premier Store (typewriters)
	Sommerville, *Siam on the Meinam*
1898	Young, *Kingdom of the Yellow Robe*
1900	Bangkok Manufacturing Company founded
1901	Royal Bangkok Sports Club founded
1902	Campbell, *Siam in the XXth Century*
1903	British Club opens
	Siam Society founded
1905	National Library founded
1908	Lindenberg, *Kurt Nettelbeck* (novel)
1904	Antonio, *Guide*; Carter, *The Kingdom of Siam*
	Siam exhibit at the Louisiana Purchase Exposition, St Louis
1905	Act for the Regulation and Control of Hackney Carriages
	Christ Church opened
1906	Thompson, *Lotus Land*
1907	Landon, *'Mid Pleasures and Palaces*
1908	*Twentieth Century Impressions of Siam*; Young, *Siam*
1909	Anglo-Siamese Treaty
	First Bangkok Census
1910	Phathanakorn Film Company founded
	Frankau, *Let the Roof Fall In* (novel)
	Death of King Chulalongkorn, accession of King Vajiravudh (Rama VI)
1911	Coronation of King Vajiravudh; visit of Prince William of Sweden
	Siam exhibit at the International Exhibition of Industry and Labour, Turin

	Exhibition of Agriculture and Commerce
1912	Graham, *Siam: A Handbook*
	Siam Pineapple Factory founded
1913	Snake Farm (Queen Saovabha Memorial Institute) opens
	Reid, *Chequered Leaves from Siam*
1914	King Chulalongkorn Memorial Hospital opens
	First flights at Don Mueang aerodrome
	Great War breaks out
1916	Hualampong Station opens
1917	Siam declares war on Germany and Austria-Hungary
1918	New Assumption Cathedral completed
	Armistice, Great War ends
1919	L. G. Riganti & Co. founded
	Whiteaway, Laidlaw & Co's premises on New Road open
1920	Reid, *Spears of Deliverance* (novel)
1921	Visit of Alfred Harmsworth, Viscount Northcliffe
1922	Neilson Hays Library opens
1923	Somerset Maugham first visits Bangkok
	Frank Exell recruited by Ministry of Education
	Hervey, *The Black Parrot* (novel)
1925	German commercial interests re-established
	Pasqual, *A Trip: Through Siam*
	Death of King Vajiravudh, accession of King Prajadhipok (Rama VII)
1926	Siamese Kingdom Exhibition at Lumpini Park cancelled; *Siam from Ancient to Present Times* (souvenir volume) published
	New British Legation completed
	New Borneo Company Limited headquarters open
	Andrew Freeman arrives to edit the Bangkok *Daily Mail*

1927	Seidenfaden, *Guide* (1st edition)
	Rabindranath Tagore visits
	Rajdhani Hotel opens
1928	Dr Ang Kee Eng shot
	Teresa Lightwood arrives in Bangkok
	Centenary of Protestant Missions with exhibition
	Le May, *Siam as a Tourist Resort*; Wheatcroft, *Siam and Cambodia*
1929	Forty, *Bangkok*
	Wireless Station and Trocadero Hotel open
1930	Kornerup, *Friendly Siam*
1931	KLM airliner crashes at Don Mueang
1932	Andrew Freeman, *Brown Women and White*
	Coup d'état by the People's Party
1933	Siam Society building opens
1934	Boon Rawd Brewery opens
1935	Abdication of King Prajadhipok
	Wood, *Land of Smiles*
1939	Siam becomes "Thailand"
	Signboards Act
	Campbell, *The Bangkok Murders* (novel)
	Outbreak of Second World War
1941	Williams, *Green Prison*
	Japanese invasion; British and American residents interned
1942	Thailand declares war on the United Kingdom and the United States

Bound for Bangkok

Before the Great War, many travellers bound for Bangkok from Europe or North America sailed on ocean liners to Singapore and then changed to one of the coastal steamers plying the Gulf of Siam up to Bangkok. After the Great War, it became more usual to take trains, either from Singapore or more often from Penang (where the liners now called) or rather from its railway station at Prai. In later years, airlines offered much faster but also much more expensive alternatives. Intending residents and travellers received no shortage of advice about the climate and living conditions they could expect.

The journey from the United Kingdom to Bangkok takes roughly 24 days by the most direct route via Marseilles and Penang. The Peninsular & Oriental and Blue Funnel lines maintain a regular fortnightly service (alternate weeks) between Penang or Singapore, most of the vessels calling at Marseilles *en route*; other lines maintaining regular sailings are the Messageries Maritimes, Rotterdam Lloyd, Nippon Yusen Kaisha and East Asiatic. From Penang an International Express runs twice a week to Bangkok in connection with the mail steamer, the journey taking 32 hours. Frequent regular boats link up Bangkok with Singapore and Hongkong. All persons entering Siam require to be in possession of a valid passport bearing a Siamese visa. Visas are obtainable at the Siamese Legation, 23, Ashburn Place, South Kensington, London, S.W.7, and at the various Siamese Consulates (visa fee, valid for one year, 8s.).

United Kingdom, Department of Overseas Trade, *Report on the Commercial Situation in Siam (1931), p. 7*

From Seidenfaden, *Guide* (1932), p. 1. According to a note on the verso of the titlepage, the "decorations and illustrations in half tone" in the book were "executed by the Arts and Crafts School Bangkok".

The Danish officer Erik Seidenfaden (1881-1958) arrived in Siam in 1906 and served as head of the Royal Gendarmerie's cadet school until 1920, after which he joined the Siam Electricity Company. Although without formal academic qualifications, he was a skilled linguist and assiduous ethnographer and collector. He was also the author of the first comprehensive tourist guide to Bangkok (1927, 3rd edit. 1932).

A Traveller who does not possess a passport to Siam is advised to call on the Siamese Consul stationed in almost every important port. No difficulty will be experienced in going through the formality required.

Seidenfaden, Guide (1932), p. 19

Noel Wynyard was the nom-de-plume of Nancy Everilda Delacherois Davidson, née Irwin (1912-2005). She sailed on a Danish ship of the East Asiatic Company in 1936, landing at Penang where she married a teak-wallah who had come down from the north of Siam. Her account of her life in Siam appeared as Durian: A Siamese Interlude *in 1939. The ship passes through the Suez Canal …*

The thing that now became most noticeable was the difference in the nights: the darkness was heavier and more intense, the stars appeared lower in the heavens and more brilliant. I became conscious in a way of the East; a feeling that was more than mere imagination, more even than the obvious realization of faces that were black instead of white. From that day to this it has remained as something attractive and unusual, something exciting and different, yet at the same time containing a repellent, almost nauseous feeling, as the odour of a durian, whose taste is so seductive, they say, that once eaten it takes a strong will to resist.

Wynyard, Durian, pp. 2-4, 7

From an Ainslie album. C. B. Ainslie arrived in Singapore from Marseille on 28 January 1900 and took home leave in 1905, 1909 and 1914. Some of the photographs in the album relate to the voyage on the SS Oceana (P&O) which sailed from Singapore in June 1909.

P. A. (Peter Anthony) Thompson (1876-1947) was an engineer who describes himself on the titlepage of his book as "late of the Royal Survey Department". He had served in Siam for some three years before returning to England in 1905. His Lotus Land: Being an Account of the Country and the People of Southern Siam *appeared in the following year; an American edition with the title* Siam: An Account of the Country and People *came out in 1910. When Reginald Le May published* An Asian Arcady *about the north of Siam in 1926, he described his book as a complement to Thompson's.*

At Singapore the traveller bound for Siam quits the great liner which has brought him from Europe, and taking leave of his friends, who will be careful to let him understand that they do not expect to see him again, he embarks upon one of the small steamers which, at somewhat irregular intervals, take up the mails to Bangkok. If the north-east monsoon is blowing he will have a rough passage up the gulf, and may be glad enough when four days later he sees ahead the low mangrove-fringed shore which marks his destination. Straight for this the steamer makes, and presently he finds that he has entered the muddy Bangkok river.

Thompson, Lotus Land (1906), p. 31

Reginald Stuart Le May (1886-1972) joined the British Foreign Office's Siam Consular Service in 1907. He left the service in 1922 to become an adviser to the Ministry of Commerce (which soon added "and Communications") under H.R.H. Prince Purachatra of Kamphaengphet, with responsibility (among much else) for tourism policy. His article 'Siam as a Tourist Resort' appeared in the Asiatic Review *in October 1928 and was also separately issued.*

My own experience of coming to Bangkok for the first time from Singapore on the good ship *Nuentung* is also bound up with memories of a different kind of danger. We had only just time to catch our boat, and when we arrived on board with our luggage, the Captain met us with the news that there were no cabins available. However, some of the officers gave up their cabins for a little consideration, and that night we were safely installed in their bunks. At about four in the morning I awoke with a sense of something unusual around me, and when I opened my eyes, it was to look straight into the face of the first Chinaman I had ever seen at that close range. He was holding a lantern over my head, and his face was not more than three inches from mine. All the stories I had read as a boy of Malayan and Chinese pirates came back in a flash, and I waited for the inevitable plunge of the *kris*. But no such untimely end was in store for me. I suppose I must have started up with a cry, for the Chinaman suddenly bolted up like a rabbit, and after breakfast I discovered it was the quartermaster come to call the officer of the watch! His shock had apparently been as great as mine!

Le May, Siam as a Tourist Resort (1928), p. 4

Advertisement in Perkins, *Travels* (1909), detail.

George Payne Bent (1854-1930) was a Chicago piano manufacturer whose autobiography, Tales of Travel, Life and Love, *was privately printed in 1924.*

In the afternoon I went on board the *Kuala*, due to sail for Bangkok, Easter Sunday, March 27th. We got away at 6:00 A.M. The boat was commanded by Captain Thompson. My cabinmate was Mr. Mitarai, traveling manager for the Japanese line, Yamashita Kisen Kabushiki Kaisha. He could hardly speak English, but so far as he could go was quite cordial and companionable. I read, and played Solitaire. The next day, Monday, was fine, and the sea calm. I read and wrote and played Solitaire, but could not win. I met a Mr. Fleming, a Scotchman, who was then in the next cabin to mine – a very fine man. Tuesday was beautiful, with the sea calm. The *Kuala* was a boat of only three hundred and ninety-six tons, the smallest I ever traveled upon. It, however, was very good, and the officers were fine.

Bent, Tales of Travel (1924), p. 268

Walter Leigh Williams (1889-1955) arrived in Bangkok en route for the north of Siam in 1913, having been taken on as a "teak-wallah" by the Bombay Burmah Trading Corporation. His memoir Green Prison *appeared in 1941.*

After much preparation and buying of kit, I eventually found myself, in company with an American missionary, a French nun, two Russian ladies of dubious antecedents, and the Portuguese Chargé d'Affaires in Bangkok, ploughing up the Gulf of Siam in a small, cockroach-infested coastal steamer. On the fourth day after leaving Singapore we were leaning over the rails, observing that indefinable phenomenon known as the loom of the land. All that can be described is that the horizon is at one moment sea, the next land. The distant haze becomes a shadow, the shadow a line of palms. And now the sun picks out the golden spire of a pagoda. We have crossed the bar!

Williams, Green Prison (1941), pp. 10-11

The Federated Malay State Railways and Royal State Railways of Siam run express trains between Bangkok and Singapore via Kuala Lumpur and Prai. There are two express trains leaving Singapore daily for Penang, one in the morning, and one in the late afternoon.

	To Bangkok.
Dep. Singapore (Tank Road)	7.28 o'clock daily.
Arr. Prai (Penang)	6.07
Dep. Prai	9.36 o'clock Fridays and 8.00 o'clock Mondays
Arr. Bangkok	19.00 o'clock Satur.
	19.00 o'clock Tuesdays

Travellers will find the services between Singapore and Bangkok quite comfortable as the Federated Malay States Railways and the Royal State Railways of Siam pay the utmost attention to their sleeping and restaurant car services. The scenery along the line will give the traveller a good impression of British Malaya and Siam.

Seidenfaden, Guide (1927), pp. 11-12

Major W. R. (William Robert) Foran (1881-1968) was a British army officer, big-game hunter and prolific travel writer. His articles on 'Fascinating Siam' were published in The Straits Times *in March 1925. They were later revised and incorporated into the Siam chapters of his* Malayan Symphony *(London 1935).*

We left Prai for Bangkok punctually at 9.36 in the morning, and we arrived at 7 o'clock on the following evening, also punctually on time. Punctuality of Siamese State Railways is one of their many strong points. This International Express train is really a fine one, and the accommodation is excellent. I shared a two-berth sleeping compartment – roomy, comfortable and well-fitted. The service throughout the journey was courteous and efficient; the restaurant and the food were first-class in every particular; the track was well-laid and the running smoothness itself; and the cleanliness, chiefly attributable to the consumption of wood fuel instead of coal, was remarkable. Another favourable impression I formed was of the great politeness of the train staff and officials en route. They were courtesy personified. They also spoke very tolerably good English, which was a relief. But this is equally true of the Siamese in Bangkok, for as a race they are very polite and obliging.

The Straits Times, 5 March 1925, p. 9

The American journalist Andrew A. (Aaron) Freeman (1898-1974) was born in Baltimore and studied at Johns Hopkins and Columbia Universities. He travelled to Bangkok with his wife in 1926 to take up the post of editor of The Daily Mail, *returning to the US in 1928. In 1932, he published his unfortunately (and misleadingly) entitled book,* Brown Women and White.[1]

It was late afternoon when we arrived at Pedang Besar. The compartment was clean and roomy and contained a wash basin, chair and the usual pullman lower and upper berths over which mosquito bars were suspended. A few minutes after the train got under way I pressed the button for the attendant. A smiling face showed itself. I ordered a stengah (Malay for large whisky and soda) and settled down for the long run to Bangkok. It was hot. I looked out of the window at a harsh landscape

---

1 Two years previously, he had published an account of his experiences in the periodical Asia and the Americas ('A Tabloid in Bangkok. An American Chapter in the History of a Paper Owned by the King of Siam').

with a scrub growth terminating in sharp rocky hills. My fellow travelers were Europeans; a salesman for an Italian artificial silk firm; another for automobile tires, toothpaste and shaving cream; another selling farm machinery; two young Dutchmen going to join a Dutch firm in Bangkok; an American missionary and his wife; and a tall, young Englishman, dressed in shorts, who was returning from home leave to the teak forests of northern Siam. I saw them only at meal times when all of us would emerge from our compartments like so many sacred cattle being taken to pasture. The tall Englishman sat at my table. "Beastly train, isn't it?" he said putting down his whisky and soda.

Freeman, Brown Women and White (1932), pp. 14-17

Paul Drennan Cravath (1861-1940) was a wealthy New York lawyer. His account of a visit to Bangkok during a cruise in the Far East in 1927 was published in early 1928.

We soon found that the coolest spot on the train was our table in the dining car. There we established relations with our neighbors. A talkative young Siamese, who had been a student in the United States and was now a motor-car salesman in Bangkok, introduced himself. Next to the auto salesman we saw most of a voluble young man. All of these Siamese had been educated in Europe or America and most of them spoke English with little or no foreign accent.

Cravath, Notes on the Cruise of the Warrior (1928), pp. 118-119

"Siamese Railways' Excellently-Equipped Restaurant Car" from *Siam from Ancient to Present Times* (1926), reprinted in *Royal State Railways of Siam. Fiftieth Anniversary* (1947).

Bound for Bangkok 29

J. Antonio (Joaquím Apolinário António, 1862-1912)[2] was born in Macao but was resident in Bangkok from 1889. In 1893, he opened the "Charoen Krung Photographic Studio" on New Road. He published the first travel guide to Siam in 1904, a work that was to be superseded only by Seidenfaden's more systematic guide in 1927.

We may here remark that as a rule no difficulty whatever is experienced in getting one's luggage passed by the Customs. The bringing of opium or spirits into the country without permits obtainable from the Opium and Spirit Farms is, of course, illegal, and all goods brought for sale must be entered at the Customs in the usual way. As to firearms and ammunition, any such must be left with the Customs officers who pass the baggage until the formality of obtaining a written permit for their landing shall have been obtained from the Director General of Customs.

Antonio, Guide (1904), pp. 14-15

The American dentist Harry Earle Blunt (1877-1968) arrived in Bangkok in 1910 with his servant Abdul.

We arrived at 10 o'clock opposite the customs house, where we anchored, as there was no dock to tie up to, I went ashore in a motor launch, to be landed in the customs house enclosure. My arrival with a full outfit of dental equipment created quite a commotion at the customs house, as it was a new experience for them. I was ushered into the presence of the head of the customs, a Scotchman, for an interview. He demanded an itemized declaration of my equipment, and the value; as he said I would have to pay a 3 per cent duty *ad valorem*. I told him that I had visited many countries with this equipment, and this was my first experience of having to pay duty on it. He was still adamant, and I made an estimate of the value and paid the three per cent duty on it. However, this event produced quite a different story. Mr. Scotchman later became a patient, and eventually informed me that when I left for a holiday, my three per cent duty would be refunded. This was done, and ever afterward, whenever I returned, they never brought up the question of duty on my dental equipment.

Blunt, An American Dentist's Unique Experiences (1968), p. 96

---

2 The form of his name used here follows Bautze: *Unseen Siam*.

The Customs House, from *Twentieth Century Impressions of Siam* (1908). The building has been preserved and is currently under restoration.

Major Foran finds Siamese Customs most obliging. Rather surprisingly, being a big-game hunter, he seems not to have had any firearms with him.

At Padang Basar, the frontier Post, the two railways meet. Here polite customs officials board the train and enquire if you have anything to declare and more particularly if you have any firearms. Both here and at Bangkok Noi the customs examination is merely perfunctory. The European traveller's word is accepted without question, and no examination of luggage is made.

The Straits Times, 5 March 1925, p. 9

Hualampong Terminus appeared to be a gigantic pipe cut horizontally in half and set down over the trains. There was a festive mood in the great shed. Crowds of Siamese, Chinese, Indians and Europeans, many carrying garlands of flowers, lined the platform eagerly peering into car windows for friends or relatives. There was no kissing or hugging or handshaking. The Siamese bowed to each other, placing their hands together in the attitude of prayer. Having assured customs officials that I carried no firearms, my baggage was passed.

Freeman, *Brown Women and White* (1932), pp. 37-38

Bound for Bangkok 31

Mail bags arriving at Hualampong Station on the Southern Express from Penang/Prai. From *Siam: General and Medical Features* (1930). The station, built in the "Italian Neo-Renaissance" style, was opened on 25 June 1916. Architect: Mario Tamagno (1877-1941) with Alfredo Rigazzi..[4]

J. C. (Joseph Christopher) Pasqual (1865-1941) was a Eurasian businessman with interests in tin mining. He was resident in Penang, though his roots are said to have been in the Portuguese-speaking Catholic community of Phuket. He published books and articles on a range of topics, including A Trip: Through Siam *which appeared in 1925.*

The arrival of the mail train from Penang at Bangkok-Noi station in the afternoon is an important event, and crowds of Siamese and Europeans are gathered on the platforms to meet their friends and relatives among the passengers.[3] Bangkok-Noi is an unimportant village of floating houses in a creek on the right back of Menam, so most of the arrivals are ferried across on motor launches of "*rua-chang,*" boats that are propelled like gondolas, to the business and residential side of the city.[5] Not knowing the ropes, I followed the line of least resistance and soon found myself the sole occupant of the Railway Rest-House which is within a stone's throw of the station.

---

3 Bangkok-Noi in Thonburi was opened in 1903 as the original terminus of the Southern Line.

4 For some reason, the builders (the Bangkok Dock Company) were not invited to the official opening (*The Bangkok Times*, 26 June 1916, p. 3). Tamagno left Siam in 1926 after twenty-six years' service. The farewell dinner was at the Royal Hotel.

5 Bangkok's river (the "Maenam Chao Phraya", the "Chief River of the Kingdom") was commonly referred to by foreigners as the "Menam" (which simply means "river").

Fairly commodious and comfortable the R. H. lacks in one essential, and that is food, unless the caretaker is warned beforehand by wire.

Pasqual, A Trip: Through Siam (1925), p. 54

Margaret Dorothea Landon, née Mortenson (1903-1993), was an American Presbyterian missionary who was resident in Siam from 1927 to 1937. She is best known today as the author of the novel Anna and the King of Siam *(1944).* Never Dies the Dream, *her novel about missionary life in modern Bangkok, appeared in 1949. Here, India Severn, its protagonist, waits for a delegation from the Board of Foreign Missions at Bangkok's main station.*

At noon on December 16, India waited on the platform of Hua Lampong Station with the other missionaries for the arrival of the International Express, which came twice weekly from Penang. Comings and goings in Bangkok still had something of the festival character of the old days. Arrivals could look forward to seeing friends waiting for them. It was a pleasant experience to step off the express and find oneself surrounded by familiar faces. Someone always brought coolies to help with the luggage. Someone always said: "My car's waiting. You're coming home to lunch with me."

Landon, Never Dies the Dream (1949), p. 200

Francis Younghusband Thompson (1909-1991) taught English at Chulalongkorn University from January 1931 until summer 1932. He later published two novels based his experience: Engagement in Bangkok *(1951) and* Water-Lily *(1952).*

The station approach was jammed with vehicles pointing in all directions, rickshaws, carriages, cars, lorries, taxis, handcarts, and milling around them were people clamouring for hires or searching for their drivers, and coolies pushing along with great bales and baskets swinging from poles balanced on the shoulders. The sun was still high, and a hot glare beat down. The noise was terrific.

Thompson, Engagement in Bangkok (1951), p. 58

Climate

The couplet about Bangkok in Noel Coward's celebrated cabaret song 'Mad Dogs and Englishmen' is witty but fanciful.

> In Bangkok, at twelve o'clock, they foam at the mouth and run,
> But mad dogs and Englishmen go out in the midday sun.
>
> First public performance, New York, June 1931

The climate of Siam is tropical, divided into a wet season (June to October), and a dry season (November to May). The best time of year for a visit may be said to coincide with the latter part of the cool season (November to February).

United Kingdom, Department of Overseas Trade,
Report on the Commercial Situation in Siam (1931), p. 7

Dr Hugh Campbell Highet (1868-1929) served as physician to the British Legation and then as Principal Medical Officer of Health for Bangkok from 1901 to 1919. His 'Advice to New Residents' appeared in Twentieth Century Impressions of Siam *in 1908.*[6]

April is the unhealthiest month of the year as well as the hottest, and February is the healthiest. The line of sickness closely corresponds with the range of highest mean temperature and the period of the rains. If possible, then, no arrival should be made during any of these hot, wet, and most unhealthy months. Not only is it very hot during March and April, but the sanitary conditions of Bangkok are then at their worst. It is better, then, not to arrive before the end of August, preferably not until the beginning of October.

Twentieth Century Impressions of Siam (1908), pp. 129-130

Francis B. (Bowes) Sayre (1885-1972) was an American jurist who served as Foreign Affairs Adviser to the Siamese Government during the 1920s.

After April the rains began; almost every day there was rain. "You bake all winter, and stew all summer," we used to say. Some of the rains were torrential. Every pit or depression would fill up with water. And the fact was stoutly vouched for by some of my friends who ought to know, that

---

[6] *Twentieth Century Impressions of Siam* was a part of a series of richly-illustrated surveys of Asian countries. In his preface, Arnold Wright, the general editor, claims that "no trouble has been spared to ensure completeness and accuracy, and in every section of the volume the various articles have been written by the highest authorities". The book gave "a pictorial representation of Siam upon a scale which has never been attempted before". The publication was supported by the Siamese government through the offices of Prince Damrong.

sometimes in summer swimming fish could be found in pools of water that had been dry pits through the winter-time.

Sayre, Glad Adventure (1957), p. 93

The British nun Sister Teresa née Ada Lightwood (1906-1995), arrived in Bangkok in autumn 1928.

According to the prophets, three or four days of heavy rain about mid-February (to help the mango fruit to grow) was the most that could be expected. But the Bangkok experts, like many another weather forecaster, were dismally wrong. All through January there was rain, rain, rain, on every day that was scheduled to be dry, and our open-air kitchen soon became a bog. Wood planks were laid on the mud to prevent us from slithering while we worked. And somehow, soaked to the skin four or five times each day, with my habit and floppy headdress spattered all over with a nice blend of mud and cooking fats, I discovered that in an altogether unexpected way I was enjoying life as never before.

Lightwood, Teresa of Siam (1960), pp. 32-33

The Hot Season is Coming.
BE PREPARED WITH ELECTRIC FANS.
All types of Fans in stock at attractive Prices.
Siam Electricity Co. Ltd.
Advertisement in The Bangkok Times, March 1923

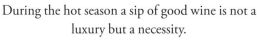

During the hot season a sip of good wine is not a luxury but a necessity.
You can find a variety of preserves, wines and liquors to suit both purse and taste at
THE INTERNATIONAL STORE.
Telephone No, 570. Corner New Road and Custom House Lane.
Advertisement in The Siam Observer, April 1918

In Landon's novel, India experiences the sudden onset of the monsoon ..

After the first scattered drops, there was a breathless interval of doubt before the storm broke. India did not move. She stood with her hand still on a pile of vouchers, waiting for what she knew would come. In a few minutes the monsoon was upon them, thunderous torrents of rain that lashed the trees with sadistic fury and catapulted from the roof. It shot in along the verandas, drenching chairs and floor and several pieces of forgotten embroidery. The wide double doors that took the place of windows rattled and banged in a dance of their own. The endless clanging of trams on Bamrung Muang Road, the constantly blowing motor horns, the cries of hawkers, the shuffle of wooden clogs were cut off as if a switch had been pulled, and the monsoon was supreme.

Landon, Never Dies the Dream (1949), p. 17

After a spell of dry weather high winds and heavy rain generally cause some interruptions to the electric light service and the telephones. The telephones suffered severely on the west bank where falling trees brought down the cables and this morning no fewer than 230 installations were reported out of order. Samsen Power Station and the S.E.C. services were in part interrupted temporarily.[7]

The Bangkok Times, 13 November 1925, p. 5

It is strange how a few degrees drop in temperature will affect the lives of people accustomed to sweltering. Eighty degrees late at night will start hundreds of Occidental tongues wagging about the cold. People will talk about sleeping under sheets and some will claim the distinction of having to protect themselves with a blanket.

Freeman, Brown Women and White (1932), pp. 199-200

Bangkok weather encourages lotos-eating. Low latitude, high temperature, low altitude, high humidity – against forces of nature so formidably deployed only rickshaw-coolies exert themselves, and theirs is a short life and a sweaty one. For the Siamese, and for the Europeans who live among them, life is like a mango, sweet, soft, and sun-warmed.

Thompson, Water-Lily (1952), pp. 37-38

---

7 S.E.C.: Siam Electricity Company, which also ran the trams.

Mr. Somerset Maugham has arrived in Bangkok and, interviewed this morning, he said that he was under the impression, when arrived in Bangkok, that he was in the tropics – but he regretted the fur coat he had left behind.

The Bangkok Times, 7 December 1927, p. 7

A Perfect Death-Trap?

Johannes Wilda was a German journalist and travel writer with a nautical background.

Foreigners living in Bangkok dispute the fact that the city is unhealthy. Nevertheless, cholera seems not to have been completely eradicated. When I began to suffer from a digestive disorder myself, a Danish officer gave me "Chlorodyne", an American medicine, explaining that it was invariably effective, but only if taken immediately the symptoms appear. I believe it worked for me too.

Wilda, Reise auf S.M.S. "Möwe" (1903), p. 276

Dr. J. Collis Browne's Chlorodyne
The Only Original and Genuine
Acts like a Charm in Diarrhoea and is the Only Specific in Cholera and Dysentery.
Sole Manufacturers: J. T. Davenport, Ltd., London S.E.

Advertisement in The Bangkok Times, January 1926

Twenty years ago, when the only method of travel was by sea from Singapore through the rough Gulf of Siam, it was the custom for the hotel proprietors to shake hands with a guest bound for the port of Bangkok. They explained at some length that it was a privilege which they never expected to have again. Sometimes they were right, for the Menam river then formed much of the drinking water, and at times when it became brackish occasioned cholera.

Forty, Bangkok (1929), pp. 15-16

Donald Eric Reid was born to Scots parents in Ceylon. In 1907, he joined Britain's Siam Consular Service. He left the service in 1913 to become the editor of The Siam Observer. *In the same year, he published his short-story collection* Chequered Leaves from Siam. *His novel about foreign life in Siam,* Spears of Deliverance, *appeared in 1920. In Reid's story* Audi Alteram Partem, *Juggins meets a young man called Hardcase who has previous experience of Bangkok.*

"What!" exclaimed Juggins, "is it such a fearful place?" "Oh my! Yes! A regular black hole, why, when I was there last, three years ago, on a trip, I vowed I would never go back." Mr. Hardcase now waxed magniloquent. "Oh yes, a regular Hades, Bangkok. If you don't catch cholera in your first month you will get typhoid in the second, and if you escape these, you will fall a victim to dysentery or rabies in a year.

Reid, Chequered Leaves (1913), pp. 3-4

Sir Josiah Crosby KCMG KBE CIE (1880-1958) spent much of his career as a diplomat in Siam/Thailand, having joined the Foreign Office's Siam Consular Service in 1904. He was British Minister in Bangkok at the time of the Japanese invasion in December 1941 and Thailand's subsequent declaration of war. His book Siam: The Crossroads *appeared in 1945.*

In 1904 Bangkok bore a most evil reputation for unhealthiness, and I was not a little perturbed, when passing through Singapore on my way out from England, by a resident there who expressed the hope that I had brought my coffin with me!

Crosby, Siam (1945), p. 42

W. A. R. (William Alfred Rae) Wood CMG CIE (1878-1970) joined the British Foreign Office's Siam Consular Service in 1896, serving in Bangkok and various other places until settling as Consul (later Consul-General) in Chiang Mai in 1913. After his retirement in 1930, Wood wrote an anecdotal memoir injudiciously entitled Land of Smiles *(Bangkok 1935). This was reprinted in London in 1965 with some extra material and the equally injudicious title* Consul in Paradise.

When I was first in Bangkok, the months of March, April and May were usually known as the *cholera season*. Driving along the New Road, as the central thoroughfare was (and is) called, one sometimes passed whole rows of Chinese coffins being borne along. As for Europeans, deaths among them were quite frequent, in spite of all the precautions they took. At the United Club one would ask in the evening: – "Where is A?" and be told he was dead of cholera. "And B?" "Dead too." "And C?" "Laid up with cholera."

Wood, Land of Smiles (1935), p. 13

Agnes Barland was an American Presbyterian missionary nurse who visited Bangkok en route for her station in the north.

It appeared to promise little but filth, nakedness, and ignorance. The people have absolutely no idea of sanitation. Bangkok has, along the sides of its streets, canals in which one woman washes her rice, another bathes, another throws her sewage, another drinks.

Letter dated: 21 January 1922, quoted in Bartlett: Female Medical Missionaries, p. 25

There was only one remedy for such a distressing state of affairs, and that was the installation of a scientific water supply system. Happily, this was achieved somewhere about the year 1907 and the result was almost magical. Cholera ceased to be the haunting terror that it had always been at the close of the hot season; epidemics became rare and it was soon evident that, but for this scourge, Bangkok was by no means an unhealthy city, if account were taken of its tropical situation.

Crosby, Siam (1945), p. 42

Whatever abnormal dangers the past may have held, they are almost non-existent now, and the visitor may be assured of an excellent water supply in Bangkok, and a complete absence of jungle-life in the principal cities of Siam.

Le May, Siam as a Tourist Resort (1928), p. 4

We announce with very great regret the death of Dr. Hugh Campbell Highet, who was Medical Officer of Bangkok for eighteen years (1901-1919). The street drains and the inconspicuous sanitary inspectors may recall to us what is perhaps his biggest accomplishment of all – the increased cleanliness of the capital.[8]

The Bangkok Times, 1 August 1929, p. 7

Bangkok is a healthful town. The rate of mortality is 29.5 per thousand which compares favourably with most of the cities in this part of the world.

---

8 Highet had lost a young son in Bangkok (Douglas Athelstan, April 1900) and also his first wife (Lilias, March 1906).

The city has an excellent water supply and several well-equipped hospitals and health centres.

Siam: General and Medical Features (1930), p. 153

Keeping in the Best Condition

C. L. (Cecil Lilliott) Watson (1879-1939) was a Legal Adviser to the Ministry of Justice from 1905 until 1929. On his retirement, he shared some advice with young recruits …

Mr. Watson has been fit all the years of his residence in Siam, and his suggestions for keeping in the best condition are worth noticing by a younger generation which is oft-times heard lamenting the trying nature of the climate. It is a recipe which even the youngest griffin on the smallest salary can observe – plenty of exercise, plenty of fruit and as much sun and as few clothes as you can bear.[9]

The Bangkok Times, 10 June 1929, p. 6

Lt.-Col. C. H. (Cecil Heber) Forty (1880-1967) was appointed to the Royal Siamese Gendarmerie in 1907 and apparently stayed in Siam after retirement. When he died, a funeral book in the Thai tradition was issued.

The following advice may be worth the perusal of intending residents to the tropics. It applies to Bangkok in particular:

> Eat plenty of fruit. Salads if taken should be perfectly cleaned, not merely rinsed. If unclean they are often dangerous.
> Water is a good drink if uncontaminated. If there is the slightest reason to suppose that it is not absolutely pure, filter and boil it.
> Wear as few garments as possible; they should be of cotton, linen, or silk.
> Bath in cold water. Never forget to wash the hands before a meal.
> Exercise daily. Evacuate a couple of times a day, certainly not less than once.

Forty, Bangkok (1929), pp. 66-67, 71-72

Tropical white suits are worn all the year round. A topee is necessary between the hours of 8 a.m. and 4.30 p.m.

United Kingdom, Department of Overseas Trade, Report on the Commercial Situation in Siam (1931), p. 7

THE "BANGKOK" White Topee
for men, quite a new shape, low crown fitted, neat White Puggaree.
Light in weight. All sizes.
PRICE TCS. 11.50 EACH.
ALWAYS SOMETHING NEW
AT WHITEAWAY'S
Advertisement in The Bangkok Times, April 1923

The young trainee teacher Frank Kingsley Exell (1902-1974) was recruited by the Siamese Ministry of Education in 1923 to teach in Bangkok schools. He later became a manager with the Siam Commercial Bank. His memoir Siamese Tapestry *was published in 1963.*

Breakfast over, Beaumont decided that my wardrobe must be attended to.[10] I gathered that if I had about six white tunics, six white coats, twelve pairs of white drill trousers, six pairs of white shorts, a dozen singlets and half a dozen short-sleeved shirts I could just about carry on. Payment, apparently, did not matter much. That could be dealt with later. Tipped off by the boy, a tailor was already on the premises. The boy, no doubt, would get his rake-off. The grinning tailor apologized most profusely for the fact that it might be a couple of days before the order was completed.

Exell, Siamese Tapestry *(1963), pp. 20-21*

AH SEEANG TAILOR

Begs to solicit the patronage of the public. White and other suits of first-class style, fit and quality, at moderate prices. Customers attended at their residence, on receipt at his address of a postcard, giving their name and

---

9 Griffin: a young racing horse, hence a new recruit.
10 A. G. (Archibald George) Beaumont (b. 1878) was an Assistant Master at Suan Kularb College from 1916 and later Principal of the Commercial School "at Wat Kaeo Fa". He had previously taught at schools in Malaya (where he had been imprisoned briefly for embezzlement) and China.

place of residence. Opposite Tram Junction, Banrak.[11]

Advertisement in The Bangkok Times, February 1909

Dr Campbell Highet advises …
For night-wear thin flannel, viyella, or a mixture of silk and wool makes excellent sleeping suits. The cholera belt should always be worn when asleep in order to protect the abdominal organs from chill. Sleep, which is one of the greatest recuperative influences in temperate climates, is even of greater value in the tropics. "Early to bed and early to rise" is a golden rule.

Twentieth Century Impressions of Siam (1908), pp. 130-131

Hansen declined a drink, and Ah Seeang was beginning to feel cheated. White men who refuse hard liquor in Siam are either missionaries or stern and rock-bound Yankees from New England, though young bachelors occasionally find themselves restricted to soft drinks on doctor's orders. He hoped this young fellow was human to this extent, for he drank fresh lime-and-soda and ate sparingly of the special menu of the Hoa Tin Lao Hotel. "You sick?" Ah Seeang inquired. He gave the word the special inflection it has acquired in Bangkok.

Thompson, Water-Lily (1952), p. 16

Build up your strength, your vigour,
your vitality!
Take Wincarnis the Tonic Wine that
for over 40 years had been famous
for its body building qualities.
Start taking Wincarnis today – the sooner
the better for you.
Sole Distributing Agents for Siam:
KATZ BROTHERS LTD., BANGKOK

Advertisement in The Bangkok Times, February 1927

---

11 Ah Seeang advertised regularly in *The Bangkok Times* and *The Siam Observer* over several decades; in 1926, his address was "ON NEW LANE, Klong Po Yome, Opposite Tramway". It seems unlikely that F. Y. Thompson's ruthless character "Ah Seeang" is intended to be a portrait of the tailor.

First Impressions

Charlton B. (Bristol) Perkins (1873-1930) was an American businessman and travel writer who spent much of his adult life in China. He published his grandiloquently entitled Travels from the Grandeurs of the West to Mysteries of the East or from Occident to Orient and Around the World *under his own imprint in San Francisco in 1909.*[1]

Bangkok (city of wild fruit trees) is situated on both banks of the river Menam (mother of waters), about twenty miles above its mouth. The entrance of the river is like a placid lake, draped on both sides with impenetrable jungles of tropical growth, whose reflections cast upon the water a picture that will linger in your memory through a lifetime. Should you approach the mouth of the river during the night, you will have an opportunity of witnessing a sight seen nowhere else in the world, and that is the wonderful vividness of the phosphorescent water, which has ofttimes been so great that the passengers could read a newspaper with perfect ease.

Perkins, Travels (1909), pp. 325-326

Harry Hervey (1900-1951) wrote novels, short stories, travel books and screenplays. Here, Lhassa Camber, the protagonist of his novel The Black Parrot (1923), *arrives in Bangkok.*

The Menam widened as though to accommodate the many craft that rocked gently on its yellow surface; the sampans, junks, and lighters, the attap-thatched canoes, the river-boats and few freighters from other ports. A swift tide ran beneath floating houses and wharves, past warehouses and mills, and skirted a wilderness of many-colored tiled roofs and golden obelisks. Ramshackle huts, built on poles, crowded down to the numerous klongs (canals viscid with stagnant water) that contributed substantially to the Oriental atmosphere. . . . That was Bangkok as it first appeared to her: a brilliant polychrome.

Hervey, The Black Parrot (1923), p. 37

---

1 Perkins seems to have given a false date of birth on at least one passport application (making himself two years younger than he was). The spelling of his second name varies in the sources, sometimes appearing as "Bristow".

Harry L. (La Tourette) Foster (1894-1932) was an American travel writer. In his books, he chose to present himself as a "tramp", a "vagabond" or (as here) a "beachcomber".

It was a quaint river, this gateway to Bangkok. Along the shore beneath the graceful palms the yellow robes of hundreds of priests were hanging upon the branches of the sacred Bo tree, and the roofs of many Buddhist temples rose above the green vegetation, their inlaid glass and gilded spires shining and sparkling in the sunlight. And then, as though to destroy the whole delightful barbaric picture, a great pall of smoke appeared ahead, the nipa-shacks and temples gave way to a cluster of European buildings - the structures with which the unsentimental European business man is constantly destroying the native beauty of all foreign lands – and the company's launch carried me shoreward, in my newly washed suit, to land me at the water-front garden of a big modern hotel.[2]

Foster, A Beachcomber in the Orient (1923), pp. 119-120

John H. (Hutchinson) MacCallum Scott (1911-1985) was a British barrister who became active in Liberal politics. His Eastern Journey *was published by John Gifford in summer in 1939 and simultaneously issued by the Travel Book Club. He seems to have travelled to the East with his wife Nora in the mid-1930s.*

Unfortunately there was no train at Packnam to greet us, and it was not until after the tug had gone on its way that we discovered that there would not be another for half an hour. The station was not a pleasant place in which to have to wait. It was only a long shed, and did not even boast any seats on which we could rest. What it lacked in appointments, however, it made up in the number of people who came to stare at us, and beg of us. A crowd began to collect almost as soon as we arrived, and we were soon surrounded by twenty or thirty gapers who considered us in a ruminative fashion, chewing betel-nut, and occasionally spitting out blood-red streams of juice on to what passed for a platform. It was not a pleasant experience.

Scott, Eastern Journey (1939), pp. 80-82

Bangkok is about fifteen miles up-river. At each bend the banks are more populous and the buildings more substantial. That hideous harbinger

---

2 Nipa-shack: roofed with palm leaves.

Frederick Samuel Harrop (1887-1947), The Temple of Dawn (Wat Arun). Harrop was a British artist resident in Bangkok in the 1920s; the 1925 Bangkok Directory lists him as "organising Art Master, Ministry of Education". From *Siam: General and Medical Features* (1930)

of civilisation, corrugated iron, begins to displace the picturesque native huts. The feeling of romance is nearly dead by the time we enter the reach known as the Port of Bangkok. The whole river is a hive of commercial activity, and everyone seems in a hurry. But the turbulent scene is flanked on one side by the pagodas of Wat Arun, and on the other by the spires of the Grand Palace. Romance is saved, but it has been a narrow squeak!

Williams, Green Prison (1941), pp. 12-13

In an advertisement for her book The Newest Way Round the World *(1908), the publishers name Celeste J. Miller (1845-1928), a wealthy resident of Chicago, "The Most Traveled Woman in the World".*[3]

Never was I so astonished as when I arrived at Bangkok and found that I had been laboring under several misapprehensions. It is true that Bangkok is hot, and that there are plenty of mosquitoes, but there are just as many in other parts of the world and there are hundreds of oriental cities much dirtier. It has been so modernized in the last few years that it has not the appearance of an oriental town, but resembles a well-built foreign city.

Miller, The Newest Way Round the World (1908), pp. 138-139

The modernisation of Bangkok has quite obliterated the few places of interest within my recall on my last visit.

Pasqual, A Trip: Through Siam (1925), p. 55

---

3 She is said to have travelled thirty-three times around the world.

First Impressions 45

The French diplomat and writer Paul Morand (1888-1976) was posted to Bangkok in 1925. His travel book Rien que la terre *(Paris 1926) was translated as* Nothing but the Earth *(New York 1927).*

Bangkok lies flat under the eye, but it is difficult to grasp. There is no sign of that succession of ascending levels that makes certain cities so easy to understand. The highways are concentric but illogical, for the streets came last and had to adjust themselves to the whims of the canals which preceded them.

Morand, Nothing but the Earth (1927), p. 104

John Gordon Drummond Campbell (1864-1935) had been one of Her Majesty's Inspectors of Schools when he was seconded to advise the Siamese government on education policy in 1899. On finishing his term, he published Siam in the XXth Century *(1902) which recorded his impressions of the country and his opinions about its prospects.*

The expectant visitor, after sailing up twenty-five miles of the broad and stately Menam, will probably derive much disappointment from his first experience of Bangkok. His earliest acquaintance will most probably be with a long, dingy, squalid road, running for several miles parallel with the river. With a further knowledge Bangkok will win on his affections. The broad roads and open spaces in the city, with the picturesque gables of the temples, the pagodas and tapering *prachadees* peeping through the foliage, the effective masses of colour against the backgrounds of white and green, the lovely glimpses of water and trees as he crosses the canal bridges, cannot but appeal to his artistic imagination.[4]

Campbell, Siam in the XXth Century (1902), pp. 53-54

The article 'Bangkok Days' in the American Presbyterian missionary periodical Woman's Work for Woman *is unsigned.*

What is Bangkok like? What remains to one after a brief visit there? What is Siamese atmosphere? I shut my eyes and see temple and palace roofs spread out under the sky, like beautiful rugs with harmonious borders, their graceful curves and finials unlike those of any other land. I see the boats and waterways, palms of many species, naïve human life in the open air, soft bamboo bowers, ragged, betel-chewing respectability lounging on verandahs, dirty surroundings of homes, ugly women, languid motion,

---

4 Phrachadee or phra chedi: holy stupa.

houses slipping down banks into water, brilliant-blossomed trees, religion towering into wats, embodied in multitudinous images and chiming bells.
Woman's Work, May 1903, pp. 101-102

Sir Henry Norman Bt (1858-1939) was a British journalist and later a Member of Parliament.

On dropping anchor in mid-stream at this strange town of Bangkok, one realises at once that it is to trade, and trade alone, that Siam has owed, and must ever owe, her chance of figuring among the people of the East. To the silent palm-groves and virgin jungles of 1850, have succeeded today the forest of masts, the towering chimneys, and the humming "godowns" of the pressing British trader. Rice-mills and saw-mills, docks and ship-yards, stores and banks, houses and schools, alike display the energy of the Anglo-Saxon, hand in hand with the industry of the Mongol, forcing new life into native indolence.
Norman, The Peoples and Politics of the Far East (1895), p. 410

Lucie Chandler's article 'The Sights and Sounds of Bangkok' (illustrated with her own photographs) appeared in the New York magazine Travel *in November 1916.*

Bangkok is a more than dual personality. This first Bangkok, the Bangkok of commerce, where merchants from Bombay and Burma ply their trade in teak; where the mysterious packets of the Orient are despatched to foreign lands; where the customs official is enthroned. The second Bangkok is the city of consulates and foreign settlements, where fair-skinned Europeans in spotless white wear soldier-like pith helmets to guard against a tropical sun and ride like nabobs in aggressive motor-cars from some Western mart. The Bangkok of the bazaars is called Sampeng. But all this is extraneous Bangkok, the Bangkok imposed by the foreigner. The real life of Bangkok is the life of the *khlongs*.
Travel, November 1916, pp. 26-28

E. (Edward) Alexander Powell (1879-1957) was an American journalist and travel writer. Where the Strange Trails Go Down *is an account of his travels in Southeast Asia in 1920. Powell's publishers were sued for "grossly libellous and untrue statements" made in the book, not – it should be said – about Bangkok, but rather about the British North Borneo Company.*

I might as well admit frankly that my first impressions of the Siamese capital were extremely disappointing. I didn't expect to be conveyed to

my hotel atop a white elephant, through streets lined with salaaming natives, of course, but neither did I expect to make a wild dash through thoroughfares as crowded with traffic as Fifth Avenue, in a vehicle which unmistakably owed its paternity to Mr. Henry Ford, or to be bruskly halted at busy street crossings by the upraised hand of a helmeted and white-gloved traffic policeman. Nor, upon my arrival at the hotel – there is one in Bangkok deserving of the name – did I expect to find on the breakfast table a breakfast food manufactured in Battle Creek, or beside my bed an electric fan made in New Britain, Connecticut, or behind the desk a very wide-awake American youth – the son, I learned later of one of the American advisers to the Siamese Government – who eagerly inquired whether I had brought any American newspapers with me and whether I thought the pennant would be won by the Giants or the White Sox. ...[5]
Powell, Where the Strange Trails Go Down (1921), p. 217

With my rigid code of convent modesty behind me – a code which forbade the nun even to undress in the presence of another sister – the sight of this woman naked to the waist and talking casually with a young man on the public highway was disturbing to say the least. True, it was not long before the beauty of olive skins and the bodies that moved without artifice began to impress me. But on that day, cluttered as I was by bony stays, a long-sleeved shift and serge petticoats, I failed to appreciate the natural graces. I was in fact outraged.
Lightwood, Teresa of Siam (1960), pp. 27-28

Ebbe Kornerup (1874-1957) was a Danish artist and writer who travelled to Siam in 1926. Unsurprisingly, in view of the fact that his trip was more-or-less sponsored by the Siamese government, his book Siam *(1928; English translation:* Friendly Siam, *1930) promoted the country as "the newest holiday land".*

---

5 In its review of Powell's book, *The Bangkok Times* highlights Powell's more improbable stories and remarks drily: "Another traveller has visited Bangkok and written of what he saw in our midst. The description of the land we live in by visitors and newcomers seldom fails to interest the resident, often indeed provides amusement" (22 July 1922, pp. 4-5).

Bangkok on a moonlight night, in the avenues or out among the rice-fields, is an adventure.

Kornerup, Friendly Siam (1926), pp. 238 240-241

Sister Marie de Lourdes writes to her family in 1927.

I suppose you are thinking of Bangkok as a capital like New York. But one look at our main street would make your illusions fly. There are a few big stores – English ones – but the others can't compare with our Chinese laundry. We have a trolley system but only one track. One has to get out at nearly every switch.

Quoted in Mahoney, Far Country, p. 54

ROBERT, HOWARD AND BONZO

Bangkok is a very big city, and has all kinds of vehicles. Some of them are cars, carriages, tramcars or trolleys and rickshas. My father is the principal of Bangkok Christian College for boys. It is a school for Siamese boys with American and Siamese teachers. There are about 400 miles of good roads in Bangkok and there are many European and Siamese stores here. Siamese money is not much different from American money. Two and half ticals make one dollar. Ticals and satangs are the names for Siamese money. The climate is so hot that you have to go away from the city for two months to the seashore where most missionaries go. At that, it is quite hot. If you do not wear a topee you would get sunstroke. A topee is a hat to protect you from the sun. I think that is all.

ROBERT PALMER[6] Auburn, N.Y.
Child Life, April 1929, p. 205

---

6 Robert Palmer (10) and his brother Howard (8) had previously written to Miss Waldo of the magazine *Child Life* enclosing a photograph of themselves with their dog Bonzo, and explaining they lived "in the Bangkok Christian College in the capital of Siam" (*Child Life*, September 1928, p. 576). Their address was "1523 Pramuan".

Frank G. (George) Carpenter, an American journalist and travel writer, visited Bangkok in the early 1920s.

Once landed in the streets of Bangkok, what a city of contrasts I found it! Palaces and hovels side by side. Straight, wide, tree-shaded boulevards set with substantial houses, and evil-smelling canals lined with tumble-down huts perched on piles or floating on bamboo rafts. The honk of the automobile and the clang of the trolley car mingling with the cry of the rickshaw coolie and the shouts of the driver of the horse-drawn gharry. Fine hotels, luxuriously appointed, with native food-stands at their very doors. Everywhere I go in this capital I am surprised by the modern character of a city that is at the same time so strange and picturesque.

Carpenter, From Bangkok to Bombay (1924), pp. 3-5

Bangkok! Horned temples. Slim pagodas. Shaven, yellow-robed monks. Heat. Trams. Pigs on the road. Scarlet panungs, yellow panungs, brilliant blue panungs. Little brown, smiling policemen. The sickly smell of durian. Vendors of rice-cakes. Chinese ricksha coolies. Rotting vegetation.

Campbell, The Haunting of Kathleen Saunders (1938), p. 114

Such is the hodge-podge of Bangkok – a network of canals where the lower-class Siamese live in carefree, contented poverty, a smoky European district where a few Europeans sit and sip their whiskey-and-soda and look vastly important, a filthy reproduction of China where ol John Chinaman does most of Bangkok's work and takes most of its money, and finally this aristocratic section where royalty dwells among splendors that suggest the Arabian Nights. Comparisons are inadequate.

Foster, A Beachcomber in the Orient (1923), p. 127

The colourful life of Marian Gilhooly Curry (1889-1929) included travel and subsequent travel writing. Her article 'Nights and Days in a Siam City' appeared in the magazine Asia and the Americas *in June 1917.*

Bangkok has a dual personality, a sort of a day and night shift, if one may resort to factory parlance. When the lower classes are seeking the native equivalent of the downy couch, shortly after sundown, society, officialdom – what you will – which has remained in seclusion during the persistent mid-day heat, is just yawning and stretching itself and preparing to come to life, for daylight is aristocratic Bangkok's time for rest. The day comes in with a bang. One has no adequate conception of the possibilities of just plain noise until one has awakened thus involuntarily in Bangkok.

Asia and the Americas, June 1917, p. 295

It is at night that the thin veneer of the Occident and the gloss of Western atmosphere is stripped from this quaint city. It is a silent blue-white night. Hot, windless, almost breathless. It is the original Bagdad – the Bagdad of fabled fantasy of Haroun al-Raschid – more like the Bagdad of old than Bagdad itself is to-day.[7]

The London & China Express, 22 March 1928, p. 204

There was very little time in which to explore Bangkok – a city so horribly filthy and smelly that it was impossible to describe, and yet so full of interest that one could live there indefinitely without penetrating its inner secrets to the fullest extent. At night it was a fairyland of twinkling lights on water, a city of canals, waterways, and bridges, of strange sounds and aromas. In the daytime it was crude and disgusting, at times strangely beautiful in its *wats* or temples. But there was about the whole place an unfriendly, alien atmosphere, in its teeming multitudes, its clashing trams, its hordes of bicycle taxis, and even its innumerable *pi* dogs. When I questioned a friend about Bangkok, he said, "You will hate it. It is indescribably filthy and repellent, but it has a deadly fascination for those who can see it; it will be your first sight of the real East."

Wynyard, Durian (1939), pp. 22-23

---

7 From an article entitled 'Eastern Night Life. A Romance of the Orient. By W. S. L. B.' Like a previous article ('An Eastern Venice: English Life To-Day in Bangkok'), it was originally published in *The Daily Express*. "W. S. L. B." also published articles in a similar vein about Ceylon, Singapore and French Indo-China.

Allister Macmillan was a prolific author on the geography of British colonies and other territories. He arrived in Bangkok in November 1922 to research a new edition of his Seaports of the Far East *with "historical and descriptive, commercial and industrial facts, figures & resources".*[8]

To attempt adequately to describe Bangkok is almost embarking on an endeavour to achieve the impossible, for in reality it is indescribable. But why? The answer is that it constitutes in itself such a mass of contrasts and contradictions that any species of evolution in the shape of order appears hopeless. But, mass of contradictions as Bangkok is, there is yet the charm of unconventionality about it; and though this does not by any means outweigh the disadvantages, yet it helps considerably to condone the faults.

Macmillan, Seaports of the Far East (1925), p. 495

The Cornish writer Crosbie Garstin (1887-1930) is probably best remembered today as a Great War poet, though he also wrote novels and travel books and was a contributor to Punch. *In February 1926, he set off "in search of local colour" in the Far East. His resulting book* The Dragon and the Lotus *was published in 1928 with extracts appearing in* The Bangkok Times *(11 August 1928, pp. 9-10). A popular edition was published in 1930, the year in which Garstin mysteriously disappeared.*

I am that human pest, a hearty breakfaster. At my first breakfast in Bangkok the boy offered me the choice of kedgeree, sausages, kidneys, ham, bacon, eggs – fried, boiled or scrambled, supported by cereals, grapefruit, bananas, oranges, mangosteens, butter, toast and marmalade. After months of dry rolls and coffee this sudden plenitude overcame me and I believe I wept. As these repasts continued day after day my experience of Siam may appear a trifle roseate, but it couldn't be helped. Day after day I determined to sally forth breakfastless and get the darker side of the picture. But my resolve invariably weakened at the dining-room door and a glance at that menu finished it – "kedgeree, sausages, kidneys, eggs fried, boiled or scrambled."

Garstin, The Dragon and the Lotus *(1930), p. 303*

---

8 The first edition had appeared in 1907, the second edition following in 1925 and a third in 1926.

Ice

Are You a New Comer to Siam?
Then come to us and we will tell you where to get the purest water, the best ice, the most popular and best aerated waters, the most delicious and tasty cold storage products.
Bangkok Manufacturing Co., Ltd.
Advertisement in The Bangkok Times, October 1912

Nothing in the tropics is more delectable and appreciated than ice, that triumph of scientific invention by which man has been able to improve upon Nature for his requirements and produce in the sweltering countries of the equator the product formerly associated only with winter in the temperate zones and the eternal zero of the polar regions. The Bangkok Manufacturing Co. are the largest manufacturers of ice in Siam, and produce daily about 100 tons of it in blocks of 300 and 400 lbs. each.

The business was established in 1900 and carried on under the name of The Bangkok Manufacturing Co., Ltd., until 1920, when it was purchased by the present proprietress, Gam Hoon Trakul, and is under the general management of her sons, Hoon Kim Huat and Hoon Kim Hua.[1]
Macmillan, Seaports of the Far East (1925), p. 513

About twenty minutes past ten o'clock this morning an outbreak of fire occurred at the works of the Bangkok Manufacturing Co., Ltd. The fire originated in the ice cream manufactory, and the fire spread rapidly, the roof soon being ablaze. The efforts of the Company's staff, therefore were directed to the preservation of that part of the building and it is pleasing to record that they were successful in keeping the machinery intact. After about an hour and a half the flames were extinguished and the danger averted.[2]
The Bangkok Times, 11 August 1910, p. 4

---

1 In other words, BMC had been acquired by the firm H. Swee Ho. The acquisition price was 320,00 Ticals (*The Bangkok Times*, 10 January 1920, p. 3). Nai Lert, a well-known Bangkok entrepreneur, had left BMC in 1910 to open his own ice factory.
2 It was later reported that a major disaster had only been narrowly avoided.

When you are down in the Mouth
Think of Jonah
He got out all right
So did
The Bangkok Manufacturing Co.
OUT OF THE FIRE
With a full stock of ICE, AERATED WATERS AND FROZEN MEAT.
Advertisement in The Bangkok Times, August 1910

B.M.C.
IN STOCK TODAY: -
FISH: Smoked Blue Cod, Smoked Murray Cod, Codroe Caviare
CHEESE: Australian, Stilton
HAM: Boiled Ham on cut, Raw (ditto), French (ditto), Breakfast Bacon Snipe (from time to time), Beef Dripping, English Margarine, Turkeys Fresh Australian Butter and Finest Australian Pure Butter in 3/4 lb. Tins. Picnic cases containing Ice, Aerated Water and Well Water for travellers by Railway or boat. Delivered free at Railway Station or any Bangkok landing.
Advertisement in The Bangkok Times, 13 February 1918, p. 4

In Landon's novel, Mr Denniscort brings supplies from B.M.C. to tempt the convalescent Angela's appetite.

Mr. Denniscort took the napkin from the basket with a flourish. "The manager at the B.M.C. helped me pick the things out," he explained. "I bought a leg of lamb for broth." India melted with suppressed laughter. "Goodness!" she said weakly, thinking of the extravagance of lamb from Australia at five or six dollars for broth!

"And here's lettuce and celery. It came from San Francisco, so it's perfectly safe. The manager said if you'd wrap it in a damp cloth and keep it in the refrigerator it would stay crisp a week." India felt her amusement tempered with awe.

Landon, Never Dies the Dream (1949), pp. 155-157

Advertisement in *The Bangkok Times*, 15 January 1926, p. 2.

Protect your health. Enjoy the convenient servant which needs no watching or care … the modern Frigidaire automatic refrigerator. It protects health by stopping food spoilage … halts the rapid growth of dangerous mould and bacteria … makes ice for cooling drinks … and frozen salads and desserts. Let us show you a Frigidaire in operation. Come in any time. The Anglo-Siam Corporation, Ltd. Siam Electric Corporation. Butler & Webster.

Advertisement in The Bangkok Times, August 1929

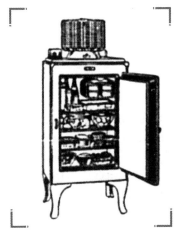

From and an advertisement for a General Electric refrigerator in *The Bangkok Times*, June 1931.

Ice 55

The Sudden Death of An Engineer

W. E. M. van Cuylenberg was a former manager of the Cold Storage Department of the Bangkok Manufacturing Company. He was taken ill on a February afternoon in 1918 as his tram car passed their premises "beside the Phitsitien Bridge spanning the Klong Kut Mai (Canal), which crosses New Road". Sadly, this was not the only misfortune to afflict the van Cuylenberg family.[1]

Bangkok, Feb. 26

The Siam Observer regrets to record the death of Mr W. van Cuylenberg which took place yesterday owing to heart failure. It appears that the deceased who was apparently in the best of health was proceeding in a tram car about 3 30 yesterday afternoon towards the city. When the tram had passed the BMC he complained to a friend who happened to be in the same tram that he was feeling a bit unwell and before the tram reached the Samyek junction Mr van Cuylenberg expired. The body was taken off the tram at the Pla Pachai junction and removed to the Police Hospital. The deceased came to Siam from Ceylon in 1904 and was working in the Siam Canals and Irrigation Co. Leaving this company he joined the BMC Ltd. as manager of the Cold Storage Department. Until very recently he was working for Messrs Swanson and Sehested. He was making arrangements to work on his own account as a surveyor and contractor. He was about 44 years of age. He leaves behind a wife and four children. The funeral takes place at 5 o'clock this evening in the Protestant Cemetery.

Malaya Tribune, 8 March 1918, p. 2

Mrs van Cylanberg [sic], a Eurasian leper came up for treatment about a year ago. She has had severe reactions from the medicine and has been very discouraged and to add to it a telegram came last week saying that her husband died suddenly in the street car. They have four little children, one in Burma and three in Bangkok. The S.P.G. School has taken the children but her income is cut off but we hope to persuade her to stay and try to get well because the children are in good hands and we shall try to raise the funds here to keep her going.[2] Of course she has to be fed as a foreigner. But it does seem as if some people had more than their share and had to suffer more than others. She is a Catholic but the children are with Church of England people.

Mabel Cort, letter dated: "Chiengmai, Siam. March, 5th, 1918"

A large collection of Household Furniture and other Effects, property of late Mr. W. E. M. Van Cuylenberg, will be sold by Public Auction, at his residence near Wat Samokrang, Samsen Road, on SATURDAY the 25th May 1918. Commencing at 2 p.m. Benjamin A. Periera.[3]

The Bangkok Times, 22 May 1918, p. 5

The Eurasian, Mrs. Vancuylenberg, who is down at the Island is getting better. She is very much happier than she was.[4]

Mabel Cort, letter dated: 16 June 1919

---

1 As we learn from letters by the missionary Mabel Cort, his wife was an inmate at Dr J. W. McKean's Leper Island near Chiang Mai. Van Cuylenberg's relationship with other Bangkok residents of the same name is unclear, for example the surveyor with the Royal Irrigation Department (also a British subject from Ceylon) who was attacked while working in 1906, or the Homan van Cuylenberg (1908-1942) who is buried in the Protestant Cemetery (Block N).

2 S.P.G: Society for the Propagation of the Gospel maintained mission schools for boys and girls (see 'In School' below).

3 B. A. Periera's name is spelt thus in the sources; cf. his fellow auctioneer E. M. Pereira.

4 In late 1924, a "Mrs F. van Cuylenberg" left Bangkok on a train bound for Penang (*The Bangkok Times*, 5 November 1924, p. 4). Whether this was the wife of the late engineer, now perhaps cured of leprosy and able to rejoin her children, is unknown.

The Sudden Death of An Engineer

Palaces and Royalty

The Grand Palace always presents a most picturesque and charming view, a view seen best either in the early morning or at sunset from the river, for then the rising or sinking rays of the sun transform the spires of the palaces and temples into flames of molten gold, while the inlaid gables flash and glitter as though they were encrusted with the choicest diamonds.

Seidenfaden, Guide (1932), pp. 133-134

The moon is up and shines down over a palace, the King's palace, *Grand Palace*, which rises behind battlemented walls among turrets and temples, fantastically lovely, with concave glazed roofs, pointed gales, and three spires. Do we dream or wake? Siam reveals herself enchanting, unique.

Kornerup, Friendly Siam (1926), p. 240

The British teacher A. (Arthur) Cecil Carter (1866-1921) was headmaster of King's College, Bangkok, from 1896, having previously been tutor to the Crown Prince of Siam. He edited (or indeed largely wrote) The Kingdom of Siam *which was published in connection with the Louisiana Purchase Exposition at St. Louis in 1904. After his retirement, he served as Superintendent of Siamese students in England.*

The nucleus of Bangkok is the royal palace, situated on a bend of the river. The outer walls of the palace enclose an immense area, but the ground devoted to the actual residence and garden is comparatively small. Within the walls are various ministries, namely, the Foreign Office, the Treasury, the Ministry of the Interior, the Ministry of the Household, and, in addition, the Royal Library, Legislative Council, a magnificent Buddhist temple, barracks, etc. Surrounding the palace on the land side is the city proper, formerly surrounded by a massive embattlemented wall and pierced by lofty gates. Next to the palace is a large open space of grass of an oval shape surrounded by trees. This is the *Premane* ground, formerly used for the royal cremations, but now used for drilling troops, kite-flying, cricket, foot-ball matches, and golfing.[1]

Carter, The Kingdom of Siam (1904), pp. 106-107

Go where one would, and when one would, in this strange medley of departments, bureaus, and government offices, every passage and every room was all unswept and littered with the daily mess, the cast-off cigarettes, the decaying betel-nut, and all the indescribable débris of the countless hangers-on and ragged retainers who attend the footsteps of every official. In not a single office but that of Prince Damrong – a brilliant exception to the general slovenliness of Siamese ministers in this, as in many respects – did I observe the slightest desire for neatness and order, or even an idea of common cleanliness.[2]

Norman, The Peoples and Politics of the Far East (1895), pp. 414-415

Harry L. Foster visits the palace of the late King Chulalongkorn.

The throne hall was a handsome structure of marble, designed by a famous Italian architect, and considered the finest building east of Constantinople. Everything except the throne was done in European style; the marble pillars, the decorations, even the mural paintings of Siamese scenes were European in design. It was beautiful, but there was nothing Siamese about it, and I was preparing myself for further disappointment, when the *panung*ed courtiers led me through a gate into the palace, and ... that palace surpassed all my wildest dreams.[3] It was magnificent, astounding, bewildering, fascinating, and so on throughout the dictionary!

Foster, A Beachcomber in the Orient (1923), pp. 143-145

Rachel Wheatcroft (1869-1942) was an English artist who travelled to Siam independently in 1925. In Bangkok, she taught drawing at St Mary's Mission schools and, in August, exhibited her pastels of "flame trees & temples in Siam & Angkor" in the Team Room of the Oriental Stores. In early 1928, she exhibited sixty examples of

---

1 Pramane or Premane Ground: the Cremation Ground, the open space near the Grand Place. The space is marked on the 1914 map as "the Kite-Flying Oval". Today, it is generally known as Sanam Luang.

2 Prince Damrong: H.R.H. Prince Damrong Rajanubhab (1862-1943) was Minister of the Interior, 1894-1916, and thereafter President of the Royal Institute which encompassed the National Museum and National Library. He was exiled in 1932. Prince Damrong is known today as "the Father of Thai History".

3 Panung: traditional garment. See below.

her Asian paintings at the Goupil Gallery in London. Her illustrated travel book Siam and Cambodia in Pen and Pastel *appeared in the same year.*[4]

It was a great disappointment to find that apparently all Bangkok freely entering, my way alone was barred – with gestures of regret and courteous smiles, it is true, but quite definitely barred. There seemed to be no official who spoke English, and, alas! I had no Siamese. However, an appeal thrown across the sentry towards a group of young men passing in found a student of English glad to practice the language. It appeared that, although open on that day to the public, without special permission foreigners were not included. ... "You do not appear to be Siamese," was an amusing comment.

Wheatcroft, Siam and Cambodia (1928), p. 113

Hermann Norden (1870 or 1871-1931) was a German-born American businessman, traveller and travel writer.

Everyone knows by now that white elephants are not white, but even though fortified with this knowledge, one expects something far lighter than one finds. I found them on their daises, ponderous, patient but bored. I was permitted to feed hay to the venerated creatures, a distinction gained by paying one tical (about thirty-nine cents) to the keeper.

Norden, From Golden Gate to Golden Sun (1923), pp. 115-116

Most visitors try to obtain a few hairs from the tails of these impotent beasts to make a good luck charm. I considered myself particularly fortunate in securing a ring from the hair of the whitest and therefore the most sacred.

Miller, The Newest Way Round the World (1908), pp. 147-148

Charles M. Hendley (1852-1927) was a government official and businessman in Washington, DC. Trifles of Travel *is based on letters written to his son in 1922-1923. They were privately printed in 1924.*

---

4 On this occasion she was finally permitted to enter the grounds of the Grand Palace but not to sketch, despite being in possession of a permit to do exactly that. The Royal Pantheon is a building in the Temple of the Emerald Buddha. It had been restored quite recently.

Emil Eduard Groote, 'A Royal White Elephant', from *Twentieth Century Impressions of Siam* (1908).

The flag of the country has upon it the figure of an elephant, and elephants are always associated with Siam.[5] I expected to see them about the streets doing all sorts of work and carrying people back and forth. The only ones in Bangkok are five so-called white ones, having a white streak about their ears, belonging to the King and kept for state occasions. By slightly subsidizing the keepers I had the distinction of feeding each of these animals with sugar cane of which they are extremely fond.

Hendley, Trifles of Travel (1924), p. 200

In Margaret Landon's novel, India Severn *and her head teacher Darun Buranda, visit the palace of a princess.*

It was large but nondescript. A servant girl ushered them into a reception room and crawled out backward on her hands and knees to announce them to her mistress. The room was oval with niches along the walls where marble figures of Italian workmanship, modestly draped, had been set. On the floor was a thick carpet in a design of red and yellow roses. There were carved and gilded tables, and carved and gilded chairs, sofas covered with petit point that looked French, and a profusion of distended pillows richly embroidered in the Siamese style. Several bronze heads stood on marble pedestals, among them a likeness of Princess Sandhya's late husband. Twenty minutes passed, and no one came. The air in the room was fusty.

Landon, Never Dies the Dream (1949), p. 23

---

5 In fact, the White Elephant flag had been replaced by the present national flag in 1917.

Dr Victor G. Heiser (1873-1972) was Far East Director of the Rockefeller Foundation's International Health Board. His entertaining if somewhat self-serving memoir, An American Doctor's Odyssey, *appeared in 1936.*

One hot June afternoon I set out along the Charun Krung, the New Road, for the palace of the King of Siam, in 1916 one of the few remaining absolute monarchs in the world. Though the thermometer was at ninety-five I had necessarily attired myself in heavy broadcloth morning coat; the hottest places in the tropics seem to have a predilection for formal dress on official occasions.

I was shown at once into the presence of the King, who was dressed as a colonel of a British regiment. The room was almost filled with admirals, generals, ministers, and other officials, all adorned with gorgeous uniforms. The short, stout, moon-faced monarch graciously motioned me to a chair and seated himself on a wicker settee. After the usual inanities about the weather had been exchanged, he suddenly asked, "What do you think of our medical school?"

Heiser, An American Doctor's Odyssey, *(1936), pp. 480-481*

The Swedish Prince William (Carl Wilhelm Ludvig, Duke of Södermanland, 1884-1965), represented his father, the King of Sweden, at the coronation ceremonies for King Vajiravudh in 1911.

During my long stay in Siam I learned to know him as a man of progressive ideas, whose first thought is his country's welfare and prestige. It was with real regret that I pressed his hand for the last time, for during our long, almost daily companionship I had learnt to value not only the monarch and autocrat, but also the man and the friend.

Prince William, In the Lands of the Sun *(1915), pp. 89-90, 140-141*

Alfred Charles William Harmsworth, 1ˢᵗ Viscount Northcliffe (1865-1922), was a newspaper magnate and a person of great political influence in contemporary Britain.[6]

From The Bangkok Times …

Lord Northcliffe had a busy day on December 21, but contrived to see a good deal of Bangkok, driving all over the town. He said that he did not notice the roads were particularly dusty. (They have been well watered – *Ed.*) At the Royal Bangkok Sports Club the distinguished visitor enjoyed a round of golf, Mr. Graham being his opponent. In the evening he was guest of His Majesty the King at dinner at the Ambara Palace. He stated that the game played yesterday was played in the hottest weather of the tour so far. The temperature was ninety degrees on the course. The appearance of Bangkok he found unlike that of any other city in the world.

The Bangkok Times, 22 December 1921, p. 8

From Harmsworth's Diary ...

Wednesday, December 21st, 1921

In the evening I dined at the Royal Palace with the King, a short little man, who is very well informed. Here is the greatest royal style I have ever seen anywhere. Footmen, wearing magnificent liveries and silver facings, stood behind every chair. I was glad to see the old-fashioned punkah swinging across the great table, instead of the electric fans. Here is the menu, cooked by French chefs, except one Siamese course, which I have marked *. (I hear that the King has two of the best French chefs in existence.)

MENU.

Consommé Alexandra. Médaillons de Kabong Nelson. Mousselines de Caille au Champagne. Tournedos Melba. Dindonneau Truffé. Salade des Lords. * Plats Siamois. Coupes Victoria. Corbeilles de Friandises. Fruits.

Thursday, December 22nd, 1921

Thinking over last night's banquet, I have come to the conclusion that I have not yet seen anything so magnificent. With the exception of the garlands of flowers, it was entirely European. Etiquette here is kept strictly very Edward VII, though our late monarch had not the loose cash that this King has. Siam is a very rich country.

Harmsworth, My Journey Round the World (1923), p. 201

A national fair was being held at the time of my visit, and I was told that the King attended it each night. In fact, the fair opened upon the

---

6   He is said to have undertaken his world tour in order to regain his health, arriving in Bangkok shortly before Christmas 1921, but he died some months after returning home. His travel diary was published as My Journey Round the World in 1923.

King's arrival, and closed whenever he went home, but all Siamese are great night-birds – most of the government offices are run during the cool evening while the officials sleep in the day-time and since the King was the greatest night-bird of all, the fair was apt to last until the wee small hours of the morning. The fair, while open to the public, seemed to be a society event. There was scarcely a native *panung* to be seen. Even the ladies were in European dress, in the latest Parisian gowns.

The exhibits consisted mainly of stores run by the local merchants, who evidently had received a royal edict to open booths here, since none of them acted as though they expected to sell anything. Only the shows and particularly the gambling games drew patrons. There was a Burmese opera, a Siamese drama, exhibitions of the Red Cross and the

Wild Tigers, – the last named organization being a form of Boy Scout Movement instituted by the King, – a European dancing pavilion, restaurants and drinking places, and even a scenic railway. But there was little merriment.

I walked about, looking for the King, but could not find anyone who looked like him. Finally, I hit upon the idea of following one man, a particularly handsome nobleman in plain white uniform. He walked quietly about, returning the salutes of his fellows, and I never suspected his identity until an old woman, evidently a scrub-lady of some sort, fell to the ground, wriggled across ten yards of dirt, and kissed his foot. I had been following the King.

Foster, A Beachcomber in the Orient (1923), pp. 141-143

Saturday, 24th December 1921

Afterwards we went to the theatre, where we saw a French play performed chiefly by local French people, one part being played by an English lady. It was very well done.[7] The King was brought up in England, speaks and writes French and English perfectly, and is a rather remarkable monarch. He writes plays in English and French, and leading articles in the local

---

7 The performance was organised by the Alliance Française and was given at the Theatre Royal in honour of the French Marshal Joffre.

newspapers. The King sent for me during the theatre performance to present me with his photograph. I had to go and fetch one of mine from the palace we are in. (I was glad to get out of the heat in the theatre.)

Harmsworth, Voyage Round the World *(1923), p. 207*

Crosbie Garstin has attended the cremation ceremonies for King Vajiravudh.

An hour later I stood on a high balcony and looked out over the dark tree-tops of the Pramane to where the tower, under its steady searchlights still shone like a pillar of gold against the night. With memory's eyes I saw myself, a mere child, returning in a hansom-cab from a prize-fight in the East End of London, my companion an Oxford undergrad. At his behest, crossing Leicester Square, we picked up another undergrad, an Oriental. He sat on my knees all the way down the avenues of lamps that are Piccadilly and Knightsbridge, to Queens Gate, where we dropped him, a plump, agreeable fellow, with a pleasant, ready laugh. His remains were in that urn yonder, among the leaping dragon-tongues, a handful of grey ash.

Finis.

Garstin, The Dragon and the Lotus *(1928), p. 343*

Left: A photograph of the cremation of Rama VI from Seidenfaden, *Guide* (1932). Right: A watercolour of the same scene from almost the same angle by Hilda May Gordon (1874-1972). Courtesy of the Martyn Gregory Gallery (London).[8]

8 Gordon had arrived in Bangkok with her friend and fellow artist Hilda Trefusis only a few days before. The watercolour was probably exhibited among the works she showed at the Oriental Hotel in April 1926. *The Bangkok Times* reported they were "hung in a fairly good light in the entrance hall and ladies' room" and were "moderately priced", though the buying public in Siam was regrettably small (7 April 1926, p. 7; 8 April 1926, p. 4).

Palaces and Royalty 65

Doing the Wats

All the principal *wats* are readily accessible to visitors, but in visiting them it is well to have a guide to explain their beauties. In some *wats* one sometimes comes across priests who have a knowledge of English and these are generally only too willing to act as cicerones to the stranger, free of all charge, but it is as well to make a small donation to the *wat* funds when leaving. Although the priests are not supposed to handle money, in many cases the custom is more honoured in the breach than in the observance.

Antonio, Guide (1904), pp. 46, 48

Mary Landon's book 'Mid Pleasures and Palaces (1907) is best described as a travelogue in the form of a novel. Set in Bangkok and later Japan, it is dedicated to "my fellow-travellers" and illustrated by photographs apparently taken by the author herself.[1]

Jim and I have been doing the *wats*, and I am more in love with them and the big benign Buddhas than I can say. I believe I prefer the desolate, forsaken ones, in their neglected gardens, where the quick jungle growth is beginning to swallow up what there once was of paths and orderliness. Some broken steps, some shimmering white

The Temple of the Emerald Buddha in the Grand Palace. Postcard with inscription dated: March 1924. The Editor's Collection.

---

1 On the titlepage, Landon is identified as the "author of How the Garden Grew", but that book (assuming it is the title published in 1900) is attributed on its titlepage to "Maud Maryon", making Landon's actual identity uncertain. There is no reason to believe she was related to the American missionary Margaret Landon.

66 In Bangkok

pagodas, the bell-tower, and the main dilapidated building are hidden away amidst the greenery. You push open a creaking door, beautiful in its time with inlayings of mother-of-pearl – a work the Siamese excelled in – and there, in the dimness caused by partially closed windows, faintly the outline of the big Buddha looms through the shadows. He is quite calm, he still smiles there in the uninterrupted twilight.

Landon, 'Mid Pleasures and Palaces (1907), p. 76

Although the article 'Wats of Bangkok' is unattributed, it was trailed in the April edition of Asia and the Americas *as being by C. Wilson Smith, "who lived in Siam".*

Behind high white stucco walls and above the green masses of Buddha's own tree flame the gorgeous roofs of Bangkok's *wats*. Yes, flame! They are covered with tiles of red, green, blue, yellow, the primary colors found in flame, and they break at the edges into dragon-forms like twisting golden tongues of frozen fire. These white walls, with the vivid green of the bo-trees and the barbaric splendor of the roofs, which rise tier above tier in serried ranks of straight lines broken only by wriggling dragons and by the curve of the swan at the gable ends, strike the most distinctively Siamese note to be found in all Bangkok.

Asia and the Americas, May 1922, p. 379

A General View of Wat Po. Postcard issued by J. Antonio. The Editor's Collection.

Whatever may be said of their architecture, their shapes and colours are very effective, and most suitable to the setting in which they are placed. There is little of artistic or other merit as a rule inside the buildings, with the exception perhaps of the temples containing the famous emerald Buddha and the great sleeping idol, which are unique in their way and well repay a visit.

Campbell, Siam in the XXth Century (1902), pp. 54-55

Although their most obvious charm is that of colour, Siamese temples are fine in line and proportion. The steepness and importance of their roofs recall those of the extreme north of Europe. They rise stage above stage, double, treble, or even quadruple at the edge, each stage becoming steeper as it rises to the high line of the ridge, tipped with the Naga.

Wheatcroft, Siam and Cambodia (1928), p. 110

We went to Wat Sutat on the 17th of May – Buddha's birth-day and death-day – in the middle of the night. The lamp-lit temple shone from a distance. It was white with people who pressed forward with flowers and nose-gays. A big gilded Buddha stood inside the temple, lit up by hundreds of wax candles that made the air vibrate. All was peaceful, calm, solemn, inside the temple. People came and went, settled down, squeezed in somewhere or other; or candles guttered. Girls adorned with flowers sat beside their mothers, themselves looking like flowers gracefully drooping on their stems. The place was thick with yellow robed monks with shaven heads, sweating till the water poured off them.

Kornerup, Friendly Siam (1926), p. 244

G. G. van der Kop was the editor of Sluyters' Magazine, *an English-language magazine published in Batavia in the Dutch East Indies. His article 'Bangkok. Asia's Temple City' appeared in* Mid-Pacific Magazine *in 1926.*

The temple in Siam is a living thing to them where the Buddha has been incarnated and where things draw to contemplation and thought, which are both inseparably bound to all true life. Proof of this attitude towards life is also the custom that at some period of his life the Siamese becomes a monk, and strives to live for a certain time in accordance to the teaching of the Master. Then he dons the yellow robe and how general this custom is, is evident from the large numbers of monks one meets with throughout the country and the capital. Yet, they are not immune from foreign influence, for occasionally one may see them prefer the luxuries of a motor car, to the more becoming walking along the streets, but in the end it shows only that they are human, as we all are.

The Mid-Pacific Magazine, July 1926, p. 137

I went there one morning and called on the reverend chief priest of the temple, Phra Damadhada Chariya.[2] The lean little man discussed politics and other worldly matters with great animation, but he was not really in his element until the conversation turned upon different religions. On the way down I looked into his little house. The rooms bore a certain resemblance to dusty storerooms, and on shelves and presses stood long rows of Buddhas, porcelain bowls, lamps, teapots, etc., of which articles he loaded me at parting with as many as I could carry. He was an interesting and genial old man, and after exchanging photographs we parted the best friends in the world. For friendliness is a distinguishing trait of the Siamese character.

Prince William, In the Lands of the Sun (1915), pp. 84-85

Ernest James Young (1880-1953) was a teacher who later entered politics. His Kingdom of the Yellow Robe *appeared in 1898 and was reprinted several times; on the titlepage he is described as "late of the Education Department, Siam".*

The cells in which the monks live are small whitewashed rooms, with practically no furniture. There are a few mats, perhaps a bedstead – or, failing that, a mattress on the floor – a few flowers, and an image of the Buddha, the founder of their religion. In a little cupboard the monk keeps a teapot and a few tiny cups, and he is always glad to give a visitor as much tea as he can drink. Most likely he possesses a chessboard and a set of chessmen, for most of the Siamese are fond of this ancient game.

Young, Siam (1908), p. 37

---

2 Apparently, the abbot of "Wat Sakase".

I do not know that these Siamese wats have beauty, which they say is reserved and aloof and very refined; all I know is that they are strange and gay and odd, their lines are infinitely distinguished, like the lines of a proposition in a schoolboy's Euclid, their colours are flaunting and crude, like the colours of vegetables in the greengrocer's stall at an open-air market, and, like a place where seven ways meet, they open roads down which the imagination can make many a careless and unexpected journey.
Maugham, The Gentleman in the Parlour (1930), pp. 154-155

Though Wat Pra Keo is the most magnificent, it was to Wat Poh that I went most often. It is cut up into courts and dotted with pagodas, pavilions and chedis. But it is less crowded, less blindingly brilliant; the mosaic is tarnished and dropping out, weeds sprout between the red flagstones, and there tuberoses grow, oleanders, yellow honey-suckle and a form of passion flower called by the Siamese the bell-flower. There are also jack-fruit and fig-trees and still larger trees spreading friendly green umbrellas between you and the smiting sun. A restful, shady, flower-scented place, gently decaying, little frequented.
Garstin, The Dragon and the Lotus (1928), pp. 321-322

On the west-bank of the Menam and on the banks of the numerous canals that intersect the "hinterland" of Dhonburi, are found a great number of beautiful and interesting temples of which, however, only a few can be mentioned here. The most important of all is Wat Chang or Arun, which signifies "the Temple of Dawn." This temple, which is of quite a unique design, is one of the most conspicuous and pretty landmarks of the capital and whether seen by day in the glare of a blazing sun or by night in the light of a brilliant moon it is always of a most striking and picturesque aspect.
Seidenfaden, Guide (1932), pp. 272-273

James Saxon Childers (1899-1965) was an American journalist and university teacher, and also a prolific author. His oeuvre included a number of travel books.

Siamese builders have one style of architectural adornment probably unique: they decorate the entire exterior of temples and palaces with broken bits of crockery. At a distance, the effect suggests the work of the della Robbias in fifteenth-century Italy; nearer, the decorations prove to be pieces of old plates and chips from saucers.

Childers, *From Siam to Suez* (1932), p. 20

We ended our tour with a visit to Wat Arun. From a distance it glitters and looks as if it were covered with jewel-encrusted mosaic. Unfortunately, as one approaches, the jewels turn out to be bits of glass and pottery glued to the masonry in shoddy fashion. One ought never to look closely at Bangkok wats. But from a distance they are magnificent.

Rickover, *Pepper, Rice, and Elephants* (1975), p. 161

Helen Churchill Candee (1858-1949) was an American journalist, writer and traveller, probably best remembered today as a survivor of the Titanic disaster in 1912. On her trip to the Far East she was accompanied by her friend Lucille Sinclair Douglass (1878-1935) who provided the drawings for the subsequent book New Journeys in Old Asia *(1927).*

'Wat Arun at Night', signed (in Thai): "Prayoon", and dated: "3/20/25". From Seidenfaden, *Guide* (1932).

In all other places in the East one runs to see the works of old masters in architecture, the modern ones lacking purity of style and the inimitable touch of time. But in Bangkok the unimaginable beauties are new. That is what makes them so preposterous. They are not legends of an enchanted long ago, they are alive, they are of the moment. Nowhere else do people dare to employ such fantasy, and nowhere else is one so thrilled with startling new beauty.

Candee, *New Journeys in Old Asia* (1927), p. 164

Doing the Wats

Built Upon the Waters

The title of "The Venice of the East" is often applied to her more in irony than seriousness. Anyhow, in a prosaic sense the analogy holds more than good. Bangkok is built upon the waters. The great majority of her population live in floating houses. The shops and bazaars open on to the waterways, and boats supply far the easiest and most popular means of communication.

Campbell, Siam in the XXth Century (1902), p. 54

The Siamese themselves live mostly in houseboats or in the thatched houses of the suburbs. For generations they have lived upon the water, and here they still prefer to live; they have their floating stores, as fully stocked as the native stores upon land; peddlers ply their trade in canoes; families move the home from place to place by simply poling it along the river or the canal and tying it to a new areca palm; the women sit upon the floating front porch and exchange gossip with the women next door; the men loaf

"Gay Life on the River." Postcard issued by Royal State Railways. The Editor's Collection.

in the shade of the trees along the bank and smoke rank tobacco wrapped in banana leaves; the children splash and swim and laugh and shout in the water; the geese and ducks quack about it; the water-buffalo stand silently in the cooling water. Truly, it is an idyllic existence.

Foster, A Beachcomber in the Orient (1923), pp. 122-123

The best of all is the river traffic which is a bewildering, kaleidoscopic movement of all sorts of crafts – motor launches, steam launches, dug-outs of all sizes and shapes, ferries, barges, and the padi boats which bring down the padi from the interior to the rice-mills. Excepting for the dug-outs which are paddled, all other craft are impelled by a forward push of the oar like in a sampan or gondola. This continual movement over the water has made the river folks hardy and muscular.

Pasqual, A Trip: Through Siam (1925), p. 56

The river is hardly less crowded than the New Road. Both sides for miles above and below the palace are lined by floating houses, most of which are occupied by traders, who, taking down their front shutters, wait quietly for their customers to arrive in boats or launches and take their purchases away with them. These houses consist generally of several rooms and are supported on pontoons; the row is only broken by landing stages and the mouths of canals. Built in Siamese style, with the curious gable characteristic of Siamese architecture, they form one of the unique and interesting sights of Bangkok.

A noticeable feature in the river life is the water markets at certain places along the banks; a regular market is held which begins soon after midnight and lasts till seven or eight in the morning. Both buyers and sellers are chiefly women. The sellers come in small boats bringing fish, eggs, fruit, etc. which they have themselves grown, and one may see two or three hundred small boats, each with its little lamp, the owners talking and laughing with their neighbors. Then as soon as the sun has risen they begin to return home, and what was a busy market is now an open space of river.

Carpenter, The Kingdom of Siam (1904), pp. 108-110

Walter B. (Burton) Harris (1866-1933) was a British journalist and travel writer long resident in Morocco.

Everywhere are children brown and naked, in the water and out of it, for it seems a matter of indifference to them whether they paddle a canoe or swim – and they dive and swim like otters, laughing, splashing and shouting with sheer pleasure. At one spot a school, itself afloat, was dispersing after the morning's work and slates and books in hand the children jumped into their little canoes and paddled off home.

Harris, East for Pleasure (1929), p. 75

From an Ainslie album.

Frank G. Carpenter (1855-1924) was an American journalist who published a series of popular geography books entitled Carpenter's World Travels. From Bangkok to Bombay *appeared in 1924.*

All through Bangkok are canals, or *klongs*, as they are called, bridged over at frequent intervals and crossed by modern highways lined with trees and electric lights. Once they were the main lines of communication between different parts of the city, and they are still alive with traffic. I find that the canals are responsible for two features of Bangkok – the croaking of numerous frogs and a variety of bad smells.

Carpenter, From Bangkok to Bombay (1924), pp. 7-8

In Bangkok

And as you pass down a *klong* you get a sight of little creeks running out of it, only large enough for a sampan to enter, and you have a glimpse of green trees and houses sheltering amongst them. They are like the secluded courts and alleys that you find in London leading out of a busy thoroughfare.

Maugham, The Gentleman in the Parlour (1930), pp. 183-185

One of the sights of Bangkok are the clumps of water-hyacinths drifting down with the current in thousands to the sea. The weed has got a stranglehold of the canals and waterways and is threatening to clog them, and the Government is spending a large amount of money in casting chunks of it adrift to perish in the brine of the ocean.

Pasqual, A Trip: Through Siam (1925), p. 56

Major Foran hopes the days of the klongs are numbered …
Bangkok's *klongs* are gradually being filled up and converted into streets and lanes. This is wise, for they are insanitary places and only breed mosquitoes and sickness.

The Straits Times, 10 March 1925, p. 9

Suddenly it was quite dark … then the miracle happened: lights were lit on the Menam; there were oil-lamps on the sampans and the houseboats, long rows of coloured lanterns with reflections that rocked on the water like swaying streaks. The air was warm and yet refreshing after a broiling day. We sat dozing on the bank, caught up in the irresistible power of the tropics. A flute sounded from some boat a long way off, then it ceased; and a moment later there was perfect silence.

Kornerup, Friendly Siam (1926), pp. 252-253

The City of Magnificent Distances

It is a distinctly modern city, laid out on a most pretentious scale with numerous public squares and several wide avenues flanked with rows of trees. So great are the distances one wonders how the business of the city was carried on before the advent of motor cars with which the dusty streets now swarm.
Cravath, Notes on the Cruise of the Warrior (1928), p. 121

Bangkok has been described as "The city of magnificent distances," which is another way of saying that it takes half an hour to get anywhere.
Garstin, The Dragon and the Lotus (1928), p. 304

The town is one great maze through which one rushes in motors without ever gaining the least idea of the plan.
Candee, New Journeys in Old Asia (1927), pp. 155-156

The streets of Bangkok are crowded with vehicles of every description – ramshackle and disreputable rickshaws, the worst to be found in all the East, drawn by sweating coolies; the boxes of wood and glass on wheels, called gharries, drawn by decrepit ponies whose harness is pieced out with rope; creaking bullock carts driven by Tamils from Southern India; bicycles, ridden by natives whose European hats and coats are in striking contrast to their bare legs and brilliant *panungs*; clanging street cars, as crowded with humanity as those on Broadway; and motors of every size and make, from jitneys to Rolls-Royces.
Powell, Where the Strange Trails Go Down (1921), p. 220

The procession of man-hauled vehicles, ox-carts, and petrol-driven machines forms a striking and unforgettable combination of ancient and modern transport. For its better regulation, there are now white lines, and the constables stand on point duty in raised concrete and iron islands, which prevent them from being run over, and automatically divide the traffic into two fair-ways.
Forty, Bangkok (1929), pp. 25-26

A Rickisha.

From Seidenfaden, *Guide* (1927).

Street Conveyanes and Fares in 1909...

Apparently there is no tariff governing these street conveyances; however, it is customary to pay as follows:

Short ride, say fifteen to thirty minutes, ½ Tical, full hour 1 Tical, and each subsequent hour or part of an hour 2 Tical. Owing to the roughness of the roads, and great distances from place to place, the traveler is advised to in all cases take a carriage.

The best horses, carriages and drivers are to be procured at the livery stables of Mr. Nai Lert, situated on the New Road.

Perkins, Travels (1909), p. 261

The streets were unpaved and dusty though partially lit by electric lamps. Electric trams – the carriages of which were always full to overflowing – provide the means of transport through the main streets. The European can hardly make use of them, however, nor the dirty rickshaws. He is obliged to hire a two-horse gharry at one of the many stands. That is tiresome, and in the long run, expensive too. The great distances and the heat mean that one is always looking for a means of transport. If spending the evening in society or at the club, one often turns up several hours late.

Wilda, Reise auf S.M.S. "Möwe" (1903), p. 277

The City of Magnificent Distances

Though the roads are atrocious and foul odours are not uncommon, Bangkok has shared to the full in the general improvement of the country during the last ten years, and the next decade may witness even greater changes. It is even rumoured that a new Hackney Carriage Act is being enforced. Should this be so the safety of a drive through the streets of Bangkok will doubtless be increased, but much of its romance will be lost.

Thompson, Lotus Land (1906), p. 50

An Act for the regulation and control of hackney carriages in Bangkok came into force on 1st June, 1905. The following summarises some of the provisions:

All carriages kept for hire have to be registered.

Drivers have also to be licensed, and to renew their license every six months. They must be at least 18 years old or apparently so. Before receiving a license each driver has to satisfy the registrar that he knows how to drive, that he has a sufficient knowledge of Siamese, and that he knows his way about Bangkok.

Bangkok Directory (1914), p. 45

At the British Court for Siam this morning before His Honour Acting Judge Crosby, one Bara Khan was summoned for allowing an unlicensed person to drive one of his carriages on the 27th March. Nai Nuen, the gharri driver referred to, said he was employed by the defendant. He corroborated the police evidence. The defendant made no defence. His Honour explained to defendant the use of the licence and what procedure must be followed if ever it was lost. Defendant must be fined Ticals 10.

The Bangkok Times, 2 April 1909, p. 4

The mornings were cool enough before ten o'clock to enjoy driving, and Dum and Dee, as I named the ponies, suppressing the "Tweedle" and thereby reducing the names to very correct Siamese (dee means good), were exhilarating in their dash and speed. The sice, in cool white livery with green collars and cuffs, and a small green forage cap stuck cockily over one ear, cracked his whip and hooted and whistled until I felt as important as a motorist; but nothing got out of our way until death was imminent, and my heart was in my throat. I should like to have stopped at every turn and had my camera hard at work; but no one would have permitted that, Dum and Dee least of all.

Landon, 'Mid Pleasures and Palaces (1907), p. 90

Yesterday afternoon about five o'clock the trap of Mr. Atkinson was standing outside Messrs Tilleke and Gibbins' office.[1] The pony was frightened by something flapping about its legs, and the sais got down from the trap in order to stand at the animal's head. He had not yet reached it, however, when the pony bolted off along Si Phya Road and before it could be secured had knocked down an old Siamese woman, who sustained some cuts on the face.

The Bangkok Times, 21 February 1911, p. 5

Before my arrival I had been told that to go about Bangkok in anything less aggressive than a motor-car was impossible, nay, suicidal. However, gharries and ricksha better suited my purse, and so received the honour of my patronage.

Wheatcroft, Siam and Cambodia (1928), p. 95

A few of the missionaries brought their bicycles with them to aid them in their touring. The Siamese were keenly interested, and when an American dentist imported several wheels to sell in 1896 they were quickly bought.[2] Now there are 3,000 wheels in Bangkok alone. The King frequently rides one. The Minister of the Interior is president of a bicycle club of 400 members. Princes and Government officials make runs into the country.

Speer, Report (1916), p. 3

---

1 Thailand's oldest law firm was established by William Alfred Goone Tilleke (1860-1918) who was joined by Ralph Gibbins in 1902. Tilleke served as Attorney-General, 1912-1917, and was granted the style Phraya Attakarnprasiddh. On entering government service, he sold the firm to Samuel Brighouse (1881-1944) and Reginald Douglas Atkinson (1881-1953).

2 The reference is to George McFarland.

Bangkok now possesses about a dozen miles of electric tramways – one line running from Bangkolem to the Palace and the other from the bridge near the Paknam Railway station to Samsen.[3] In the front portion of each car a small "first-class" portion is reserved, for which double rates are charged. One the main line, which was first worked by electric power in 1894, the fares charged are: -

	1st class.	2nd class.
Bangkolem to Bangrak Bridge	8 atts.	4 atts.
Klong Poh Yome to Sam Yek	8 atts.	4 atts
Sam Yek to Palace	8 atts.	4 atts

These tramways are an immense boon to the Bangkok public and are in every way a success; so much so that another line is projected. The Siam Electricity Co, the tramway proprietors, is a handsomely paying concern and shares rarely come upon the market in any quantity nowadays. The Company has been fortunate in having had but few accidents, these merely minor ones.

Antonio, Guide (1904), p. 21

Bangkok Tramway from Carter, *Kingdom of Siam* (1904).

Lucy Chandler describes the trams …

    All along the street leading from New Road to the Palace crawls the tram-car, like a mechanical toy on the verge of a strike.

Travel, November 1916, p. 27

Today the Borispah Court, Talat Noi, gave judgment in the case in which the Siam Electricity Co. Ltd. sued Mr. F. Dean for Tcs. 75 damages for stopping a tramcar in Bahurat Road in August last.[4] It appeared that Mr. Dean took off the starting handle to prevent the departure of the car before he received his change. Originally a criminal action was brought but this was dismissed. Today the Court awarded the Company Tcs. 10 as damages, Mr. Dean to pay Court costs and lawyer's fee (Tcs. 10). Mr. W. A. G. Tilleke and Mr. D. Atkinson appeared for the Company, and Mr. Soon Kim for Mr. Dean.

*

Between half past eight and nine o'clock Saturday evening, one of the brackets supporting an electrum wire at the corner of Song Wad and New Roads, broke, and the live wire being released coiled up in part, swinging into the middle of the road. Some of the Electricity Co.'s officials from the Sam Yek office were almost immediately on the spot and warned all drivers of vehicles and pedestrians of the danger of approaching the wire. One Chinese, however, pulling a second-class rikisha refused to believe there was any danger. He attempted to get past but became entangled in the live wire and was killed instantaneously.

The Bangkok Times, 20 February 1911, p. 4

    By using the tramways only, the visitor can cheaply and easily reach nearly every place of interest in Bangkok, besides which trips by the tram

---

3 Bsankolem: the area at the southern end of New Road.

4 F. Dean was an engineer with a motor garage which may explain his antipathy to the tram. He later opened the Bangkok Employment Bureau at "189, Surawongse Road, behind British Club".

are full of fascination for the visitor who wishes to learn something of the peoples of Bangkok. We say "peoples" because the trams are always found packed with passengers belonging to a variety of races, nations and creeds, all of whom find shelter within Siam's hospitable shores. Here will be found sitting together yellow robed Siamese monks, long bearded Arabs, sarong clad Malays, voluble Chinese who would appear to keep no secrets from the outside world and yet keep many, dark-skinned Tamils, Burmese, Mon, the *panung*-clad Thai and members of a host of other races. These, for the newcomer, form a picture of unending interest.

Seidenfaden, Guide (1932), pp. 35-36

Waiting for a tram. From an Ainslie album.

The tram-cars offer certain advantages to strangers, since at any rate they are compelled to follow the lines laid down for them, and cannot, like the rickshaws, turn and twist with him through the most impossible streets, from the maze of which it may be difficult to find a way out.

Prince William, In the Lands of the Sun (1915), pp. 78-79

It was obvious I could not confess in French, so it was decided that I should make weekly or fortnightly visits to Père Gigout who was the only English-speaking priest. These expeditions involved a cross-town ride in a Bangkok tram, and during the rains it was a trial of endurance; the trams were flimsy single-deckers open at the sides and without windows;

sometimes canvas flaps were let down in an effort to keep off the torrent, but with a full load of steaming wet passengers it was a regular ordeal.

Lightwood, Teresa of Siam (1960), p. 31

Domingo, being a Eurasian, scorned tramways for the reason that they were patronized almost wholly by natives.

Hervey, The Black Parrot (1923), p. 47

The arrival of the train did not raise our spirits. To call it a train at all was really going far beyond the necessary demands of politeness. It was little more than a glorified tram-car with hard, wooden seats, the first-class portion being exactly the same as the rest, but cut off by a wooden partition. When the "train" started to move it achieved a speed of twenty miles an hour with considerable difficulty, and bumped its way over the uneven track in a bone shattering manner.

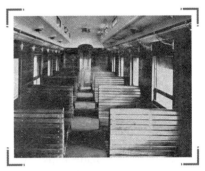

"Interior of bogie third class carriage No. 14-22", from *Royal State Railways of Siam. Fiftieth Anniversary* (1947).

Scott, Eastern Journey (1939), p. 82

Along the left bank of the river ran a small-gauge railway which looked strangely out of place. The toy-like wooden coaches were drawn by a diminutive wood-fired engine of ancient vintage. It was by this line that the fish caught in the Gulf were rushed to the Bangkok markets. It was, in fact, the first railway ever to be constructed in Siam. I was to travel on it daily during my first few months in Bangkok. The line runs almost wholly through paddy-land until it reaches the outskirts of the city at Klong Poh Yome. I learned from Beaumont that the terminus was at Hualompong and the name tickled me. It had a sort of "tiddely-om-pom" air about it which was in keeping with the self-important little engine.

Exell, Siamese Tapestry (1963), pp. 16-17

Bangkok is a city of avenues, and its avenues are lovely; they close high up like Gothic arches. The road gleams yellow in the lights of the car; only when we meet other cars these are lowered on both vehicles, the lamps shine brightly towards us, and glide past.

Kornerup, Friendly Siam (1926), p. 240

The streets of Bangkok will agreeably astonish the visitor from Canton or Peking by their width, their condition, and comparative cleanliness; while the excellent state of the many cross-roads also in the city, such at least as are near the Palace, speak well for the efforts made by the Government during the past ten years in this direction. These owe their existence to the energy of the various European employees of the Siamese Public Works Department.

Norman, The Peoples and Politics of the Far East (1903), pp. 423

From the *Phra Meru* Ground the broad and stately called *Rajadamnoen*, or the Royal promenade, flanked with rows of stately tamarind trees leads out to the Throne Hall and the Dusit quarter where it ends.[5] A certain foreign prince who has visited Siam several times likened this fine avenue to the Champs Elysées of Paris and it certainly vies in beauty with that famous thoroughfare, only so far for it lacks the fine buildings which flank the latter, but these will undoubtedly appear in time.

Seidenfaden, Guide (1927), p. 249

'A Street in Bangkok', from Carter, *Kingdom of Siam* (1904).

---

5 "Phra Meru": Premane. An alternative way of transcribing the Sanskrit word.

84 In Bangkok

This boulevard consists of three carriageways, separated from one another by double lines of trees and bordered by shady footpaths. The palace is surrounded by ornamental gardens open to the public, and the whole quarter is laid out as a purely residential district, the houses being occupied by the princes and noblemen of the court. Between this quarter and the river runs the Samsen Road, corresponding to the New Road below the palace, but far less densely populated. It has a good service of electric trams. Running between these two main roads are many subsidiary roads; the total length of carriage roads being some one hundred and twenty miles.

Carter, The Kingdom of Siam (1904), p. 108

In the afternoon Mr. Bovo drove me through the Dusit Park, which the late King Chulalongkorn a few years ago presented to the people.[6] "Dusit" means Paradise – and truly these tropical gardens, dotted with miniature lakes and cool winding canals, are most beautiful.

Besso, Siam and China (1914), p. 25

The city is not growing so much to the north as to the east and southeast where big plans for settlement and road making are now maturing. The future will see Bangkok as a vast well laid out, park-like town intersected with a network of broad shady roads running in all directions and it will then have become much more even than now "the city of great distances", by which name it is already known.

Seidenfaden, Guide (1932), pp. 89-90

What they have aimed at you see in the broad avenues, straight dusty roads sometimes running by the side of a canal, with which they have surrounded this conglomeration of sordid streets. They are handsome, spacious, and stately, shaded by trees, the deliberate adornment of a great city devised by a king ambitious to have an imposing seat; but they have no reality. There is something stagy about them, so that you feel they are more apt for court pageants than for the use of every day. No one walks

---

6 Goffredo Bovo "who is a journalist and businessman at the same time" (p. 25).

in them. They seem to await ceremonies and processions. They are like the deserted avenues in the park of a fallen monarch.

 Maugham, *The Gentleman in the Parlour (1930), p. 153*

The Ford Car has now arrived and can be seen and trial runs arranged at the Agents' Garage. The Ford Car is the best value in motor cars ever offered and is very cheap to run. It is cheaper to run than a carriage and its first cost is only Ticals 3,150. It has the comfort, smoothness and quiet running of a car costing twice as much.

The Bangkok Dock Company, Limited. SOLE AGENTS.

Advertisement in The Bangkok Times, August 1910

Advertisement in *The Siam Observer*, January 1916.

Since the liquidation of postwar stocks, imports of automobiles have advanced steadily and the American car now dominates the market. Motor traffic is increasing in Bangkok, both in the use of passenger cars and busses. Total registration of motor cars in Bangkok as of January 1, 1928, was 4,388 of which 3,265 were passenger cars.

United States, Department of Commerce, Economic Development of Siam (1929), p. 35

A reader has asked us to draw to attention the bad state of repair of New-road from Banrak to Ban Tawai. He writes: It is getting full of holes and owners of motor cars are having their cars rattled to pieces.

The Bangkok Times, 22 July 1922, p. 6

In Singapore you have your traffic problems, but for sheer unadulterated congestion come to Bangkok.
The Straits Times, 15 June 1923, p. 9

The traffic-control policemen are no less efficient than those in British Malaya. But, like all modern places, Bangkok has many grave traffic problems to be solved and overcome. Many of the streets are far too narrow to accommodate the increasing volume of traffic; and the practice of placing electric street-lamp standards and telegraph poles in the centre of the highway only serves to accentuate the dangers. There are many of these obstructions at the junction of two roads, these compelling motor vehicles and transport to make a wide detour round them. Accident follows accident, for the view of the road ahead is badly obstructed.
Foran, Malayan Symphony (1935), p. 125

There is a growing demand for all forms of motor transport both in Bangkok and the provinces, a significant feature of this development being the recent introduction of taxi-cabs for use in the capital where hitherto casual transport requirements had been met by rickshaws which are now being steadily ousted.
United Kingdom, Department of Overseas Trade, Report on the Commercial Situation in Siam (1929), p. 29

For longer trips than are possible by the tram, such as to the Throne Hall and Wat Benchamabopitr, motor cars or horse carriages are necessary, either of these can be ordered through the hotel in which the visitor is staying.
Seidenfaden, Guide (1932), p. 35

The taxis already have created a very serious problem. At the moment there are no recognised stances, and no special rules whatever governing taxis. Thus we have introduced into our daily life an additional element of danger.
The Straits Times, 5 November 1927, p. 12

There are plenty of motor cars, no speed regulations, and no tar on the roads.
"A. R. M.", quoted in: The Bangkok Times, 4 April 1923, p. 6

The motor has suddenly invaded the country and the driving of the young chauffeur is stupendous. The Government was taken by surprise at the sudden influx of cars, and no traffic regulations were ready. A good many people were taken by surprise also in a still more unpleasant way. The Siamese drives well, it must be allowed, from a trick-driving point of view. He escapes ninety-nine accidents by a hair's breadth for every one he indulges in.

Harris, East for Pleasure (1929), p. 64

To the Editor of "The Bangkok Times."
Dear Sir,

It is unfortunate that so few motor-drivers seem to know the elementary rules of the road, that the driver of a car coming out of a drive or side-road on to a main road must first see that the road is clear before coming out, and that the risk is entirely his. Drivers seem to think that if they blow a horn they can then come out with impunity.

Yours Faithfully,
MOTORIST
The Bangkok Times, 19 February 1929, p. 4

Of 101 cases admitted to the Central Hospital in November, motor accidents accounted for 24, and of outpatients treated during the same period 93 out of a total of 1,699 were motor accident cases. It is said that a man who can drive up New Road in the rush hours when tramcars, rikishaws, horse gharries, heavy lorries, baby cars and limousines are all struggling homeward, and the air resounds with blasts from a dozen differently tuned horns, without accident, can get a driving license anywhere in the world.

Singapore Free Press, 4 January 1929, p. 13

> 6 Cylinder 17 H.P. 25 miles per gallon.
> Any comparison will satisfy you that such automobile values were never before offered.
> Butler & Webster
> Seekak Phya Sri
>
> *Advertisement in The Bangkok Times, 5 February 1927, p. 3*

> Mr. C. L. Watson met with a nasty accident last evening returning from the Sports Club. He was in a five-seater Essex car and collided with the red lamp place where Hua Lampong, Suriwongse and Sports Club roads meet, the car apparently swerving then into a tree by the klong fronting the Chulalongkorn Hospital. The car was severely damaged. A leak was also started in the petrol tank located in the rear of the car. Mr. Watson was thrown against the wind screen and received a nasty gash on the forehead, which necessitated his receiving medical attention.
>
> *The Bangkok Times, 19 January 1926, p. 4*

> We regret to record that Mr. Charles Edward Bulpitt of Messrs. Barrow, Brown & Co. Ltd., was killed last night in a motor cycle accident, which occurred in Hualampong road twenty yards or so to the left of Si Phya road. Precisely how the accident occurred is not quite clear. Apparently, in attempting to avoid a vehicle of some description which was passing out of Si Phya road, the deceased swerved to his right. His right-hand foot-rest struck a tree in front of the row of Chinese shops. The cycle then crashed head-on to another tree. Mr. Bulpitt's head striking the tree, the force of the impact smashing in the top of his skull, and killing him instantaneously. The deceased served in the Army throughout and after the War. He was engaged for the firm out here by Mr. H. Leatherbarrow and reached Bangkok about the end of last December. He was only 29 years of age. Of a most cheerful disposition he will be sadly missed by his people at home and the many friends he made in Bangkok.
>
> *The Bangkok Times, 23 May 1923, p. 4*

The Balharry Case

An accident occurred at New Year's Day at about six o'clock in the morning outside the In-Gate of Chulalongkorn Hospital, when a girl of sixteen named Nangsao Luan Gong-charoen, her little brother of eight, two other girls of thirteen and a youth of sixteen were knocked down by an Essex Super-Six two-seater car driven Mr. J. R. Balharry. All the five juvenile victims were carried into Chulalongkorn Hospital for immediate treatment, but the first named died of internal haemorrhage due to broken loins an hour later. Her little brother and the youth of sixteen sustained serious injuries, while the other two girls received slight injuries. We gather that Mr. Balharry was driving out from the Race Course road towards Sala Daeng. He had swerved to avoid hitting a milk cart trying to pass one of the green 'busses. He himself fortunately escaped with relatively light injuries.

The Bangkok Times, 3 January 1933, p. 6

J. R. Balharry, an accountant with Barrow, Brown and Co. was sentenced here today with six months' imprisonment and fined Tcs. 800 for negligently driving a motor-car on New Year's morning whereby a young girl was killed and two children injured. He was further fined Tcs. 50 for not being in possession of a driving licence at the time of the accident.

It was announced that the defendant is appealing. He has been released pending the hearing of the appeal on bails of Tcs. 8,000.

The Straits Times, 1 April 1933, p. 6

The Appeal Court this week has reversed two judgments both of which concerned foreigners, and both of which have aroused much interest in the foreign colony, albeit it is nowadays of such small dimensions. The first concerned Mr. J. R. Balharry. There was no suggestion that plaintiff was anything other than perfectly normal at the time of the fatality, and he rendered whatever assistance was possible. Mr. Balharry had been waiting for the result of the appeal before going on leave this week, and has received many congratulations on his acquittal. Singapore football players who recently came to Bangkok for the interport matches will remember Mr. Balharry, who had a good deal to do with the successes of the visit.[7] The second case concerned Mr. J. C. Warner of International Engineering Co. and he was found guilty of negligent driving in Christmas week, and fined also for being without a driving licence. The Court of Appeal also in this case reversed the judgement of the lower court as to the charge of driving negligently.

The Singapore Free Press, 28 June 1933, p. 5

---

7 While on leave in Scotland, John Ross Balharry (1907-1986) married. On returning to Bangkok, he resumed his career and continued to play for the Sports Club's football XI. He and his wife finally left Siam in 1939.

Post and Telecommunications

The numbers of civil, genial postmen in their yellow khaki uniforms faced with red, and carrying big Japanese umbrellas under their arms, are sufficiently numerous and busy to testify to the efficiency of this branch of the Civil Service.

Young, The Kingdom of the Yellow Robe (1898), p. 18

There are eleven post and telegraph offices in Bangkok. Their locations and the hours during which they are opened for the transaction of postal business are as follows:
> Post Office No. 1. In the Post Office Lane off Chakrpetch Road opposite the Siam Electricity Co., Wat Lieb, 8 to 17 o'clock.
> Post Office No. 2. Custom House Lane, 8 to 18 o'clock. Telegrams are accepted at his office at all hours.

On Sundays and some of the Government holidays the counters are open only from 8 to 9 o'clock. In the event of a European mail arriving at Bangkok after the ordinary business hours, the Post Office No. 2 (Custom House Lane) is opened for delivery of correspondence as soon as possible after the mails have been sorted and is kept open for one hour, up to 22 o'clock.

Seidenfaden, Guide (1927), pp. 41-42

"Licensed Post-office in business district" from *Siam: Nature and Industry* (1930).

There is a weekly outward and inward mail to and from Europe arriving on Saturday night and closing on Tuesday night. Telegram rates, Bangkok to United Kingdom, are Ticals 1.10 to Ticals 2.00 (2s. to 3s. 8d.), according to route.

The Bangkok wireless station was opened to the public in January, 1929, and telegrams are now received for transmission by wireless to all European countries and to America. The charge to most of the countries in Europe is, for ordinary telegrams, about 2s. 1d. a word, triple rate for urgent and half for deferred. A wireless telephone service between Siam and Europe through Nauen has also been sanctioned and will probably be opened to the public in the near future. A Telefunken unit has been ordered for this purpose. The radio fee for every three minutes connection will be 150 gold francs, to which must be added 12 gold francs for the use of the German land lines and the local charges of the various countries providing facilities.

United Kingdom, Department of Overseas Trade,
Report on the Commercial Situation in Siam (1931), p. 22

The London mails of January 28th via Bombay and Negapatam arrived in Penang by B.I. steamer in time to catch the international express which left Penang this morning and is due in Bangkok to-morrow evening. There are 120 bags.

The Bangkok Times, 19 February 1926, p. 4

General Post Office, Bangkok. "Opening" and "Sorting the European Mail under the Supervision of the Courteous Postmaster Phra Sanasrethra (Nai Fak Sanasrethra)". From *Siam from Ancient to Present Times* (1926).

Post and Telecommunications

The first telephone exchange was established in Bangkok in the year 1886 with 61 subscribers, using the magneto instrument on a single wire system. This installation served satisfactorily until the introduction of electric lights and electric trams into Bangkok. The system was tolerated for 20 years and then abandoned for the present central battery double wire plant. The growth of the system was rapid, but due to the lack of funds, it was not possible to lay down a comprehensive scheme based on best methods or materials. The Government therefore has decided to replace the present system with a complete new underground cable net and modern instruments and equipment.

Siam: Nature and Industry (1930), p. 291

ACCELERATED BI-WEEKLY SERVICE.
Mails closing at G.P.O.
Burma, India, Europe, America: Thursdays 9.30 a.m. Saturdays 4 p.m.
Effective from 12th June
BANGKOK – EUROPE 4 ½ DAYS.

Announcement in The Bangkok Times, August 1935

Along New Road

The New Road is the main artery of the city, five miles long, and it is lined with houses, low and sordid, and shops, and the goods they sell, European and Japanese for the most part, look shop-soiled and dingy. A leisurely tram crowded with passengers passes down the whole length of the street, and the conductor never ceases to blow his horn. Gharries and rickshaws go up and down ringing their bells, and motors sounding their claxons.

Maugham, The Gentleman in the Parlour (1930), p. 151

And what shall I say of thee, Bangkok? Of merits a many, of faults also, not a few. But I could forgive thee all thy faults, were it not for the new road. The new road, why, the very name brings to the lips the scornful smile. Do you know why it is called the new road? Because, at the time it was made 40 years ago, it was the only road! Even more incongruous is its native name "The Road of the Happy City". Always grimy, unlovely, and squalid. Never a glimpse of beauty anywhere, nothing picturesque, nothing to be seen of native architecture – from one end to the other drab and dirty and this is the main road of Bangkok.

Singapore Free Press, 23 August 1917, p. 117

The endless chain of electric cars, which constantly make the air hideous by an automatic fish horn which is always blowing to warn the populace of their approach, carriages, jinrickishas, bullock carts, automobiles and thousands of pedestrians constantly pass in a never-ending stream, making this street a special study in human characters and modes of transportation.

Perkins, Travels (1909), p. 269

New Road cannot boast of any architectural beauty, most of its buildings on both sides being plain or ugly two-storied brick houses without any saving features whatsoever. However, in spite of these obvious drawbacks, this noisy street through which, so to speak, throbs the life blood of the capital, is not without interest, especially for the new-comer.

During a single drive through it one will upon the faces of at least a dozen different races or nationalities.

Seidenfaden, Guide (1927), p. 27

"Central New Road". With Whiteaway, Laidlaw & Co (at left) and H. Swee Hong (at right). Wikimedia Commons.[1]

In the down-town section, fronting upon the river, is the Europeanized business district, where the thatched dwellings are replaced by stone banks, consulates, embassies, stores, and office buildings. The district itself is colorless, but the traffic upon its streets provides plenty of color. There are Siamese government officials, Chinese laborers and merchants, Hindu money-lenders, Japanese dentists or photographers, European employees of foreign commercial houses, all mixed together in a jumble of dilapidated carriages and assorted humanity, a disconcerting mixture of the ancient and the modern, the native and the foreign. The rickety tramway, leading northward parallel to the river, carries one from the European

---

1 Starting in 1906 as a grocery shop, by 1926 H. Swee Hong had become an "extensive and progressive establishment" dealing in "wines, spirits, cigars, cigarettes, confectionery, toilet requisites, etc., etc". Not to be confused with the firm H. Swee Ho though there was clearly a family connection.

business district into the Sampaeng or Chinese quarter, a community of narrow lanes and smelly shops that reproduces Chinese Canton. And finally, from all these drab and disappointing scenes, the dinkey little tramway continues northward, passes through an opening in the ancient city wall and emerges into a strikingly different Bangkok, with wide shady boulevards modeled after those of Paris or Vienna, with parks and gardens and statues, with the handsome palaces of Siamese nobility, with modern office buildings to house the departments of the government, with marble temples surmounted by golden spires and glittering porcelain roofs.

Foster, A Beachcomber in the Orient (1923), pp. 123-127

"Tramway crossing [on] the New Road near entrance to Nagor Khasem Cinema, Bangkok." From *Siam from Ancient to Present Times* (1926).

An Up-to-Date Building for Business

The Borneo Company Limited (BCL) was a general trading company incorporated in London with branches in Bangkok (established 1856) and Chiang Mai. Its operations in Siam included banking, insurance and shipping; the export of rice and hardwoods (especially teak); and the importation of automobiles, engineering equipment, petroleum and numerous consumer products. It acted as local agent for overseas companies, a list of which covered several pages of contemporary commercial directories. Work on a representative new Bangkok headquarters began in early 1924.

The Borneo Company, Limited. (Incorporated in England.)
Head Office – 28, Fenchurch Street, London, E.C. 3
BANGKOK BRANCH

Rice & Timber Merchant. Textiles, Metals, Machinery & General Importers. Telephone "Borneo" – 6 Lines
General Manager for Siam – A. R. Malcolm. Forest Manager – R. W. S. Ogle Commercial Engineering Department. Saw Mill. Borneo Wharf. Banking. Lloyds, Shipping. Fire Insurance, Life Insurance, Motor Car, Personal Accident, Burglary and Plate Glass Insurance.
Bangkok Directory (1930), pp. 350-351

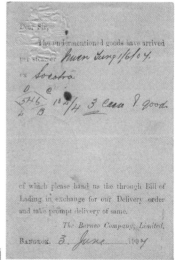

A pre-printed card dated 3 June 1907 in which the company informs the merchants Diethelm & Co. that goods they had ordered have arrived from Singapore on the Nuen Tung of the East Indian Steamship Co. (Bangkok). This happens to have been the ship which brought Reginald Le May to Bangkok in the same year. The Editor's Collection.

Business premises in Bangkok conforming in style and size to the importance of the port are rare. The handsome building in course of construction by the Borneo Company at Bantawai therefore is not only a matter of interest to the company. The building is a three-story structure constructed in ferro-concrete and brick throughout so being entirely fireproof. The methods of construction are entirely up-to-date and in many respects unique, being designed to obtain the best use of materials and labor conditions available in Bangkok. The total length of the building is about 200 feet and the height over 50 feet, the lower floor being about 19 feet. The exterior is treated in free Renaissance style, the main portico being composed of a colonnade of double Ionic columns running through the height of the first two stories. The orientation of the building is so arranged that the fullest advantage is gained from the prevailing hot season winds and the sun passes over the long axis of the building, so avoiding excessive heat from this source, in the working portions of the office. The interior consists mainly of a completely open space covering almost

the whole area of the building, at floor, together with necessary offices, lavatory spaces, strong rooms and staircase spaces. The staircase wells at each end of the building are provided with Waygood-Otis electric lifts, serving all floors of the building.

An Up-to-Date Building for Business 99

The architect of the scheme is Edward Healey A.R.C.A., London, of the Siam Architects, and the contractors are United Engineers Ltd.[1] This is the first time a business firm in Bangkok has built really suitable and adequate premises and we think the community will appreciate their enterprise in this matter.[2]

The Weekly Underwriter (New York), 15 August 1925, p. 297[3]

The new offices of The Borneo Company Limited were formally opened on March 29th, 1926, by His Highness the Minister of Commerce.[4] His Royal Highness said:

"It is a great honour to me that one of the most important firms in Siam has asked me to perform the ceremony of declaring open the new offices. I rejoice, indeed, to see the growth of the Company for the growth of business firms means the growth of trade; and the growth of trade is an index to the prosperity of the country. That the Borneo Company has contributed a share – a large share – towards the making of present-day Siam, I do not think anybody will dare to deny".

The Borneo Company, Seventy Years in Bangkok (1926), pp. 6-7.

The Shipping and Insurance Departments, from *The Borneo Company, Seventy Years in Bangkok.*

---

1 The lighting was installed by the Siam Electricity Company.
2 Healey's building was destroyed by Allied bombing during the Second World War.
3 Much of the description was supplied by BCL and was later printed in Seventy Years in Bangkok.
4 H.R.H. Prince Purachatra.

Almost a Danish Colony?

Leigh Williams explains the importance of the Danish connection with Siam.

Other afternoons were spent buying kit and provisions in a large emporium known as "The Oriental Stores." This concern was run by the Danish "East Asiatic Company," which has branches all over the world and runs its own fleet of motor-driven passenger and cargo vessels. This company is, in a way, the Danish equivalent of our old East India Company, and in those days Bangkok was, commercially, almost a Danish colony. An adventurous young Dane turned as naturally to Thailand as our forefathers to India. In addition to this big company, most of the public utility services in Bangkok were run by Danes, including tramways, river transport, and electric lighting. At that time, too, all the executive posts in the Royal Siamese Provincial Gendarmerie were held by Danes, and a Danish ex-army officer was Director-General of this corps.

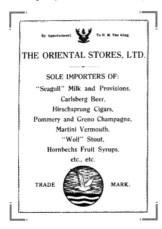

Williams, Green Prison (1941), p. 24

THE LARGEST WHOLESALE STORES IN SIAM.
Large Assortment of Gentlemen's Outfittings, Stationery, Books, Novels, Travelling Implements, Camp Outfits, Glass and Porcelain Wares, Aluminium and Enamelled Wares, Household Goods, etc., etc. Always Large and Fresh Stocks of Provisions, Wines and Spirits, Chocolates, Tobaccos, Cigars, Cigarettes etc., etc.
Cable Address: "Oriental Bangkok."
Advertisements in Seidenfaden, Guide (1927, 1932)

One of the largest import and export businesses in Bangkok is that carried on by the East Asiatic Company, Ltd., who succeeded Messrs. Andersen & Co. in January, 1897. They are largely interested in the teak

The headquarters building of the East Asiatic Company on the river, with the Oriental Hotel on the left. Around 1916. From The American-Scandinavian Review, January 1917. The building has been preserved and is currently under restoration (2023).

trade, holding concessions from the Government over some of the finest forests of Siam, and owning and operating a large sawmill in Bangkok. Their imports consist chiefly of building materials, especially cement, of which no less than thirty to forty thousand casks are imported yearly; while they export, besides teak, such valuable products of the country as sticklac, rubber, gum benjamin, hides, horns, &c. They were the first company to carry teak to Europe by steamer, and now, with characteristic enterprise, they have established a new line of vessels – five in number, and of four to five thousand tons each – which have been built specially for the teak trade, and maintain a regular monthly service from Copenhagen, Middlesbrough, and Antwerp to Bangkok, and from Bangkok to London and Copenhagen.

The East Asiatic Company's offices in Bangkok form an imposing building on the east bank of the Menam.

Twentieth Century Impressions of Siam (1908), p. 143

The Siam Electricity Company, Ltd.[1]

---

1 From 1911, the Managing Director was William (or Vilhelm) Lennart Grut (1881-1949), a former Swedish naval officer. In 1906, he had married Helen Aiko Conder, the daughter of the British architect Joseph Conder, "the father of modern Japanese architecture". Grut became one of the undisputed leaders of Bangkok's foreign business community in the following decades and served as Swedish Consul.

Undated photograph of the European staff of S.E.C. (and Indian watchmen). The location is the company's Wat Liap Power Plant, which is currently under restoration. Wikimedia Commons.

ELECTRIC LIGHT AND POWER SUPPLY
Cheap Rates to Large Consumers.
ELECTRIC TRAMWAY CONCESSIONAIRES.
SUPPLIES OF ELECTRICAL MATERIALS of Every Description,
ELECTRIC INSTALLATION DEPARTMENT.
ELECTRIC AND MECHANICAL WORKSHOP.
Advertisement in Seidenfaden, Guide (1927)

EXHIBIT OF THE SIAM ELECTRICITY CO., LTD. (1911)
This exhibit was divided into three sections, the most attractive of which occupied a site in the north-west quadrant of the Exhibition. Facing the central mound was a signboard, consisting of the name of the Company in Siamese worked out in coloured electric lamps. The internal illuminations were effected by electroliers and brackets of artistic design, while a chain of minute lamps festooned the back wall. At one end an electric motor-car was shown, described as having a capacity of 50 miles for one charge, and a speed of 14 miles per hour. A small charging plant accompanied this exhibit.

Almost a Danish Colony?   103

In another part of the stand was a small sitting-room furnished with ornamental electric lamps, electric kettles, electric cigar-lighters, etc. Among other exhibits were an electric washing and wringing machine, an electric oven, electric flat-irons, and a switch-board with various types of switches, cut-outs, instruments, etc. On the opposite side of the stand was a row of motors of powers varying from ¼ to 10 H.P., and a triplex pump with a capacity of 720 gallons per hour delivered to a height of 75 feet. This was driven by a ¾-H.P. motor. Electric ceiling- and desk-fans were distributed throughout the stand.

Report of the Second Exhibition of Agriculture and Commerce Held in Bangkok (1911), pp. 50-51

The Siam Electricity Co. Ltd. have just imported an electric trolley for use in conveying their men and goods in Bangkok. Three years ago the Company did all their transport by horses; today they have five lorries, petrol and electrical, and further additions will be made shortly. The Company have thoroughly tested the lorries in use, and have arrived at the conclusion that electric driven lorries are more satisfactory than petrol driven ones. The new trolley is a Baker and runs 50 miles without recharging.

The Bangkok Times, 19 May 1911, p. 5

Germans and the Great War

Founded in 1873 as Windsor, Redlich & Co., this old-established house was one of the first European firms to start trading in Siam. Its progress is traced through the periods when Windsor, Redlich & Co. became Windsor, Rose & Co., to remain finally Windsor & Co. The firm carry on a large shipping trade, "Windsor's Wharf" being one of the best known on the river, while the huge stacks of cases, bags and bales prove the size of their import and export business.

Twentieth Century Impressions of Siam (1908), p. 143

Paul Lindenberg (1859-1943) was a German journalist, novelist and travel writer whose journey round the world in 1900 included a sojourn in Siam. In Kurt Nettelbeck, *his novel for young adults (as we would call it today), the firm of Siebold under its proprietor Erwin Siebold is presumably meant to resemble Windsor & Co. under Christian Brockmann or Falck & Beidek under Christian Kramer.*

Kurt had been warmly recommended to Erwin Siebold, the firm's proprietor, and had been amiably received by him. Kurt deeply admired a man who, despite being only a little over forty, had already secured for his firm a sterling reputation. Thanks to a character marked by reliability, propriety and indefatigable energy, and his calm manner, he had won the friendship of the King of Siam himself who had come to rely on his advice in commercial matters.

The interior of the main building resembled a department store, the goods of which, however, were destined for rich Siamese and Chinese customers (there being several hundred thousand of the latter in Bangkok) rather than Europeans. Apart from modern hunting equipment and equestrian gear, fine textiles, precious stones and time-pieces, there could be found musical instruments, optical and pharmaceutical instruments, music

Kurt with two wealthy Chinese customers.

boxes, phonographs, mechanical toys and Parisian puppets. One room was even rigged up with a baldachin of purple silk, richly decorated in gold. It had been ordered by a Siamese prince, a close relative of the King, who had however died before the wonderful creation had completed its long journey from Vienna to Bangkok.

Lindenberg, Kurt Nettelbeck (1903), pp. 4-5

The social centre and general meeting-place for German residents in Bangkok is the Deutscher Klub, which was founded, with an original membership of 40, some eighteen years ago. During the first years of its existence the Klub had a small rented house as its headquarters, for its present premises in Suriwongse Road were not erected until 1896. The building is surrounded by well-laid-out grounds, containing tennis-courts, &c, and the Klub has now 135 members, which means practically every German resident in Siam. They have their own reading-room, and are entitled to make free use of the library, which is an excellent one, comprising German, English, and French books. The club is also provided with billiard-tables, a bowling-alley, and a gymnasium for the entertainment of the members. The management of the Klub is vested in a committee, elected annually.

Twentieth Century Impressions of Siam (1908), p. 252

The German Club. The knowledge that there was such a thing raised our spirits and brought us somehow nearer home even at this great distance. A Chinese boy drove us there. Suddenly, a shimmer of light and the sound of German voices and songs. These were coming from an attractive villa-style building. We had reached the German Club – and an authentic piece of our homeland. Apart from the proprietors of the largest trading companies in Bangkok, we find more Germans working as architects, engineers, apothecaries, booksellers, ship captains, goldsmiths, photographers, etc., and – what makes a particularly good impression – they all come together in the previously-mentioned club and cultivate there a sense of nationhood and a love of their native land.

Lindenberg, 'Deutschland und Siam', in: Asien. Organ der Deutsch-Asiatischen Gesellschaft, Vol. 1, 1902, pp. 14-17

Although Lindenberg's novel *Kurt Nettelbeck* ends with a rendition of the German national anthem, this is followed on the final page by Martin Ränicke's illustration of the young Siamese Maha-Kien and the White Elephant.

The Weber Case

Until "extra-territorial rights" were cancelled under revised treaties, consulates and their officials had a judicial function.

At the German Consular Court this morning the hearing was resumed of the case in which W. Weber is charged with defrauding a Javanese woman, whose name is given as Marie Mina, with whom he had stayed in a local hotel. It will be remembered that about two months ago prisoner was brought back to Bangkok from Singapore, where he had been arrested on information received from Bangkok. He has since been in custody. The Consul, Baron Rudt von Collenberg, accompanied by Mr. H. Habenicht and Mr. H. Schüngel as assessors, and Mr. K. Zobel as Registrar, heard the case.[1] The proceedings were conducted in German.

Prisoner first gave evidence on his own behalf, addressing the Court at length, and replying to occasional questions by the Consul. He said that he met the complainant in the train from Kuala Lumpur. His boy acted as interpreter and he did not know all that was said. Complainant spoke Malay. She had not a thousand dollars in her possession. He did not ask her to come to Bangkok. She wanted to come. He understood complainant was the widow of a certain Dr. Day, who died in Kuala Lumpur and left

---

1 The German Vice-Consul, Heinrich, Freiherr Rüdt von Collenberg-Bödigheim (1875-1954), was transferred to Winnipeg in Canada in 1913; he later became an active member of the Nazi Party. Zobel: Student Interpreter at the Legation, later chargé d'affaires; Habenicht: manager of A. Markwald & Co. in Bangkok; Schüngel: local representative of Norddeutscher Lloyd.

her his property. Prisoner gave details of work he had done in various places, including Colombo, Calcutta and Singapore.

Complainant was the next witness, Mr. Landau acting as interpreter.[2] She declared that a cheque for one thousand dollars, which was the result of the sale of Dr. Day's property, was taken from her by prisoner at Bangkok. She said she was born in Singapore. When she met prisoner in the train, he proposed to take her to Java, and then they would go to America, where they would be married. When they got on the boat to go to Bangkok she understood they were going to Java. Complainant added that prisoner took some other money of hers at Singapore and some jewellery at Bangkok.

Mr. Prufer, of the Bristol Hotel,[3] gave evidence to the effect that prisoner and complainant came to his hotel. Prisoner gave the name of Eckhardt and said the woman was his wife, and the bill was Tcs. 196, of which Tcs. 60 had been paid. Mr. Rosenberg of the Europe Hotel stated that he had known the prisoner in Singapore as well as his wife, who was German, and considered him a very respectable man.[4] Prisoner called on him at his hotel. Prisoner strongly denied taking the cheque from complainant. The only thing he had done wrong, he said, was giving a wrong name to Mr. Prufer.

The court decided to inflict sentence of two months imprisonment for taking money to Singapore, one month for taking the jewellery, and fourteen days for going to the Bristol Hotel when not in a position to pay for board. Fourteen days being deducted according to German law, a month was left to be served, as prisoner had already been two months in prison. He had the right to appeal. As the appeal would have to go to Germany the prisoner elected to undergo the third month's imprisonment. Prisoner was found not guilty with regard to the alleged cheque.

The Bangkok Times, 4 June 1912, p. 5

---

2 Adolphe Landau, who spoke Malay.

3 C. Prüfer, the manager.

4 Maurice (Mordechai) "Max" Rosenberg (1864-1930), proprietor of the Europe Hotel, is buried in the Protestant Cemetery (Block E1).

The Great War and After

Anglo-German rivalry in Siam was becoming sharper around the turn of the century.

The largest part of the carrying trade between Siam and the outside world is in German hands – a fact due almost entirely to the enterprise of one company, the Norddeutscher Lloyd. They have what is to all intents and purposes a monopoly. They also engage largely in the coast trade, and the extent and importance of their interests may be calculated from the preponderating number of steamers flying the German flag which may any day be seen in the river Menam.

Twentieth Century Impressions of Siam (1908), p. 143

When the Great War began in August 1914, Siam at first remained neutral. In July 1917, however, Siam declared war on Germany and Austria-Hungary.

At daylight this morning four Naval gun boats, in company with two fire floats and a number of launches and other small craft filled with armed naval parties went down the river and took possession of the German steamers and lighters now lying there.[5] The officers on board were taken away for internment and armed parties were left in charge of each ship, which is now flying the Siamese flag. The German business premises were today all in charge of a party of police and military, with sentries with fixed bayonets outside.

All the German and Austrian men were taken to the internment camp in motor cars under escort of police officers.

The Straits Times, 28 July 1917, p. 9, quoting the Bangkok Daily Mail of July 22

Auction Sale.
Instructed by the CUSTODIAN OF ENEMY PROPERTY,
I will sell the Furniture and Household Effects including TWO MOTOR CYCLES, belonging to Messrs. O. Knoepf, E. Rosenburg [sic], A. Falck, W. F. Schmidt, A. Jurgensen, A. Fitz, F. Lampe, W. Lampe, A. Ulrich and S. Goertzen.[6]

---

5 The ships had lain idle in harbour since August 1914.

6 Most of these interned "enemy aliens" had been minor government officials or assistants in German firms. Similar auctions were held in the following weeks and months.

On Thursday, the 25th, Saturday 27th, and Monday, the 29th October 1917. Commencing at 2 p.m. each day.
At the show rooms of the City Auctioneering Co., Unakan Road, opposite S.A.B. City. Benjamin J. Periera, Auctioneer.

Advertisement in The Siam Observer, October 1917

WAR LOAN LOTTERY.
To be held under the auspices of the Patriotic League of Britons Overseas. (His Majesty's Government has kindly sanctioned the holding of this Lottery.) The amount of the Lottery will be TICALS 250,000 Or such lesser or greater amount as may be subscribed Tickets Ticals Five Each. HAMILTON PRICE (President)[7]
ANDREW R. CARSON (Hon. Secretary)

The Bangkok Times, 5 December 1917, p. 3

The examination of the different businesses, etc. by the officials of the Custodian of Enemy Property has led to certain facts being ascertained, and the Civil Court will shortly hear how Mr. C. Kramer, the wealthy head of the late firm of Falck and Beidek, disposed of some of his property. It appears that shortly before the declaration of war by Siam Mr. Kramer transferred the title-deeds of the land and premises upon which he carried on business in Chartered Bank Lane to Nang Plaak, as guardian for his children by her. In a similar manner he also transferred certain shares to Nang Plaak, and a mortgage from Messrs. Markwald and Co. Ltd. All the transfers are, we understand, alleged to have been made by way of gift, and the Custodian is applying to the Courts to reject these transfers.

The Straits Times, 22 March 1918, p. 9

German and Austrian residents were interned on the declaration of war and, with very few exceptions, were expelled to British internment camps in India in early 1918. In 1920, most were repatriated to Germany. Only in 1923 were Germans allowed to return to Siam and could German firms be reestablished.

---

7 Hamilton Price was manager of the Bombay Burmah Trading Corporation in Siam; Carson was accountant to the Bangkok Dock Co.

110 In Bangkok

The enemy alien prisoners of war interned since the 22nd July last left Bangkok yesterday by the *Den Samud* and *Pia Samud*.[8] The men were accommodated on the *Pia Samud* and numbered 180. The women and children to the number of 90 were placed on board the *Den Samud*.

We have heard of English people who cried when enemy children under their care were taken away. This spirit of *songsaan* was too prevalent; happily now the cause has been removed, it may well be that the circumstances will be viewed in the right light.[9]

The Bangkok Times, 13 February 1918, pp. 4-5

FREEZING OUT THE BOCHE

At an extraordinary general meeting of members of the Royal Bangkok Sports Club what was probably the biggest attendance since the Club has been in existence gathered, there being about 140 present. The Chairman said the first thing before them was the consideration of the proposed new rules to read as follows: (1) No German or Austro-Hungarian Subject shall be eligible for election to the Club, either as an Ordinary or honorary Member. (2) No German or Austro-Hungarian Subject shall have extended to him any of the privileges relating to "Visitors and Strangers," specified in Rule 29 of the Club.

The amendment to the rules on the agenda was then put. Upon the Chairman asking those in favour of it to stand up, practically the whole gathering rose, and on those opposed to it being asked to rise no one moved. The Chairman then declared the amendment carried, amidst cheers and applause.

Englishman's Overland Mail, 29 November 1918, p. 13

There follows the text of a postcard in the editor's collection which was written (in German) in reply to a letter from an unknown person who was presumably in internment and awaiting repatriation.

---

8   Former German-owned ships, renamed.

9   "Songsaan": sympathy, feeling sorry for someone.

Geinsheim, 13 August 1919

Many thanks for your greetings. We are still well. We are thinking a good deal about the dear Siamese soldiers ("die guten Soldaten Siamoises").

Best wishes from Papa, Mama and Cäcilie. I wish you a safe journey back to the homeland, dear Sir, and send you warmest greetings. Until we meet again ("Auf Wiedersehen").

Your Marie.[10]

The Re-Establishment of German Interests

Germans are now permitted to reside in this country and carry on trade.
The Bangkok Times, 17 February 1925, p. 4

Representative of a well-established HAMBURG house desires first-class connections for export and import STOCKS of high-class LACES and TRIMMINGS for immediate disposal at Bangkok. Please call EUROPE HOTEL Room No: 11.
Advertisement in The Bangkok Times, 18 February 1925, p. 4

We regret to announce the death of Mr. Karl Zobel, Chargé d'Affaires for Germany, which took place about midnight last evening. Mr. Zobel was at dinner with his wife when he complained about not feeling well. Mrs. Zobel went to his assistance and he was conveyed to his bed unconscious. Mr. Zobel passed away without regaining consciousness. Death was due to a heat stroke. Much sympathy will be felt with Mrs. Zobel and their young daughter Margarethe, so suddenly bereaved. Since Mr. Zobel's return to Siam he had been a very busy man, and told the writer a few weeks ago he would be glad when he had assistance as he was feeling the strain of the work consequent on the reestablishment of German interests in Siam.[11]
The Bangkok Times, 12 June 1925, p. 4

NOTICE IS HEREBY GIVEN BY THE UNDERSIGNED
THAT THEY HAVE TO-DAY RE-ESTABLISHED THE FIRM OF
B. Grimm & Co.[12]
As an open partnership in this city. They further beg to notify that they have taken over the firm of L. Bohensky. Bangkok 1st January, 1926.

An advertisement in another column sets forth the re-entry into the business community of Bangkok of the firm of B. Grimm and Co. Messrs. B. Grimm and Co. were a big firm before Siam's entry into the war brought an end to their trading here, and the big three storey building now occupied by the Siam Electricity Co. Ltd. was built for the occupation of Messrs. B. Grimm and Co. Mr. L Bohensky, who has been successfully established here since 1922 as general importer and representative of the Hamburg firm of B. Grimm & Co., and Mr. J. K. Hanhart, the former manager of the said Hamburg firm, have joined Mr. A. Link, the former sole proprietor of B. Grimm & Co., as partners, while the firm of L Bohensky has been amalgamated with B. Grimm & Co.

The Bangkok Times, 2 January 1926, pp. 5, 7

Emil Eisenhofer (1879-1962), who had been expelled with his colleagues in 1918, returned to Siam in early 1929 with a new job in business.

The German railway engineer Mr. E. Eisenhofer who arrived on the last *Deli* has come out from Germany for the firm of Paul Pickenpack and Co. Before the war Mr. Eisenhofer was in the Royal Railway Department. He superintended the construction of the Kao Plung tunnel and had a great deal to do with the boring of the Khoon Tan tunnel. After an absence of several years he finds Bangkok a changed city.

The Bangkok Times, 18 January 1929, p. 4

---

10 As it happens, Geinsheim was one of the villages that had been allocated to the Siam Expeditionary Force under the Allied occupation of the Rhineland between December 1918 and July 1919. One of the nineteen members of the Siam Expeditionary Force to die in Europe died in Geinsheim in April 1919. "Marie" was a conventional name in German-speaking Europe for a female servant, and the letter uses formal pronouns (Sie/Ihr). It is written in cursive rather than German script, presumably because the letter would otherwise have been illegible to censors. The card is franked "DE 21 07", perhaps suggesting it arrived in Siam long after German internees had been repatriated from India in early 1920.

11 Zobel is buried in Block H. The inscription on his memorial appears to have been deliberately removed.

12 In 2023, the firm celebrated its 145th anniversary, having established "the first modern pharmacy in Thailand" in 1878. See https://bgrimmgroup.com/history/.

The People of Bangkok

The first Bangkok census was carried out in 1909, with the following results:

Bangkok Town – Males, 379,118; Females, 249,557; Total 628,675. Provinces in Monthon Bangkok – Males, 108,863; Females 129,913; Total 238,776. The whole Bangkok Monthon – Males, 487,981; Females 379,470; Total 867,451. The different nationalities: – Siamese 639,920. Chinese 197,918. Indians and Malays, 20,764. Europeans 1,604. Other nationalities 7,245.

Bangkok Directory (1914), p. 190

The spectator is struck by the diversities of nationality that make up this huge city of half a million souls. The Siamese themselves form the chief element. Next to them come the ubiquitous Chinamen, who are variously estimated as constituting from one fourth to one half of the population; then, too, there are Laos and Shans from up country, kinsfolk of the Siamese, and not easily distinguished from them, Annamites

"Siam. A Type of the People", from a series of postcards issued ca 1905. The Editor's Collection.

114 In Bangkok

and Cambodians, Malays, Burmese, Singhalese, and Indians, a regular anthropological museum, and what is very noteworthy, almost all with their special occupations and provinces of work.[1] Nowhere, too, in the East is to be found such a representative gathering of European nations, the smaller communities, such as the Belgians and Danes, being well to the fore.

Campbell, Siam in the XXth Century (1902), pp. 55-56

Let the Roof Fall In *is a novel published in late 1910 by Julia Frankau, née Davis (1859-1916), writing as "Frank Danby". Although there is no evidence that Frankau herself visited Siam, As a reviewer remarked, the novel includes, "some sketches of life in Siam that seem to have been studied from the real thing".*[2]

A babel of polyglot tongues is heard in the streets, not only by the side of the mud-banks, the wharves, and the jetties, where the floating Asiatic population of Chinese and Malays, Annamites and Siamese dominate the river, but up in the town, where there are Javanese, Singalese and Bengalee, men from Bombay, and gem-dealers from Burmah.

Frankau, Let the Roof Fall In (1910), p. 213

The Japanese have a large community domiciled here, and are chiefly engaged in trades or professions. There is more than an average proportion of Japanese among the medical and dental professions; and many more are either chemists or photographers. They are to be found in almost every township – watchful, polite and yet inscrutable.

Foran, Malayan Symphony (1935), p. 126

On arriving at the Merchants' Wharf or the Hotel Quay, or when looking up one's acquaintances in the busy town, one's first question is,

---

1 Annamites: Vietnamese.
2 The Standard, 28 October 1910, p. 5. The most plausible explanation for the "sketches" is that Frankau drew on letters sent from Bangkok by her niece, Benita ("Nita") Eugénie Thompson, née Aria (1885-1923), or perhaps on Thompson's later recollections. Aria had married Harry Alec Thompson (1881-1912), an assistant in the Royal Survey Department, in December 1908. She lived with her husband in Bangkok for about two years, returning with him to England at the end of his contract in early 1910.

Where is Siam? Where are the Siamese? Everywhere are Chinamen, or Malays, or Indians. Do the Siamese have no part in all this scene of activity and commerce? A very small share. In one's wanderings one sees at first but little of Siam and the Siamese.

Norman, The Peoples and Politics of the Far East (1895), p. 410

But where all this while are the Siamese? Here and there in the crowd we have picked out a Siamese of the better class in white linen coat and *panung*, a graceful garment this, of shot silk draped so as to look not unlike loose knickerbockers; and in the city we may have seen officers of the army, possibly even a prince, in uniform. Perhaps a lady has driven by.

Of the humbler classes three out of every four whom we have met so far have been Chinese. To see the Siamese we should walk through the city at daybreak, when the streets are thronged with yellow-robed monks slowly moving on and stopping only when some devout person steps forward to put in their bowls a little rice, or sweetmeats or dried fish.

Thompson, Lotus Land (1906), p. 36

The Siamese are a good-looking, polite little people. There is at least as much etiquette as in any place I have been to, and they are most particular about it. Siamese ladies are very pretty, very tiny, and very misleading as to their age. A girl I thought was thirteen was twenty, and so on. They are the youngest-looking people in the world, and among the smallest. Siam is a nation in miniature.

Harmsworth, Voyage Round the World (1923), pp. 205, 207

The features of the Siamese are strongly Mongolian. A wide head, flat at the back, a prognathous jaw, a flat nose very broad at the nostrils, long and slightly oblique eyes, large ears and high cheek bones, are the usual physical characteristics. The result is not very prepossessing, while the customs, common to both sexes, of wearing the hair short and erect in a stiff black brush and of blackening the teeth either by the constant chewing of betel or by the application of a dye obtained from burnt coconut shell, still further detract from the general appearance.

Graham, Handbook (1912), pp. 141-142

Major Foran was also unimpressed by the physical charms of the Siamese ...

The Siamese, both men and women, are not endowed by nature with much physical beauty, but they are very sturdy. Their faces, generally speaking, are almost ugly; and they heighten this with the beastly practice of chewing unlimited quantities of betel nut mingled with lime.

The Straits Times, 5 March 1925, p. 9

They prefer the darker colours, and many of them dress in pure black. In spite of that, however, the scene was far more picturesque than anything Malaya had to offer, simply because it was far more Oriental.

Scott, Eastern Journey (1929), pp. 81, 86

The common classes are very filthy in their habits. The immorality of the Siamese women is really deplorable; there are few oriental countries where they have fallen so low.

Miller, The Newest Way Round the World (1908), p. 143

One of the most unmistakable signs that Siam is a stronghold of the aristocratic spirit is the complete absence of any exclusiveness in school. Young princesses sit side by side with foundlings, and bring their little servants to receive identically the same education as themselves.

To the English idea a very curious custom is that of addressing every person be he child or servant by the prefix Mr. or Miss, Nai or Meh. I was told that it is because so very many names serve both sexes – but as most people know their own sex it more probably has to do with the national love or ceremony.

Wheatcroft, Siam and Cambodia (1928), pp. 203-204

The skin is not tattooed except here and there with tiny charm-marks.

Graham, Handbook (1912), p. 142

I saw a good many men with tatooed [sic] arms and breasts and upon inquiry was told that on account of the perishable nature of their records, or inability to keep any, often the salient events of a family are thus preserved. To show their respect, the people, especially those of the more subservient kind, have a habit of placing their hands together in what would be with us an attitude of prayer and bending their knees slightly. The children usually do this if they are given any favor or attention.

Hendley, Trifles of Travel (1924), p. 206

The politeness of the Siamese, I was to find, is ingrained in all classes, and is not a mask, as in the case of some Oriental races. These smiling, friendly people are as scrupulously polite to each other as to strangers. Instances of discourtesy among pure-bred Siamese are extremely rare, and were confined in my experience to "other ranks" in the army.

Williams, Green Prison (1941), p. 13

One very pleasant token of respect in Siam is the lowered voice, which makes even holiday gatherings, gay though the Siamese naturally are, quiet compared to most crowds, notably to Chinese and Indian crowds.

Wheatcroft, Siam and Cambodia (1928), p. 106

The Siamese greet one another charmingly, their hands joined in prayer and their bodies bent at the waist. When inferiors come into the presence of their superiors they prostrate themselves and advance by crawling on their knees. The head is sacred in Siam. One of the reasons why there are no multiple stories in Siamese houses is that it is not proper to walk over the heads of others.

Morand, Nothing but the Earth (1927), p. 142

Traps for the unwary are many and various in a land with traditions so different from our own. It was only at the very end of my stay that I discovered that to point with the foot is considered rudeness' depth. Most probably too I may have tapped the floor with my foot in efforts to wake up the class, which must have been paralysed with horror!

Wheatcroft, Siam and Cambodia (1928), p. 206

The *panung* combines in an admirable degree the qualities of usefulness and gracefulness, at any rate in the case of the male sex. It leaves the

limbs bare from the knees downwards, and has the appearance of loose knee-breeches or knickerbockers. The *panungs* of the rich, being often of beautiful silk, are very handsome, their very simplicity adding to the effect. They are to be seen of all hues – orange, green, blue, red, and purple in every shade – each day of the week, it is said, having its appropriate colour, and this variety greatly enhances the picturesqueness of a Siamese crowd, all classes alike wearing the *panung*. It must, however, be admitted that it is not so becoming to the women, whose figures no more than their faces are their strong points of attraction.
Campbell, Siam in the XXth Century (1902), pp. 137-138, 140

The custom is derived from Brahminism, and the colours are those of the planets. Siamese who can afford the luxury wear for:

Sunday	Red
Monday	Yellow
Tuesday	Light Mauve
Wednesday	Green
Thursday	Dark Orange
Friday	Blue
Saturday	Dark Purple or Black

On *Wan Phra* – Holy Days – the days of the Moon's changes, Rose may be worn.
Wheatcroft, Siam and Cambodia (1928), p. 184

A word must be said for the really exquisite toilettes of the Siamese ladies, who possess the faculty of being able both to combine styles and to blend colours.
Macmillan, Seaports of the Far East (1925), pp. 480-481

Scantiness of clothing is the prevailing mode among the lower classes, and the peasantry still retain the national costume of the *panung* with next to nothing above the waist. But the aristocracy and the bourgeoisie have struck out new lines, so tentatively and hesitantly, however, that the fashions of Bangkok may be said to be in a state of flux. While some cling tenaciously to the *panung* and adopt the European fashions of exquisite creations without the skirt, a few others are following the Parisian styles "in toto". It is gratifying to note that, while most women wear their hair cropped short like men, the fashion in the upper classes tends in the direction of bobbed hair and long tresses – and white teeth.

Pasqual, A Trip: Through Siam (1925), p. 61

Siamese flappers are the American girls of the East – pretty, boyish, insouciant. They Charleston, smoke, drink a wee bit, and play golf. They do almost all the "Western" things except wear hats. Sometimes a shawl – but never a hat!

The London & China Express, 22 March 1928, p. 203

They believe in ghosts, in *Phi*. These spirits and many others play a great rôle in their lives. They are the spectres of those who have died of cholera or have been eaten by wild beasts, or have had no sepulchre. They must be looked after and fed. The most dangerous of all are the ghosts of women who have died in childbirth and of those who loved life too well while they lived.

Morand, Nothing but the Earth (1927), pp. 143-144

Lucie Chandler describes "spirit houses"…

In front of each house, whether it borders a khlong or creeps up on the flat plain that approaches the palace grounds, there stands a tall bamboo pole, topped by a sort of bird house. These miniature aerial domiciles are detention houses for the *pees* – the evil spirits of Siam. The superstitious natives believe that if furnished with a private residence outside, the pees will refrain from encroaching upon domains so hospitably on the defensive. At night bright lanterns swing upon the poles, not by way of invitation, as in the daytime, but by way of a flaming sword at the gate. For the pees a quarantine by day, but by night complete exclusion!

Travel, November 1916, p. 29

When not plunging into the mud the boys are generally smoking cigarettes of the coarse native tobacco.

Thompson, Lotus Land (1906), p. 41

AN INVETERATE SMOKER

Everybody in Siam smokes – men, women, and children. The favourite place for carrying cigars and cigarettes is behind the ear, just as our American grocery clerks carry their pencils. Yesterday I saw a naked boy of four smoking a cigarette. He was puffing away lustily at the one in his mouth, and he had two others yet unlit, one behind each ear. He apparently enjoyed his tobacco, and smoked and spit and spit and smoked as though it were an every-day matter, as I doubt not it was. His brown-skinned father stood beside him and when he started away he picked up the still smoking youngster, set him astride his hip, and walked off.

Carpenter, From Bangkok to Bombay (1924), p. 10

Smoking is commenced at a very early age, and every little boy has his own tobacco supply and packet of cigarette-papers. As he trots to school in the morning he puffs away vigorously, occasionally passing his cigarette to a friend that he also may take a few whiffs. As soon as school is over, out come the matches and the cigarettes again, and the little chimney puffs off home to lunch.

Young, Siam (1908), p. 16

The children are charming and go naked, their little bellies filled to bursting with rice. Sometimes they smoke cigars, stopping only long enough to suckle their mothers.

Morand, Nothing but the Earth (1927), p. 146

The staple article of food is of course rice, as it is in all Southern and Eastern Asia, Siam being one of the greatest rice-producing countries of the world. The usual accompaniment of this is fish curry, meat being practically never used by the poorer Siamese, who have not acquired the Chinese predilection for pork. Still fish affords scope for a considerable variety of dishes. The people are also not averse to decayed prawns and salted eggs, and are skilled in the making of various hot sauces and condiments, the favourite one of which is called *namphrick*, and contains several ingredients, among them red pepper, brine, and ginger.

Campbell, Siam in the XXth Century (1902), pp. 142-143

Caspar William Whitney (1862-1929) was an American journalist and travel writer.

Siamese food principally consists of dried, frequently rotted fish, and rice, done into curries which comprise a little of about every kind of condiment, and especially a very popular sauce called *namphrik*, a chutney-like and thoroughly mixed thing made of red pepper, shrimp, garlic, onions, citron, ginger, and tamarind seeds. I must confess that when the fish in the curry chanced to be dried instead of decayed, I found the concoction toothsome.

Whitney, Jungle Trails and Jungle People (1905), pp. 11-12

'Siamese Women Milling Rice'. Part of a set of postcards printed by Raphael Tuck in England for E. M. Pereira, the stationers and auctioneers, in Bangkok. The Editor's Collection.

When the members of the family sit down to take a meal, they squat on the floor. A big bowl of rice is placed in the centre of the ring, and round it are arranged smaller basins of curry. Everybody helps himself, so that the fastest eater gets the biggest share. Forks and knives are not used, and very often spoons also are lacking. In such cases fingers take the place of spoons, and they seem to serve the purpose equally well. Of course, the fingers get greasy and sticky, but they can be put in the mouth and licked clean again quite easily and quickly.

Young, Siam (1908), p. 53

The morning meal usually consists of rice curry, vegetables, and peppers, mixed with salt and garlic. The noon meal is about the same as the breakfast. The evening meal is largely of rice curry. It usually lacks the hot flavoring ingredients used at breakfast. The rice curry of the evening meal is generally of chopped meat and fish. A small amount of fermented fish oil may be added. Among the wealthier classes, fresh native fruits usually conclude the meal. The use of sweets between meals is common throughout all of Siam among people able to purchase them.

Crocheron and Norton, Fruit Markets (1930), p. 184

Although the leading characteristic of the Siamese may be a disinclination for any hard and sustained form of labour, it must be confessed that this is generally shared by those Europeans who live in hot countries. Moreover it is only true of the men in Siam, for the women are hard workers, keen business people and the backbone of the country. As to the men then, one of their best friends was indignant that they should be called "incorrigibly idle," but when asked to substitute a phrase he could only suggest as an alternative "incurably indolent."

Thompson, Lotus Land (1906), p. 199

I have been told that in Bangkok, at any rate, the Siamese now work much harder than they did a generation ago. With the influx of Europeans and the increasing competition of the Chinese, and with the spread of. the town, the price of necessaries has greatly increased, and life involves a harder struggle for everyone, so that it may well be that many individual Siamese are now confronted with the choice of doing some work or starving.

Campbell, Siam in the XXth Century (1902), pp. 101, 104

Rosaleen had a secret sympathy with the Siamese natives. She had found great happiness at Bangkok, and perhaps that softened her judgment. What Mrs. Huxted called lying, she and Derry had agreed to regard as merely a habit of circumlocution. And the natives were only idle when they were not set to work. Derry had two Siamese clerks under him in the office, and could not speak sufficiently highly of them. She did not think they were vicious.

Frankau, Let the Roof Fall In (1910), p. 217

We liked the Siamese people. The rank and file of them are gay, good-natured and orderly. Their faces are intelligent and alert.
Cravath, Notes on the Cruise of the Warrior (1928), pp. 127-128

The natural kindliness of the Siamese also comes to light in their treatment of their children. One of the most pleasing sights, among much that is squalid and ugly in the streets of Bangkok, is to see not only the mothers, but also the fathers carrying in their arms and fondling their little soft-eyed, brown skinned children, who have at that early age a distinct attractiveness.
Campbell, Siam in the XXth Century (1902), p. 110

The Siamese are a gentle and lovable race.
Sayre: Glad Adventure (1957), p. 90

Beaumont's knowledge of Siam and the Siamese was inexhaustible. The Siamese, I learned, were a cheerful, happy, polite people, not over fond of work; easy enough to get on with, but determined to go it their own way. They had never been colonized and resented nothing more than lofty Western criticism. They had an intense national pride and the younger generation was feeling its way cautiously and uncomfortably towards political development.

"Learn their language and their customs," advised Beaumont. "Then you'll earn their respect and close friendship."
Exell, Siamese Tapestry (1963), p. 15

W A. R. Wood receives some advice from Prince Damrong ...

In 1905 I made my first trip up to the North. When I went to say good-bye to Prince Damrong he was extraordinarily kind to me, and gave me a good deal of excellent advice, some items of which I have attempted to act upon ever since. I will give one example. I happened to say that a certain man had deceived me. Prince Damrong gave me the following warning: – "Before accusing one of my fellow-country-men of deceit, make quite sure that he is not merely trying to be polite." I have never forgotten this advice, which has often saved me from judging my Siamese friends unjustly.
Dedication to Prince Damrong of Siam (1947), pp. 6-7

My travels have never brought me among a people seemingly more contented, more happy, than these Siamese.
Whitney, Jungle Trails and Jungle People (1905), p. 43

The people of the country are hospitable and very pleasant – the whole atmosphere is friendly. Bangkok itself is amusing, full of colour and unpretentious. The city may present no very remarkable features, but it possesses many things that please and are its very own, that give colour and character to the place and that reflect the contented spirit of the population.
Harris, East for Pleasure (1929), p. 79

Chinese Bangkok

If you turn out of the main road you will find yourself in a network of small streets, dark, shaded, and squalid, and tortuous alleys paved with cobble-stones. In numberless shops, open to the street, with their gay signs, the industrious Chinese ply the various crafts of an Oriental city. Here are druggists and coffin shops, money-changers and tea-houses. Along the streets, uttering the raucous cry of China, coolies lollop swiftly bearing loads and the peddling cook carries his little kitchen to sell you the hot dinner you are too busy to eat at home. You might be in Canton. Here the Chinese live their lives apart and indifferent to the Western capital that the rulers of Siam have sought to make out of this strange, flat, confused city.
Maugham, The Gentleman in the Parlour, pp. 152-153

'A Street in Sampeng' from *Twentieth Century Impressions of Siam* (1908).

Almost every house is a shop of some kind and an immense amount of trade is carried on in the quarter by a population herded together under the most revoltingly insanitary conditions.

Graham, Siam (1912), p. 26

Sampeng was China. It was narrow and cobbled and full of the quick and ceaseless clatter of wooden clogs. Overhead pieces of matting and cloth shut out the sun so that the lane was in perpetual twilight. The shops were side by side in an unbroken row with their fronts open to the lane. Ancient and lecherous-looking dogs prowled the gutters. On chairs in front of the stores old men nodded, some thin and yellow with sparse beards, others round and fat with faces as blank as the full moon. Long pipes with tiny bowls were in their mouths. The lane had many secrets. They hung in the air like the musky odor of spices and dried fruit and the sickly sweetness of opium.

Landon, Never Dies the Dream (1949), pp. 98-99

Chinese New Year fell on February 8, a warm day – it is always warm in Siam. In a trip through the native market, we were able to judge of the large amount of business in the hands of Chinese, by the multitude of New Year red papers pasted over the shops, the many places where "we do not sell to-day", the throngs of Chinese men in the streets, clad in fresh, delicate blue, lavender, or pink silk and pongee garments. We saw the efforts of dragon processions and heard their discordant musical instruments.

Woman's Work, May 1903, p. 105

Sampeng is a street of character; it is the Bowery of Bangkok.

Whitney, Jungle Trails and Jungle People (1905), p. 41

The Sampeng is a long, narrow, winding street, two miles long, and so narrow you can touch the shop counters on both sides with outstretched arms. Looking down the long vista, it certainly forms a most picturesque sight, and is also, it cannot be denied, full of powerful whiffs from the rubbish heaps and little open gutters that border the road. Unless from a balloon, no one could sketch in the Sampeng. One would be mobbed and

stifled by the good-natured interest of the garlic and betel loving people, and even a photograph was nearly an impossibility.
Landon, 'Mid Pleasures and Palaces (1907), pp. 101-105

Dogs, men, women, and children swarm through the twisting alleys, the filthiest of people in the filthiest of cities. Yet here is a throbbing of busy life unequaled in the other parts of Bangkok. Every Chinaman is carrying something, selling something, buying something, making something, doing something. Shopkeepers in the narrow booths haggle over their merchandise with prospective buyers or scream the virtues of their wares in shrill, unmusical voices at the passing throngs. Where the Chinese live, in no matter what Asiatic city, will be found the noise and the stench and all that is vile, yet there also will be found the activity and the industry and the greater part of the city's commerce.
Foster, A Beachcomber in the Orient (1923), pp. 125-126

In a dark alley the public scribes, silhouetted in candle light against a background of red paper, tame the demons who live in their writing. They write with amazing concentration, their noses down on the paper, so that you see only their black hair parted in the middle and their round, bare shoulders. Nothing approaches the gravity of the tracer of letters.
Morand, Nothing but the Earth (1927), p. 110

Major Foran did not enjoy his visit to the Sampeng...
The Sampeng quarter, where is situated the Chinese bazaar, left me cold. There was nothing of interest in its filthy and narrow lanes.
The Straits Times, 10 March 1925, p. 9

The area swarms with children and beggars, flies and mosquitoes; one noise attempts to out-vie the others; beastly smells to out-smell others equally nauseating; and beggars to out-whine the rivals' shrill supplication for alms. And I had heard so much in praise of the Sampeng quarter!
Foran, Malayan Symphony (1935), p. 123

In Bangkok and in every large village there is a strong Chinese element. Almost the entire retail trade of the country is in their hands, for they possess a sound business capacity, and a native honesty to which the lower class Siamese can lay no claim. How often has it been said that a Chinaman's word is his bond?

Thompson, Lotus Land (1906), p. 58

In Bangkok half the inhabitants are Chinese and they constitute the back-bone of the population. All the stores and many of the industries belong to and are conducted by the Chinese. They are industrious and prosperous, sleek and comfortable.

Hendley, Trifles of Travel (1924), p. 202

When I first went to Siam in 1904, the Chinese question, though it was already attracting notice, was not a very urgent one, chiefly because in those days the Chinese immigrant usually took to himself a wife from among the women of the country. But the situation changed radically after the rise to power in China of Dr. Sun Yat Sen and the Kuo Min Tang Party, accompanied as it was by an assiduous cult of Chinese nationalism. The day of the "luk chin", of the Sino-Siamese of mixed blood, thus passed away and the members of the Chinese community, who even when left to themselves had always shown a tendency to lead a separate life of their own, now carried this tendency still further and made no attempt to assimilate themselves to the people of the country of their adoption.

Crosby, Siam, (1945), p. 71

"The Siamese are annoyed because the Chinese are so much better, and naturally they get all the best jobs", said Susan Hedley. "That's because they aren't afraid of work. That's why they'd practically run Siam, if it weren't for the Europeans. The Siamese are nice people, but they don't like work very much."

Thompson, Water-Lily (1952), p. 159

As far as the casual observer can judge, in this capital of Siam there are no Siamese engaged in any hard manual labour at all. There are of course, many Siamese employed in various kinds of domestic or official work, but

"Chinese Merchants of Bangkok" from *Siam from Ancient to Present Times* (1926), p. 173.

in the streets nearly every workman is Chinese.

Young, The Kingdom of the Yellow Robe (1898), p. 9

My room at the lodging house was reached through the back yard and up a flight of steps to a balcony from which I could look into the houses next door. On one side dwelt a Chinese family – pajama-clad girls in braided pigtails, and raw-boned men with close-cropped hair. When I first arose in the morning, they were already at work, sitting at a table and making something with their hands – I could not see just what, but when I retired at night, they were still at work. On the other side dwelt a Siamese family, *panung*-clad girls with long black hair falling gracefully over their shoulders, and plump indolent men who loafed in any old garment. When I arose in the morning, they were doing nothing, and when I retired they were still doing the same thing.

Foster, A Beachcomber in the Orient (1923), pp. 130-134

A high proportion of the boys in the class were *luk chin* – child of a Chinaman. Born of a Chinese father and a Siamese mother, they had inherited the physique and energy of the Chinaman, the harshness being tempered by the serenity and kindliness of the mother. Whilst most of them had inherited their father's ambition and dedication to hard work, they had also the cheerfulness and love of pleasure so typical of the Siamese. They were an altogether admirable product and regarded themselves as one hundred per cent Siamese.

Exell, Siamese Tapestry (1963), pp. 25-26

Every shop has a signboard and every signboard is a picture, with its skilfully designed characters, gold on black, or black on gold. A Chinaman will pay the writer-expert the price of a picture for the composition of one of these works of art.

Harris, East for Pleasure (1929), p. 63

The Signboards Act of April 1939 was passed largely to allay the irritation felt by the Thais at the ubiquitous Chinese signs, which gave Bangkok the appearance of a foreign city. In July 1939 there began a campaign, punctuated by police raids, against Chinese newspaper offices, banks, schools, and secret societies' headquarters, followed by the arrest and deportation of thousands of Chinese, ranging from opium addicts and vagrants to such prominent businessmen as the managers of the Overseas Chinese Bank and the Bank of Canton.

Thompson, Thailand (1941), pp. xvii-xviii

Eurasians

Every cosmopolitan port offers large opportunities to succor the stranded waifs, or repair the damages, of Western civilization, but it is rather particularly a part of Bangkok traditions to do this, so I was not surprised to find Mrs. Snyder adding to the care of her own four children an Englishman's sick and motherless baby. Down at Sumray, Miss Galt had surrounded herself with seven small boys who have been specially committed to her charge and attend the school. They eat at her table, she teaches them manners, morals, watches over their health and studies, protects, in short, mothers them. Some of them will derive from her, more than all other sources, whatever respect they have for woman or virtue. God bless the seed sown in that precious field! I saw three of the boys. One was a brown Asiatic, son of a Siamese governor in the north. One was half fair, bright, alert, could learn anything, and his name, "Fritz," proclaimed his father's lineage. The third was an amiable lad with Scotch eyes and hair.

Woman's Work, May 1903, pp. 103-104

Among the children sheltering at Jasmine Hall are a number of mixed race …

Howard and Jeannie Ansel had an English father who thought them too young for regular boarding school, but would not trust them to their Siamese mother during his furlough. Mo Tek and Mo Kiang were there because their parents were in China for a year. Then there was Eng Siow. She was older than the other boarders – fourteen, in fact – and went with Pastor Rasami's children to Jane Hayes School.[3] Her father was a Christian Chinese. Her mother was a low-class Siamese and an inveterate gambler. Eng Siow was at the school for a year, while her father was on business in China, because he refused to leave the girl, his only child, in the care of her mother.

Landon, Never Dies the Dream (1949), pp. 44-45

The Mission Chapel is at St. Mary's, though services are also held at the boys' school in the town. The congregation is chiefly Eurasian, who are by no means all *Anglo* Siamese, so that no other convenient name exists to designate people of mixed European and Asiatic descent. It has never been clear to me why the name "Eurasian" should now be barred in India. The fact is concisely stated in the name. That which we ought to face is that the quality of contemptibility is bred by contempt. What is to be expected of people held at arm's length by both their parent races?

Wheatcroft, Siam and Cambodia (1928), p. 203

In Hervey's novel, Lhassa arrives at the house of the mysterious Dr Garth where she encounters Domingo, the "number one boy".

A ghostly form materialized on the veranda as the carriage came to a halt. It was a house-boy who took her hand-bag and slunk soundlessly into the hall ahead of her. "The doctor is in his study," he announced suddenly, in liquid tones. He was young, barely twenty she judged, with ivory yellow skin and eyes that were slightly oblique. A Eurasian she decided. "Will you go to your room first – Miss Camber?" He pronounced her name as though he considered his knowing it an accomplishment. His every movement was so noiseless, his manner so secretive, that she expected to see him vanish before her eyes, like a shade instead of a person of substance.

---

3 A Mission school for girls, founded in 1917.

Later, Dr Garth explains the presence of Domingo …

"Domingo" – again reading her thoughts – "is one of my treasures. He is the boy who showed you in. I picked him up in Macao when he was a little chap. His father was a Portuguese, and his mother – Chinese or Malay. In either case, I'm sure he inherited his gentle nature from her. He reads to me, attends to the garden; does almost everything."

Domingo's nature, however, turns out to be rather less "gentle" than Dr Garth believes.
Hervey, The Black Parrot (1923), p. 41

Apparently Dulcie still believed that someday, somehow, she would recover her father's property. And she had all the pertinacity of the wronged and helpless combined with the deviousness of the Eurasian. Not even the possibility that she might forfeit her livelihood seemed able to deflect her from the central passion of her life.

*

Mani was a pretty Eurasian, with the soft beauty that sometimes follows the mixing of East and West. Her face was a delicate oval, her skin a dusky off-white. She had large eyes, and a heavy sweet mouth, which she painted coral. Her high-heeled shoes were foreign, and the style of her blouse, but she clung to the Siamese *pasin*, worn tight around her hips, which gave her height. Grace looked at her with open distaste. Mani was one of her failures.

Landon, Never Dies the Dream (1949), pp. 3, 53

The British lawyer Gerald Sparrow (1903-1988) was appointed to the International Court in Bangkok in 1930. He published several memoirs about his life in Siam/Thailand during the following decades.

If Mr Borge was a Eurasian, he never admitted it. He was determinedly Dutch. He drank Dutch beer, smoked small Dutch cigars, turned up at the Netherlands Legation on all high days and holidays, and was in every way a loyal and devoted subject of Queen Wilhelmina. It is possible, of course, that this attitude was dictated by the fact that in the free and opportunistic Bangkok market Eurasians were paid less than those accepted as Europeans. Mr Borge was accepted as a European. He therefore could command the goodly sum of twenty ticals a night.

Sparrow, The Golden Orchid (1963), p. 18

Mr. Louis Windsor is the son of Khun Smudh Gochara (Captain Garnier Windsor) master of one of the steamers belonging to the Alfred Holt fleet plying between Singapore, Hongkong, Swatow, Hankow and Bangkok. While trading in these ports, he became acquainted with His Majesty King Rama IV who conferred upon him the title Khun Smudh Gochara. When Siam was about to conclude a treaty with France, he was appointed interpreter of the mission to Paris. After the treaty was signed, he returned to Siam, and, in partnership with his friends, he founded the firm of Windsor, Rose & Co., with the King's patronage.

The Captain had many children, Mr. Louis Windsor being one of them by a Siamese mother. At twenty years of age, he became a teacher at Assumption College, and, after leaving that institution, he joined Messrs. Kim Seng Lee & Co. who were then doing an extensive business in rice and teak. He afterwards quitted that firm to join the Royal Opium Department where he was appointed Chief Preventive Officer. He is now established in trade and is well-known to princes, notabilities and merchants in Bangkok. Mr. Louis Windsor has a wide circle of friends and is popular.[4]

Siam from Ancient to Present Times (1926), p. IV

---

4 In 1901, Windsor had himself been arrested after a launch under his command belonging to Kim Seng Lee & Co. was found to be carrying some 50,000 ticals-worth of illicit opium. He forfeited the opium and was fined 2,000 ticals by the French Consular Court (*The Straits Times*, 27 November 1901, p. 2). When he died in 1927, the Bangkok correspondent of the *Singapore Free Press* described him as a "devout Catholic" who would be "much missed in church circles".

Louis Windsor's house ("Baan Windsor") was "located in a small Catholic community in Kudeejeen" on the river in Thonburi near Santa Cruz Church (*Bangkok Post*, 17 January 2016). According to local information, that house was demolished long ago; the "gingerbread house" which remains on the site (and is in need of restoration as of 2024) was brought at a later date from a different location. Photograph: The Editor.

Mr. Marican

MOONA THABISAUBOO MARICAN (M. T. S. MARICAN)
Diamond and Cloth Merchant and Commission Agent, General Importer and Exporter.
2615 & 2617 Rachawongse Road, BANGKOK.

The firm of M. T. S. Marican was founded by the late Mr. Moona Thabisauboo Marican of Karikal, French India. During the latter portion of the nineteenth century, M. T. S. Marican began his business career in dealing in diamonds, precious stones of Siam and other gems, and by his perseverance and keen business methods, worked up quite a large trade in Bangkok.

Subsequently, he opened the piece-goods line and established the business on a small scale in Wat Koh Street, and in addition thereto he founded another firm in the same line in Rachawongse Street, which was then newly opened. At these two places, all sorts of woollen, linen, cotton and silk are being imported from all parts of the globe. Mr. Merican deals very considerably too in English flannels, velvets, serges and cottons and other fancy goods. The goods are always sold wholesale and also enormous supplies are furnished to the Siamese military department, whenever required. The Wat Koh branch conducts retail business also. Mr. Marican does a vast business in piece-goods, in which he stands first among the Southern Indian community here. The late founder died at his native place, Karikal, in August 1924. His only surviving brother, Mr. Moona Kader Moheideen Saiboo Marican, and his son-in-law, Mr. Seena Kader Moheideen Saiboo Marican, are now the proprietors of the firm. Mr. Marican's name and reputation has stood in Bangkok, the Straits Settlements, Karikal, in French India, and also many places in British India, for the last thirty years or more.

Siam from Ancient to Present Times (1926), pp. LXXXVI-LXXXVII

On Tuesday, I went to a bank, found it open, and drew money with which to pay my obligations, both at Singapore and at Bangkok. I had selected an antique ring from an assortment shown me by a Mr. Marican, a dealer at Bangkok, telling him that I had no money and could not then get any on account of the bank holidays, but that I would remit as soon as possible, so that he could send the ring to me. Again my "face" was good, showing what a wonderfully good "face" I had, for he insisted on my taking the ring anyway, saying I could pay later. I sent him the money from Singapore.

Bent, Tales of Travel (1924), p. 269

The People of Bangkok 135

One of the Truly Great Men of the World

The visit to Bangkok of Rabindranath Tagore (1861-1941), the Bengali writer, thinker and Nobel Prize laureate, in October 1927 was one of the most remarkable "celebrity visits" of the period. During the ten days he spent in Bangkok, Tagore was presented to the King and Queen, met various princes (most importantly, Prince Damrong, with whom he had tea), addressed assemblies of the Indian and Chinese communities, and visited educational, scientific and cultural institutions.[1]

Dr. Rabindranath Tagore arrived in Bangkok on Saturday night by the express from Penang. Dr. Tagore descended to the platform surrounded by his countrymen, and his progress to the exit was really a pilgrimage. It was with the greatest difficult that he was able to progress at a snail's pace along the length of the platform. Standing in the gaily-decorated car and acknowledging the raucous salutations of his admirers, his fine features relaxed and the eyes smiled appreciations the voice could not hope to convey over the over-excited crowd. Dr. Tagore and his car emerged into the open space in front of the terminus to receive another welcome from the hornblowers of Bangkok.

The Bangkok Times, 10 October 1927, p. 6

A thing, remarkable to those who have lived in India, or to those who have given study to Indian religious, social and political questions, was that the gathering included people of different faiths who ordinarily are not ready to mix together. But a bond of unity was provided in the desire to pay tribute to one of the few truly great men of the world.

The Siam Observer, 10 October 1927

---

1 The visit was part of a four-month tour of Southeast Asia. See Sawitri Charoenpong, 'Rabindranath Tagore in Thailand', URL: https://embassyofindiabangkok.gov.in/public/assets/pdf/Rabindranath%20Tagore.pdf.

2 A. R. Salebhai & Co.: "Largest Paper Importers in Siam, Wholesale Stationers, General"; A. E. Nana & Co.: "Merchants" (*Bangkok Directory*, 1925, pp. 295, 299). According to information at the Bangkokian Museum, Dr Francis Christian was "the coordinator in welcoming the great Eastern philosopher". Dr Christian was one of the "attending physicians" of the Jawarad Company Limited (Banrak Branch).

A new Dodge car (of Messrs. A. R. Salebhai & Co.), beautifully decorated and illuminated, was waiting in readiness to escort the poet to Phya Thai Palace. Tagore was accompanied in the car by A. E. Nana.[2]

The Siam Observer, 10 October 1927

An appeal for tolerance, world-wide good will and the interchange of cultures was made by Sir Rabindranath Tagore, noted poet and philosopher, yesterday to an audience of over a thousand residents of Bangkok at the Phya Thai Palace.[3] The assembly included members of the diplomatic corps. Government officials, the Indian community and numerous laymen.

Promptly at five o'clock Dr. Tagore was escorted to the chair of honour. His arrival was the signal for the gathering to stand and applaud. Mr. D. A. Pestonji introduced the distinguished guest, after which Mr. A. E. Nana, chairman of the Indian reception committee, then presented an inlaid silver box containing the address of welcome to Mr. Lall who, in turn, read it to the Poet.[4]

The Bangkok Daily Mail, 12 October 1927, p. 1

---

3 Tagore had in fact renounced his knighthood in 1919 in protest against the Amritsar Massacre.

4 D. A. Pestonji was an accountant at Nai Lert. Mr. Lall: Nand Lall, a representative of the Sikh community.

To Siam

(The latest poem from the pen of Dr. Tagore was read to Their Majesties at the palace last night where Dr. Tagore lectured).[5]

[Translated from the original Bengali]

The final stanza ...

I come, a pilgrim, at thy gate, O Siam,
to offer my verse to the endless glory of India
sheltered in thy home, away from her own deserted shrine,
To bathe in the living stream that flows in thy heart,
whose water descends from the snowy height
of a sacred time on which arose, from the deep of my country's being,
the Sun of Love and Righteousness.

Phya Thai Palace, Bangkok.
October 11, 1927.
The Daily Mail (Bangkok)

---

5 Tagore was scheduled to deliver his speech to the King and Queen on 13 October.

Dinner at the Room of the Moon

Then as now, Bangkok offered a variety of cuisines (Siamese, Chinese, European) and a variety of settings to enjoy it. Here, Lucie Chandler describes a "perambulating restaurateur"…

Regardless of all obstacles, the perambulating Siamese restaurateur trots doggedly ahead. Over the restaurateur's shoulder is swung a bamboo pole, from one end of which depends a portable charcoal stove, and from the other his box of condiments. He stops his jogging only long enough to sell his queer concoctions of curry, dished up in unwashed bowls and seasoned by remnants of prehistoric feasts.

Travel, November 1916, p. 27

'A Portable Restaurant' from Exell, *Siamese Tapestry*.

Pushing their way through the crowded thoroughfares, their raucous cries rising above the clamor, go the ice cream and curry vendors, carrying the paraphernalia of their trade slung from bamboo poles borne upon the shoulders – perambulating cafeterias and soda fountains, as it were. For a satang – a coin equivalent to about a quarter of a cent – you can purchase a bowl of rice, while the expenditure of another satang will provide you with an assortment of savories or relishes, made from elderly meat, decayed fish, decomposed prawns and other toothsome ingredients, which you heap upon the rice, together with a greenish-yellow curry sauce which makes the concoction look as though it were suffering from a severe attack of jaundice.

These relishes are cooked, or rather re-warmed, by the simple process of suspending them in a sort of sieve in a pot of boiling water, the same pot and the same water serving for all customers alike. By this arrangement, the man who takes his snack at the close of the day has the advantage of receiving not merely what he orders, but also flavors and even floating remnants from the dishes ordered by all those who have preceded him.

Powell, Where the Strange Trails Go Down (1921), p. 219

THE PLACE TO EAT IS AT LANDAU'S RESTAURANT. CLEANLINESS IS MY MOTTO.

Advertisement in The Bangkok Times, August 1910[1]

The building known as Café Norasingh situated in Dusit Park will be opened from the 8th October 1922. Refreshments of all kinds including tea can be obtained daily from 2 p.m.

The Bangkok Times, 26 September 1922, p. 7

The Norasingh Café in Dusit Park was opened to the public on Sunday afternoon. A large number of guests were received by Phya Bidaks Nantanikor and the Royal Entertainments Department and were entertained to tea in the Café grounds. The department's orchestra played selections throughout the afternoon, assisted by a military band. The building itself is a very fine one and is the work of the Royal Fine Arts Department. When the Café comes to be known there is no doubt it will become a popular rendezvous for evening motorists.

The Bangkok Times, October 1922

---

1 Landau: Adolphe (or Aaron Adolf) Landau (1873-1947), who had moved to Bangkok from Singapore in 1909. He was the proprietor of the Astor House Hotel (where the restaurant was presumably located). The restaurant offered "Fass Bier" and "special dinners" on Saturdays, the latter for two ticals. Later, the firm of "A. Landau & Co." were active as an "auctioneers and commission agents"; Landau also served as manager of the Siam Pineapple Factory.

2 Presumably "Norasingh" and "Narasingh" were accepted alternative spellings. The name of the present Norasingh Café at Phya Thai Palace was evidently chosen to recall the former café in Dusit Park.

Advertisement in *The Bangkok Times*, October 1927.[2]

        YOUR SIAMESE DINNER.
Your friends will be delighted if you entertain them to a Siamese dinner.
        SOODHA BHOCHANA SATHAN,
        The only Siamese Restaurant.
At Bambhen Boon Market, opposite Narasingh Studio, New Road.
After dinner step to the Bambhen Boon Casino: Entertainment nightly.
Advertisement in The Bangkok Times, August 1929

    Lise was bent on a pleasant outing in Lumbini Park, with ice-cream, and late Saturday night supper. Lumbini Park had originally been Hans's idea of an occasional Saturday evening treat for her. She had preferred the rare Sunday morning outings, when Hans hired a taxi at Bangkolem Wharf and they drove round Dusit Park, and had mangosteen ices and listened to the Royal Band. The European ladies drove there after church or club. It was nice, because only grown-ups went to Dusit Park. Lumbini was silly. Just a lot of shops in the Chinese quarter, and nobody but Chinese and Siamese, drinking red lemonade and watching theatres. Then, almost by accident Lise had discovered she was a privileged person. The girls at school were envious: they weren't allowed at Lumbini Park. Since then, Lumbini was a delectable land, forbidden to everyone who had not a farang to herself.

                          Thompson, Water-Lily (1952), p. 142

The Dining Room at the Oriental Hotel (ca 1926).

LUNCH AND DINNER AT THE HOTEL ROYAL.
Menus for Saturday, 10th August 1929.
Lunch: Potage Isan, Omelette Parmentier, Steak & Kidney Pudding, Côtes de Veau Nouilles, Maïs en Pain, Curry Siamois, Viande Froide Assortie, Jalousies, Fromage, Fruits, Café

Dinner: Hors d'Œuvres, Consommé Ox Tail, Timbale de Poisson, Filets Mignon Macédoine, Haricots Blancs à la Crème, Dinde Farcie Rôti, Pommes de Terre Pailles, Glace Pralinée, Fromage, Fruits, Café
Advertisement in The Bangkok Times, August 1929

THE POPULAR CAFÉ
(British Dispensary Building New Road.)
When you are free from office, do not forget
The Popular-Café
A clean and airy space for ladies and gents, for cold drinks, sandwiches and popular drinks, and cold beers of different brands.
DO NOT FORGET.
Advertisement in The Bangkok Times, June 1933

Advertisement for the restaurant at the Hotel Rajdhani in *The Bangkok Times*, August 1935.

It was a gay party of men and women that assembled in the Room of the Moon – the largest private dining-room in the smart new Chinese restaurant. Waiters flitted about, giving to each of us a hot, damp, perfumed towel; most welcome they were to me, for I cannot remember a moment during my stay in Bangkok when I was not dripping with perspiration. Tea was served. Some passed it by in favour of Scotch. Others reclined on couches, and enjoyed a whiff or two of opium which had been deftly rolled into pellets by the Cantonese girls, passed through a flame, and dropped into the pipes of the lotus-loving friends. Though the women all had cigarettes, I did not see any of them smoke opium. I fancy it is not done. [join up:] Above the hum of talk rose the shrill songs of the Cantonese girls, and the strains of the Khim, zither-like instruments which they played. But in spite of the gaiety of the entertainment and the beauty of the picture, as the evening wore along I became more and more uncomfortable.

I was getting terribly hungry, and no food appeared; I began to see good reason for that national greeting, "Kin Kao Rue Yang." More tea; more wet towels; more Scotch and opium cocktails. It was not until ten o'clock that the first course of the dinner was served. But when it came, it was truly amazing. Here is the menu, given in the order of service:

Chicken kidneys. Mushrooms. Shrimps. Cheese. Shark's ears soup. Fish. Onions. Macaroni. Chinese bird's nest soup. Duck. Barley soup. A sweet fruit soup, made of the milk of cocoanut.

My friend confided to me that the dinner committee had sat up until all hours combining this menu for gourmets. I can readily believe it.

Norden, Golden Gate to Golden Sun (1923), pp. 121-124

The ice cream vendors drive a roaring trade in a concoction the basis of which is finely shaven ice, looking like half-frozen and very dirty slush, sweetened with sugar and flavored, according to the purchaser's taste from an array of metal-topped bottles such as barbers use for bay rum and hair oil. But, being cold and sweet "Isa-kee," as the Chinese vendors call it, is as popular among the lower classes in Siam as ice cream cones are in the United States.

Powell, Where the Strange Trails Go Down (1921), p. 219

We soon found ourselves in Yawarad Road, the Broadway of the Chinese quarter. Even at that late hour lights glared. Blaring orchestras from restaurant balconies dinned an invitation to dine into the ears of the milling crowd which overflowed the sidewalk and mingled with rickshas and automobiles. Those who laughed were Siamese. There was a sober intensity about the Chinese that made one wonder why they came to this street of pleasure. "Let's have an ice cream soda," said Louis.

Ice cream soda! There was something depressing about it; something one hundred per cent American. It was an intrusion; the wrong piece in a jig-saw puzzle. We turned into Ice Cream Soda Street, a block with half a dozen shabby-looking stores before which a score or more of cars were parked. Chinese boys with trays were carrying chocolate, vanilla, strawberry and raspberry drinks to the occupants who blithely sipped the beverages through straws. This American institution was introduced into Bangkok by a Chinese who had been a soda fountain clerk in a San Francisco drug store.

Freeman, Brown Women and White (1932), pp. 81-82

Food Production

The article on 'Rice' in Twentieth Century Impressions of Siam *was written by A. E. Stiven, the manager of the Borneo Company's rice mill in Bangkok.*

As an instance of the growth of the rice trade at Bangkok one has only to look at the enormous increase in the number of mills during the past ten or fifteen years. The Chinese have always predominated in the rice trade, and quite naturally so too, seeing that the bulk of the crop has formerly gone to Hongkong and China ports. In recent years there has been more business done by the mills for Europe, and the European element seems likely to become stronger as the trade expands. The active partners and general managers of this important industrial undertaking are Nai Tom Yah and Leang Chai Chaninan Niti, a man known in business circles throughout Siam.

Twentieth Century Impressions of Siam (1908), p. 146

The tourist and traveler who would learn more of this great industry should by all means pay a visit to the enormous rice mills of Messrs. Luang Chai and Tom Yah, situated on the west side of the river, and of easy access by steam launch from your hotel. No conception of this great mill with its throbbing machinery can be gained unless first visited, whose present magnitude is entirely due to the enterprise of Mr. Tom Yah.

Perkins, Travels (1909), p. 268

How the West Serves the East. What is Sterilized Natural Milk?

On account of the fact that it is almost impossible to obtain fresh cow's milk in the tropics, a process has been discovered by which the milk given us by perfectly healthy cows can be STERILIZED and put up in air-tight tins and conveyed to us here at regular intervals, so that STERILIZED MILK is really THE IDEAL DRINKING MILK FOR TROPICAL USE.

ALWAYS ASK FOR THE RELIABLE BRAND
Milkmaid Natural Sterilized.

Bangkok Depot: DIETHELM & Co. LTD., Rachawongse Road.[1]

Advertisement in The Bangkok Times, November 1913

The supplies of canned foods are furnished largely by European manufacturers, and the greater proportion is sold in Bangkok, the capital and principal city. The Anglo-Swiss Condensed Milk Co. has practically absolute control of this market, and with an agent on the ground is intrenching itself securely. A large amount of advertising is in evidence, all of the street-car lines of Bangkok carrying signs advertising the "Milkmaid Brand." That the Siamese recognize the value of canned food may be inferred by the establishment of a factory for canning Siamese fruit in Bangkok.

Shriver, Canned-Goods Trade in the Far East, 1915, p. 63

BY ROYAL APPOINTMENT.
LARGEST SALE IN THE WORLD.
Perfectly safe. No risk whatever.
Buy the brand with the reputation behind it:
MILKMAID.
NESTLÉ AND ANGLO-SWISS CONDENSED MILK CO.,
(London).
Bangkok, Rachawongse Road, (Diethelm & Co. Ltd.)

Advertisement in Bangkok Directory (1914)

Keeps in any climate

Although it is only in recent years that the possibilities of canning pineapples in Siam have attracted much attention, the industry has already developed to a considerable extent. Those engaged are confident of still further growth, and there is no reason why Siam would become as celebrated for for its pineapples as for its other productions. Beside those in the

---

1 Other brands advertised in the period include "Natura-Milch" (distributors: Behn Meyer & Co.) and "Bear Brand Milk" (Bernese Alps Co.).

146   In Bangkok

provinces, Bangkok has a factory itself on the most up-to-date lines at Samsen in the Siam Pineapple Factory. Luang Chitr Chamnong, one of the most enterprising of Siamese businessmen, is the proprietor, and the works are under the control of Mr. A. Landau who, it may be mentioned, was the first to export pineapples from Siam. All the machinery is of the latest design, and every part of the work is done on the premises, making and stamping the cans, canning the pineapples, and packing. The utmost cleanliness is observed throughout. Last year, when the factory was working for seven months, several shipments were consigned to Europe.

The Bangkok Times, 5 March 1913, p. 4

Three years ago Mr. Landau interested Luang Chit Chamnong, also known as Tom-Yah, a wealthy Chino-Siamese rice-mill merchant, in the canning of pineapples, and as a result Mr. Landau was engaged under a five-year contract to develop a canning factory at Sam Sen, a suburb of Bangkok, where one of the four rice mills belonging to Luang Chit Chamnong is located. This plant was operated for the first time during the season 1912 and its first real pack was put up in 1913. It is well arranged and better equipped than any of the Singapore factories. His Excellency, Phya Anudhutvadhi, a Siamese of rank and related to the King of Siam, became interested a couple of years ago in re-establishing, under the name of the Bangkok Canning Co., the factory first started by Mr. Landau. His idea is to develop not only pineapple canning but also the canning of other native fruits of Siam that are of particularly good quality, such as the mango, the papaya, the durian and the Jack fruit.

Shriver, Pineapple-Canning Industry (1915), p. 31

Both the Siamese and Chinese of the better classes are sympathetic toward imported articles. They like sweets. They are fond of fruit. The limiting factor in the past has been that American canned fruits were beyond the range of purchase of all but a very minute percentage of the population.

Crocheron and Norton, Canned Fruit (1930), p. 189

Ceremonies and Festivals

The Siamese year is an almost continuous succession of shows and festivities. In fact, the life of the Siamese is one long round of play, only broken by short periods of work.
Campbell, Siam in the XXth Century (1902), pp. 161-162

That the Siamese do not take life sadly is a conviction forced upon everyone who has even the very briefest of acquaintances with them. A very slight pretext always serves them for occasion to "call out a holiday" and few persons visit Siam without being present on one of these gala days. The Siamese official year commences on April 1st and at about that date, according to the phase of the moon, occurs the KRUT THAI, or popular New Year's Holiday.[1]
Antonio, Guide (1904), p. 38

If one of Siam's typically gorgeous festivals or ceremonies can be seen, you need bother about nothing else. I cannot hope to explain how sumptuous they are. A wedding, when there is rank and wealth, is prodigally resplendent and is celebrated with elaborate theatrical spectacles. A funeral is even more glittering in its amazing display.
Kirtland, Finding the Worth While in the Orient (1926), p. 272

This cutting of the top-knot is undergone by practically every girl in the land, though, as regards boys, it is usually confined to the upper classes. In the case of royal children the ceremony lasts as long as three days, and it seems to mark, as one writer has put it, the entry of the Siamese child into individualism.
Macmillan, Seaports of the Far East (1925), pp. 481-482

One day there came to my room the sounds of music and revelry from the house next door, and from my balcony I could see priests and guests assembling. Incense was burning before the statue of Buddha, food was being served, gifts were being received by the family, and in the center of

---

[1] A festival celebrated ten days before Songkran.

148 In Bangkok

the whole affair, upon a throne-like chair covered by a kingly pagoda-like umbrella, sat the twelve-year-old son of the family, all dolled up in skirts of rich brocade, his wrists and ankles so laden with ornamented rings that he could scarcely walk. Little Dhip Borihar Pramonda Banaraks, it seems, was about to have his top-knot cut.

The celebrations next door lasted for three days. This ceremony usually precedes the youth's entrance into the priesthood. Every Siamese, from king to peasant, spends a portion of his life in a Buddhist monastery – usually about three months of it – which accounts for the large number of temples and priests to be seen throughout the country. There are reported to be 10,000 monks in Bangkok alone. Presently Dhip will be dolled up again, and escorted to the temple, where the chief priest will ask him innumerable solemn questions as to his virtue, including such – to us – ludicrous inquiries as, "Are you troubled with fits or leprosy?" and "Have you ever been bewitched by magicians?" and if Dhip hasn't, he will don the garment which has won for Siam its nickname of "The Kingdom of the Yellow Robe," and for three months or more will live the life of a saint, meditating upon the evils of the world, after which he will leave the monastery, return to civil life, and enjoy all the evils to the utmost.

Foster, A Beachcomber in the Orient (1923), pp. 134-136

The hairs that have been cut off are separated into two bundles, long and short. The short hairs are put into a little vessel made of plantain-leaves, and sent adrift on the ebb-tide in the nearest canal or river. As they float away, they carry with them all the bad temper, the greediness, and the pride of their former owner.

Young, Siam (1908), p. 47

Whether illuminated by electricity or with the soft glow of cocoanut oil, for H.M.'s birthday the streets in every direction were decorated as they might be in England on the occasion of a jubilee or coronation, as were also the palace gates of princes and nobles; but best of all were the open spaces round the Old Palace, crowded with people in gay attire, the rich in cars and the poor in double rickshas or on foot. Everywhere bright-coloured pasin and panung were visible, and the priestly yellow; for priests and students are prominent figures by reason of the robe that sets them apart. In the streets were itinerant vendors, too, sellers of foodstuffs, sellers of sweetmeats, and, best of all, the men running in and out among the people, their hands full of those familiar joys, great brightly coloured air balloons, held high for safety above the heads of the crowd. Few Western toys seem equally at home and appropriate in every part of the globe. The crowd, though so gay, was astonishingly quiet, even the Chinese noisiest of the noisy in their own country, seemed under the spell of national quiet. There were bands, and here I made my first acquaintance with Siamese music, very pleasing rhythmic melodies, in which the problem of perpetual motion seems to have been solved in contrapuntal themes of great charm and ingenuity. The interwoven threads of sound appeared to me to have much analogy with the beautiful designs on the lacquered bookcases, collected in the National Library by H.R.H. Prince Damrong, interlacing lines without beginning or end, enriched with a thousand fantasies.

Wheatcroft, Siam and Cambodia (1928), pp. 124-125

On the last day of our visit the celebration of the anniversary of the King's accession to the throne began. Bangkok was *en fête*. The streets thronged with merrymakers. Tens of thousands of them were gathered in the brilliantly lighted palace enclosure where amusements of every kind had been organized. There were several theatrical performances, military bands playing European music, Siamese bands playing music, and dancers and jugglers galore. I was never jostled by a happier and more good-natured throng.

Cravath, Notes on the Cruise of the Warrior (1928), p. 127

In a letter dated: "Bangkok, Oct. 26, 1910", the Presbyterian missionary teacher Edna S. (Sarah) Cole (1855-1950) describes the ceremonies that followed the death of King Chulalongkorn and the accession of King Vajiravudh.

Rachel Wheatcroft, 'The King's Birthday Illuminations', from *Siam and Cambodia* (1928).

Last Sunday morning, news came that the King of Siam had died during the night. It was a great shock to us all, and we could only look into each other's faces with genuine sorrow.

The King died in his summer palace, and with a great procession, was brought down to the royal palace. The procession was to have passed at 3 o'clock in the afternoon, but did not arrive until 8 o'clock, and it took the better part of an hour to pass a given point. The soldiers came twelve abreast, completely filling the wide royal road, and each bore a lighted taper in his hand. The army has been greatly augmented, so there were thousands of men in the escort. The bands all played the sweetest music I have ever heard. The streets were lined with people, who stood silent and sad. After the army came the catafalque, the golden jeweled urn borne high on the shoulders of men in ancient costumes. The urn was supported by two of the King's sons of highest rank. In front and around were the Chow Phyas, the Siamese nobles of highest rank, dressed in cloth of gold, and the princes followed, all clothed in white. The marines came next with the policemen. Over the catafalque was held The White Seven-Storied Umbrella that is, I believe, used only at the death of a king. As they reached the royal palace, the white umbrella was lowered, and as the urn passed through the gate, all the bands played the National Anthem; and so, for the last time, His Majesty passed through the long lines of his people who almost worshiped him. The night, the silence, with only the light of the flickering taper, borne by each, made an impressive scene that no words can adequately picture. Now we must wait and see what this little kingdom will become in new hands.

Woman's Work, February 1911, p. 42

The customs differ in various places, but cremation is the usual practice resorted to, and families have been known to spend as much as one million ticals on a single burial; for provision has to be made for free entertainment for a week or more, while theatricals, pony and foot races, etc., are also provided. The advancement in civilisation is evidenced by the fact that a short time ago the bodies of dead paupers were placed in open spaces to be devoured by the pariah dogs and vultures, whereas now provision is made for their being cremated in certain wats.[2]

Macmillan, Seaports of the Far East (1925), p. 482

This festivity of the royal cremation had been long talked of in the town. The ceremonial itself – more than a thousand years old, a legacy from Buddha – was not made less striking by the example of modern science introduced. The Queen arrived in a motor-car quite up to date, the chassis English, but the coach-work from Paris and in quiet Parisian taste. The car was closed, and she sat back in the corner of it, without bonnet or veil, still, strange Eastern figure, quite immobile. Then came the Siamese band, playing the Siamese anthem, a most dire and discordant chant. The band preceded His Majesty King Chulalongkorn who made his appearance in a European uniform. He was, however, accompanied by a bodyguard of eight Siamese, holding over him an enormous umbrella of cloth of gold that glittered in the sunshine. The urns that contained the corpses were two tall vases, Greek in form. They were probably of lacquer, but looked flimsy, as if made of gold paper. The ceremony consisted of the king setting fire first to one and then to another of these vases. The whole thing was much more like a wedding than a funeral, with perhaps a dash of a country fair thrown in to add to the other incongruities.

Frankau, Let the Roof Fall In (1910), pp. 156-157

The American missionary Henry Hale Bucher (1907-1998) describes a Royal Cremation in 1929…

The ceremony was extremely elaborate and impressively royal. For this cremation there were four long, low pavilions which formed a hollow square with two main openings; an entrance on the north and an exit on the east. In the center rose the funeral pyre, a beautiful and majestic structure of Singapore wood coated with pointed paper-stencil, looking very much like gold tiles or mosaic. Its beauty was crowned by a handsome spire many feet high. The most striking feature of the spire was the beautiful cupola on its extreme top, put on with great ceremony several days before the cremation. His Majesty, the King, the Supreme Council of the Realm,

---

2 Helpfully, Sommerville provides photographs of a dead body being devoured by vultures.

and the foreign advisors, were seated upon a raised platform facing the pyre, with the princes. Just south of the section occupied by His Majesty, the King, the Queen was surrounded by all the royal princesses. They were separated from the men by an exquisite curtain woven of gold cloth with metallic embroidery. The north pavilion was given over to foreigners, and one small section was occupied by an Italian Black Shirt delegation.

The Siam Outlook, October 1929, p. 369

A typical Siamese ceremony is the rice planting ceremony each spring, when half the population of Bangkok follows the Minister of Agriculture out into the country to watch him plow a field with a gilded plow drawn by white bullocks.

Foster, A Beachcomber in the Orient (1923), pp. 136-138

The auspicious hour has arrived. The great crowd of people that have been accumulating since early dawn for the eventful occasion suddenly becomes quiet and expectant. The procession approaches slowly, guided by the plaintive three-barred refrain on the flageolet and the pulsing beats of the deep-throated drums. Several conch shells are blown as the procession draws close. The crowd leans forward with interest as it approaches.

The Siam Outlook, August 1927, p. 154

Ploughing and planting done, the bulls were turned loose, and left to graze. They, too, were watched by the soothsayers, for the manner of feeding plainly indicates to those versed in these matters, whether the yield will be big or small. So soon as the ceremony was over, the people scattered, to finish the day in festivity. I looked about to fix the scene in memory.

Norden, From Golden Gate to Golden Sun (1923), pp. 104-106

'The Ploughing Ceremony' from Carter, *The Kingdom of Siam* (1904).

Ceremonies and Festivals 153

The Foreign Colony

The foreign colony in Bangkok is quite small. There are about five hundred English, about one hundred Americans, half of the latter being missionaries, so that the American business and official circles have in them not more than twenty or twenty-five men. There are several Danes and a few French.

Hendley, Trifles of Travel (1924), p. 205

A group of mostly foreign young men. Bangkok, ca 1895. The man sitting at left may be G. R. Ainslie. From an Ainslie album.

The European residential quarter is to the south and south-east of the town where many of the foreign consulates, now nearly all raised to the condition of Legations, have been, or are being, rebuilt. All the main streets are lined with shade trees and provided with electric tramways while the whole town is lit by electricity.

Graham, Siam (1912), p. 25

The residences, clubs and business establishments of the foreign population were practically all located together in the southern part of the city along wide, well-kept streets.[1]

Blunt, An American Dentist's Unique Experiences, p. 100

---

1 For "lifestyles", see also Van Beek: *Bangkok Then and Now* (2008), pp. 77-84.

This district is cut through by several roads running roughly from west to east between New Road and Rama IV Road, namely, in order from north to south, the Si Phya, the Suriwongse, the Silom or Windmill and the Sathorn Roads. The last two run alongside canals of the same name. The upper part of this triangle is called Bangrak, the lower part Sathorn and here live the majority of the European residents.

Seidenfaden, Guide (1932), p. 77

The foreign colony is a feudal municipality, most of whose members regard themselves as martyrs elected by those at home to be standard bearers of white civilization. Fate has appointed them to suffer the trials and hardships of an alien existence while they attempt to knock some sense into the heads of slant-eyed heathens. They believe that they are the prototypes of Captain Cook and Raffles, but before they make a move they give deep consideration to what their neighbor will say and how it will affect their social standing. The complacency and smugness on Main Streets of American small towns become insignificant when compared to similar qualities existing in Oriental white communities. Who are these couriers of Western culture? For the most part they are merchants exploiting a naïve people. About ninety per cent of their number are recruited from Europe's middle class. The majority are clerks and business workers whose limited abilities made competition too one-sided for them at home. They were forced by economic necessity – not by the lure of the East – to make a living elsewhere and readily signed a three-year contract with passage paid guaranteeing them a larger salary than they could earn at home.

Freeman, Brown Women and White (1932), pp. 193-194

John read the letter three times before he put it down. He was on the short-list for a job at the other end of the world! The first job he had ever tried for. Where was that cutting? He took out a small slip of newsprint and smoothed it out on the letter.

BANGKOK, SIAM: Asst-Mgr, Gregory & Potter, Importers, W'sale Prov. M'chants. Thor. exper. trade essential. Age 25-35. £400 x £50 – £500, p.a. 3 yr. contract. Passage single paid. Applics. by personal letter only. No refs. Before March 31st.

Thompson, Engagement in Bangkok (1951), p. 13

The "down-town" *farang* – the Siamese word for every foreigner – though full of rumours, gossip, stories, and his own ideas about the Siamese and their ways, the Palace and its intrigues, the princes and their policy, knows practically nothing about the real Siam.
Norman, *The Peoples and Politics of the Far East (1895), pp. 410-411*

So well has the Siamese adventure into commerce developed that European traders are beginning to feel the pinch. Where they once had a monopoly they now find that they are subject to competition.
Scott, *Eastern Journey (1939), pp. 88-89*

To the average European, especially the Englishman, it must be confessed, whose one object is to make money and lead as comfortable and enjoyable a life as the circumstances of his exile will permit, Bangkok is not the most agreeable of residences. It has one advantage, perhaps, over many of the other big towns of the East. With its diplomatic body and consuls from all the chief civilised states, and with Government officials drawn from divers quarters of the globe, it affords a more varied and interesting society than is to be found in, at any rate, the big colonial capitals of the British Empire. But this point of superiority apart, existence is dull and limited it must be admitted, from the strictly Western aspect. There are the usual recreations of lawn tennis, golf, bicycling, riding and racing, which are always to be found wherever a certain number of Englishmen are gathered together; but these are not of a very exciting nature, and gay ladies will miss the garden parties and the dances, the excursions and the picnics which help to pass time pleasantly in Singapore and Hongkong.
Campbell, *Siam in the XXth Century (1902), pp. 56-57*

It was the custom in Bangkok for a newly arrived foreigner to obtain a list of the married foreigners, and their addresses, and then take a two-horse *gharry* and leave his calling card with address, and the upper left corner bent over.

I got busy on this job at once. It took me about a week to complete, as custom prescribed that social calls of this nature should only be made between 5:00 and 6:00 P.M. Within two weeks after completing these social cards, my appointment book, which till then had been practically blank, began to fill up.

Blunt, An American Dentist's Unique Experiences (1968), p. 98

In the early evening, attired in the correct "club" clothes, we proceeded to patrol the European residential area in a slow-moving car. The syce, having been given the objective – Mrs. Williams - drove warily towards a pair of open wooden gates. On one gate-post was a small wooden notice "Mr. and Mrs. A. B. Williams – not at home", underneath was a small wooden box. The car came to a standstill at the entrance to the compound. Two cards were dropped surreptitiously into the box and then a hasty retreat. As the car moved off, Mr. and Mrs. Williams waved from the veranda. And so we proceeded to visit the houses of the "best" people. This game was known as "calling".

Exell, Siamese Tapestry (1963), p. 22

THE "SIAM FREE PRESS" COMPLETE ARRANGEMENTS HAVE NOW BEEN MADE WHICH WILL ENABLE THIS OFFICE TO UNDERTAKE ALL KINDS OF JOB PRINTING AND VISITING CARDS,

Prospectus Forms, Debit Notes, Labels, Programmes of Entertainments, Trade Circulars, Reports, etc.

Advertisement in Cartwright, Elementary Hand-Book (1906)

I did not install a "Not At Home" box when I moved into my house and I recall only one occasion when a member of the foreign colony came to pay a formal visit. I was entertaining our advertising manager, a Scotch man, and one of our photographers, with whisky sodas. We had had two or three drinks when a shiny, new sedan was driven into the compound. From the auto there emerged a well-dressed, rather portly lady whom I did not recognize. Unaware that she came only to leave her card, I asked her in and called to the servant to bring a drink. She declined and even refused to let me order a lime squash.

I noticed that the advertising man and the photographer were uneasy and stiffly turned down another drink. In the spirit of banter I ventured a polite remark that it was a good thing that there was no prohibition law in Siam. At that the lady arose, smiled very icily and took her departure. Puzzled, I saw her to the car and when I returned I found my guests convulsed with laughter. "Didn't you know that Mrs. Black is the wife of the richest missionary in town and that she and her husband are the founders of the prohibition movement for Siamese and Chinese converts?" the advertising manager blurted out.[2]

The resident of the foreign colony becomes a slave to good form and must do everything *comme il faut*. His mottoes are "is it done?," "go slowly," "what will the firm say?" And he acts as if he were under the lorgnette of a thousand Mrs. Grundys. And what are the consequences should he do otherwise? If he displays originality, he is eccentric; if he is sure enough of himself to follow his own inclinations and shows initiative, he is dubbed "common," or "selfish," or, if the critics are feminine, his wife is "ambitious."

Freeman, Brown Women and White (1932), pp. 194-197

Sometimes it seems that life in Bangkok is all European, so thoroughly does one get caught up in the whirl of little events of friendliness. There is a dinner at a big house, there is a luncheon that joyously lingers on for half a day, with collectors' treasures brought out, and excited talks on art ensuing. And always there are more men than women around the tables, for the men are legion who have left Old Europe to find occupation in New Asia.

Candee, New Journeys in Old Asia (1927), pp. 165-166

Reginald Campbell (1894-1950) was a naval officer before joining the Siam Forestry Company as a forest assistant in 1919. After leaving Siam on grounds of ill health in 1924, he established himself as a professional (and prolific) writer. His novel The Bangkok Murders *(1939) may have been inspired by a return visit to Bangkok in 1938. The protagonist is Rosie Temple, a former typist.*

I awoke to the sensation of heat, to the knowledge that a harsh and blinding glare was beating on my eye-balls. I glanced at my wrist watch,

---

2 In 1925, Mrs W. G. McClure was the President of the Bangkok Women's Christian Temperance Association, and Mrs P. A. Eakin its Treasurer and Secretary (Bangkok Directory, p. 253).

which showed nine o'clock, slipped through the mosquito-net, rang for the boy, yawned, scratched my arms, scolded the fierce Bangkok sun for not allowing me to sleep another hour or two longer.

This was life, romance with a capital R, and it was strange to think that but for the accident of a small legacy and the fact that I possessed a brother working in a merchants' office in Bangkok, I, Rosie Temple, would still have been acting as typist in the dingy and dusty offices of Messrs. Stiggins & Stiggins, brokers, of Mincing Lane, London.

"Yes, Missie ..." Ah Loo, my brother's Chinese boy, was calling through the door. "Some tea, Ah Loo," I answered. "Quick time."
The tea, when brought, was delicious as only tea consumed in Bangkok can be. That, together with a cigarette, completed my breakfast. By the time I had dressed it was ten o'clock, and the bungalow simmered under the glare of the May hot weather sun. Sprawled out on a long cane-chair, I read periodicals until eleven-thirty; there was nothing else to do. Officially I "kept house" for Tony my brother, but in a country where Chinese servants wait upon you hand and foot, and where the cook would bitterly resent your slightest intrusion into his domain, this meant rather less than nothing. Nor, must I confess, was I losing much sleep through the knowledge thereof. At eleven thirty-five I had a gin sling, ice-cold and cockle-tingling, then put on my topee and walked over to Ruby's place.

Campbell, The Bangkok Murders (1939), pp. 2-3

Advisers

Most of the Government departments are now administered with the assistance of European advisers, and a staff of European officials. Lest any European nation should obtain an undue share of influence in Siam these Government posts are distributed amongst men of many nationalities, and even within the limits of a single department this cosmopolitanism prevails. Since, however, the administration of a department is more efficient when men of the same nationality are working together, the tendency is for each department to draw its officers from some one nation in particular. Thus the general adviser to the Government is an American; the State Railways and the Postal and Telegraph Services are managed by Germans; the officers in the Navy and the Provincial Gendarmerie are Danes; Italian engineers are employed on the Public Works and Frenchmen in the Sanitary Department; in the Ministry of Finance, the Customs, the Bangkok Police and the Education, Mining and Survey Departments, the majority of the higher posts are filled by British officials, whilst the Ministry of Justice, to which Belgians were formerly appointed, is now advised by an Englishman and a Frenchman who, in theory at least, have equal powers. It must be clearly understood that any measure suggested by a European adviser is subject to the approval of the Siamese Minister of his department. Nevertheless, even if their proposals do not meet with favour, the mere presence of Europeans in high quarters acts as a wholesome check upon the Siamese official classes, and the Siamese themselves are the first to admit that were this check removed corruption would be rampant amongst them.

Thompson, Lotus Land (1906), pp. 52-53

MASAO, Tokichi (BANGKOK,) LL.D.

Tokichi Masao from *Twentieth Century Impressions of Siam* (1908).

Legal Adviser to Siamese Government; Judge of Supreme Court of Appeal; b. Nov. 17, 1870; at Ozu, Iyo, Japan; m. Nov. 4, 1898, Mitsuko, d. of Baron Kuhi, Privy Councillor, *Educ*.: Waseda University, Tokyo; Yale University, U.S.A.; LLB. (1st in class) 1895; LL.M., *cum laude*, Yale University, 1896; D.C.L., *cum laude*, Yale University, 1897; LL.D., given by Imperial University, Tokyo, 1903. Is at present Legal Adviser to Siamese Government; appointed 1897; Judge of Supreme Court of Appeals, appointed, 1900; on Commission on codification of Siamese laws, appointed, 1898; Vice-President of Siam Society since 1905. *Decorations*: Knight Commander of Order of White Elephant. *Publications*: Civil Code of Japan; Draft Law of Siamese Partnerships and Companies, etc. *Club*: Nippon, Tokyo. *Address*: Bangkok, Siam.

Who's Who in the Far East, 1906-1907, p. 218

> I met a Dr. Eldon James, the American adviser to the Government of Siam. I think that they are wise to have an American adviser.
>
> Harmsworth, *My Journey Round the World* (1923), p. 201

D. R. S. (Dermot Richard Southwell) Bourke-Borrowes (1884-1968) served as Adviser to Siam's Chief Conservator of Forests for a relatively short time during the mid-1920s. His article 'Siam' was based on a lecture he had given to the Royal Central Asian Society.

> Such success as has been achieved has been due in part to the fact that the Government has been wise enough to employ and to co-operate with European and American expert officials in many branches of the Administration. But the Siamese are now reaching the same stage that the Japanese arrived at many years ago, and in the future they wish to run their country without the assistance of white officials. The process of getting rid of foreign officials has already started.
>
> *Journal of the Royal Central Asian Society*, vol. 15 (1928), p. 316

"H. H. Prince Brom Bongs Adhiraj, together with W. A. Graham Esq. and W. F. Williamson, Esq," from *Siam from Ancient to Present Times* (1926), p. 205. At this time, Graham was "Adviser, Ministry of Lands and Agriculture" and Williamson, "Financial Adviser, Ministry of Finance". With others, they formed a committee of "Inspectors of Revenue" under the chairmanship of the prince.

The Foreign Colony 161

With advisers of many nationalities often giving conflicting counsel, it was plain how the Siamese had been pulled first in one direction and then in another, all efforts lacking coordination. They had developed into a set of apologists, and were constantly confronted with the necessity of giving the least offense to those whose advice they did not accept. The game of the different legations was to have their nationals appointed to office. The amount of intrigue and countermoves that went on backstage was unbelievable. The community presented the picture of a few whites quarreling among themselves, and a huge native mass that did not know what it wanted.

Heiser, A Doctor's Odyssey (1936), pp. 484-485

The services rendered by all of these counsellors to Siam have been conspicuous, and without their aid the Siamese monarchs would certainly have been unable to carry out their successful policy of depriving Western Governments of any excuse for intervening in the internal affairs of the country. In recent days, however, the tendency of the Siamese Government has been to rely less and less upon the counsel of the advisers, and for a long time past the custom has been discontinued of appointing foreigners to executive positions.

Crosby, Siam (1945), p. 37

Legations and Consulates

Foreign governments were represented in Bangkok by Legations headed by Ministers or chargés d'affaires. The latter sometimes doubled as Consuls, though Britain maintained a separate "Siam Consular Service", a service which (confusingly) also covered the Dutch East Indies and French Indo-China. Only after the Second World War were Legations made into full Embassies headed by Ambassadors.

Almost every nation has its consular representative. Consular Bangkok is distinguished by its verandahed houses, its club, and tennis and cricket grounds. The palm and the bamboo dominate the gardens, and the note is of the higher civilization, the civilization of hot and cold baths and electric light. Here the Stars and Stripes are conspicuous, and the Tricolor floats in the breeze. The Union Jack is unfurled side by side with the national emblems of Denmark and Germany; Italy runs up its red, white, and green in friendly rivalry with the yellow of little Holland.

Frankau, Let the Roof Fall In (1910), p. 213

Very soon the Legations will abandon the river side, fly from the noise and reverberation of the water, the evil smells, and the excessively costly ground, and take refuge in a new and more sanitary quarter. How we shall miss our old Legation then, with its old fashioned colonial design, its modest enclave of French territory planted with banyans and bougainvillias and a one-hundred-seventy-five-foot mast flying our colors in the midst of the croaking of toads and bullfrogs!

Morand, Nothing but the Earth (1927), p. 105

"In this dilapidated building are the offices of the American Legation and Consulate" and "American Consul's Office in Bangkok. Note the furnishing". From Perkins, *Travels* (1909), p. 264.

The diplomat Maurice P. Dunlap (1882-1964) describes the American diplomatic presence in Bangkok in the early 1920s.

The office of the Consulate is in a good-looking concrete building situated only a few steps from the main street which runs for miles parallel to the winding river. The office consists of two enormous, airy rooms and a store-room. It is immaculately kept with polished teak-wood floors, the trim furniture sent out by the Department being tastefully supplemented by teak cabinets, tables and screens, all finished to match the oak tone. One notices this fine wood everywhere in Bangkok; it is very decorative and seems to take light, dark, dull or glossy finish equally well. There are two Siamese clerks and a coolie who acts as janitor.

It has been a pleasure to find so many Americans associated with different interests in Siam. They meet in goodly numbers every Monday at the Legation when the Minister's wife, Mrs. Brodie, has her afternoons at home. Real American ice cream is a prominent feature of these gatherings.

The connections between Consulates and Legations in Bangkok are very close, as most of the ministers or *chargés d'affaires* are also in charge of the consular activities. There is a great deal of calling to be done in Bangkok and there is considerable official entertaining.

American Consular Bulletin, January 1923, pp. 4, 15

The celebrated American "adventurer" Richard Halliburton (1900-1939) turned up at the United States Legation in Bangkok shortly after Dunlap's arrival.

The secretary, being a rather young man, was greatly embarrassed when I first called on him, dressed in my usual shorts. He prayed inwardly that the minister would not come into the office and find him entertaining a khaki-clad vagabond. Of course that's exactly what happened. But to the great relief of the secretary, instead of being treated coldly by our envoy because of my outrageous costume, I was invited to dine that evening at the legation. A rented coat, a pair of borrowed trousers, a purchased tie, and a few apologies prepared me for the occasion. That dinner proved a sort of social "début" in Bangkok. During the ten days that followed I became acquainted with everybody in town but the king.

Halliburton, The Royal Road to Romance (1925), pp. 288-289

In Landon's novel, India Severn attends a reception at the American Legation.

Chinese boys in the livery of the Legation – white coats buttoned to the neck and wide white trousers gathered into black socks – were hurrying about replenishing the supply of elaborate cakes and sandwiches. There was no one in the garden, but there were benches and a pleasant calm. The modulated cadence of voices floated from above. The lawn had been watered earlier in the afternoon, and there was a sweet smell of hay from a pile of freshly cut grass that the gardener had not yet removed.

Landon, Never Dies the Dream (1949), pp. 3-4, 8-9

I arrived in Bangkok as a Student Interpreter in July 1896. I was just eighteen and half years old – the youngest Consular Officer who ever came to Siam, or, I think, to any Eastern post. There were two of us, M. being a couple of years my senior. Originally a Student Interpreter was a person who studied to become an Interpreter. In Siam such posts never existed, so that a Student Interpreter was, in effect, a Probationer Vice-Consul. The one thing he was, and is, most unlikely to be required to do was to interpret. We had to do all kinds of office work. M. was factotum to the Consular Court, whilst I helped with the accounts and shipping,

Staff of the British Legation when Sir Herbert Dering (centre) was Minister (1915-1919). To Dering's right are the chaplain, Rev. H. J. Hillyard, and Reginald Le May, the Vice-Consul for the Bangkok Consular District; to his left is the Consul-General, T. H. (later Sir Harold) Lyle. Behind Dering stands Brigadier-General R. C. Stevenson, the Military Attaché. According to *Siam from Ancient to Present Times* (1926), Dering had been "a trusted representative of the foreign community" (p. 211).

Legations and Consulates 165

besides acting as typist and Secretary to the Minister. I was the first typist the Legation ever had, and a pretty bad one, I fancy; but the Minister was delighted with this rare accomplishment of mine.

Wood, Land of Smiles (1935), pp. 9-10

Bangkok, Friday (received yesterday).
The British Consuls in the Far East are usually badly housed and grossly overworked, said Lord Northcliffe at a banquet given in his honour by the British clubs here this evening. One result of his world tour was to convince him that the British Empire was short of administrators and had more territory than it could properly direct. Consular arrangements were often totally inadequate. It was impossible, for example, that the small Consular body could properly administer, even temporarily, British business affairs in a group consisting of such widely scattered but important centres as Java, Sumatra, and Siam.

Weekly Despatch, 25 December 1921, p. 7

Until recently, New Road had one oasis, the British Legation. Brilliant with Flame-of-the-Forest in the hot weather, it stood on a beautiful site overlooking the river on its far side; a site which had been presented to the British by King Mongkut, a great, learned and good man, grandfather of the present monarch. It was probably intended as a compliment to her hosts that Queen Victoria should sit in a bay just outside the Legation Gardens, facing the street; but she wore our best inimitable English air of owning all she surveyed. Now the beautiful site has been sold for a large sum and the Legation removed to the new residential quarter, a practical step, but lacking in grace, as many think, towards the givers.

Wheatcroft, Siam and Cambodia (1928), pp. 96-97

A soirée is on at the British Legation. For a mile along the lotus-edged road a crowd is pushing onward toward the big compound away out on Rama Road. Every motor-car in Bangkok is on the way, and in these are ladies in their prettiest evening frocks and men in the absurd white Eton jacket that one grows to like after learning that it is not a ship steward's dress. All the compound of the Legation is gay with lights and flags waving over the lawns and over the innumerable open-air theatres. Here are all the people with whom you have dined and tiffined, and here is all the diplomatic corps smart and engaging as at every capital. The house is in good British taste with rare bits of bronze, of porcelain, of all the Eastern crafts of long ago.

Candee, New Journeys in Old Asia (1927), pp. 166-168

Trade

One of the tasks of members of the Siam Consular Service was to compile reports on the commercial situation of their consular districts and the prospects for British trade. In 1921, Josiah Crosby was confident that Britain could retain its dominant position.

Direct exports from Bangkok to the United Kingdom in 1920-21 amounted to Ticals 7,868,466, valued at £821,343 or nearly 12 per cent. of the output of the port for the year. The United Kingdom ranked third upon the list of receiving countries. In the matter of imports, the United Kingdom again headed the list. Imports from the United Kingdom exceeded those from any other country in respect of the following classes of goods: – Cotton textile manufactures; cotton yarn; iron and steel manufactures; machinery; paper; carriages, cars, cycles and parts; precious stones, unset; goldsmiths' and silversmiths' work. The above figures indicate the gratifying way in which British trade continues to hold its own in Siam, such business as was lost during the war now having returned again. There is every reason to suppose that, so long as they can meet competition in prices, United Kingdom manufacturers will be more than able to maintain their ground. Whilst they have nothing to fear on the score of the quality of their merchandise, the question of prices is, however, a capital one, and it remains to be seen whether, in face of existing industrial conditions at home, it will be possible for them to keep the cost of production low enough in the future to compete successfully with their American, Japanese and German rivals.

United Kingdom, Department of Overseas Trade, Report on the Commercial Situation in Siam (1921), pp. 15-16

From *Siam: Nature and Industry* (1930).

Legations and Consulates 167

The Englishmen in Siam, I discovered, like most Englishmen in the Orient, were antagonistic toward Americans. They regard us as intruders who have started to invade with our commerce a territory wherein they have so long held a monopoly that they feel entitled to continue monopolizing it. They particularly resent the fact that during the earlier years of the war, before America entered the conflict, our own merchants took advantage of the opportunity by trying to capture British trade in the East.

Foster, A Beachcomber in the Orient (1923), pp. 129-130

The United States exported to Siam in the calendar year 1919 goods worth $1,938,000, or 5% of the Siamese total; our imports were only $224,000 or four-tenths of 1% of Siam's foreign output. Our leading exports to Siam include cigarettes of which we sent $281,070 worth in 1919; electrical goods, machinery, metal manufactures, oil, tools and motor cars. Siam's purchases of oil from the United States exceed $250,000 a year, or about 20% of her total oil importations. The country needs coal, saws, axes, tools of all kinds, knives, forks and spoons, scissors, enameled ware, cooking utensils, knives and razors. Most of her imports are from the United Kingdom.

Irving National Bank, Trading with the Far East (1920), pp. 264-267

Character of the Trade. – In the capital, Bangkok, are located the principal wholesale houses. These supply the smaller distributors in the capital and practically all of the other buyers throughout the Kingdom. The principal industrial plants are also located here. Between 85 and 90 per cent of the trade of the Kingdom passes through the port of Bangkok. To canvass Bangkok thoroughly is to canvass all Siam.

Importing Retailers. – In Bangkok are certain retailers who are in a position to import direct. They should be called upon when the representative carries a line of merchandise for which the wholesalers cannot be depended upon for adequate distribution.

Agencies. – Local agencies are always established in Bangkok. Many of the firms, both European and Chinese, already have their agents in the principal towns.

Business Centers. – The chief business center is the capital. Nearly all of the smaller firms in the towns are dependent on the firms at the capital. Practically no merchants in the other important towns of the Kingdom import direct, and it is useless for salesmen to canvass the smaller places.

Purchasing Power. – The purchasing power of Siam is not great; the larger part of the native population is poor with few material wants. Rice is the principal staple of food.

Import Duties. – All goods are charged 3 per cent ad valorem with the exception of spirituous liquors, which are charged roughly 8 per cent. The customs requirements are not exacting or complicated.

Hints for Travelers. – The conditions in the interior of Siam are still rather primitive. It is quite useless for the average commercial traveler to go outside of Bangkok, as to canvass the capital thoroughly is to canvass the whole Kingdom.

United States, Department of Commerce, Commercial Travelers' Guide to the Far East (1926), p. 229

Siam Advertising Co. Klong Kut Mai & New Road, Bangkok, Siam. All kinds of advertising, billposting, pamphlet distributing, newspaper and magazine advertising, tramway and railway advertising. We control all the advertising rights on the Railways and Tramways in Siam and also in the City of Bangkok. An expert staff of "ad" writers and translators at your disposal.

Advertisement in Cartwright, Elementary Hand-Book (1906)

The business problem of today is not the manufacturing, but the selling end of your business. Anything that increases sales is of importance to the business man – and advertising is the great sales increaser. The "*Observer*" specialises in advertising that sells goods and develops trade. For rates etc. inquire from the manager or ring him up on the 'phone.[1]

Announcement in The Siam Observer, 1916-1918

---

1 In fact, the rates are supplied elsewhere in the paper: a single insertion cost two ticals or thirteen ticals if repeated each day for a month.

At Home

The roads are well kept and in part shady being lined on both sides by cosy cottages and bungalows each standing inside its own garden plot shaded by the foliage of the big trees or almost hidden behind a wealth of flowering shrubs and creepers, while every afternoon the fresh sea breeze makes life in this quarter more than bearable, in fact, quite enjoyable.

Seidenfaden, Guide (1932), p. 78

When I saw to what fate, in the way of houses, some people were condemned, I said a little daily grace for the big verandah overlooking the patch of green grass that ran down to the broad shining Menam. To live in the East, and specially in Bangkok, and not have a verandah as your principal room, is as bad as living in the country without a garden. I blessed then the broad long verandah where openness and light, and what air there was, kept the pest at its lowest. There a variety of cane chairs, light tables, groups of palms, ferns, and Eucharist lilies, gave a comfortable and cool invitation; a flight of wooden steps led down to the garden, and the

'The Author's Residence in Bangkok' from Campbell, *Siam in the XXth Century* (1902).

170 In Bangkok

simplest way of entrance for a visitor was to walk up and see if anyone was at home

Landon, 'Mid Pleasures and Palaces (1907), pp. 35-37

On landing it was a disappointment to find squalid pseudo-European streets, which moreover are spreading. Still there is plenty of room in the seventy square miles of Greater Bangkok, and to my pleasure I found that the mission which for the next eight months was to be my home was almost in the country. It opened on to one of the fine avenues planted by order of that fatherly monarch, King Chulalongkorn. Houses in this part of the town were almost all Western looking, but by no means all inhabited by Europeans; for though the left bank of the river is now fashionable among the Siamese, the beautifully fashioned wooden house of old Siam hardly exists on this side. In this Western quarter the more modern type of house seems to disregard the drawbacks of tropic sun and storm, while the older and more picturesque are lifted out of the danger of flood on columns and surrounded by deep verandahs to give much needed shelter from the sun and from storm driven rain. The mission, I am glad to say, was definitely of the old type, and a stretch of paddy fields was separated from us only by a canal.

Wheatcroft, Siam and Cambodia (1928), pp. 89-90

In Landon's novel, the missionary India Severn has established her modest school in a house known as "Jasmine Hall". It has seen better days.

Jasmine Hall was a sprawling two-story building, painted gray, and encircled by verandas upstairs and down. Those on the second story jutted out beyond those on the first and were supported by wooden trusses. The resulting effect was vaguely reminiscent of a Swiss chalet. The inside design was basically simple. It was one of the "wagon-run-and-haymow" houses common to Siam. The rectangle formed by the exterior walls was divided upstairs and down into three sections by wooden paneling a single board thick. The top thirty inches of this were an elaborate scrollwork designed to permit free passage of air. Spiders claimed this region as their own. The central sections of the rectangle were the wagon runs and went across the width of the house, uninterrupted with walls. The sides were divided to make the haymows. Verandas encircled the whole. Segments of the upstairs veranda at the back and sides had become sleeping porches, bathrooms, and a kitchen for India, while a part of the veranda downstairs, farthest from the entrance, had been walled and screened to make an apartment for Darun.

Landon, Never Dies the Dream (1949), pp. 15-16

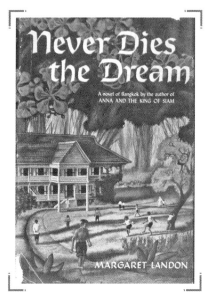

In Hervey's novel, Lhassa arrives at the house of the mysterious Dr Garth …

Dr. Garth's house, or villa as the proprietor had called it, lay beyond the congested quarters, near a canal smothered with lotus and water-hyacinth. It was a rambling house, almost hidden by banians, tamarinds, and betel-palms; and the approach, a road where white dust arose under the horses' feet, ran between hedges of bamboo. She followed the "boy" into a large, dusky room. The shutters were closed, but a sky-light arrangement diffused a twilight upon linen-covered furniture. This half-tone included in its somber glow an oil painting, the portrait of a woman who looked down wistfully from her frame, even sadly Lhassa thought, as if each shrouded chair was the ghost of a dream.

Hervey, The Black Parrot (1923), p. 41

The flat was in Siphaya Road. It was noisy, dusty and had no outlook. During the day it did not matter. In the evening I could go to the club. Night time was the problem. Bangkok never slept. Opposite was a row of Chinese shops and, at night, the pavement became a sort of public sitting-room. Everyone seemed to prefer squatting on the pavement and all talked at once. Anyone who thinks that Chinese is a musical language because it has tones is making the mistake of his life. The men's voices were raucous and the women favoured a high-pitched squawk. Though they were three storeys below, they might just as well have been in our lounge. When they were not arguing their wooden sandals clip-clopped about on the stone paving like a grandfather's clock with hiccoughs. Indian watchmen helped things along by calling the hour but their timepieces never seemed to synchronise. Calling the hour started at about a quarter to and carried on until a quarter past. They also had a habit of suddenly bursting into song for no apparent reason and this started up all the pariah dogs in the district. To add to the discomfort there was no main drainage and receptacles were placed at night along the pavement edge. Since I was practically teetotal at the time. I played games each night, had a late dinner at the club, a hundred-up at billiards and then strolled over to the flat hoping for the best.

Exell, Siamese Tapestry (1963), pp. 37-38

Rachel Wheatcroft describes her room at St Mary's Mission.

Each of the large rooms had two big window doors giving on to the verandah at either end. The choice for the inmate was a considerable lack of privacy when the doors were left open, or stewing in artificial light if they were shut. Mine was the furthest back of the large rooms, and in most respects the best placed for privacy, being behind the staircases. Privacy, as understood by us, is the comfort most missed by Europeans in a life in any small measure common with natives of the East. The room's drawback was that the small slice, the linen room, was beyond me, with a door between, and without keeping my room doors shut it was almost impossible to prevent the boarders from making a passage of it. I had, for refuge, a beautiful bathroom with two windows, one or other of which could be kept open in nearly all circumstances. It was the best bathroom in the house, with a tin hip bath as well as the zinc sink, which served most people for their ablutions.

Wheatcroft, Siam and Cambodia (1928) pp. 209-211

The American Presbyterian missionary Althea Lyman Eakin (1865-1951) was the second wife of Dr John A. Eakin. They retired in 1925 but stayed in "in the field".

My seven years of retirement in Bangkok have "seemed but a few days". And contentment, tranquillity and thankfulness have filled those days. Money was given us by friends to build a house in the suburbs of Bangkok. A motor bus passes my door, reaching the city in about twenty minutes. I live within the sound of the bells of one Buddhist temple, only (I say one only, at Petchaburi I live within the sound of twelve.) My neighbours are Chinese gardeners, Siamese employees of a large engine shop, and a few officials. In this group the human sorrows and joys go on as in any group anywhere. Colourful weddings, births, sudden and sad deaths, cremations, young men entering the priesthood – all these enter into my daily life, and I try to share their pleasures and sorrows. The kindness and consideration of the Siamese people to me during these seven years is beyond description.

Women and Missions, November 1933, p. 260

THE HOUSE BY THE SIDE OF THE ROAD

At night we always knew when one of the horde of frogs had been trapped, caught and consumed by a snake in the gardens. From the veranda I saw it happen several times, but this was not so chilling to the soul as hearing the slaughter take place while lying in bed. The familiar croaking of the frog would change to a higher pitch, producing a note that was almost a cry. Somehow the cry was identifiable as one of fear and pain. Finally the snake would strike, and if you were near enough you could still hear a muffled yelp as the frog was swallowed.

Lightwood, Teresa of Siam (1960), pp. 36-37

Bertha McFarland writes about her husband's search for a house with his first wife, Marie, around the time of the end of the Great War.

Search as they would, there was no house for rent that seemed even adequate. Just at this time, Dr. Hugh Campbell Highet, Medical Officer of Health, was retiring and returning to England. He had built himself a home in a new and desirable section of the city, some five miles from Siriraj Hospital, and wanted to sell. The deal was made and Holyrood, as Dr. Highet called his home, changed hands. The grounds comprised some five or six rai (more than two acres) bordering on Sathorn Road. The house was of brick with a second story of teak. Above was an attic covering the whole house, room to store all the treasures George and Marie had acquired or ever would accumulate. The grounds had been well laid out, with the house set back from the street, facing due east and being so arranged that it caught the breezes from the south-west in hot weather and from the northeast in the cool months – the secret of a comfortable house in Bangkok. A trellis covered with bridal wreath broke the expanse of lawn, giving them a secluded inner garden with vistas through the arches in the trellis. It was with very grateful hearts that George and Marie settled down to life in their own home.

B. McFarland, McFarland of Siam, pp. 189-190

The bungalow allocated to Derry was fully furnished; his predecessor had evidently luxurious tastes. The beds were English, and there was enough glass and china, considerably damaged, as it was. Before they

Holyrood, the house of George and Bertha McFarland in Bangkok. Originally built by Dr Campbell Highet.

At Home 175

had time to go through the four rooms and big veranda of which the residence consisted, it seemed to Rosaleen that the neighbours began to call. Certainly they were met with kindness or was it curiosity? She fell easily into the habits of the place, and her domestic qualities developed rapidly. She made war against ants and cobwebs, learned to leave the cook to his own devices, and express no surprise when her little brown maid was courted by an aspirant, who sat on his haunches and watched her without speaking, at all hours of the day and night. The price of foodstuffs appalled her, and all the ways of the coloured servants were strange at first. It irked her that if she went shopping, for instance, she should be followed by an Indian watchman with a big stick; but she submitted to it, as it was Derry's wish, and apparently not unusual.

Frankau, Let the Roof Fall In (1910), pp. 142-143

1st Cl House to Let
For 2-3 yrs. at 160 p.m. H cl furniture. Md. conv. inst. u-t-d. Rooms 4 big 2 small bath toilette verandah terrace. Lar gdn. Sit facing S. Silom N side near Saladaeng. Apply Box 74.

Advertisement in The Bangkok Times, 5 August 1935

I found a little house in the paddy fields of the Phya Thai section that seemed to have been built especially for my needs. Its owner was a Siamese lawyer who lived in it with his wife, five children and several relatives. He was willing to move into smaller quarters in the rear and let me have the house completely furnished for one hundred and fifty ticals a month. A real estate man would have called it a bungalow but to me it was an Asian idyll.

Inside were four large rooms furnished in Occidental fashion. The living room walls were lined with sectional bookcases containing Siamese volumes and standard English sets: Dickens, Thackeray, Jack London, an encyclopedia, books on home building, interior decoration, gardening and other subjects. One case contained priceless Siamese pottery from the provinces of Sukhodaya and Svargakoloke. In a corner was a rosewood desk alongside which stood a bronze cuspidor three feet high. There were also a rug, divan and several easy chairs. The dining room was screened and in addition to a large table at which eight could sit, there was a sideboard with a complete set of china, glassware, silver and napery. In the bedroom were two beds with canopies of mosquito netting, a wardrobe and a dressing table. The bathroom, equipped with a modern tub, shower, basin and sanitary toilet, was tiled in the best American style. A rear porch with teak furniture looked out upon a pond in the center of which was a Chinese tea house with tables and stools of rosewood inlaid with mother of pearl. Lotus flowers and lilies floated on the surface and occasionally a small fish would ripple the water. Across the pond, hidden by tall bushes, were the kitchen and quarters for servants. It would be easy to become a lotus eater here.

Freeman, Brown Women and White (1932), pp. 242-244

George F. Worts (1892-1967) was an American novelist and short-story writer specialising in what is probably best described as "pulp fiction". His story 'A Message for the Maharaja' concerns Judy van Dorn, a young American recently arrived in Bangkok.

Dr. Dill warned her to conserve her energies, and as a result of ignoring that warning she spent several days in her room, a victim of sun fever. But the room was delightful. A huge box of copper screen of very fine mesh, two thicknesses. It overlooked the garden, and the air in it was agitated by a slowly flapping, electrically animated punkah. There one could recline and look out over the tops of mahogany and tamarind and olive trees at shining temple spires which stabbed the sky, and ponder amazing things.

Collier's, The National Weekly, 13 December, 1924, p. 11

Arriving in Bangkok in 1910, the American dentist H. Earle Blunt soon found premises.[1]

There was a very large empty room on the second floor, but the only entrance to this room was behind the drugstore. I found the room was so large that, by putting up some light partitions, I could have an operating room, reception room, laboratory, kitchen nook, bathroom, and small room for Abdul. While these partitions were being put up, by diligent searching I was able to find the necessary simple furnishings. This was fortunate, as there were no furniture stores for foreigners. Foreign residents had three methods of procedure in furnishing a room. First, order it made

---

1 As we know from his advertisements in *The Bangkok Times*, Blunt's premises were first located "over the Lotus Dispensary" (at the corner of Custom House Lane); two years later he was "located at Dr. Petersen's Consulting Room, New Road".

from designs in a furniture catalogue by a Chinese expert; second, order it from England; third, buy out a whole houseful of furniture from someone departing for another post.

Blunt, An American Dentist's Unique Experiences (1968), p. 97

THE BANGKOK HOUSE FURNISHING CO.[2]
Cable Address: "FURNISHING." – Postal Address: Si-Phya Road. – Phone 917. Cabinet and High-Class Furniture Manufacturers, Wholesale Furnishers.
IMPORTERS AND EXPORTERS. GENERAL CONTRACTORS.
All furniture is made from thoroughly seasoned Teakwood (Highly polished) Estimates and plans free.
Furniture made according to plans and specifications of the Clients.

Within two days the ghosts of my predecessor's mutilated romance were driven from the house and in their place were furniture, lamps, rugs, a few books, a kitchen stove, a cook and a house-girl. All I did to put my house in order was to spend an afternoon with Louis at an auction where the household effects of a farang leaving for England were put on sale. He had been Number Two in the branch of English banks and was quitting after six years. His wife and two children, both born in Bangkok, were going with him. The auctions of these departing guests are monuments to the ephemeral existence of the white man. He comes, buys furniture, auctions it off to others who have recently arrived, and they in turn eventually do likewise.

The sale was held in the garden of the farang's home. A dapper Eurasian in a red tie and a bowler hat banged his gavel on the veranda rail.[3] Those waiting to snap up the bargains included venerable Indians with white beards, and young Indians with blue-black beards, Siamese in varicolored panungs, Chinese in black trousers and coats, Malays in bright-colored sarongs and Europeans in spotless whites. The sun, the jungle, the East, had taken its toll of another white man and we were a pack of good-natured wolves haggling over the kill.

---

2   Proprietors: W. Ming For, W. Ming Doa.
3   Possibly, E. M. Fereira.

"Chet bhat, chet bhat, pet bhat, pet bhat, seven ticals, seven ticals, eight ticals, eight ticals," rattled on the auctioneer in Siamese and in English with the fervor of a radio announcer, and a perambulator was sold to a Chinese who wheeled off his purchase with a great show of pride. Since Oriental babies do not know the luxury of perambulators, I remarked to Louis that the buyer must be a modern father. "Not so modern," said Louis. "His baby will never ride in that carriage. He'll turn it into a pushcart for iced cocoanuts or bananas or make a lunch wagon out of it."

The baby carriage was about the only object put up for sale on which I did not bid. Here I accumulated chairs, beds, chests of drawers and other necessary pieces of furniture. They were carted off to my house and when I saw them again they were all installed in their proper places. Linens were on the beds and table. Towels, dishes and all the paraphernalia for keeping house were also there.

Freeman, Brown Women and White (1932), pp. 68-71

For Sale and On Hire.
All kinds of Furniture, Writing Desks, Bookcases, Travelling Trunks, Iron Safes, Mosquito Houses, Dinner Sets, Gramophone and Records, English Books, Saddle and Bridle, Violin, Camera, Iron-Beds, Mattresses, Electric Table-Fans and Lamps, Filters, Tracing Papers, etc. etc.
I buy and exchange everything. Money advanced on goods entrusted to me for sale.
D. FROIMAN
Second hand Furniture Store
Si-phya Road.
Advertisement in The Bangkok Times, December 1919

Excellent house furniture (mahogany and wax polished.) mostly made to special design and almost new. – An unusual opportunity for THOSE DESIRING to furnish a first class home.
Mr. Apcar will sell by auction on a/c of Meh Taram, at her residence Wind Mill Road next to Roman Catholic cemetery, on Saturday, 16th. January 1926, commencing at 2 p.m.
Terms: C.O.D. a deposit of 25% will be demanded on fall of hammer.

Delivery the following day from 9 to 12 noon.

T. S. Apcar
Auctioneer and Valuator
(Opp. British Legation)
'Phone No. 542

Advertisement in The Bangkok Times, 15 January 1925, p. 4

The Siam Observer says that Mr. T. S. Apcar, the auctioneer, was the victim of an unprovoked assault in the auction rooms of E. M. Pereira & Co. It appears that he was examining a sideboard which he intended to buy when a second-hand furniture dealer – one Froiman – came from behind and assaulted him, and it would seem rather savagely, with a new kind of weapon in the form of a mincing machine. Mr. Apcar was taken unawares, but he managed to ward off some of the blows though he had suffered considerably about the head. A complaint has been lodged with the police.

The Straits Echo Mail Edition, 10 December 1919

Sale by Auction.
Favoured with Instructions by R. F. Smyth Esq.
I will sell by Public Auction
At his residence at Luang Muang
At 2 p.m. sharp
On Saturday 5th February, all his HOUSEHOLD FURNITURE & EFFECTS including exceptionally fine wardrobes, upholstered sitting-room and highly-polished drawing-room and bedroom furniture, gramophone, ice-chests, camera, hammocks, meat-safes, curio cabinets, book-cases, tables, chairs, mosquito-houses, 2 writing desks, silver bowls, picture, glass, crockery, cooking utensils, stove, pot plants, clock, el. lamp, etc. etc.
A REALLY GOOD LOT. NO RESERVE.
R. D. Brainbrigge, Auctioneers etc. etc.
Keo Fah House, New Road.[4]

Advertisement in The Bangkok Times, 1 February 1927, p. 4

---

4 R. F. Smyth had been an engineer with Siamese State Railways since 1898; his two brothers also worked in Siam as railway engineers.

Shopping

To lady visitors who desire to go a-shopping, the firms of Badman and Co, J. Sampson and Son, and the Bangkok Outfitting Co, all in the City, may be recommended, whilst the Indian *pinwallah* and Chinese tailor abound.[1] For jewellery, either of foreign or Siamese pattern, Graehlert and Co. and Tisseman and Co. will be found to supply all needs, whilst the traveller or sportsman will find much to his taste in the premises of Messrs. Falck and Beidek and the East Asiatic Co's store, both near the Oriental Hotel. There are also many excellent Chinese owned general stores where practically everything is sold, the chief of these being the firms of Kiam Hoa Heng, Kiam Hoa Seng, Yong Lee Seng, etc. etc.

Antonio, Guide (1904), pp. 26-27

On the bank is a most interesting market, Talaat Plu, the market of the Betel leaf. From the point of view of the sightseer the quantities of Manchester goods on sale, encouraging though they may be as to the prospects of British commerce, seem out of place; but in the flower and fruit sections it is a joy to linger. Here are flowers by the trayful, great mounds of blossom and of blossom only, never gathered by the spray as in the West, but picked flower by flower and heaped in gorgeous piles of colour and scent.

Wheatcroft, Siam and Cambodia (1928), pp. 91-92

The shops are decked out with black and red flapping signs covered with gold lettering, and as I move forward through this hanging waterfall I am conscious that with only one head and two eyes it is impossible for me to see everything. Shopkeepers and clerks, naked at the waist, smiling and inscrutable, surround one at each attempt to affect a sale. Under the awnings that almost touch and let through zigzagging and broken lines of sky, the heat is terrific.

Morand, Nothing But the Earth (1927), pp. 109-110

---

1 For department stores, see also Van Beek: *Bangkok Then and Now* (2008), pp. 74-75.

From Crocheron and Norton, *Fruit Markets* (1930), p. 191, with the caption: 'Merchandizing in Siam is in the hands of Chinese who control the commercial enterprises of the kingdom'. Also published in Exell, *Siamese Tapestry* (1967) with the caption: 'A pedlar of toilet requisites'.

Boon Chui's shop was a cheerful place, full of things from all over the world. There were great piles of snowy enamelware from Sweden, and a cupboard of cheap earthenware from England. In one glass case were dozens of flashlights from America, toothbrushes, tooth paste, and baby powder. In another there were tennis shoes from Japan, lacquered boxes and trays from China, and hundreds of other small articles.

Landon, Never Dies the Dream (1949), p. 99

A pre-printed and stamped order card for the firm Falck & Beidek. Editor's Collection.

It is no exaggeration to say that practically everything which a resident in Bangkok needs, with the exception, perhaps, of piece goods, may be purchased from Messrs. Falck and Beidek, a firm of importers and wholesale and retail merchants who have been firmly established in Siam now for some thirty years past. The business was founded in 1878 by Messrs. Falck, Bramann, and Beidek, and has, since its inception, been known by the Hong name of "Hang Sing Toh." Some idea of the extent of the trade carried on by the firm and the resources at their command may be gathered from the size of their new premises, which are situated on an extensive piece of ground just off the New Road.[2]

Twentieth Century Impressions of Siam (1908), pp. 263-267

The Karachi Store into which she turned was one of several run by Indian merchants, who had almost a monopoly on the sale of yard goods in Bangkok. Some of their shops were hardly more than holes in the wall with bolts of cloth piled to the ceiling. The Karachi Store was spacious and catered to the foreign trade. It offered for sale many things hard to find elsewhere: embroidery cotton, silk hose, English linens and voiles. There were also brass trays, rugs, carved ivories, and ebony elephants for tourists. One of the sleek Indian clerks greeted the girl with an obsequious flourish as if he knew her well. "Ah, madame, and what will it be today?" "Some blue linen if you have it," India heard her say.

Landon, Never Dies the Dream (1949), pp. 46-47

---

2 Hang Sing Toh: "Lion Store". Christian Kramer, the proprietor of the firm, was interned and expelled with other Germans in 1917-1918. The firm's premises have been preserved and now operate as an antiques store known as "O. P. Place" (30/1 Soi Charoen Krung 38).

BY APPOINTMENT TO H.M. THE KING
KIAM HOA HENG & CO., LIMITED. Estab. 1879.
Head Office Address: – East Bank, River Menam, Bangkok.
General Merchants, Importers, Commission Agents, Wholesale Dealers in Wines, Sprits, Provisions, Hardware, Fancy and Soft Goods, and Contractors to H.S.M.'s Army and Navy Stores.

Advertisement in The Bangkok Directory (1925)

HORLICK'S MALTED MILK LUNCH TABLETS
For Businessmen, Lawyers, Golfers, Sportsmen, etc.
Kiam Hoa Heng & Co's SI PHYA BRANCH.

Advertisement in The Bangkok Times, December 1925

For a quarter of a century and over Messrs. Harry A. Badman & Co. have held a leading position amongst the large retail stores in Siam. The house was established by Mr. Badman on January 1, 1884, close to the Royal Barracks, and became known as No. 1, Bangkok, a name it retains to the present day. The store is splendidly appointed and the goods in the various departments are displayed in most attractive fashion. The firm do not confine themselves to any particular branch of trade, but conduct a business on the line of the departmental stores.

Twentieth Century Impressions of Siam (1908), pp. 272-273

Badman's furniture productions are worthy of the highest praise. Most of the articles are made of the native teak, which is superbly finished in different styles as desired. The popular rattan furniture is also supplied by them in charming designs. The firm's furniture workshops are behind the main building, and the Shanghai workmen employed there produce with precision and fidelity copies of any period furniture. The fact that machinery does not enter into their work, and that their tools are of the simplest description, makes their efficiency all the more astonishing.

Macmillan, Seaports of the Far East (1925), p. 516

While a cottage was being built in the suburbs of Bangkok Dr. Eakin started a small religious book store. After Dr. Eakin's passing in 1929,

> **DON'T FORGET!**
> at
> **THE EAKIN STORE**
> *866-G Windmill Road*
> there are
> **RODEHEAVER RECORDS**
> **SIAMESE RECORDS**
> **PICTURES in GREAT VARIETY**
> for the
> **HOME and CHURCH**
> and
> **AMERICAN MAGAZINES.**

the store was moved from the city to his study in the cottage. Supplying Sunday school rolls, Bible pictures for churches and homes, and religious books in the Siamese and English languages, I still carry on.

Women and Missions, November 1933, p. 260

BY APPOINTMENT TO H.M. THE KING
SIAM'S PREMIER STORE.
THE COOLEST AND MOST UP-TO-DATE STORE.
THE VISITOR'S PARADISE.
LOWEST POSSIBLE PRICES. BEST QUALITY GOODS.
ALWAYS SOMETHING NEW.

Whiteaway, Laidlaw and Co., Ltd., have been established in Bangkok since 1908, and the premises they used to occupy at the corner of Siphya Road and New Road could not be regarded as in keeping with the large and handsome stores which they had established in many other Eastern cities. The local branch, however, was brought into line with the firm's other fine establishments when, on March 31st, 1919, the new premises in New Road were opened by H.R.H. the Prince of Nakorn Sawan. The premises, three storeys high, occupy an area of 15,500 square feet, and their handsome appointments throughout are an excellent example of local workmanship. The multitudinous variety of goods are displayed in artistic and effective comparisons, and the arrangements of the various departments represent the result of long study and experience of the organisation and adaptation of supplies, so as to exemplify the maximum of convenience and the minimum of labour.

Advertisement in Siam from Ancient to Present Times (1926)

No firm throughout the East are greater adepts than Messrs. Whiteaway, Laidlaw and Co., Ltd., in accurately anticipating the public's requirements, and especially in concentrating on meeting individualised local demands and idiosyncrasies wherever they have become established. Each of their numerous markets differ in many ways. In Bangkok, for instance, they are called upon, more than in any other Eastern centre of population, for goods of the highest possible quality. Hence it is that in their New Road emporium the stock in each department ranges through all the finest grades of manufacture. This is particularly noteworthy in the sections for ladies' and gentlemen's outfitting, where fashion is followed in its latest decrees, and fancy and novelty are given an interpretation beyond stereotyped demarcations of pattern, colour and texture. All kinds of high-class boots and shoes, general household drapery, furniture, glassware, chinaware, English and French perfumery, jewellery, silver and electroplate, books, stationery, travelling requisites, and fancy goods, form departments on which much could be written if space permitted. Briefly, the establishment is one of the most popular and appreciated of Bangkok's shopping resorts, and an influential factor in the exemplification of fashion, art and utility in the extensive range of its supplies. The manager is Mr. F. J. Ford, and the assistant manager Mr. F. D'Arcy.

Macmillan, Seaports of the Far East (1925), pp. 511-512

AS A SPECIAL ATTRACTION FOR NEXT WEEK
WHITEAWAY'S WILL HOLD A WONDERFUL
FIVE TICAL WEEK.

Advertisement in The Bangkok Times, 23 January 1926, p. 10

L. G. RIGANTI & CO. COURT JEWELLERS AND WATCHMAKERS

"In these disturbing days of still rapid and great fluctuation in exchange, and, consequently, the value of commodities, then we affirm one of the most satisfactory for the investment of your floating capital is – jewellery. We offer you every opportunity to make this safe investment: but just come along and pay us a visit, and we can talk the matter over." The firm was established in 1919 by its present proprietor, Mr. L. G. Riganti, who is an expert watchmaker and jeweller, and has some twenty years' experience in Siam. His private firm employs many assistants in its various branches, and it would be difficult for anybody to find that he could not get an order executed by some branch of the expert staff under this undertaking's competent control.[3]

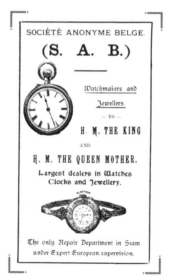

Advertisement in Cartwright, *English-French-Siamese Word and Phrase Book* (1917).

---

3 Parallel text in English and Thai.

The former S.A.B. premises on New Road (corner of Worachak Road) were designed by Fausto Pistono of the Government's Building Office. The three-storeyed, ferro-concrete building was opened in late 1921 when its "imposing exterior" and "artistic, business-like and well ordered interior" were praised by *The Bangkok Times* (19 December 1921, p. 8). In the 1950s, the firm was acquired by the Borneo Company. Today, the premises are occupied by a Chinese-language newspaper, but the clock is still keeping accurate time. Photographs: Wikimedia Commons, *Siam from Ancient to Present Times* (1926), The Editor (2023).

Chummeries

On arrival at his post, the latest employee, if he is unmarried, is generally put up at a company mess, similar to a college fraternity house. There the freshman is initiated into the secrets of the society in which he is to dwell. He soon learns what is and what is not done. He learns that the man in the retail business is on a lower social scale than the man who sells his goods at wholesale prices and that the Number One man in the biggest commercial house is the colony's social mentor. As at home, the man with money is to be looked up to, but here he is regarded with greater reverential awe. If the neophyte is not already a snob he is soon taught to be one. He discovers new powers in himself when his servant addresses him as master.

Freeman, Brown Women and White (1932), p. 194

From a private album, 1890s. K.I.T.L.V. Wikimedia Commons.

Leigh Williams describes "the bachelors' mess of The London and Bangkok Teak Company" (i.e. the Bombay Burmah Trading Corporation) as it was before the Great War.

An ornamental bridge over one of the "klongs" leads us to the iron gates of a spacious "compound." An Indian watchman, in the Company's smart uniform and armed with a stout bamboo "lathi" or stick, salutes us as we draw up in front of a large white building. This is the bachelors' mess of The London and Bangkok Teak Company, where I am to stay until I start up-country. This large, cool house accommodated half a dozen of the Bangkok Office and Sawmill staff, and was known in the Company as "The Chummery." I soon discovered that several of its inmates were not on speaking terms! At dinner, served in a large hall, we all sat at a long table in order of seniority. As any junior who spoke "out of turn" was snapped at, it was rather a gloomy meal. But it was a riot compared to breakfast next morning. Everyone sat at his own small table, facing the wall and waited upon by his own Chinese "boy." Conversation would have been an outrage, and anyone who entered with a cheery "Good morning!" would I think, have been shot, so "livery" was "The Chummery" at that hour of the day!

Williams, Green Prison (1941), pp. 17-18

In Eric Reid's story 'Profit and Loss', "Infant" finds his income does not match his aspirations.

In common with the rest of the Minor Mess, F. W. Laking, B.A, (alias the Infant), held firmly to the intention of somehow making, acquiring or saving as many ticals in as short a time as possible to enable him one day to buy a house in town, a shooting in the country and an odd motor car or two, if not a yacht. In common with everyone all over the East, he cherished the fond hope that one day these projects would be realised. Everyone knows best how he is to arrive at this happy consummation, and everyone has his own infallible method. Infant had several methods, all different and some of them devious. He found, first of all, that to save enough for his modest purpose was quite out of the question if he were to keep body and soul together, as Bangkok understands the phrase, i.e, by belonging to two or three clubs, maintaining a horse or two for driving and racing purposes, shooting snipe in their season and entertaining his friends on a lavish scale all the year round.

Reid, Chequered Leaves (1913), pp. 145-147

By what strange law of gravitation these four fellows had come to be associated in the common existence of a Bangkok bachelor mess it would be impossible to demonstrate. As a general rule, men of the same "pidgin" (calling) find it convenient to live together in the Capital of Siam; and of course circumstances or congenial tastes and sympathies play a certain part in assorting the members of a mess. But, in the case of No. 73 Suriwongse, the causes leading to such an admixture as existed there were wholly inscrutable. Certainly it would have been hard to find a more curious mingling of types than was presented by the members of the first mess that Harkness knew in Bangkok. Free and easy in all their ways, the most complaisant member of the association usually assumed the invidious task of "running" the household; that is to say, writing the "chits" to the stores for orders of groceries necessary; doling out the market-money to the cook, or fining the coolie for not sweeping the verandah clean; and at the end of the month, paying the bills, and subsequently recovering the proportion of the total expenses from each member.

In 73 they took these tiresome duties in turn, each fulfilling them as badly as a mere man might have been expected to do in such un-masculine conditions. Just before Harkness' arrival the Mess bills had been mounting up. Living is atrociously dear in Bangkok, house-rent so high, and servants are paid such inflated wages that a bachelor as a rule finds it beyond his means to maintain a separate establishment. That being so, the reason for two or three men chumming together in a single house is evident, and the result is a reduction of household budgets to reasonable dimensions.

"No. 73," accordingly, Harkness joined. The members consisted of Santall (already described), Garstin (of the Mines), and the lively little Frenchman, Jean-Marie Nempont, who lent a touch of sprightly colour alike to the Mess and to the Local Sanitary Board, to which he was more or less attached. These four men in the employ of the Siamese Government, and chosen for various reasons and various qualifications to "advise" a young nation in the way it should go towards the high ideals of European administrative methods, inhabited a large, wooden two-storey and very typical Bangkok house. A mass of pink and white Honolulu creeper did its best to cover and subdue the garish blue with which this edifice was painted; but apart from that, the house possessed compensations of convenience in its nearness to the business centre of the town and to the Clubs, and of airiness derived from a detached situation in a decent sized "compound."

Reid, Spears of Deliverance (1920), pp. 18-20

Williams describes service at the Chummery before the Great War ...

The food was good and the service, under the direction of the white-haired Chinese butler, excellent. All the "boys," many of whom of course were middle-aged, wore spotless white duck suits with high-buttoned collars, and the lower ends of their trouser legs were tucked into white socks and kept in place by a broad band of black elastic silk. No ankle

The interior of a house, probably Bangkok ca 1895. From an Ainslie album.

scratching for them! A pair of black velvet Chinese shoes with silent rubber soles completed their neat and unobtrusive outfit. These tactful and efficient "boys" are a class by themselves, and mostly come from the island of Hainan in southern China, whence they take service all over the Far East. How many a returned Easterner sighs in vain at home for their quiet industry and incomparable ubiquity! How they spoil their masters for anything but the life of a millionaire! Do you arrive home for dinner from the British Club three-quarters of an hour late and with two or three unexpected guests? It does not matter. There is no fuss, bother, confusion or black looks. The head "boy" merely whispers, "Cook he say please Master give him five more minutes." Time for a round of sherry, and the company sit down to a meal perfect in every respect, with no sign whatever that it is nearly an hour late and was originally prepared for two instead of five!

Williams, Green Prison (1941), p. 18

TO BACHELORS
ACCOMMODATION FOR ONE BACHELOR,
BRITISH, IN MESS.
Well-furnished and comfortable house, garage etc.
To pay PROPORTIONATE SHARE OF EXPENSES, about TCS.
250 odd per month, everything included.
Apply, B. B.

Advertisement in The Bangkok Times, 19 July 1922, p. 6

Beer

Pilsener Ur-Stoff Bier.
MOST DELIGHTFUL AND REFRESHING.
Price per case of 48 1 bottles.
Tcs. 20.00 delivered free to house. Fresh consignment just arrived.
Well assorted stock of cigars and tobaccos always on hand.
Hamburg-Siam Gesellschaft
Unverzagt, Bachfeld & Co.
Hamburg. Bangkok.

Illustration by Martin Ränicke from
Lindenberg, *Kurt Nettelbeck* (detail).

Fresh and Cheapest
"Sapporo" Lager Beer Specially Brewed for Export.
Dainippon Brewery Company Limited.
Tokyo, Japan.
Wholesale only from
The Mitsui Bussan Kaisha.
Advertisements in The Bangkok Times, February 1909

According to a Consular Report the only good beers obtainable in Bangkok are Dutch or Danish importations. Breweries have been established in Japan and Hong-Kong and their products are sold in Siam, but are not deemed equal to the European brands. Good water is now obtainable in Bangkok, and as there is a large demand for good beer, the establishment of a brewery would prove a profitable undertaking.

The Brewers' Journal, 13 August 1910, p. 481

A new note was struck with the formation two years ago of the Boon Rawd Brewery Company, whose brewery was opened in July, 1934. At the time of its formation, the Company experienced some difficulty in raising capital. This is a Siamese enterprise, although the machinery and the technical experts required for the erection and working of the plant were obtained from abroad. The venture has apparently been successful and the brewery now markets in Siam three brands of beer, the best of which compares favourably in quality and price with the European or Malayan product, and the cheapest of which may supersede the very widely drunk Japanese beer. The plant is said to have a capacity of 30,000 bottles a day and negotiations are now being made for export to Malaya, Burma and other neighbouring territories.

Advertisement in *The Bangkok Times*, February 1925.

United Kingdom, Department of Overseas Trade, Report on the Commercial Situation in Siam (1934), p. 20

Why drink beer that has travelled thousands or hundreds of miles when you can get the finest lager beer brewed fresh on the spot.

Advertisement in The Bangkok Times, September 1934

A friend and I were returning, somewhat late, from a party when it occurred to us – it was devilish hot – that we could mingle lovingly with some beer. We told the boys where to go,

Beer 195

but they naturally took us to quite another place. However, its proprietor declared that he had what we wanted and we went inside, into a room in which were several polite little Japanese women and a few Malays, squatting on the floor in their sarongs and tattoo-marks. We were swallowing the beer when a prosperous, middle-aged Chinaman entered, from another room, a trifle the worse for wear but most gentlemanly.

"Sir," said he to me, "you will pardon the impertinence, but I take it you are a Britisher."

"No impertinence at all," said I. "People are always taking me for a Britisher, and, funnily enough, I am."

"Then will you allow me the pleasure of singing you a Scotch song complete with appropriate gestures, accent and idiom?"

"Man," said I, "I should be tickled stiff."

And sing he did, Harry Lauder's *The Reason Why I Wear a Kilt*, complete with appropriate gestures, accent and idiom – though whether or not they would have been recognised in Scotland is another matter – delivering the classic with enormous spirit and finishing up with what I presume was intended for a Highland fling. All the while the Japanese and Malays sat quiet as mice, their eyes wide with wonderment – as were my own, for it was a truly astonishing performance.

Garstin, The Dragon and the Lotus (1928), pp. 306-307

X'mas

For the Festive Season.
X'MAS CAKES AND PUDDINGS.
Fancy Cakes. Mince Pies, Pastries, Etc. Etc.
Orders should be booked as soon as possible to
ORIENTAL BAKERY (Oriental Avenue).

Advertisement in The Bangkok Times, December 1908

Made to Order: Wedding, Christening, Birthday Cakes for the festive seasons and for all occasions. The only Bakery in Siam installed with up-to-date machinery electronically driven.

F. V. DE JESUS, MANAGER[1]

Siam from Ancient to Present Times (1926)

Julia Corisande ("Zulu") Fyshe, née Mattice (1877-1957) writes to Anna Leonowens about a Christmas dinner given by Louis Leonowens and his wife Reta in Bangkok. She had married Leonowens' nephew, Dr James Carlyle Fyshe (1880-1921) of the Department of the Medical Officer of Health, in December 1908.

---

1 "He was born in Bangkok in 1864, and received his English education at St. Joseph's Institution, Singapore, where he remained as a student from 1875 to 1879. His knowledge of various languages gives him a special advantage in handling the workmen employed" (*Twentieth Century Impressions of Siam*, 1908, p. 179). De Jesus had previously worked as manager of the saw-mill at Sriracha. His predecessor at the Bakery was G. M. de Jesus, possibly a brother, and he was assisted by Leo C. de Jesus, presumably his son. They lived at the Villa Rosa, 964 Windmill Road. On 1 August 1925, de Jesus' daughter Letitia Victoria Beatrice (1896-1980) had married William Oliver Deacon (1893-1947) of the Sriracha Company. The wedding took place at the British Legation, with Rev. Fr. Colombet officiating.

Last night we dined with Uncle Louis and Aunt Reta. There were Messrs. Milne, Anderson, Mountain, MacLeod, all in L.T.L. Ltd., and very nice boys, Mr. Milne being particularly nice. A lovely dinner in their new mosquito-proof dining room. Such a treat not to be eaten alive or have the table covered with insects. We had stuffed olives, soup, fish en cocottes, beef filet and tomatoes, roast turkey, peas and potatoes, ham and sausage, asparagus, plum pudding and sauce, fruit, champagne galore, crackers and afterwards we went to Phya Pipat Kosa, a Siamese, who had a Christmas Tree and dance on Christmas Eve.[2]

Quoted in Bristowe, Louis and the King of Siam (1976), p. 124

Kiam Hoa Heng's X'mas Bazaar
NOW OPEN.
Never has a more brilliant show of CHRISTMAS NOVELTIES been seen along the banks of the River Menam.
We cordially invite our customers to call early,
to see and select at leisure.

Advertisement in The Bangkok Times, December 1913

X'mas Convivialities and the Days of Auld Lang Syne!
The time-honoured custom of celebrating Noel-Tide in the good old traditional way has not been forgotten in Bangkok. We are now preparing photo-pictures of many of the most prominent of last X'mas' social parties, and ladies and gentlemen appearing in the groups may like to procure copies of these, as souvenirs of X'mas 1917 in Bangkok. They will come as a pleasant surprise to those who may have forgotten them, in the hurry and scurry of the more laborious functions in connection with the War, but the "Old Folks at Home" "Tommy in the Trenches" or "Jack on the Rolling Wave" will hail them with delight. Orders should be sent early. Call and inspect samples. The Talat Noi Photo Studio. Phone 208.[3]

Advertisement in The Bangkok Times, February 1918

---

2 LTL Ltd.: Louis T. Leonowens Limited. Phya Pipat Kosa (C. M. Xavier) was a senior official in the Foreign Office. Dr Fyshe had been appointed to the post in Bangkok in 1907 (*Canada Lancet*, November 1907, p. 249).

GREETINGS FROM SIAM.
Christmas and New Year Cards.
A large assortment of attractive Greetings Cards specially printed for Siam. Artistically coloured Siamese Scenes on the front with real photographs enclosed. Complete with envelopes in many shapes and sizes.
THE SIAM PHOTO STUDIO
Siphya Road, Bangkok.
Advertisement in The Bangkok Times, December 1926

Advertisement for the Bangkok Manufacturing Co., in The *Bangkok Times*, October 1927.

Not even the slump nor the economic conditions can entirely divorce the spirit of gaiety from the celebrations of Christmas, and this year's festivities appear to have been on as big a scale as ever, to all accounts. Among foreigners in general there have been two large international parties by American and British hosts, at which the hospitality was lavish, and the obvious care spent on the entertainment of the guests has been thoroughly appreciated by them. Of the public functions, all the largest hotels have had their gala nights, generally well patronised, while the smaller and newer restaurants have also made a bid for Christmas time. General regret was felt that the last fortnight's really cold spell did not extend over the

---

3 The photographers Robert Lenz had advertised "albums of Siam" as "suitable X'mas presents" in 1898 and later "X'mas cards and New Year cards with coloured views of Siam" (*The Bangkok Times*, November 1913).

festive season, but these things are not man made. However, slump or no slump, there has been any amount of gaiety, and anything that helps to take our minds off business conditions in these times is worth its weight in gold.

The Bangkok Times, 27 December 1932, p. 6

Ruth Rickover (1903-1972), the wife of a well-known American admiral, visited Siam in 1938.[4]

There were only a few hundred Europeans and Americans in Siam, but they certainly succeeded in generating much Christmas spirit in Bangkok. Everybody entered wholeheartedly into the holiday atmosphere; Christmas packages were continually being interchanged between Siamese and their foreign friends, decorations went up everywhere, and there were innumerable parties. Christmas had simply become a national holiday in Bangkok. Mr. Walter A. Zimmerman, who was in charge of the Bangkok YMCA, and his wife, Betty, took me to watch the children's Christmas party at the Polo Club. The children were all dressed like little princes and princesses. Some of them sat eating cake and ice cream at long tables, with neat Siamese nurses standing by to serve their little masters and mistresses.

Rickover, Pepper, Rice, and Elephants (1975), pp. 177, 180

---

4 For Rickover, see also Enchanted Land.

Language

The Siamese language is tonal, having comparatively few polysyllabic words. The greatest differences in meaning may be expressed merely by change of tone. Siamese consists of no fewer than 44 consonants, 15 ordinary vowel-marks, and also some other vowel and accent-signs, as well as to characters for the numbers.

Macmillan, Seaports of the Far East (1925), pp. 484-485

The language is very difficult. Words are few, but the intonations many; thus the same word may mean many different things according to the inflection that is given to it.

Harmsworth, Voyage Round the World (1923), p. 205

B. O. (Basil Osborn) Cartwright (1877-1928) was a teacher and translator in Bangkok.

A word of caution is necessary to would-be learners, and especially to those who imagine they can "pick up" a smattering of the language in a few weeks by trying to learn words or sentences in a parrot like fashion from romanised versions which are invariably most misleading. To try to do this is merely an absolute waste of time, money and frequently of temper also. The author has found by practical experience, that a working knowledge of the language can be acquired by average persons with proper tuition and diligence on the part of the learner in about 6-8 months, and by those with linguistic abilities in a somewhat shorter period.

Cartwright, An Elementary Hand-Book of the Siamese Language (1906), pp. viii-ix

Exercise 67.
TRANSLATE INTO SIAMESE.

1. Last night I saw two snakes in the road in front of my house, one of them was black. I think it must have been a poisonous one.
2. During the hot weather you should not eat so much meat; it is better to eat fish, if you know that it has just come from the sea.
3. This curry is not hot enough. Tell the cook to put about three times as many chilies in the next one he makes.

4. In Siam we never have any snow, but they say that hail fell once about five years ago.
5. Look how dark the sky is growing; I think we shall have a heavy thunderstorm this evening.
6. Walking is not pleasant in the streets of Bangkok, because most of them are rather narrow, and there are so many carriages and rickshaws.
7. If you cannot buy me a box of those cigars at that shop, go to the hotel and ask them if they keep them there.
8. Why are all those people dressed in white? They are going to a cremation at the temple near your house.
9. The thief who stole my hat has received three month's imprisonment.
10. Where did you find that umbrella? I found it on my verandah yesterday. Does it belong to you? If so you had better take it away with you.

Cartwright, An Elementary Hand-Book of the Siamese Language (1906), pp. 190-191

Jim brought me with triumph a book on the language, the only one printed, and I turned to it eagerly. It is a confusing book – I apologise to the author, but that is the truth, and not altogether his fault perhaps. However, I tried to grasp something, and this is one rule I specially noted: "In the pronunciation of all the letters there is a vocal sound of 'aw' following." The truth of that statement helped to fix it in my mind. "Aw, ong, ung, wong, tong, taw" – that might be a Siamese sentence! Then there are six different "tones" in which these same seductive sounds may be pronounced, and each variety of tone conveys an entirely different sense to the initiated ear. I shut up the book, wondering how quickly my little maid would learn English.

Landon, 'Mid Pleasures and Palaces (1907), p. 42

My teacher liked to give me trick sentences to illustrate the use of the tones. He would ask me to translate such things as "Who sells ducks eggs?" It went something like this – "*Krai khai khai khai?*"[1] Provided you said it as if you were something like Big Ben chiming the quarters, then you were all right. Say it all in one tone of voice though and it might mean – "Who

---

1 In fact, this means "hen's eggs".

eggs eggs eggs?". I rather thought my teacher got quite a bit of fun out of me but we were good friends. As soon as we got tired of floundering about in Siamese, he would drop into English. We were much happier that way. I was not a good student. His English improved enormously though.
Exell, Siamese Tapestry (1963), p. 50

In theory, we were supposed to devote most of our time for the first two years to the study of the Siamese language. In practice, we learnt Siamese when we could find the time. We had two teachers, one of whom knew some English and the other not. Neither had any idea of teaching. I cannot think how we managed to learn anything at all, but in fact we both did pretty well. At the end of our two years we could speak, read and write Siamese more or less, and we passed our examinations with flying colours, M. beating me by a few marks. Siamese writing, I may say, was an accomplishment only attained by one of our predecessors.
Wood, Land of Smiles (1935), pp. 9-10

"Are you English?" "Certainly." "I thought you were Siamese. You speak our language so well." Even in the jungle, this sop to the vanity of the traveller was offered with all the charm and sincerity that marks the same gift elsewhere. The compliment to my linguistic abilities was very gratifying to me, because I was young enough to believe it. I know now that I spoke the language atrociously. All Europeans do, especially those whose business it is to speak it best, the Government and Consular officials.
Young, From Russia to Siam (1914), pp. 66-67

On arriving in Bangkok in 1928, Sister Teresa receives advice from Bishop Perros.
"Learn the Thai language," he advised, "so that you may understand the needs and problems of the people for whom you will work." By way of a start he then pressed a pack of cards into my hands. They were not, let me add, playing cards. These were a children's classroom aid – a series of coloured cards bearing the letters of the Thai alphabet, and with their help I was to become gratifyingly proficient at the language in little more than three months.
Lightwood, Teresa of Siam (1960), p. 28

Naturally the greater part of the studies is in Siamese. In such circumstances, knowing no Siamese, it was impossible for me to be quite independent, and it was frequently necessary for me to snatch Siamese teachers from their classes to interpret in mine, a sad loss of time to both. Drawing certainly improves powers of observation, so it is important to teach it to all children regardless of taste and talent, but the lack of a common tongue is a terrible handicap.
Wheatcroft, Siam and Cambodia (1928), p. 207

Experienced Siamese teacher is now free to resume giving lessons to English-speaking foreigners. Difficulties in reading, spelling and pronouncing unfamiliar sounds of compound vowels and tones, easily overcome by new method, which is unforgettable. Lessons at any time or place to suit students. Regular students guaranteed ordinary conversation six months. A free trial is given. Curios, genuine old images for sale. Apply P.P. c/o this paper.
The Bangkok Times, 1 August 1929, p. 9

"The language," I asked, "just how difficult is it?" "All you need," Beaumont said, "is a good teacher, a good memory and the will to work. But a word of warning. Don't take on a lady teacher or, in other words, don't indulge in the luxury of a 'Sleeping Dictionary' or you'll acquire what the Siamese so aptly term a 'mosquito net accent'." Beaumont knew it all.
Exell, Siamese Tapestry (1963), pp. 15-16

An encouraging sign of American progress in certain lines is shown by a typewriter company that has built up a large business by manufacturing machines with Siamese characters.
Shriver, Canned-Goods Trade in the Far East, 1915, p. 63

In 1895, the multi-faceted George McFarland took over responsibility for the development of a Siamese typewriter from his late brother Ed.
From 1895 the typewriter became a part of the fabric of my life.[2]

---

2 An advertisement appeared in *The Bangkok Times*, dated: June 18th 1895.

In 1897, I opened the Smith Premier Store. The years since 1915 have seen great development in the Siamese typewriter. The first keyboard provided for all the characters but not for writing the natural way. The mechanism would not allow this. I worked over the mechanism until I discovered how to change it and get the machine made which would write the natural way. Then the Remington Company made it for me. The keyboard was improved and the Remington keyboard has now been taken by every other Siamese typewriter company and put on their machines. They are quite willing to profit by my effort. I now have a Siamese Portable, Siamese Standard and Siamese Accounting Machine. I have established an up-to-date Service Department under a skilled American Mechanic. I have a Typewriter School for teaching typing and a well-equipped Store and Sales Department. My staff numbers fifty, at present. During the past eleven years I have enlarged my line, to include Office-Appliances of all sorts and have had a large part in the introducing of their use into Government offices. Much water has flowed under the bridge, since I first put the Siamese typewriter on display in my dental office.

McFarland, Reminiscences (1936), pp. 12-13

The lingua franca employed in the foreign trade in Siam and also as a ready means of communication with educated natives is, as all over the Far East, English. Foreign firms usually keep their books and carry on their correspondence in English. French is but little avail, except with French trading concerns.

Gerini, Siam (1912), pp. xliii-xliv

It is to be observed that, since 1855 at any rate, English has been the only foreign language in anything like general use in Siam.

Crosby, Siam (1945), p. 54

The Siamese are excellent linguists, and the accuracy with which many of them speak English is little short of marvellous.

Macmillan, Seaports of the Far East (1925), p. 487

Mias

Philip had already heard a little about the institution of the *mia* in Siam. In a Siamese household the "*mia*" is of varying degrees. Polygamy, despite its having been recently discountenanced in high quarters in the land, is still legally recognised and, notwithstanding a slight dash of "civilisation" in many other directions, is still generally practised. As in the feudal past, even nowadays a Siamese gentleman of wealth still finds his influence and his importance estimated in the vulgar computation to a large extent by the number of women in his household. But the European too, in Siam, has generally his *mia*, a woman of the country who shares as much of the white man's lot as he permits her. That participation, in the majority of cases, is little enough, the *mia* of the European filling no larger place in his outward life than, say a favourite pet, a dainty animate plaything. Santall himself had a "girl" (most men call them "girls") somewhere in the background. He being young and human and easy going, that was almost inevitable.

Reid, Spears of Deliverance (1920), pp. 9-11

Wattana had dropped Mani after she ran away with the brother of a classmate, and Grace had never forgiven her the disgrace that had touched the school because of the incident. Mani had returned at the end of the week moderately penitent, but Grace had delivered her to her mother with a stinging rebuke. Later the mother had arranged a temporary match with a German businessman for, it was said, two thousand ticals. When he left Bangkok, she arranged another with a Dane, who was Mani's present husband. He was a kindly man and had grown fond of her. Two years before he had married her.

Landon, Never Dies the Dream (1949), p. 53

Bangkok, 16th December, 1911
On the following morning at six we left in a motor launch with Bovo for the long – and take it all round – but little interesting excursion to Klang Ransit, where amid immense rice-fields irrigated by canals lives the Italian Mazza, who has married a Siamese and who has a cloud of children, which,

strangely enough, are nearly white. His wife, dressed in simple and rough *panum*, displayed her breasts in quite an indecent manner. Perhaps with age and as a result of her frequent maternity, she has lost that grace which one finds in the younger women of her own country. Mazza calls her Madame Mazza, and it requires an effort not to laugh at that ape which in a few days will be the legalized companion of an Italian. At the birth of the twelfth child Mazza has *decided*!

Besso, *Siam and China* (1914), p. 81

In Eric Reid's story, Bobbie Featherstone reads of some startling provisions in the 1909 Anglo-Siamese Treaty. He fears he is not the only person to have become aware of them.

He opened the paper and began to read in a desultory fashion. His eye lit upon a paragraph, and he fell into a moment's silence, reading intently. At last, "What balderdash!" he cried, flinging the sheet down, but he smiled grimly in the dusk. "*Mia luang? Mia luang?*" (chief wife) he repeated, "What the deuce are they driving at? Of course the thing's impossible! There could be no conflict of laws upon such a question."

He flung his head back and pondered. Ten years ago! He did not know Alice then. It had all been very foolish no doubt, but fortunately it was all done with and buried long since. Other men had done the same; others could leave a youthful sowing unharvested by time. Days of youth! Days of youth! And now he was a married man of six years' standing, a model of all that was *rangé*, domesticated to a hair, proud and happy in his love of the charming wife for whose sake he toiled early and late.[1] But to-night he could not prevent his mind from reverting to the first days he had known in the East, those earliest hours of a natural and cradled ease filled with a simple inarticulate joy in life's gifts to youth. The night settled softly down. Featherstone lay musing on that almost forgotten period of brief infatuation. Voices whispered to him from the past; muffled steps came and went. A gramophone in a neighbouring house began softly playing "Frou-frou". The sickly sentimental air stole into his senses.

---

1 Rangé: orderly.

In a dream, Chalæm, Featherstone's discarded mia, appears to him with their son. She castigates Featherstone because he fears "the new laws which the English rajathut has made will change the old order, that you will have to give a share of your property to us". All she wants, however, is recognition from Featherstone that she (as the mother of his only child) is his mia luang, taking precedence over the childless farang wife. Alice returns; Featherstone wakes up and cries out.

Featherstone tried to answer naturally, but his throat was dry and his thoughts still on the vivid dream.

"Why, you old dear!" cried his wife, "you look wretched. You've been working too hard again at that horrid office. Come along. I've got the gharry waiting here. Let me drive you to the club."

Reid, *Chequered Leaves* (1913), pp. 33-42

Servants

The domestic servant question, though less discussed, is no less important in the East than it is at home. In England an incompetent cook may be the cause of indigestion, in the tropics his ignorance may land his master in the cemetery. Indians from Madras make the best cooks, and speak the best English, but most of those found out of India give way to drinking bouts. The majority of English residents employ Chinese cooks and boys. These are independent and expensive, but are nearly always sober and sometimes reliable. Their little failings are gambling and opium-smoking. Very few European domestics are employed: it is hardly fair to bring them out, as the stratum of society in which they can enjoy themselves is so very small.

Forty, Bangkok (1929), pp. 77-78

Ralph Parlette (1870-1930) was a publisher and author, probably best known for his The University of Hard Knocks *(1914). His main informant in Bangkok seems to have been his friend "Carl Vaseline, manager of the Standard Oil station".*[1]

A family needs a half-dozen native servants to go along at all. Vaseline has a Siamese chef who costs him 50 ticals a month, a man of all work Chinaman who gets 45, a nurse at 40, a coolie at 30, and a laundryman at 10 working part time. The natives board themselves, which means that they live off the food they can entice unbeknownst out of the employer's kitchen.

Parlette, A Globegadder's Diary (1927), p. 297

For house servants we had Chinese boys. They spoke little English, and one always wondered how much they understood. Our Number One boy would mechanically say "Yes, yes" to every order given. They took exclusive possession of the kitchen, which the house mistress could not afford to lose face by entering, so that one never knew what might be set on the table at dinner. The hostess for a dinner party might have been very particular in working out the menu and telling the boy what was wanted;

---

[1] In 1925, the manager was W. L. Blackett (Bangkok Directory, p. 333).

but often no dinner guest could have been more surprised than she by the dishes which appeared.
Sayre, Glad Adventure (1957), p. 93

The servants were all Chinese, most of whom spoke "pidgin" English, except for the night watchman who was an Indian. He was required at night because of the lack of police protection.
Blunt, An American Dentist's Unique Experiences (1968), p. 100

English people in Siam generally have Chinese servants and, as all the world knows, they can be very good indeed. However, they are very much more expensive than the less trainable Siamese, who have but little of the Chinese capacity for routine and detail. The Mission was poor – what Mission is not? So our servants were Siamese, and the national characteristics made domestic service there more picturesque if less regular than in most European houses. For instance, it was difficult to persuade the waiting maid that she should not clasp our plates to her bosom, a way of carrying them that we did not find appetizing!

Advertisement in *The Bangkok Times*, February 1911. The Bangkok branch of Fraser & Neave, "aerated water manufacturers", was in Siphaya Road.

Wheatcroft, Siam and Cambodia (1928), pp. 105-106

Siamese servants are at times even more casual than English ones. Though when they have been long in service they often show great attachment to their masters, and are greatly preferable to the Chinese in this respect, yet they always remember that they are perfectly

A Siamese servant from Crosby, *Siam*.

210 In Bangkok

free agents and stand up for themselves if they think they are not getting their full due.

Campbell, Siam in the XXth Century (1902), p. 100

The "boy," which word signifies in the East a personal attendant, was a man of forty, a Madrassee, and one of the best "boys" that ever master was blessed with. He took me under the shadow of his protection, and I can never be sufficiently grateful to him. He wore beautiful white draperies, falling in fine folds to his bare brown feet, and a white turban crowned his dark expressive face, out of which gazed deep brown eyes full of the silent wisdom born of numberless silent forefathers. When he raised a thin, sensitive brown hand to his forehead in respectful salaam, you honoured yourself. He began each morning for me by bringing tea and fruits. I, shrouded in my mosquito curtains, then watched the daily procession. "Master's boy" having said, "Missee ready for bars" he summoned two coolies, the under housemaids – men, I should say – and they, bearing large pails of water on long poles over their stooping yellow shoulders, followed him in solemn single file to my bathroom.

Landon, 'Mid Pleasures and Palaces (1907), p. 38

Louis' wife, Charoon, had hired servants while I was at work getting out the paper. Why she hired female servants I do not know. Meh (mother) Pin, the cook, was an emaciated creature of forty years. She looked sixty. She wore a black *panung* and a shabby garment like an old style corset cover. Chun, the house girl, was younger, about twenty-five. She seemed to have but one *panung*, a purple cloth, which, at least, always looked freshly pressed. The teeth of both women were black; their lips were starched with red lime, an essential ingredient when chewing betel nut, and hung open as if they were too stiff to close. When they spoke, the sounds they made were like those of a deaf mute. These two were on my monthly payroll at the rate of twenty ticals for the cook and fifteen for the girl.

I saw Chun only at meal times when she would shuffle in and out of the kitchen with the dishes prepared by Meh Pin. She seemed afraid of me. She would hurry out of my sight as soon as she had served a course and I would catch her peeping at me from behind the door leading to the kitchen. Often Meh Pin would join her and they would whisper about me as if I were a demon for whom they had to care.

Meh Pin, I had been informed, could cook foreign food, but from the dishes which Chun placed before me it was impossible to tell just what school of cookery she attended. Everything she served, including vegetables, came out of the frying pan and appeared before me floating in fat.

Freeman, Brown Women and White (1932), pp. 71-72

From an Advertisement for Sunlight Soap in *The Bangkok Times*, March 1914.

Burglaries are by no means uncommon and only those houses which, like our own, possessed a night policeman all to themselves, were generally immune. I waked without agitation on hearing our guardian's creaking boots – all officials are at once promoted into trousers and boots – tramping under my windows and up the verandah steps and down again. I knew I should not hear a soft, barefooted burglar, though I sometimes wondered if I would not have preferred him; that zealous watchman had no one to disturb but us, and he did his duty. Jim told me I must not let my mind run too largely on reforms, so I never wrestled with that watchman's boots.

Landon, 'Mid Pleasures and Palaces (1907), p. 37

Derry bought a dog-cart and a pony. In less than a week the syce ran away without notice, but before she had time to wonder who would groom the pony, a brother of the Indian watchman appeared, and announced that he was their new syce. He was an inch or two taller than the other, and not insignificant in weight, dressed all in white, even to the turban; a most princely figure. Rosaleen pitied the pony should he attempt to drive. But Derry said it was all right.

Frankau, Let the Roof Fall In (1910), p. 143

Late one afternoon on my return from the office, Ah Kin greeted me with a doleful face.

"Cook very much sick," he said.

I went with him to the servants' quarters where I found Kwong groaning on his mat. He was an emaciated man about forty-five years old whom I seldom saw. He would rise at 4:30 A.M. and go off to market to buy provisions for the day's meals, returning in time to prepare breakfast. The coolie, the cook's daughter, Song, who was six years old, and a Chinese I had not seen before, stood at the door with worried looks on their faces.

"What's the matter with him?" I asked Ah Kin. "Very much sick," he said. "How long has he been sick?" "Three days." "Who's been cooking?" "Lim," said Ah Kin, pointing to the stranger. "He cook's brother." "Why didn't you tell me before that he was sick?" "No want trouble master," said Ah Kin.

I had a feeling as I watched Kwong writhe that there was no time to lose and I drove at terrific speed to the home of a German doctor two miles away. He got into my car and we raced back to the house. We were too late. Kwong died of tuberculosis two minutes before our arrival. Kwong's death caused no interruption in the smooth running of my household. With the fatalism of the Oriental, his brother prepared breakfast the next morning and remained with me until I left Bangkok.

Freeman, Brown Women and White (1932), pp. 244-246

Flora and Fauna

To the Lotus Bloom in a Bangkok Klong
A lady bids me write an ode to you
O, beauteous bed of lotus flowers, down in the stagnant *Klong*.
Your glories, pink and fresh as morning dew,
I, a mere bard of doggerel, must weave into a song![1]

PILGRIM
The Bangkok Times, 5 October 1912, p. 8

Mary Ellen Hayes Peck (1839-1909), a wealthy lady from Milwaukee, had spent nine months travelling throughout Asia. In the foreword to her book, she expresses the hope that "these pages prove a pleasant reminiscence to those who have visited the scenes described, and an introduction to those who have not thus travelled, but some of whom may plan to do likewise".

The tropical growth of Siam impressed us only slightly, as we had just come from Java, "the garden of the earth." Otherwise we should have been enthusiastic over the beauty of the landscape and the luxurious growth of trees and plants.

There were fewer flowers than I had been led to expect, but the flora of Siam is said to be particularly rich in unusual varieties of orchids, which are found flourishing abundantly even in the jungles, and a visit would well repay a collector. A person can find a rich field in Siam along many lines of investigation.

Peck, Travels in the Far East (1909), pp. 199-200

It was not a large garden; one green square of curious tuft-like grass of poor quality lay at the back, and was given over to tennis or the less strenuous croquet. It was surrounded by mango trees whose green pod-like fruit was slowly developing, and Jim spoke of mango fool as of something worth waiting for.[2] Padouk trees were there, and they stretched bare brown branches amid the greenery as though to say, "It is only February, and

---

1 The first of only two stanzas.
2 Mango fool: a creamy dessert.

we will sleep at the proper time, however foolish other trees may be!" The padouk tree insists on this little winter of its own, and one avenue down which Jim and I used to drive almost made me chill with its wintry bareness. For the rest, the other trees made but a poor show of flowers: the cassia would hang out laburnum-like blossoms later, the golmohur show brilliant scarlet spirals, and big, red, tulip-like bloom would cover another tree. They said nothing but "wait" to my questioning eyes, and I whispered, "But don't you delay too long, or I may not be here to see your beauty. I go before the rains."

Landon, 'Mid Pleasures and Palaces (1907), p. 52

JUST RECEIVED
A Large Choice of Sutton and Sons' FLOWER-BULBS
Including the following: – hyacinths, narcissi, aconites, snowdrops, crocuses, tulips, anemones, ranunculuses, gloxiniae, begonias, lilium, Etc. Etc.
SOLD BY PIECE AND BY COLLECTIONS.
One Collection Complete of about 350 bulbs and roots: 16 Ticals.
City. S.A.B. Banrak.[3]

Advertisement in The Bangkok Times, February 1909

PLANTS, – For Sale, Roses, Palms, Ferns, Caladiums, etc., about 150 pots, apply – E. M. Pereira & Co, New Road, opposite Custom House Lane.

Advertisement in The Bangkok Times, February 1911

Bangkok in the hot weather is famous not only for its fruit but for flowering trees too. The residential parts of the city are then on fire with what Europeans there like to call Flame-of-the-Forest, the Madagascar Poinciana. In Ceylon we know it as Flamboyant and in India as the Golden Mohur. Flowers come before leaves. In the older trees they form domes of almost unbroken colour of a nearly perfect umbrella shape, the outline

---

[3] Sutton and Sons ("The Royal Seed Establishment, Reading, England") issued catalogues of "English Seeds for India and the East".

Flora and Fauna 215

sharp with the extraordinary precision of tropical trees. The bole and giant limbs, writhing uncannily, seem tortured to uphold such weight of beauty, in colour ranging from orange-vermilion almost to crimson, lightened only by the single, yellow or whitish petal in each blossom.

Wheatcroft, Siam and Cambodia (1928), pp. 100-101

To the Editor of the Bangkok Times
Dear Sir
I was painfully surprised at noon on returning to my house for tiffin that a vandal had ravaged the trees along Tejo Road including those in my own garden bordering the road by cutting off many of the larger branches. At first I thought this action might be the forerunner of the introduction of electric street lighting, owing to the many thefts of which my neighbours and I have been victims lately, but found on enquiry that the mischief maker was an official from the Sanitary Department who declared his object in cutting the branches was to "beautify" the road.

The Bangkok Times, 11 December 1919, p. 4

The compound was fresh and green. Large pools of rain water glistened brightly in the morning sunlight. A thin brown water snake wriggled out of one and glided leisurely across the grass. A restful stretch of unbroken lawn lay immediately in front of the veranda and separated it from two magnificent beds of crimson, pink and yellow cannas, backed by a hedge of deep red hibiscus. A neat semi-circular driveway separated the main lawn from the rest of the compound. From the two sides of the drive stretched larger lawns, tastefully broken by a variety of beautiful flowering shrubs. The double flowered pink and white oleanders and lantanas were in pleasant contrast to the vivid golden yellow of the bell-shaped alamander. At the far end of the lawns rose lofty pergolas over which were trained the deep rich purple bougainvillaea. Just beneath us was an hibiscus called the Rose of Sharon. In the early morning, its large peony like flowers were a pure white, by midday they would have changed to a delicate shade of pink and, by nightfall, to a deep red. Soon after sunset the flowers would fall and be replaced next morning by fresh blooms.

Exell, Siamese Tapestry (1963), p. 20

The eccentric Maxwell Sommerville (1829-1904) was "the first and only Professor of Glyptology (the study of engraved gems)" at the University of Pennsylvania in Philadelphia.[4] *He is said to have become wealthy "through publishing, and pursued collecting in two disparate areas: engraved gems and artifacts of Buddhist worship".*

We had a superfluity of mosquitoes; so vigorous were these troublesome insects that at any moment of the night, by quickly closing the hands over the forehead, on an average, eight or ten of these musical creatures would remain helpless on the palms of the hands. We thought it not prudent to speak of these executions to the Siamese room-boys, as they, being Buddhists, would not only lose respect for us, but would regard us as guilty sinners.

Sommerville, Siam on the Meinam (1897), p. 28

Newcomers talk of malaria as if it were a foregone conclusion that they would soon contract the disease; and yet, if they will only make a few inquiries, they will find that it is the exception rather than the rule for Bangkok residents to suffer from malarial fever. Malarial fever is rarely contracted by residents of this city, and those who do happen to get infected have generally contracted the disease while on a trip into the interior. The malaria-bearing mosquito, the Anopheles, is not easily found in Bangkok, even during a search for it.

Twentieth Century Impressions of Siam (1909), p. 132

When I first went to Siam in 1915, at every dinner party my hostess, upon receiving me, would, as a matter of course, hand me a small bottle filled with oil of eucalyptus which I was supposed to pour over myself in liberal quantities in the hope of discouraging insects. But mosquitoes swarmed in such numbers that the preventive was of no avail, and I usually returned to the hotel with my feet, ankles, and hands swollen beyond recognition. Guests used to cover their legs at table with bags. The last time I was there Flit had become popular, and every half hour a servant would pump a liberal supply under the table, while the guests sprinkled neck and arms with Sketalene.

Heiser, An American Doctor's Odyssey (1936), p. 496

---

4 See https://www.penn.museum/sites/expedition/the-eccentric-maxwell-sommerville/.

"W. S. L. B" writes about Bangkok's "perfumed nights"...

Evening means rest - not from the heat – but from the glare of the sun. The flowers that sleep by day are fragrant by night. The lotus, whose petals close at the first streak of dawn, fills the night with perfume. Millions of happy frogs sing in high shrill voices, perched on the banks of the klongs. In Siam the frogs never croak. The beauty of a Siamese night is as the inverse square to the ugliness of the day. It is the one compensation to the Englishman who crawls in under a suffocating mosquito net to sleep on a hard bed with a long, white bolster-like contraption that is known in Siam as a "Dutch wife." It is supposed to keep him cool.

The London & China Express, 22 March 1928, p. 204 [5]

The night insects last night surpassed anything I have ever known. I slept in a magnificently comfortable bed with a good mosquito net, and I am glad to say that nothing biting got through. This morning on the floor there are heaps of insects. I saw them being swept out of the room like dust. The frogs fairly shrieked. But I was so tired that I knew nothing from midnight until half-past six this morning. The night comes at six and the dawn at six. The cooing of the doves starts exactly at the latter time. There are, of course, no insects in the morning.

Harmsworth, My Journey Round the World (1923), p. 201

Beaumont kept very much to himself. He was tall, well built, somewhat dignified and round about middle age. His features were marred by a badly sagging cheek and I wondered if, perhaps, it made him shy and self-conscious. It looked as if he had had some sort of stroke. I had noticed, too, that one of his legs was badly swollen from knee to ankle. I was to learn later that it was all due to a failure to deal soon enough with a bite from a black scorpion.

Exell, Siamese Tapestry (1967), pp. 14-15

Towards the end of the meagre meal, armies of ants came swarming over the table and into the dishes to claim their ration. I would never

---

5 Also reprinted in the Singapore Free Press (21 April 1928, p. 6).

have believed that in a few short weeks I too would be learning to tolerate them along with the mosquitoes and a score of other insects, snakes and crawling creatures.

Lightwood, Teresa of Siam (1960), p. 30

The table was set for dinner on the upstairs veranda. India herself came out first. She sat down abstractedly, and in a moment Dulcie appeared. She too was wordless. Dom placed a bowl of soup in front of each, and each bowed silently for grace. After several mouthfuls of soup India laid down her spoon with distaste. There was too much pepper in it tonight. Then she looked more closely at her bowl. Ants! Infinitesimal red ants floated in small rafts on the surface. The dishes had not been properly washed, and the ants had been at work on the greasy plates when Plo served the soup. Ignore it or reprimand Dom? Neither did any good. What would it be like to have a maid who washed dishes clean? India glanced at Dulcie eating methodically, oblivious of the ants. Well, after all, they weren't poisonous.

Landon, Never Dies the Dream (1949), pp. 31-32

Advertisement for Flit in *The Bangkok Times*, July 1935. Distributor during the 1920s: Katz Bros. Ltd. Head office: Singapore, Bangkok branch: Anuwongse Road.

Outside the section of the palace in which I am living was something that made a sound like a person shouting "chock taw." This is a lizard about a foot and a half long.

Harmsworth, My Journey Round the World (1923), p. 201

Flora and Fauna 219

The *chin chocs* were everywhere, running up and down the walls and across the ceiling, every now and then losing their foothold; but nobody showed the slightest concern or took much note of their activities. At one moment, when a plump French sister turned to her neighbour to offer a dish of rice, a *chin choc* landed with a plop on the table and slithered into her lap. She picked the creature up by its tail, gave a tolerant "Oh là là!" as the tail came off in her hand and the lizard fell to the floor, then continued the conversation while eating her curry.

Lightwood, Teresa of Siam (1960), p. 30

One evening while preparing for dinner guests, I slipped on the living room floor and the next instant felt a score of stings on my ankle. I turned on the lights. My foot was covered with ants and nearly half the floor, the rug and one of the walls were black with the insects. Each of them had a white egg in its mouth. They had come through the front door seeking dry ground. I yelled for Ah Kin who sprayed my leg with kerosene and he, the coolie and I attacked the little creatures. It took us half an hour to spray the swarm and when the boys swept up the dead ants there was a pile over a foot high, literally millions of them. It made my flesh creep to think of the damage they could do. They could cover a sleeping man's body if he happened to be in their track and his slightest move would be a signal for hundreds of thousands to bite. That night I insulated my bed against ants by putting the posts in pans of kerosene.

Several nights later, I was awakened by the terrified squeals of the two dogs. They were leaping about as if they were obsessed. When I coaxed one of them to me, I found he was covered with red ants. After Ah Kin and I had bathed the dogs in the bathtub, I went back to see the cause of the trouble. A column of ants about two inches wide was marching across the porch into the house. Evidently the dogs had stepped on this army. As in the case of the black ants, each insect had an egg in its mouth. It was astonishing how continuous the line was. It seemed unending. Once more we attacked with the spray gun and it was an hour before we had stopped the migration.

Freeman, Brown Women and White (1932), pp. 248-249

Outside the section of the palace in which I am living was something that made a sound like a person shouting "chock taw." This is a lizard about a foot and a half long.
Harmsworth, My Journey Round the World (1923), p. 201

Immediately I bent over an old-fashioned washbasin to clean my teeth, the mosquitoes commenced a meal on my bare back. To slap was useless. There were too many of them and they were too wily. I decided to stick it out. As I bent low to swill out my mouth, there was a clammy thud on the back of my neck, followed by violent splashing in the basin. Water was flying everywhere. Two lizards about a foot long were struggling frantically to escape from the basin. My yells of terror had brought the head boy at the double, to be closely followed by Beaumont. Their sympathetic grins did not amuse me. The boy informed me that it was good luck. I could not agree. Beaumont told me it was most unusual. With that I could agree.
Exell, Siamese Tapestry (1963), pp. 18-19

Just below in the darkness runs our neighbour's klong, a dividing line to the gardens behind the trees. He is a Siamese and an unknown quantity, but he keeps geese, and they are one great disturber of the nightly peace. It is their custom to have attacks of nightmare between the hours of two and three, and they choke and quack until they have awakened the neighbourhood; then they go to sleep, but rise to gurgle over the morning meal at five o'clock. I catch a glint of their white feathers ruffling down below, and I earnestly wish their sleep were eternal.
Landon, 'Mid Pleasures and Palaces (1907), p. 84

In the remotest alley, the most secluded corner, the broadest highway, or the most open of public spaces, roam the most disreputable and degraded members of the canine family – the pariah dogs. Often it would be a kindness to the poor starved and crippled creatures to put them speedily out of pain, but the Buddhist law, "Thou shalt not kill", is all powerful here, and so the pariahs breed and multiply, giving in return for the permission to live, their effective services as vigilant and industrious scavengers.
Young, The Kingdom of the Yellow Robe (1898), p. 21

> A much more satisfactory method is now being employed to rid the town of undesirable dogs. Hitherto they were poisoned on the streets. Now the dogs are caught in baskets and taken to a depot where they are killed and their carcasses incinerated. A humane and hygienic method.
>
> *The Bangkok Times, 2 September 1922, p. 8*[6]

> The Department of Public Health was making war on pariah dogs, but in spite of enormous numbers killed (70 to 100) every week, was unable to keep up with them, partly perhaps because, as at the Mission, when called upon to take action, the response was a notification of the day and hour of their visitation. In consequence, when its minions arrived, there was not a dog to be found in the compound! The Siamese servants had seized the opportunity of making twofold merit – by saving the lives of the dogs on the one hand, and on the other preserving their employers from the crime of having them killed.
>
> *Wheatcroft, Siam and Cambodia (1928), pp, 104-105*

---

[6] Inevitably, the article led to some heated correspondence.

The Snake Farm

The houses had porches and great open windows to catch the slightest breeze or stirring of air. This meant that snakes and scorpions could also enter, so that we tried always to avoid going around the house in the dark. One of my missionary friends had a strange experience with a cobra. As she hastily opened a bureau drawer one evening to pull out a scarf she saw a cobra coiled in the drawer. It had crawled up inside the bureau and found a soft and comfortable nest. She had the presence of mind quickly to slam the drawer shut and run to the kitchen for a kettle of boiling water. Opening the drawer a crack, she poured this in and killed the cobra.

"Cobra (Naja Naja) with head and hood spread ready to strike". Photograph by J. J. McBeth. From *Siam: Nature and Industry* (1930).

Sayre, Glad Adventure (1957), p. 92

Mrs. Blunt and I were having dinner one night, when she suddenly cried out, and jumped up from her chair, saying, "Something has bitten me on the leg!" I went to see the doctor, and he said that it was probably a scorpion and gave me a soothing preparation to put on. This did no good whatever, and the pain kept growing worse, till finally the doctor came, and discovered, to his as well as our surprise, the marks of the fangs of a poisonous snake. How that snake ever got into and out of the dining room has always remained a mystery, as all the doors were screened. The wound kept getting larger and larger, and it was weeks before he was able to get it under control. In the meantime, Mrs. Blunt was confined to bed in continual pain, and the wound had to have the dressing changed every day. Finally, it began to contract and the pain to ease up. As soon as she was able to move, I took her to Singapore, and put her on board a boat for England for further treatment.

Blunt, An American Dentist's Unique Experiences (1968), p. 121

An unusually large specimen of the Banded Krait (*Bungarus fasciatus*) was recently killed in the compound of the Bangkok Nursing Home. It was trodden upon by the house coolie when going out to fetch water after dark, and was promptly dispatched by the remainder of the staff, who came to his assistance. The enlarged tip of the tail was unfortunately missing, but allowing 20 mm. for this, it measured, without stretching. 2,020 mm. (6 ft. 7½ in.) in total length, the tail being 150 mm. Malcolm Smith. September, 1913.[1]

Journal of Natural History Society of Siam, vol. 1, 1914, pp. 58-59

Bangkok, or Krungdeb, as the Siamese call their capital, is a city in the midst of the jungle. The luxuriant growth surrounding it seems like an ever-menacing octopus stretching its tentacles toward the houses. In the darkness it creeps closer to the city, constricting it with leafy coils. Cynics say that the jungle will win back what it has lost and that it already has had some measure of success. Snakes come right down to the business section showing little fear of motor cars and trams. A thirteen-foot python was killed on the veranda of one of the hotels and a cobra was beaten to death by clerks on the second floor of a department store two days before I arrived, Kosol said.

"Are many people bitten by cobras?" I asked.

"Very few," he replied. "The cobra won't attack unless you madden him in some way. And if you are bitten we have a fine Pasteur Institute always supplied with anti-venom serum."

Freeman, Brown Women and White (1932), p. 43

This afternoon I visited the snake farm as guest of a young Siamese doctor I had met one evening at dinner. He is particularly keen on tennis and joked me considerably about America's loss of world domination in that sport.[2]

---

1 Malcolm Arthur Smith (1875-1958) was a physician and herpetologist. His memoir *A Physician at the Court of Siam* was published in 1947.

2 Joked: teased.

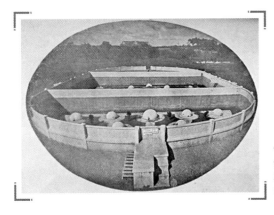

"Saovabha Institute: the Snake Park", from *Siam: General and Medical Features* (1930).

We went out of the main building, two attendants following us, toward the cement ellipse, one hundred and fifty feet long and fifty feet wide, where the snakes are kept. Immediately inside the surrounding cement wall is a three-foot moat enclosing the three compounds where the snakes live. In each compound are little cement domes, looking like beehives or miniature snow houses, that have holes in the sides through which the snakes can crawl in and out.

The doctor and I leaned over the wall and watched the attendants. They wore boots of extra thickness and one of them carried a wooden pole with a forked iron prong on the end; with no other protection they went down into the compound and handled the King Cobra as if he were a toy. They caught the snake and held a saucer before its mouth. The black, forked tongue shot out with the rapidity of an electric spark jumping between two poles. They waited until the snake opened its jaws; then they forced the saucer inside. Instantly the fangs closed upon it and the poison sacs emptied themselves through the upper teeth that are hollow like hypodermic needles. As the snake drew back, a small thimbleful of clear, creamy liquid, with the fluidity of thick gruel, slid down the saucer. Siamese doctors are no longer satisfied to work in Bangkok alone. Every morning they hurry forth with glass tubes filled with fresh antivenin. They hand them to little Siamese men who finger levers and gaze at quivering instruments.

The Snake Farm 225

From A. H. Hale's article in *The Chemist and Druggist*, 15 March 1941, p. 170.

> There is the roar of a plane
> A blast of dust
> A black speck in the heavens,
> It is Siam's answer to the King Cobra!
> Siam, little Siam, is sending life to her people!
>
> *Childers, From Siam to Suez (1932), pp. 42-46*

My children always enjoyed our visits to the "cobra farm," maintained by the Pasteur Institute for treatment against cobra bites; there they used to watch the cobras swimming up and down the small waterways, sometimes with small frogs given them for food actually sitting on their backs, enjoying the ride.

Sayre, Glad Adventure (1957), p. 88

Night Life

After work, many westerners would head for one of Bangkok's social clubs. Like any metropolis, the city also offered a variety of amusements, including concerts, plays (both Siamese and western), films, dances and performances of various kinds, often by travelling "artistes". Here, "W. S. L. B." writes about the city's night life – or lack of it.

A Londoner might say that Bangkok has no night life at all. Sometimes he attends the native cinemas, where a special enclosure is reserved for him at 6s. a seat – but he never goes during the cholera season! Three barn-like cinemas, death-traps in the event of fire, are crammed with excited natives gazing at "Wild West" films, the titles of which they cannot understand. A few travelling "shows" set up their stands in vacant lots. But it is all over by midnight, and the city streets are deserted. Twice a week a small cluster of "foreigners" and Siamese gather at the Phya Thai Palace to dance. Once a month the Sports Club holds a similar affair. Diplomatic entertaining is meagre. Three times a year the King's orchestra gives a symphony concert. During the cholera season nothing happens. There are only about six unattached English women in Bangkok. There are twenty times that number of single men. Dancing then consists of fifty men watching six others dance. The real night life in Bangkok is a life of fantasy. It is a riot of imagination in an atmosphere of romance. To the Englishman in Bangkok, with or without imagination, bored and cholera-scared, dust-choked and hungry for a head lettuce salad – that conquest cannot come too quickly!

British life in Bangkok revolves around the £100,000 British Legation and the Sports Club. The Legation "entertains" and the Sports Club "amuses." Towards evening, as the sun pales and the midday shower of fierce heat from the sky is over, the long, narrow road, hedged with evenly trimmed

Advertisement in *The Bangkok Times*, July 1929.

227

bamboo trees, that leads from town to the Sports Club is thick with dust. Car after car rolls up to the club entrance, and a steady stream of golfers in "shorts" pours on the course. Twice a week it is ladies' day, but there are few Englishwomen in Bangkok. Life for the Englishman is one of monotonous, hot, dusty regularity. A little bridge, more golf, but most of all, work. Bangkok is one of the few hot Eastern cities where business men are at their desks at eight o'clock in the morning, where they don't "lie in" at noon, where they work right up to the "golfing hour."

The London & China Express, 22 March 1928, pp. 203-204

There still remain elements of the night life of Bangkok that are a disgrace to the city. There are several places where the night life proceeds quite openly to 12-30 a.m. In these places one is permitted to dance and to pay very exorbitant prices for very inferior wine. It will be said that if a young man cares for this form of entertainment there is no reason why it should not be within his reach. But this sort of thing lowers the prestige of the European.

The Straits Times, 7 October 1926, p. 10

Despite the depression people in Bangkok seem still to have money to burn, and night life in the dance halls, cabarets and centres where Chinese gather seems to be as active as ever.

Singapore Free Press, 6 April 1933, p. 6

This letter to a friend by "a Siamese resident in Bangkok" is dated: September 1933 …
There are lots of establishments for amusement in Bangkok. Siamese girls are dancing in Cabarets, and throw their legs, sometimes in costumes that hardly show any difference from those in Hollywood. Advertising of these establishments is sometimes very amusing "do not miss your chance!" "The sweetest dancers will entertain you!" "Every night a change of Partners!" Suriwongse road is the street for amusement, jazz and dancing. Those who do not take ladies along, will find them there. In our sporting club we have a wonderfull [sic] swimming pool now. You can imagine you were at the Lido. The large water-basin contains water that is as clear as crystal. A look out of a window of our office shows the most fashionable

and largest Cinema in the far east. Temperatur [sic] inside is so cool that Siamese ladies sometimes wear fur.

The Sphere, 11 November 1933, p. 4

At the Club

Clubs and Societies in 1909 ...

Bangkok United Club, The British Club, The Société Musicale, Bangkok Gymnastic Club, Chiengmai Gymkhana Club, Royal Bangkok Sporting Club, Society of Historical Research, Siam Society, Engineers Society of Siam, The German Club, Bangkok St. Andrews Society, Bangkok Gun Club, Bangkok Cricket Club, Bangkok Golf Club, Bangkok Lawn Tennis Club, Bangkok Philharmonic Society.

Perkins, Travels (1909), p. 261

Bangkok clubs as a general thing are by no means exclusive and an acquaintance with any of their members will usually suffice to procure for the visitor a temporary admission to all their privileges.

Antonio, Guide (1904), p. 24

The United Club, which was established upwards of twenty years ago, may perhaps be considered the most popular resort for foreign residents in Bangkok. It occupies large premises, surrounded by well-laid-out grounds, at the corner of New Road and Siphya Road. The club is purely social in its character. The wives and daughters of members are admitted to certain privileges, including, for instance, the free use of the reading-room and library, and often dances and other social functions take place in the club buildings. The club contains very comfortable dining, reading, card, and billiard rooms, and possesses also a fine bowling-alley and several good tennis-courts, which are constantly in use. The affairs of the club, which in 1908 had a total membership of 225, are conducted by a paid secretary. The British Club was started in 1903 by a number of residents in Bangkok, who combined to form a proprietary club. The ownership of the club is vested in the debenture-holders, who alone are responsible for all club debts and liabilities. The membership consists of ordinary and honorary members. Ordinary members must be British residents in Siam, and are divided into those holding and those not holding debentures; honorary members comprise residents of Siam, other than British, who may be elected to the club. Candidates for admission are balloted for by the debenture-holders, but while ordinary members pay an entrance fee of 100 ticals (about £7 10s.) and a monthly subscription of 15 ticals (about £1 2s. 6d.), honorary members are only called upon to pay the monthly subscription.

Twentieth Century Impressions of Siam (1908), p. 252

In his novel Spears of Deliverance, *Eric Reid lightly disguises Bangkok's clubs before the Great War under different names: the "Racing Club" is the Royal Sports Club, the "Cosmopolitan", the United Club, and the "Britannic", the British Club.*

It is undoubtedly true that the majority of Bangkok's confirmed "club-men" uphold the club as essential to life because the languor of the climate they live amongst induces the vapidity of a mind which cannot be a kingdom to itself. Conversation scarcely reaches a higher level than unilluminating remarks on the banalities of the day; reading, of any kind more abstruse than a colonial-edition detective-yarn, becomes an impossibility; while pictures, music and the other ministering angels of the higher human sensibilities become a yawning bore and are replaced by the sensationalism of the cinema-films at one of the more or less comfortable "picture palaces" in the town.

A visit to each of these characteristic Bangkok institutions had sufficed to render Harkness indifferent to their attractions. When, moreover, he discovered how much membership and hospitality in them would work

out at per mensem, as compared with his total income at that period, he came to the conclusion that he must for a time forego their charms.

Reid, Spears of Deliverance (1920), pp. 38-42

The largest social club was the Sports Club, on the grounds of which was a golf course, several tennis courts, a social hall for bridge and dancing, and a race track. All European nationalities were eligible for membership. The British and German Clubs were more exclusive, being reserved with very few exceptions for their own nationalities.

Blunt, An American Dentist's Unique Experiences (1968), p. 100

One thing remained before I could consider myself safely launched into Bangkok society. I must join the Club. This meant the Royal Bangkok Sports Club. Its facilities were an eye-opener. Rugger, soccer, cricket, tennis, squash, golf, racing, bridge, billiards, dancing. It had everything. And all for an entrance fee of 5 Pounds and a monthly sub of 1 pound. It must have been the cheapest club in the world. Later it was to have the finest swimming pool in the Far East. It suffered from no odious colour bar and many Siamese were valuable and welcome members. It was democratic to a degree and the wonder of visiting Burra Sahibs from India and Burma.

Exell, Siamese Tapestry (1963), pp. 23-24

The colour question scarcely arises. The Club's name is prefixed by the epithet, "Royal", and His Majesty the King of Siam is its chief patron. Naturally it is open both to Europeans and to Siamese, and there is full social intercourse between the two races. Intermarriage is frequent, and carries no hint of stigma with it. In this respect the difference from Malaya is extreme, and illustrates how artificial the whole structure of colour antagonism really is.

Scott, Eastern Journey (1939), p. 88

A New Year's Party at the Sports Club, late 1930s. Collection: Maryanne Stanislaw.

Night Life 231

Leigh Williams recalls the Sports Club before the Great War.[1]

In the evenings there was a fair choice of recreations for the foreign residents of Bangkok, but there was a definite time-limit for games. Office or the heat delayed the start to well after four in the afternoon, and it was dark, practically all the year round, at half-past six. At the Royal Bangkok Sports Club there was a race-course, "rugger" field, tennis and "squash" courts and an eighteen-hole golf-course. The hazards on the latter were the inevitable "*klongs*," so we played with floating balls. Heaven knows how many of these wretched waterways intersected the course! They were generally invisible from the tee.

After a round of golf or a game of tennis, a cooling drink was generally indicated. The crowd that thronged the small tables on the lawn in front of the clubhouse was as cosmopolitan, if not as large, as one would find in Cairo or Shanghai. Nearly every country in Europe was represented, as well as the U.S.A. The foreign community in Bangkok on the whole mixed very well together. There was sometimes a little friction between the younger Danes and Britishers, which would lead to an occasional brawl late at night in some less respectable Russian "hotel." But at the Sports Club the atmosphere was very friendly. Many of the Siamese aristocracy and higher officials were members, and some of these could give the foreigner points at tennis or even at "rugger." At "soccer" the Siamese, in spite of our having an Oxford and a Cambridge "Blue" in the European side, almost invariably beat us.

A more formal resort was the British Club, mostly composed of the consular body, British advisers in the various Ministries, and "burra-sahibs" or heads of business firms. The atmosphere reminded one faintly of that at "The Chummery" in that juniors were expected to hold their tongues in the presence of their betters.

Williams, Green Prison (1941), pp. 25-26

---

1 According to the *Bangkok Directory* for 1914, J. Caulfeild James (the Headmaster of the Mahapritaram Commercial School) was the president for that year, and A. E. Stiven of the Borneo Company Limited the chairman of the committee.

"Saigon versus Bangkok at 'Rugger' on Sports Club Ground, 1923", from *Siam Ancient to Present Times* (1926), p. 248. Bangkok won 17 to 8 on a rain-soaked pitch.

Maurice P. Dunlap describes the Royal Sports Club in the early 1920s.

In an open veranda an orchestra plays for a "tea dance"; upstairs a number of bridge tables are going. A Rugby football game is posted between "Rice and Teak" and "The Rest." In other words, the rice and teak is composed of members of firms interested in these two exports while "The Rest" draws on the rest of the foreign community for its members. It is but an indication of how rice and teak overshadow every other interest in business, just as in football. There is a good race course and much interest is taken during the season in this sport.

American Consular Bulletin, January 1923, p. 45

Another turn, and the car stops in front of the modern Sports Club. Here there is music and dancing; the verandah is full of people; men in white are drinking in the bar, the billiard-rooms are full, the reading-room too are full, and a big athletic ground lies outside open to the seven winds of heaven.

Kornerup, Friendly Siam (1926), p. 242

In George F. Worts' story 'A Message for the Maharaja', Judy van Dorn goes to a dance at the Sports Club.

On her first night in Bangkok she went to a dance at the Sports Club, and her first glimpse of the dancers made her laugh outright. They reminded her of a slow-motion movie. A foxtrot was being played by the Filipino orchestra at subnormal time, and everyone on the floor was dancing half-time. She waited in vain for a really attractive man to appear. And she was even more cautious about flirting. Men took her seriously; they wanted her so desperately. She pitied them and she suffered for them. In none of them did she glimpse that indescribable something that might prove her undoing.

Collier's, The National Weekly, 13 December, 1924, p. 32

The Sports Club was the be-all and the end-all in the social life of the white colony. It was on the outskirts of the city, a long ramshackle structure with a huge bar. After several drinks the case of Mrs. Wright, the principal figure in the current scandal, came up for gossip. It seemed that her husband found her and the dashing new clerk, recently arrived from the main office of Mr. Wright's firm in London, alone in her house together. The youngster had tired of parties with brown girls in the company mess. He was homesick and sought the companionship of Mrs. Wright because she was white. Whether Mrs. Wright was bored with the round of bridge, gossip and the Ladies' Musical Society and found the company of the young man a source of relief, or whether she merely took a motherly interest in him, was not considered. The consensus of opinion was that the young man should be sent home immediately. "Wow, what a bunch of stiff-necked bimbos they are," said Dick when we got home. He poured himself a half tumbler of whisky and downed it with a shudder.

Freeman, Brown Women and White (1932), pp. 90-92

At the Sports Club much gaiety abounds. The late afternoon is filled with dancing in the ball-room and with the drinking of cool things on the lawn. The sun has gone, the eyes can be opened full without pain, and the heat is abated. But this is the hunting hour of the mosquito. The provident have brought sarongs, and those who sit at the tables on the lawn use them. A diplomat representing a Great Power sit flirting with a smartly dressed lady from London with his important feet and knees thrust in this calico bag, nor considers the refuge ridiculous. As for the pink legs which women wear at the moment, they slip gratefully within the shelter. A woman who invites a table-full of guests greets each with the right hand while extending a sarong with the left. Those who dance kick themselves free, then return to swaddle their ankles again.

Candee, New Journeys in Old Asia (1927), p. 156

In Eric Reid's story, Mac, "who was really a Lowlander", had never heard of Scotland's patron saint before coming to the East. Once there, he nevertheless becomes an enthusiastic member of the "Bangkok St. Andrew's Society".[2]

On the thirtieth day of November then Mac and his compatriots were wont to pour a libation or two to St. Andrew. They had got the idea somehow into their heads that they were rather good at libations, and they used to invite the whole of Bangkok to watch them do it. Bangkok, nothing loth, went to admire and came away to praise.

All Bangkok entered into the festivities with entire zest, contributing each to the success of the evening, as fancy prompted, or assisting in the preparations, as Mac directed. Male Bangkok shot hordes of snipe for pies, or risked their necks in hanging tartan festoons on the club walls. Female Bangkok cooked the pies or disposed Chinese lanterns gracefully about the grounds. Some superintended the proper waxing of the dancing floor, while others wrangled as to the exact position of the supper tent. Some gave their days and nights to thought on the subject of the champagne cup, some excelled in the cunning arrangement of nooks for sitting out. All bubbled with suppressed excitement for hours before, and all turned out on the night itself wearing their best clothes and their most cheerful smile. Sassenach and Gael joined hands and danced to the tabor's sound. Mirth held both hands out to all.

Rehearsals of the national Scottish dances were held for some weeks in advance by those who aspired to trip the light fantastic as it is tripped

---

2 According to the Bangkok Directory for 1914, the "Chieftain" of the club in that year was Leslie S. Smart with W. A. Graham as "Vice-Chieftain".

among the heather. Mac himself, who had nothing to learn of the intricacies of Strathspey or Eightsome, held a rehearsal of his own by inviting the Committee in a body to dinner at the Minor Mess on the Friday immediately preceding the Ball. The Minor members were excused as not knowing any better, but the Committee to a man turned up in kilts and sporrans, dirks and plaids, as imagination and vanity dictated or their wardrobe allowed.

Reid, Chequered Leaves (1913), pp. 173-177

I like the English in Siam, or rather the British, for most of them are Scotch. I must confess that it is the best that goes abroad. All carry responsibilities, all have to decide for themselves. As one of them said to me, "We are all the time on our best behaviour to show the world what we can do."

Harmsworth, Voyage Round the World (1923), p. 210

Miss Loulou Dailly and the Five-Pound Note

In June 1925, Miss Loulou Dailly, "the well-known dancer", appeared in a one-woman show at the Victoria Theatre in Singapore, having previously appeared in Manila. The Straits Times found that she "worked hard and wore very pretty dresses, but her dancing was nothing out of the ordinary".[3] A second performance was cancelled "owing to alteration in steamer dates". Miss Dailly was heading for Bangkok...

A charge has been lodged with police by the Siam Observer against Loulou Dailly, dancer, in connection with the loss of a five-pound note. The

Advertisement in *The Bangkok Times*, 4 July 1925, p. 7.

---

3 *The Straits Times*, 24 June 1925, p. 10. There appear to be a few references to a dancer called Loulou Dailly in the Paris press, but none in Britain or the United States.

charge alleges that Miss Dailly snatched the note out of the manager's hand in the Observer office and left. No warrant has been issued, but the matter is in the hands of the police.

The Straits Times, 9 July 1925, p. 9

Miss Loulou Dailly, against whom a criminal charge has been lodged in connection with the loss of a £5 note, left by the mail train for Penang this morning.

The Bangkok Times, 8 July 1925, p. 4

The following appears in the Siam Observer of July 9: – Miss Loulou Dailly should arrive safely in Penang this evening, there to cast her elusive spell for a time and to pass on to other worlds. Loulou will remain with us as an entertaining memory, and we suppose so far as she is concerned, we must be content to leave it at that. But we are not so gently disposed with the Police Authorities. We were asked to call at the Bangkok Police Station at 7 o'clock, along with a witness who had seen the snatching, in order that his statement might be taken. The manager called at the time specified, along with the witness, but when he got there he was informed that the police had obtained payment for our bill for advertising. The Manager was asked to take this money, but rightly refused to do so, on the ground that a criminal charge had been lodged. That course evidently was unexpected, and eventually he was informed that if we refused to accept the money no criminal charge could be entertained at that station.

The Pinang Gazette, 14 July 1925, p. 4

The community were informed that Loulou would perform at the Sports Club, and that she would be assisted by the world-renowned composer and violinist, Mr. Iljinsky.[4] It is said that in Bangkok we live off the beaten track. That perhaps might explain why no one had heard of Mr. Iljinsky. The unfortunate thing is that we have not been able to make his acquaintance. Mr. Iljinsky did not eventuate. It was noticeable that Miss

---

4 Advertisements in Singapore and Bangkok named him "Ilinzisky".

Night Life   237

Loulou arrived without him and departed without him. There are strange stories current of an encounter she had when engaging a regimental band here, how, like all great artistes, she gave way to a fit of temperament, and slapped the face of a conductor during rehearsal, and, if the stories be true, also that of the officer of the guard. But her best bit of work was on the day before her departure for Penang when she snatched a £5 note from the manager of the Siam Observer, and cleared. The police here did not want to have her on their hands, so they allowed her to go.[5]

The Straits Times, 17 July 1925, p. 10

Music

A Grammophone[6] That Does Not Worry "Parthenope"
The Best and Most Selected Theatre at Home
French, Italian, English, German and Siamese records in stock.
Undeniable Superiority.
TO HEAR IT IS TO ADOPT IT.
Obtainable from Messrs. G. Bovo & Co.,
New Road & Custom House Lane.

Advertisement in The Bangkok Times, August 1910

In the International Court to-day before Phya Phichet, Luang Poripoa and Mr. C. L. Watson, Victor Maclean was charged with stealing a gramophone the property of Mr. Gaudart, valued at Tcs. 95, and a number of records valued at Tcs. 35. It was stated on behalf of the Krom Ayakarn that accused took the gramophone and records from the complainant's house and subsequently pawned them. The accused denied the charge, contending he had only borrowed the machine and records.[7]

The Bangkok Times, 21 February 1911, p. 5

---

5 Dailly herself continued to tour the Far East and seems later to have assumed the name "Louisa Valdes".

6 Spelt thus.

7 B. B. Gaudart & Co.: a firm of "general outfitters" in New Road. Krom Ayakarn: the Public Prosecution Service.

> "Maxim"
> Everybody's doing it, doing it – Doing what?
> Going to Maxim to hear the Great Phillipino Band
> Direct from Manila
> Latest song success by Dixy and Yambo[8] AND
> Nightly rag-time all the time From 8 to 12
>
> *
>
> Music to Hire For all special occasions ALSO
> Lessons given for Piano, Violin, Flute, &c. &c.
> For terms apply to: DIXY AND YAMBO.
>
> *Advertisements in The Siam Observer, January 1916*

The Siamese are an exceedingly musical people, and in spite of the fact that their own scale has about seven tones to our octave and that in their own music only melody and counterpoint are considered, they enter exceedingly well into that of the west, as is proved the excellence of the King's orchestra, though the conductor is a Siam-born Austrian who has never been to Europe and all the instrumentalists are Siamese.[9]

Wheatcroft, Siam and Cambodia (1926), p. 126

Until our coming here I looked upon Siam as a wild country, filled with savages and wild animals, subdued by soldiers and whipped into submission by force. We have just returned from hearing the fifty-piece Royal Siamese Band playing the modern music of the world. The leader is Mr. Feit, an American. The orchestration and rendition was better than many bands in America. The King of Siam subsidizes his music and they practice daily from 10 to 4 p.m.

Palmer, Round the World (1926), p. 273

---

8 Dixy (or Dixie) Davis and Yambo were "two American rag-time dancers, who get through some vigorous work seldom seen out here" (*Penang Gazette*, 30 April 1914, p. 7). They had appeared in Penang with Borowsky's Circus. Yambo must have been one of the first performers of African descent to appear in Bangkok.

9 The "Siam-born Austrian" mentioned by Wheatcroft was Peter Feit, better known as Phra Chen Duriyang (1883-1967) who was a composer, writer, and conductor of the Royal Orchestra. His father Jacob Feit (1844-1909) had been born in Germany rather than Austria but had evidently migrated first to the United States and then to Siam.

In spite of the fact that many people had left Bangkok for a holiday during the Chinese New Year, many musical enthusiasts met at the Royal Theatre to enjoy the concert given on Thursday evening last by the Royal Orchestra. Phra Chen Duriyanga again showed his ability as a musical director, and conducted the orchestra admirably. Naturally, the only work on the programme based on a Siamese air, and in the Siamese mode, namely Grassi's Melodie Siamoise No. 1, was tastefully reproduced.

The Bangkok Times, 5 February 1927, p. 9

One is glad to note that Bangkok again possesses a Musical Society – this time called the Ladies' Musical Society. The name doesn't matter but lovers of music will be glad that an organisation has been formed, which if it is conducted like its predecessor, will provide its members with a good deal of pleasure in meeting together in rehearsals and practices and will from time to time invite its friends to listen to the results of such training.

The Bangkok Times, 2 November 1923, p. 4

For eleven years Bangkok boasted a Ladies' Musical Society that provided many splendid formal musical programs, the proceeds of which benefited local charities. In addition, monthly informal musical programs were provided for the members. Eventually, because of constantly changing personnel, Bangkok seemed almost devoid of musical talent; the same few women were having to bear the whole burden of the informal musical programs.

McFarland, Our Garden Was So Fair (1943), p. 116

Bangkok, Sunday 26th November, 1911
Yesterday evening at the hotel a concert was given by two tenth-rate Italian artists. They were generously applauded by the Italians who were there *en masse*, as well as by the few foreigners and the "wild tiger," invited by me. After the concert, De la Penne offered champagne to the "diva"!!! and to all the Italians assembled and to my "wild tiger".

Besso, Siam and China (1914), p. 53

Bangkok had been worked up to a fine frenzy, and tickets for the Terrasco recital had been all sold out long before the artiste's arrival.[10] The concert was a huge success. From the point of view of oddness, it exceeded anything Bangkok had ever seen, or ever hoped to see again. Terrasco appeared wearing a garland of frangipanni round his neck. The rest of his body was contained in immaculate evening dress. The great artiste, a ferocious looking fellow with Mephistophelian eyebrows, a mane of red hair and a full beard and whiskers, came forward amid vociferous applause, and announced in a broken accent that, as he was suffering from lumbago, he would confine himself that evening to one instrument and would give a piano recital only. The Great Egoist then sat down to the piano and for three-quarters of hour discoursed really divinely. There was no doubt about his genius, and prolonged applause requited him.

Reid, Chequered Leaves (1913), pp. 167-170

BUTSAPANATA SALA
The New Theatre Hall Charoen Krung Road.
Tonight! At 9.15
SYKORA Cello Virtuoso
And Miss Katherine Campbell, Pianiste
Admission price Tcs. 5, 3 & 2.

Advertisement in The Bangkok Times, 2 March 1918, p. 4

The audience went with high expectations, for both musicians were reputed to be highly talented, and those expectations were realised to the full. Mr. Sykora's technique was perfect and no one would have failed to be moved by this pure passion for music. The programme was well chosen. There was a very fair-sized audience to represent Bangkok.

The Bangkok Times, 4 March 1918, p. 4

---

10 Although "Terrasco" is presumably fictitious, "great artistes" of a similar kind came quite frequently to Bangkok, usually arriving via Singapore or maybe Penang.

At the Theatre

The Siamese love song and music, and the drama is one of the most ancient and cherished institutions of the nation. Though there are several Siamese theatres as in the capital the ancient forms of play Khun (masked pantomime), Rabam (dance in character) and Lakhon (opera ballet) are now seldom seen. The present-day taste, at least of the inhabitants of the capital, tends more towards modern play acting; the pieces played are partly translations from European dramas and partly plays written by Siamese authors, the "mise en scène" being quite European. Notwithstanding the difficulties of the language, tourists are recommended to visit the Siamese theatre which possesses several charming and clever actresses well worth seeing. The old drama is, however, the more interesting, and may be seen during the cold weather when a troupe of the Royal Theatre appears before the public.

Seidenfaden, Guide (1932), pp. 55-56

From Seidenfaden, *Guide* (1932).

Soon we stand before an establishment occupying five or six times the space required for other business, a temple where, through Thespian sources, men are trying to obtain all the enjoyment possible in life. This is a Siamese theatre. It is scarcely necessary for a visitor to go inside, for the actors are all "touters." During fifteen minutes at a time the decorated curtains are drawn up, revealing a bewildering scene of color, gilding, mirrors, and gaudy costumes; not a natural face is there. A rampant variety show is thus given gratis, with a view of bringing in a paying audience from the crowd assisting at the free entertainment.

Sommerville, Siam on the Meinam (1897), pp. 86-87

To an ordinary Siamese it is the height of happiness to sit jammed in a dense crowd on the floor, from seven p.m. to two a.m., watching the same play – or rather portion of a play, for it is a matter of several such nights in succession before the drama is completed. The plays are usually adaptations from old Hindu mythology; the plot and every incident of it are familiar to all in the audience – the more so, the better. The attraction consists in the manner of its presentment, the long-drawn tension of the "love" episodes, the realism of the *dénouements*, the gorgeousness of the dresses, and the minute skill of the numerous dances. The actors, with the exception of a few clowns, are all young girls. They are subjected to stringent training from the age of four years, and in their prime at seventeen and eighteen years of age are a possession of immense money value to their "owners," in spite of the much-vaunted but unenforced slavery reforms of the present reign. The dances are entirely posture-dances, great pleasure being taken in the abnormal bending-back of elbows, wrists, ankles, and finger-joints, which is carried to an extent that would be impossible to even a "double-jointed" European. The dances are accompanied by loud music from the orchestra, assisted sometimes by the hard voices of a chorus of some twenty old women, and heightened in the impassioned moments by the voices of the danseuses themselves.

Norman, The Peoples and Politics of the Far East (1895), pp. 421-422

In the *Lakon Luang* – the Royal Lakon – the repertory is Brahman mythology or legendary history, and the heroes all gods and princes, so it follows naturally that they act in a traditional manner, and conventional gestures be used to express the emotions. The convention in singing is peculiarly unpleasant to us, being loud and nasal, but although the spectator who has not the advantage of understanding what he hears may easily wish himself deaf, to the eye all is enchanting.

Wheatcroft, Siam and Cambodia (1928), p. 163

Salvatore Besso (1884-1912) was an Italian jurist who travelled to Bangkok, where he was present during the coronation ceremonies for King Vajarivudh, and afterwards to Beijing where he died. His letters and articles were printed as Siam e Cina *(1913) and translated into English in the following year.*

Bangkok, 6th December, 1911

At 10 o'clock last night we went to the gala performance at the Royal Theatre at Dusit Park. It looks like a bon-bon box in Rococo style and has the ceiling painted to represent the sky flecked with tiny fleecy clouds. The audience was very stylish and many well-known Siamese ladies were there wearing their national baggy trousers as worn by the men, and bodices encrusted with gems. And the performance? you will ask me. Beautiful for a while, very beautiful, but finally most monotonous.

Besso, Siam and China (1914), pp. 72-73

I went one day to spend a morning at the Royal Ministry of Entertainments. Great halls filled with properties opened their treasures. All these masks, chariots, strange trappings seen hitherto at a distance in the magic of processions or performances, became mine in the flat light of a rainy morning. Ranged in perfect order in a series of glass cases I saw masks of deities, and of animals, grotesque, pierced with blind eyes, the masks which the dancing girls hold by a string caught between their teeth. Here was the livid face of Hanuman, the brave, astute, very generous general of the monkeys, the green face of Rama, the black head of Ngo, the ugly man. There were dancing costumes in gold and silver cloth, admirable red scarves that float crosswise over the shoulders and brighten the gold; stoles, *cache-sexe*, thigh pieces, false finger-nails, leggings, all the sections of those gold carapaces which leave bare only the face and feet of the actor, effecting thus a marvelous contrast. Europeans are too prone to believe that these Asiatic dances are lascivious. As a matter of fact, Asia is chaste; it dissembles the wealth of its body as it does its other wealth.

Morand, Nothing But the Earth (1927), pp. 150-151

The Siamese are extremely fond of the theatre. Of late years all kinds of Western innovations have been introduced onto the Siamese stage, and it is fashionable to regret this; but I, for one, think it a very good thing, for I will admit that I found the old style of Siamese classical drama almost insufferably boring.

Wood, Land of Smiles (1935), pp. 89-30

Once, by lucky mischance, we were present on such an occasion, we being the only Europeans at a Siamese rendering of Moliere's play 'Les Amants Magnifiques.' A mistake had brought us there that evening instead of the next with our fellow Europeans, but we were warmly welcomed, and I greatly prized the opportunity of seeing Siam at home. The King arrived two hours late, so, as we could not leave unperceived, we were there from 8 p.m. till 5 a.m., and to keep open eyes as the hours grew from late to early against a lullaby of never-ending Siamese tunes, heard without understanding, took heroic effort! Yet the scene was not one to be missed. Western touches transposed, and, in so different a setting, were almost as new and delightful as pure Oriental. Ungratefully, of the whole interesting evening the clearest picture in my mind is that of the King's departure, when he motioned the lady who had accompanied him to pass in front of him into the motor car, while she, not to be outdone in Western fashions, first dropped him a little curtsey.

Wheatcroft, Siam and Cambodia (1928), pp. 122-123

One Performance only. For the benefit of the Cruiser Fund.
THEATRE ROYAL.
Dusit Park. On Saturday, the 8th July, a play will be staged in English.
Under the Patronage and Direction of His Majesty the King.
"Freezing a Mother-in-Law."
(A FARCE IN ONE ACT.) By T. E. Pemberton.
"The Earl of Claverhouse"
(A FARCICAL COMEDY IN 3 ACTS.) BY SRI AYUDHYA.
Performed by Officials in His Majesty's Service.
Booking at the office of the Siam Import Co. Ltd.
every day between 9 a.m. and 5 p.m. except on Sundays.
BOOK EARLY TO AVOID DISAPPOINTMENT.

Advertisement in The Bangkok Times, 28 June 1916, p. 3

Officials in His Majesty's Service presented a couple of plays on Saturday evening for the benefit of the Cruiser Fund, and they had the satisfaction of feeling their efforts met with the warm appreciation of a large audience. "The Earl of Claverhouse" is a farcical comedy by Sri Ayudhya which was originally written in Siamese, and has been produced on several occasions under the title "Noi Indasen".[11] The present English version has been prepared by the author himself. The story is slight enough. It is a play of character and as such received a highly intelligent presentation. Prince Siddhibara's rendering of the part of the foolish and foppish youth Archie was probably most enjoyed, and it was admirably played. But he was not by any means alone.

The Bangkok Times, 10 July 1916, p. 5

UNDER THE PATRONAGE of HIS MAJESTY THE KING
A Special Performance of The Slaves of Liberty,
a Comic Opera in two acts
Words by Wilfred Thornely. Music by A. G. Beaumont.
Will be given at THE ROYAL THEATRE, DUSIT PARK
on SATURDAY JUNE 30TH overture 9.25 p.m., curtain rises 9.30 p.m.
The proceeds will be devoted to the Cruiser Fund.
Seats may be booked at Messrs. the Siam Import Co. Ltd.[12]

The Bangkok Times, 2 June 1917, p. 3

---

11 "Sri Ayudhya" was one of the noms-de-plume used by King Vajiravudh. He had himself appeared in at least one production of a play by Pemberton in England. Apart from acting, Prince Siddhibara was also active in the scouting movement and was Vice-President of the Football Association of Siam.

12 The first performance was on 16 June; the King had sent a thousand ticals "towards the proceeds". Percival Wilfred Thornely (1880-1926) was an Appeal Court judge. He died of sunstroke in the Nursing Home in March 1926 (despite having recently returned from holiday "very fit") and was buried in the Protestant Cemetery. According to an obituary, he had "done more for the cause of the stage in foreign circles in Bangkok than any one else" (*The Bangkok Times*, 9 March 1926, p. 5).

We have received a copy of the book of *The Slaves of Liberty*. Mr. Justice Thornely has a happy facility of producing light verse of a decidedly Gilbertian flavour, and it is probable that the opera could be presented to a larger public than that of Bangkok with equally good results.[13]

The Straits Times, 30 July 1917, p. 13

I was present at an excellent performance of *A Pair of Spectacles* by the English Dramatic Society, to which His Majesty had leased the theatre.[14] The King was present. The Royal box was above the parterre immediately opposite the stage, so that, as the Siamese National Anthem struck up, the audience rose as one man and pivoted on its axis. Commonsense, but comical.

Wheatcroft, Siam and Cambodia (1928), p. 162

When we took our seats we found ourselves witnessing a performance of "The Lilies of the Field" by a company of English amateurs before an English audience such as one would expect to find in an English provincial city.

Cravath, Notes on the Cruise of the Warrior (1928), pp. 119-120

Bangkok amateurs last Saturday staged "The Lilies of the Field" at the Theatre Royal, and scored a great success. Their Majesties were present, and the King who saw the play when it was originally produced in London enjoyed the production in Bangkok.[15] The royal benefaction of one thousand ticals to the funds in aid of which the play was staged was very welcome, for despite a crowded house, the expenses of producing a play and mounting and dressing it for one night are bound to be on the heavy side.

Singapore Free Press, 4 March 1927, p. 9

---

13 In May 1918, the St George's Minstrels performed Thornely and Beaumont's musical comedy "When Music Charms". It was followed with a "screaming farce" entitled T"he Bangrak Dramatic Agency".

14 The popular play by Simon Grundy had been performed at Windsor Castle in 1907. A silent film version was released in 1916.

15 John Hastings Turner's comedy was first staged at the Ambassadors Theatre in 1922-1923.

The Sanuks will give a performance in aid of the British Red Cross on Saturday, 3rd November 1917, at The Royal Bangkok Sports Club. The Sanuks (through no fault of their own) have not been heard in five continents nor on the beach at Brighton. The performance will start at nine fifteen p.m. precisely with a short play "Lights Out". The audience, if any, is requested to be in his seat punctually if not before, as parts of the play are very subtle. Seats may be booked at Messrs. the Siam Import Company's office at the Sports Club. No Lotteries. No Auctions. No Extras. Programmes almost free! If the audience does not like the show he has full permission to ask for his money back.[16]

The Siam Observer, 25 October 1917, p. 4

At the Movies

The Japanese Cinematograph at Wat Tuk.
Every Monday and Thursday we change full programme;
partial change every night.
First and Largest Show in Siam.

*

Krung Thep Cinematograph Co.
FULL HOUSES EVERY NIGHT.
Don't miss our present Grand Programme.
COME EARLY IF YOU WANT A PLACE.

Advertisements in The Bangkok Times, February 1909

The Royal Japanese Cinematograph has an excellent week-end programme including a number of novelties. Special attention was directed to a lengthy film of an episode in the life of Cardinal Richelieu which has been especially staged and acted by eminent French artistes for reproduction on the cinematograph. There were also a selection of comical pictures. The Phathanakorn Cinematograph has a very interesting series of films including some notable incidents in the life of the late King Edward

---

16 The performance was postponed "owing to high tides".

and the manoeuvres of the German Fleet, and the sugar cane industry, and others.[17]

The Bangkok Times, 8 August 1910, p. 5

In Eric Reid's novel, Bennett has a suggestion.

"There's a damn funny fake-film of a Jack Johnson fight at the Cinematograph," he mentioned. And when Watts added the items, "Twenty thousand feet long too, in five acts and a kidney punch," the proposition was taken up with acclamation.[18] Followed a scramble for vehicles, *en route* to the "pictures," and a sorting out of the company in two's and three's.

Reid, *Spears of Deliverance* (1920), p. 22

We drove back into the town through the brightly lighted streets of Bangkok and finished up at a cinema. It was great fun to sit in the picture palace with them and listen to their comments, now on one subject, now on another. It was incredible, the things they noticed; amazing how they thought about everything they saw. When a girl was kissed on the screen they hugged themselves, looked askance at each other with the hint of a smile, or gave vent to a quiet "h'm," and wiped themselves under the nose and round the lips with the back of a rough hand.

Kornerup, *Friendly Siam* (1926), pp. 255-256

There are all kinds of entertainment in the town, the most popular being the picture palaces where women and girls throng, and emerging from them quite on their own, jostle you on the street. Women have long ago emerged from the seclusion and thraldom of man, and the Feminist movement is strong in Siam.

Pasqual, *A Trip: Through Siam* (1925), p. 57

---

17 The Phathanakorn Film Company was founded in 1910 and soon became the leading distributor of films in Siam. Its Cinematograph was in New Road "near Cantonese Temple, above Samyek Police Station". Manager: Siow Siong Wan (formerly of the Siam Electricity Company).

18 Jack Johnson was an African-American prize-fighter whose bout with James J. Jeffries on 4 July 1910 was billed as "the fight of the century". A film of the fight was banned in several US states.

In her article 'The Heavenly-Royal City of Siam', Florence Burgess Meehan describes Bangkok's movie theatres. She was in Siam "getting material for moving picture scenarios and working on Bray-Powell travelogue pictures" (The Music Trades, 21 May 1921, p. 28).

The Siamese drift laughing through life. They are called the French of the Orient, because of their gaiety. They love music and the drama and the "movies". They flock to Bangkok's motion-picture theaters. The King often comes for the première of a new picture. Usually the film is a well-worn French or American product, which has been broken so often and pieced together so quaintly that following the story becomes an acrobatic feat. The Siamese follow it eagerly, unmindful of strange gaps in the plot. But Charlie Chaplin may gambol in vain if the King is in the theater, for the audience turn their backs on the screen to look at royalty.

Asia, January 1921, pp. 208-209

The picture houses change their programmes three times a week. In view of the considerable number of venues, film fans can therefore go to pictures every night of the week. This is something I've often observed myself, not only among young unmarried men (who may have no alternative forms of entertainment), but also among women and whole families. In fact, it's not proved possible to move away from the thrice-weekly change of programme and any attempt to do so has so far failed. A cinema that adopts this system can reckon with sold-out houses every night. You won't be disturbed by the kind of crude calling out during love scenes in a Siamese cinema you have to endure in India. The security staff would quickly throw perpetrators out onto the street.

Der Kinematograph (Berlin), July 1928, p. 13

De Forrest talking, singing and musical films were shown for the first time in Bangkok last evening to a crowded and appreciative house at the Pathanakorn Cinema. Although possibly a large percentage of the audience was not able to follow the film in its entirety, as all the turns were given in English the producers had varied their programme with a nice discretion, and the full features of this epoch-making invention were conveyed by means of episodes which need no actual language for their

assimilation. The first effect of a sound-film is an indescribably weird sensation.
The Bangkok Times, 26 August 1928, p. 36

Paramount "Stereoscopiks," the newest sensation in motion pictures, will be shown at the Phatanakorn Theatre, in Bangkok, to-night and to-morrow. They are a marvellous development in the art of the moving picture.
The Bangkok Times, 30 August 1929, p. 46

Their Majesties the King and Queen were unexpected guests at the Phathanakorn last night, coming to see Bebe Daniels in "Love Comes Along". The singing they liked very much. The singing of Miss Daniels itself was worthwhile. Another visit is expected of Their Majesties on Sunday night to see the new picture.
The Bangkok Times, 18 October 1930

The Presbyterian missionary Josephine Albert Tate writes about 'Movies and the Youth of Siam'…

"Have you ever been to Hollywood?" and "Have you ever seen a movie star?" were the first questions asked me by Siamese youth upon my arrival in Bangkok. It is evident that the strongest impression of America upon these youth is that of her wealth and luxury. Money is the thing and any means is justifiable to obtain it. That this condition is only too prevalent in America no one can deny, but is that the philosophy which we wish to pass on to other peoples?
The Siam Outlook, April 1933, pp. 141, 143

Afterwards we went to the cinema which is the most modern building in Bangkok and boasts an up-to-date system of air-cooling. The latest American films were fascinating to watch, regarded anthropologically as an illustration of "how the other half lives". They portrayed a mode of life which from this distance seemed as fantastic and unreal as a fairy story, as indeed a film of Oriental life would seem in a London cinema.
Balfour, Grand Tour (1935), p. 264

The recent outrages have given rise to a very substantial movement in favour of establishing some form of censorship. In two of the cases the work was carried out on real Wild West lines, and while it might not be correct to attribute the crimes to the influence of the cinema, there can be little doubt that suggestions as to the details were obtained from the screen. All things considered, there is need of a censorship.

The Straits Times, 17 October 1923, p. 10

There are now many halls in Bangkok, where nightly are shown diverting exploits on the part of "farang" which may well inspire impressionable Siamese youths with a desire to imitate them. There is something wrong with the control of cinematograph enterprises, which permits these ridiculous and melodramatic films to find their way to the East, where they are viewed by thousands of uneducated Eastern folk.

Le May, An Asian Arcady (1926), p. 159

Midnight finds Bangkok at its most wide awake. Movie houses and theatres have emptied their crowds into the streets. Ice cream and soda shops are filled. Food, cooked and uncooked, is snatched from street stands. There is much tooting of auto horns; much scurrying of rickshaws and gharries to save themselves. The Rajah Wongse Road is as busy after the show as any theatre street in the Western world.

Norden, From Golden Gate to Golden Sun (1923), p. 128

Advertisement in *The Bangkok Times*, August 1928.

Vice

I shifted my quarters to the city proper within twenty-four hours of my arrival, and for nearly three months I lived in the very centre of it, within a stone's throw of the Palace wall. To the opportunity of doing this I owe whatever intimate knowledge of Siam I possess. As you drive through the one main street to the city wall you see many of the worst aspects of Siamese town life – the pawnshops and brothels, the spirit-dens and gambling-houses, the reeking alleys and the heaps of refuse, the leprous beggars and the lounging peons.
Norman, The Peoples and Politics of the Far East (1895), pp. 411-412

His voice was drowned as the sampan shot into the noise and confusion of the area occupied by Bangkok's floating population. Colored lanterns hung from gently rocking eaves like tremulous moons of some weird solar system, multiplying their number on the black water. In the mingled glare and gloom were shops, fruit and toddy boats, restaurants, gambling-houses and floating theaters. On platforms in front of the theaters were musicians and men who waved torches; within, seen in smoky light, were dancers, rice-powdered and red-mouthed. These quaint little creatures, dressed in gold-cloth and gaudy silks and wearing tapering gilded head-dresses, looked like figures transposed from old Cambodian prints. "This is the real Siam," remarked Barthelemy, his voice raised above the clamor, "not the Siam of guidebooks".
Hervey, The Black Parrot (1923), p. 56

George F. Worts' 'The Panther of One Claw' is "a highly colored story of dramatic events in a tropic seaport", namely Bangkok. It begins with a description of the Blue Grin, an establishment on the banks of a klong.

Lucrative and foul and sinful was the Sign of the Blue Grin. Peopled with yellow phantoms and white fools, it was perched like a bird of prey, an evil, sprawling bird, on the bank of a blackish, gurgling klong which floated garbage and sewage from the City of Brilliant Diamonds into the coffee-colored Menam Chow Phya when the tide ran out – and which,

253

when the tide ran in, drank back the garbage and sewage again. There was no form of recognized vice that you could not indulge in at the Blue Grin as long as your money lasted, whether your tastes inclined toward strong drink, the black smoke, fan-tan, or merely painted ladies – or all four![1] In the old days a sailor from a ship in port overnight could spend a month's pay handily – and get his money's worth in the Blue Grin.

The Blue Book Magazine, June 1923, p. 105

Our next port of call was a Siamese brothel. A substantially built native house was reached through a door in a high bamboo fence. We climbed up a steep wooden staircase on to a broad verandah lighted by a single kerosene lamp. The sole occupants were a toothless old woman who puffed at a green cheroot and took an occasional pull at a bottle of "Beehive" brandy, and a small boy. The small boy dashed out as we arrived, and the old dame invited us to squat on some grass mats on the floor. In about ten minutes the youngster returned with three Siamese girls. They had regular features and almond eyes, and their faces were slightly powdered to please the "*farang*" (European). They were obviously young, and none of them was over five feet in height. Their figures were well developed, and they were dressed in cotton bodices and silk "panungs" of the gayest colours. One of them had thick silver anklets, and they were all heavily perfumed with bazaar French scent. They stood on the verandah pretending to be coy, then started to laugh and chatter. Jones and I, of course, could not understand a word, but the other man gave them each a silver coin, and they started to dance.

Williams, Green Prison (1941), pp. 30-31

He and Gerald drove to Bangkok, a city of green-roofed temples, klongs (canals) and street touts, one of whom handed them a card that said: "Oh, gentleman, sir, Miss Pretty Girl welcome you Sultan Turkish bath, gentle, polite massage, put you in dreamland with perfume soap. Latest gramophone music. Oh, such service. You come now! Miss Pretty

---

1 "Black smoke" betokens smoked opium; "fan-tan" is a Chinese gambling game.

Girl want you, massage you from tippy-toe to head-top, nice, clean, to enter Gates of Heaven."[2]

Morgan, Maugham (1980), pp. 266-267

Anybody who desires to inform himself upon the normal condition of Eastern prostitutes should pursue inquiries into the lot of the young women who are sold into slavery and who pass a great part of their lives in the district of Bangkok known as Sampeng, behind barred windows and padlocked doors, from which they never emerge until, dead or alive, they leave the place for good.

Norman, The Peoples and Politics of the Far East (1895), p. 43

In 1930, there were 151 licensed brothels in Bangkok, of which 126 were Chinese, 22 Siamese and 3 were Annamite, as compared with 203 brothels in 1928, of which 167 were Chinese, 30 were Siamese and 5 Annamite. The Chinese brothels thus constituted approximately 80 per cent of the total, the Siamese 18 per cent and the Annamite 2 per cent during this period. In 1930, there were 649 licensed prostitutes in Bangkok, as compared with 978 in 1928 in the same proportion, as to races, as existed in the case of the brothels. The customers of the Chinese prostitutes are exclusively Chinese, whereas the Siamese and Annamite women receive men of any race. In addition to the licensed prostitutes, the police estimated that there were in November 1930 about 200 Chinese sly prostitutes and 100 Siamese sly prostitutes. One official witness estimated that there were many times this number in Bangkok, perhaps as many as 2,000. There were, in 1930, eight or more Russian so-called dancers and barmaids who were regarded by the police as prostitutes and carried

---

2 He and Gerald: Somerset Maugham and Gerald Haxton. This oft-repeated anecdote is not derived from Maugham's own *Gentleman in the Parlour*, as some have claimed, and the story may be apocryphal. The earliest reference I can find is in Ted Morgan's 1980 biography of Maugham where Morgan supplies his source as "Wilmon Menard to author". Menard had known Maugham and was the author of the first Maugham biography (*The Two Worlds of Somerset Maugham*, 1965), although he seems not to have published the quotation himself. Maugham and Haxton did not of course "drive" from the north to Bangkok (there being no roads) but came down on the Northern Express.

on this business secretly with their clients in bedrooms in hotels where they worked or elsewhere. There were some Siamese café girls, but none of any other race were discovered. Little was known about the method of recruitment of clandestine prostitutes either for secret brothels or for the cafés and bars above referred to except in the case of the Russians who were known to have been brought from Shanghai. Solicitation in streets was said to be extremely rare, and this accords with the observation of the Commissioners. There are no private organisations or institutions in Siam doing protective or preventive work for girls and women. As regards health education measures, a good beginning had already been made on the initiative of the Health Department.

League of Nations, Commission of Enquiry into Traffic in Women and Children in the East, Report to the Council (1932), pp. 312-315

Those who know the East are fully aware that at race meetings or at great carnival gatherings, most of the clubs – especially the great Liberal German clubs – throw open their doors, in truly friendly fashion, to visitors, who are at liberty to saunter in and out, drink, play billiards, cards, or bet on races. It was at one of these gatherings that the "pimp" elbowed himself amongst the horse racing fraternity – all honest, straight men, who work for their living and despise the unclean monster who lives on unfortunate women's earnings.

The "pimp" was busy talking about his own ability, when one horse trainer – an Australian – being disgusted with the fellow's talk, stopped him by remarking, "If half one hears is true, the game you're at is a bit over the odds. I know what they would do with your sort in my country." The "pimp" became indignant, and actually defended his trade. He said, with much vehemence, "It's all sentimental humbug about girls coming out here. In the first place, they want to come out; in the second place, they know what they are coming for and they get what they expect. Here they get money, good clothes, good food, and a good time. If the life is short, it's merry. If they remain in England – well, they get what they're looking for, without money, or food, or clothes. If I bring a girl out here, I see she knows the business before we start."

MacKirdy and Willis, The White Slave Market (1912), pp. 269-270

We next drove on to a Russian "hotel" on the fringe of the residential quarter. An Indian watchman opened a door in a wooden fence in response to our knocks, and conducted us up a flight of stairs, along a passage, and into a large room. The centre of the floor was cleared for dancing, and around the walls were small tables and an occasional plush settee. Some large and "blowsy" Russian women lolled about, and a couple of lugubrious Scandinavian supercargoes sipped drinks at opposite ends of the room. An ancient gramophone ground out some forgotten dance tune. Our entry caused something like a sensation. We sat down at one of the tables, and very soon two of the "girls" (they must have been nearly forty) came across the floor to join us. They suggested champagne, but we told them it would be bad for their figures, and ordered whiskies-and-sodas all round. The impassive face of the Chinese "boy" who brought the drinks somehow contrived to register contempt of his employers. We did not stay long, and left the two Danes or Norwegians to their fate.

Williams, Green Prison (1941), p. 30

As we walked through the narrow, vile-smelling alleys, I did not enjoy being so tightly sandwiched in between my rough-neck escorts, but when they explained that, so walking, there was less chance of my being stabbed in the back, I hugged them tight. Vice is cut after much the same pattern the world over. It was more than sufficient to get a glimpse into the hovels along the river banks, and on the raft; hiding places for vice of every vileness; crime of every enormity – disgusting, appalling, unnatural.

We had paddled about a mile downstream before we boarded a raft, on which a square, wooden house was built. This house proved to be a theatre of the underworld. There was a stage, probably twelve by twenty feet, covered with a Brussels carpet. Whatever colour it had once had was quite lost in dirt. At the edge of the carpet sat the orchestra – two boys that made a terrific noise by picking instruments that resembled banjos. A dozen players, men and women, were on the stage, but I did not linger long enough to find out what the play was about. The noise, smoke, and generally hideous atmosphere stifled any desire to extend my studies in the dramatic art among the cut-throat fraternity of Siam.

I only wanted to get out of the hellish place; wanted, too, to get away from my guides.

Norden, From Golden Gate to Golden Sun (1923), pp. 129-131

It was under the guidance of the Chief of Police of Bangkok that I made a little round of the city's opium-dens and gambling-hells, a round which certainly no tourist has ever made before. Late one evening we went off in a jingling rickshaw down the broad streets, which were brilliant with electric light. But soon we left these great arteries behind us and came into narrow, winding alleys, very sparsely illuminated by paper lanterns here and there before the doors. For it was the "shady side" we were bound for. All was still and deserted. We scarcely met a human being, and only now and then the melancholy howling of a dog disturbed the silence. The low, ruinous houses became closer and closer, and their dark shutters grinned at us like the empty eye-sockets of a spectre. I had long ago lost the way, and would certainly never have been able to get out of this winding labyrinth by myself. The lanes became ever narrower, and the neighbourhood ever more mysterious and ugly. It was a good thing to have the Chief of Police in one's company and a Browning pistol in one's hip-pocket.

Prince William, In the Lands of the Sun (1915), pp. 96-97

At lunch at the British Legation we met the chief Englishmen here, most of them Government employees and public school and university men. I am asked exactly what I would like to do and see. I see it at once. There are no excuses or delays. I asked to see the opium factory, of which they are not particularly proud. It is a large tall building, which looks like a small-arms factory. All the machinery came from Birmingham, I noticed. The opium is inserted in little tubs and sold at various prices. The Siamese wish to get rid of the opium monopoly, but can't do it at present, as one-third of their income comes from opium.

Harmsworth, My Journey Round the World (1923), p. 204

An opium den, under strict surveillance, as opium is a government monopoly, was one of the interesting things we saw at Talaat Plu. An uncomfortable-looking place even by the standard of a butcher's shop which it vividly recalled to me, only, instead of mere joints, *people* lay about the slabs, their heads on porcelain supports. They were Chinese, or Siamo-Chinese, almost all; and dreams were the last thing suggested by their attitudes and expressions. They would need to be particularly pleasant dreams to compensate the bleakness of their surroundings. The smoking, too, was such a restless performance. The pill to be made, two puffs to be enjoyed, and the whole proceeding over again. Even the pipe was not an old friend; it had to be hired and the stuff bought on the way in. We were at any rate a godsend to the curiosity of the smokers, who were quite as much interested in us as we in them, and we decided that the Englishman who showed the place in turn to us ladies would be credited with an oriental number of wives!

The bliss of opium-smoking remains something of a mystery even to present-day science. What is there in the smoke to comfort? I am told that, on analysis, there is little if any morphia in the smoke- the morphia is all collected in the large tubular cavity of the pipe stem as are the alkaloids of the opium.

Wheatcroft, Siam and Cambodia (1928), pp. 92-93

In September 1938 the opium dens of Bangkok were raided by the police, and 5,223 smokers were arrested. They consisted of 491 Siamese, 3 Indians, 1 Annamite, and 4,728 Chinese. Such as were found to have homes of their own were leniently treated, but those proved to be aliens whose registration papers were not in order were sentenced to deportation.

Thompson, Thailand (1941), p. 741

While drunkenness is not very common, there is a great deal of drinking, and the "Spirit Farmer," who has the Government concession for the manufacture and sale of liquor, is one of the mighty men in every community. With humiliation I must record that, with other foreign commodities, Scotch whiskey, French brandy and Australian beer have made their appearance. I saw shops with rows of foreign bottles in the remotest towns, and several times in Bangkok I read the English sign: "Place for the Drinking of the Delightful Juice." Some of the Siamese nobles who were educated abroad have learned not only European manners but European intemperance, and one of the highest judges of the land has died as the result of the excessive drinking which he began in England.

Speer, Report (1916), p. 6

In Bangkok and in the larger provincial towns today, the bottle shop has become one of the most familiar objects along the principal streets. Shelves filled with imported wines and liquors of every kind are in evidence everywhere. The drink habit has increased greatly in recent years, as is proved by the large increase of the traffic. Temperance work is being done in Siam, but not in an organized way or to any great extent. In the mission schools a special effort is being made to teach the truths of scientific temperance. Temperance tracts have been issued by the mission press and distributed freely. The sale and manufacture of alcohol, as well as opium, is in the hands of the government.

The Anti-Saloon League Year Book 1920 (Westerville, Ohio), p. 262

Opium-smoking is rare, except among the Chinese, but gambling is the national vice.

Speer, Report (1916), p. 6

'A Gambling Place off the Sampeng in Bangkok. In the background a band is hard at work entertaining the patrons'. From Whitney, *Jungle Trails, Jungle People* (1905).

Lucie Chandler visits a gambling den...

Through a labyrinth of dark alleys bordering on Sampeng we were conducted to a huge, barn-like structure, where a few pennies, judiciously bestowed, procured an unchallenged entrance. The entire floor was covered with straw mats, arranged in squares, each square offering a different game of chance, and around each, squatting on their heels, groups of Siamese, their bodies bare to the waist. Oil lamps with round reflecting shades, suspended from the rafters by long chains, hung about a foot and a half from the floor, just above each group of players, and the air was stifling. All one could see was a mound of small snail shells alternately scattered and gathered up by the long rake of a croupier, while the gamesters, each with a small pile of coins on the mat before him, guessed at the probable number of shells and thereby increased or depleted their piles of coins. It seemed dull sport to the onlooker, but doubtless the "ticker" on our stock exchange would fail to thrill the heart of a Siamese, particularly the uneducated peasant.

Travel, November 1916, p. 29

Eric Reid describes a visit to the Rong Bawn, a "Siamese gambling hell", shortly before the Great War.

The casino, as Jones grandiloquently styles it, is a huge building in a state of horrid dis-repair, seething with people, and of an odour - whew! On the corrugated iron roof the rain-storm rattles like hail. Money-changers' tables are placed at intervals along the walls whose rotten beams, slimy with fungus, seem to be exuding beads of perspiration in the thick heat of the room.

There are no seats. Everyone squats on haunches round the mats, and money may be placed opposite little buttons of wood bearing the numbers, or may be flung into the centre. The croupiers astonish us with their dexterity in wielding the long scoops with which they claw in the money. The skill of these men in throwing a handful of money half across the room to the person for whom it is destined elicits the plaudits of every visitor.

It is noteworthy that nearly all the gamblers are Siamese; this would seem to bear out the statement one so often hears about the besetting vice of this nation. It is strange, too, that the majority of those present are women. One sees Chinese, young and old, of course, but most of the faces round the central mat are those of withered old Siamese crones, who follow the play with a dull show of indifferent interest that betrays little of their inherent passion for the vicissitudes of chance.

Reid, Chequered Leaves (1913), pp. 219-221

The special branch of the local Police raided a gambling den at the rear of Wat Jang Saeng in the Rama I. Road at 1 p.m. on the 28th inst. and took into custody thirteen men and women, including a private of the police. The games indulged in were dice, "high-low" and *po-kam*.

The Bangkok Times, 30 July 1929, p. 7

Pawnshops

The pawnshops of Bangkok held me for many an hour. They are incredibly numerous; incredible, that is, until one traces their connection with gambling – the dearest vice of the Siamese. Sandwiched among the open bazaars in the alleys that branch from the Sampeng – the shopping street – they are kept by Burmese and Chinese. The Siamese are the pawners; never the brokers. They are too gay in spirit; glide too easily between the rock of life to succeed in this business which is essentially one of thrift. On the shelves and counters of these pawnshops lie jewellery, old crowns,

A street, ca 1920. The sign over the clock of the building at the centre reads "pawnshop". K.I.T.L. Wikimedia Commons.

weapons, embroideries – rare old bits that might find a place in great museums. All are covered with dust. Often while I stood turning them over, a coolie would bring in a panung, and borrow on it a satang or two, that he might try his luck again.

These pawnshops are open to the street and contain the most varied assortment of articles that can be imagined. Besides being crammed with things, they serve as the dwelling of their respective proprietors, and are at the same time bedroom, dining-room, and parlour. The floor is crawling with dirty-nosed youngsters, and the youngest of the family lies shrieking in a corner among a heap of other rubbish, while the mother sits calmly chewing betel at the entrance and smiles a jet-black smile upon the passersby. But the husband looks after the business and blinks his oblique and cunning eyes at the visitor from behind a pair of colossal horn spectacles.

Prince William, In the Lands of the Sun (1915), pp. 79-80

There were, in my early days, an enormous number of pawnshops in Bangkok. They were all owned by Chinese, many of the pawnbrokers being British or French subjects, and a good number of Macao Portuguese Chinese. There were then no pawnshop Regulations, and many (I fear most) of the pawnbrokers were little better than "fences", ready to take anything in pawn, no matter how suspicious the circumstances. When one was burgled, one waited a bit, and then went round the pawnshops, when the stolen property would quite likely be seen exposed for sale. I had one or two Chinese pals in the business so was often able to get back my own and my friends' stolen property on favourable terms; but the ordinary victim had the choice between losing his valuables, or buying them back on the pawnbroker's terms.

I once had a valuable silver vase stolen, which I met with later in a pawnshop. I knew quite well who was the thief, and that he was a person whom the pawnbroker could not possibly have supposed to be the owner of the vase, so I uttered a few rather censorious remarks on the subject. The pawnbroker appeared very contrite, and begged me to accept the vase without payment. As it was my own, and as I looked upon the pawnbroker as an accessory to the theft, I took it. A few days later, the pawnbroker came to the Consular Office and asked me to register him as a British subject. He had no evidence whatever to show that he really was a British Subject, but he clearly thought that he had placed me under such an obligation, by giving me back my own vase, that I could not decently refuse his request.

Wood, Land of Smiles (1935), pp. 29-30

In September 1925, Raymond Clément Plion-Bernier (1902-1993), a young French diplomat who had just arrived in Bangkok accompanied (rather unusually) by his mother, reported the theft of jewellery (presumably Mme Bernier's) from his room at the Trocadero Hotel.[3]

On the 10th inst., Mr. Raymond Plion, Student Interpreter of the French Legation, informed the Bangrak Police that jewellery to the value of about Tcs. 500 had been stolen from his room at the Hotel Trocadero in Suriwongse Road. He suspected a young Siamese boy to whom he had given some biscuits earlier that day. On the police moving, some of the articles were found in a pawnshop. The small boy was also found, and he said he got these things from a man to pawn for him. This man, whose name he gave, had been called away to Potaram on business. Two police officers were promptly despatched to Potaram and got their man out in the country, in the Commune of Chet Somian. He was still in possession of some of the articles stolen. Quite smart work.

The Bangkok Times, 15 September 1925, p. 4

Virtuous Bangkok

Lt.-Col Forty, now retired, felt that Bangkok had become more "virtuous" by the late 1920s. Nevertheless, some ten years later, Virginia Thompson, still found "the red-light district - green in Bangkok – very extensive", observing that "many religious leaders have called the Siamese capital a spiritual morgue" (Siam, p. 687).

The huge gaming houses, in former days one of the most remarkable sights of Bangkok, no longer exist. Gambling is now prohibited by law. But in spite of every effort to stop it a certain amount continues, for the Siamese

---

3   Mme Bernier also accompanied her son when he was posted to cover for the French consul at Chiang Mai, but died there after what seems to have been a stroke.

are by nature fond of all games of chance. Nearly opposite the spot where the largest of these establishments stood is a large collection of pawnshops.

Bangkok from a moral point of view compares favourably with other capitals, and when contrasted with the great Eastern ports might even be described as virtuous. Solicitation is severely discouraged, and there are none of those whining touts and pimps who pester the stranger to buy their filthy photographs or to accompany them into diverse haunts of sin. The flaring bars, with their tawdry sordid women, once to be found in profusion near the foreign legations, no longer exist. Departed also are the white slavers, callous and furtive brutes, who regarded the unfortunate females who kept them as animals to be beaten, bought, sold, exchanged or gambled for as circumstances dictated. Public opinion, the abolition of extraterritorial privilege, passport regulations and other exigencies caused by the Great War, all aided in wiping out an industry which at one time flourished exceedingly.

Visitors to Bangkok who expect to find the hectic scenes of vice and depravity sometimes described by novelists as the usual things of the East will be agreeably surprised at their absence, or chagrined as the case may be. But as elsewhere reasonable provision is made for all the wants of the stranger within the gates. Opportunities if wanted can be found for indulging in the night-out, binge, or jag, which even the oldest and steadiest-looking traveller sometimes feels himself entitled to.

Forty, Bangkok (1929), pp. 32, 38-39

Bangkok is said to be a moral cesspool, but I do not think it is worse in this respect than other metropolises in the East and Europe.

Pasqual, A Trip: Through Siam (1925), p. 57

Crime and Punishment

The Bangkok police are a smart khaki-clad force. A large proportion are Sikhs, but these are rapidly being replaced by Siamese. There is nothing that the Siamese policeman enjoys more than exerting his authority over a Chinaman, and at times of religious enthusiasm he may be seen herding off to jail a dozen turbulent Chinese coolies at once, all tied to a long rope by their wrists. Each one of his prisoners is his physical superior, but they never make an organised effort to escape.

Thompson, Lotus Land (1906), pp. 49-50

"City Police Station" from *Siam from Ancient to Present Times* (1926). The well-preserved building in Maharat Road is known today as the Royal Palace Police Station.

Two men, Nai Dang and Nai Pherm, and two women, Nang Sai Phoon and Nang Hai, were prosecuted in the International Borispah and the Borispah Courts this morning, on five charges of theft in all.[1] As the owners of goods stolen in the two cases before the International Court had not turned up, both cases were adjourned. But they were tried in Borispah Court No. 1 for having stolen goods to the value of about Tcs. 300 from Messrs. F. A. Pratt and E. L. Longway in the Siphya road.[2] In this case the

---

1 Borispah Court: Police Court.
2 Rev. E. L. Longway and Rev. Forrest A. Pratt were American missionaries of the Seventh-Day Adventist Church who had arrived with their wives in Bangkok in December 1918.

owners were allowed to receive some of the stolen goods back after they had been identified. The accused denied having stolen the goods, but admitted having received them as stolen goods.

The Bangkok Times, 4 December 1919, p. 5

In Bangkok the foreign community is living in a state of terror. These are days when the housebreaker and the thief are abroad, and no man knows when his house will prove the attraction. During the last six months the gentry have been exceedingly busy and exceedingly daring, and the victims do not like it the least little bit. There is a district in the midst of which is a police station that has proved peculiarly attractive to the thief. I do not know if the thief selects this district by way of a joke, but if he does he has a sense of humour recognised by his victims but by no means shared by them. The police sit in the office and wait for the criminal calling to give himself into the hands of the law. At least, that is the impression of the householders living in the district. And, after all, they may be forgiven if they are inclined to be a little caustic. With a police station so close at hand, they cannot understand why there should be so many burglaries.

The Straits Times, 15 June 1923, p. 9

Of course the European does not suffer more than anyone else. Both Chinese and Siamese have been complaining of late the local beggars move about with too much freedom in the streets and lanes of Bangkok and take every opportunity of pilfering.

The Bangkok Times, 17 October 1929, p. 5

The Bangkok police, as well as the provincial constabulary, is composed of conscripted men. They are drilled with rifles, taught to march and salute, are given brief instructions as to their duty and assigned to station houses at a salary of four ticals a month for two years. The police are unarmed except for a small night stick. When a policeman faces an armed outlaw he is forced to run back to his commander and ask for a rifle. Although the odds are against the conscripted policeman, he often displays unusual bravery in coping with armed men. If he overlooks the capture of a criminal, however, he is not blamed for inefficiency or called a coward. If he is wounded or killed he is more often than not called a fool to risk his life for four ticals a month. As a result, Siam has its full share of gangsters and bandits.

Freeman, Brown Women and White (1932), pp. 225-226

The police inspired little respect. Inasmuch as they were recruited by conscription and virtually unpaid, it was no wonder that they balked at night duty and did little to regulate the numerous opium and gambling dens, where most crime originated.

They seemed unable to differentiate between different categories of offenders, and zeal verging on brutality was often misplaced. Although murder and theft were frequent in Bangkok, few arrests were made; but a ricksha coolie had only to run excitedly over to the wrong side of the street to have the police belt him within an inch of his life and drag him in shackles to prison.

Thompson, Thailand (1941), pp. 177-178

About a month ago, Mr. E. Healey, the director of the Arts and Crafts School, who lives at Samsen, was, with Mrs. Healey, entertaining friends to dinner. Mr. Healey is in the habit of keeping a small rook rifle on his verandah for the purpose of shooting at pariahs. After dinner, one of the guests asked Mr. Healey if the weapon made much noise. He replied that it did not and then fired a shot at the bank of the klong by the house. About a week or so later a policeman served him with a paper in Siamese. It appears this was a summons, but as Mr. Healey could not read it he would not sign the receipt but asked the policeman to leave the paper and he would have it translated. On Thursday, Mr. Healey was arrested on a warrant for refusing to accept service of the summons. He was taken to the Borispah Court and bail was allowed in his own recognisances, the amount being fixed at Tcs. 200. The original summons was for firing off a gun without any cause.

The Bangkok Times, 6 May 1911, p. 5

Mr. John F. Johns the British Consul-General, while walking on the outskirts of Bangkok, in the company of the British Minister, Mr. R. H.

Greg, was hit in the back of the neck with a knife by a Siamese peasant. The injury was not serious and there is no political motive for the act.

The Straits Budget, 25 February 1916, p. 12

This morning the assailant was taken to the British Legation where he was identified by Mr. Johns; and he was then formally charged by the Police. He refused to say anything in answer to the charge. The accused, by name Nai Choon, will be brought before the Courts when further evidence has been obtained. Nai Choon is a young man of twenty-four years, and is the son of a wealthy *pu-yai ban*.[3] The accused man, it is said, had a hidden grievance against no one in particular. He was formerly a conscript policeman, and was under the command of Captain S. P. Groves, who made him a traffic controller. He was discharged from the police force in B.E. 2466, and shortly after he was discharged his father-in-law and a friend were attacked on precisely the same spot where Mr. Johns was struck down. His father-in-law was badly injured and lost a leg, and the friend was killed.

The Bangkok Times, 23 February 1926, p. 5

"A Group of Professional Criminals, with Guard" from *Twentieth Century Impressions of Siam* (1908).

---

3 Pu-yai ban: village headman.

Crime and Punishment 269

I arrived in the thick of an epidemic – no, not cholera, – hooliganism of hat snatching, and men were going about the streets with their hats tethered to their button holes with elastic. It was a common thing to see a crowd chasing a "hat snatcher" in broad daylight, with the crows, which infested the city, joining in the chase and adding to the general melee and din with their cawing. What hats were wanted for I never knew. Hooligans are by no means dead, but they go for the more thrilling pastime of head snatching if one can believe some of the police stories going round, that gang robbers, who terrorise the city to-day, have been known to cut off the head of a fallen comrade to prevent identification when they are hard pressed by the police. A wave of crime is sweeping over the city, and it is just a toss-up whether Bangkok is as bad as Singapore or Singapore as bad as Bangkok. The street societies and cinemas are violently at work here.

Pasqual, A Trip: Through Siam (1925), p. 55

That was Bangkok – clamour erupting furious and intense at a street-corner, by a street fountain, in an eating-house, in a rickshaw rank, and a few seconds bedlam and all hell let loose – then silence.

Thompson, Water-Lily (1952), p. 230

Anyone parking his car of an evening before a Bangkok entertainment hall has to fight off a crowd of hoodlums who battle for the privilege of "guarding" it and who exercise effective revenge if they are not tipped. The Government has made little effort to deal directly with these juvenile groups. There are vagrancy laws, but they are so ineffective that diseased beggars roam the city streets and country roads. The government reformatory at Kohsichang has been far from adequate in tackling the problem of youthful criminals. A new reform school is projected for the near future, and there has been a general quickening of interest in the whole problem.

Thompson, Thailand (1941), p. 690

On the 29th ult., six boys from the reformatory school at Kohsichang commandeered a small sailing boat left unguarded on the beach by the postal authorities and set sail, making a bid for liberty. The police, however, succeeded in capturing the juvenile party at Jolburi on the 5th inst., and took them back to Kohsichang.

The Bangkok Times, 9 August 1928, p. 5

The prison buildings and the accommodations for the detained compare unfavorably with like institutions in India, Burmah, and the Straits Settlements. Like them, they are conducted on the principle of making the criminals support the house of their incarceration. Daily, and in every direction, numbers of these prisoners are to be seen at labor in the streets or on other public works. They are always in irons. Some of the worst characters, who are constantly detained within the prison walls, are forced to wear about their necks a broad, flat, wooden collar, somewhat similar to those worn by vicious cows in Northern Europe. The prison shop offers a curious variety of stock. This shop is the principal source of the open-work split rattan balls used in the game of raga-raga, or foot shuttle-ball.

Sommerville, Siam on the Meinam (1897), pp. 83-85

The gaols, as recently as within the last twelve years, have been described by observers as the foulest holes imaginable. In the best of them men and women were condemned to sleep in the same den, with a chain run through their leg-irons at night, while the stench was intolerable. This has all been changed, at least in Bangkok and the nearer provinces, and if any criticism is to be made now, it is that the prisons are almost too comfortable for the inmates.

Carpenter, Siam in the XXth Century (1902), p. 182

George W. P. Hunt, former Governor of Arizona, now United States Minister to Siam, has written an interesting letter from Bangkok, to Frank Walsh of Bisbee.

I made application through the foreign office and after nearly two weeks I was notified that they would be glad to let me inspect their prison. Yesterday I went with the official interpreter of the legation. I found all the lifers and the long term men assembled. They all had on leg irons. There were 381 lifers and 201 long term men. About 2642 prisoners and all the buildings are in the heart of the city and cover 12 acres. While everything looked clean and there was no prison odor, I thought that it was run on hard lines. They seemed very anxious to please, and when I left he intimated to my interpreter that he would be pleased if I could say a good word. In that bunch of prisoners there were 20 who were heavily ironed, and they were brought out. These are the ones that will have to suffer death and the way they kill them here is to cut off their heads with a huge sword. All the prisoners were working, making furniture, baskets, mats and inlaid furniture. They had a hospital, and I must say the prisoners looked rather plump.

The Bisbee Daily Review (Arizona), 26 July 1920, p. 2

Visitors to Bangkok desirous of taking away with them mementoes, or souvenirs, of their visit may be interested to learn that they can obtain numerous useful and decorative articles made in the gaols at very reasonable rates. Really beautiful grass mats and baskets can be made and coloured in accordance with any pattern supplied. At the Prapatoom prison the basket work turned out is of such a quality as to probably defy competition anywhere.

Antonio, Guide (1904), pp. 82-83

The Menace of the Gunman

Bangkok has just had its first taste of the Chinese gunman. For many years past the secret societies have thriven and from time to time have had serious feuds with one another but in practically every case hitherto either knives or big sticks have been the weapons used. In the present instance the victim, a young Chinese doctor, was sitting in the shop of his father, a well-known Chinese chemists, about noon. When three well-dressed Chinese came along and one of them fired at the breast of the victim. The three then running off down the labyrinth of lanes which constitute Bangkok's veritable Chinatown. It seems that only a few weeks before the victim had been kidnapped with a view to making him either join or subscribe to the "Blood and Iron" Society. The victim, though badly injured, is said to be recovering, but the criminals are still at large.

The Straits Times, 21 August 1928, p. 12

A. SIAH LENG DISPENSARY.
Nos. 403-409, Sam Yek. New Road BANGKOK, (SIAM).
Established 1900. Wholesale and retail druggists, chemists, and sellers of surgical and dental instruments.
Dr. A. KEE ENG. Dr. A. CHIA SEW.

The A. Siah Leng Dispensary. Advertisement in *Siam from Ancient to Present Times* (1926).

Regarding the audacious crime committed yesterday on the person of Dr. Ang Kee Eng of the Siah Long Dispensary, we were today informed that his father has offered a reward of Tcs. 2000 for the arrest of the gunman, and the Bangkok police are also offering Tcs. 1000. The patient is being cared for in a special ward of the Central Hospital, and a nurse is on constant duty.

Two probable motives have presented themselves – that it was part of the boycott campaign against the sale of Japanese goods; or otherwise that it was a demonstration of the powers of the society which is insisting on receiving subscriptions from patriots.[4]

The Bangkok Times, 7 August 1928, p. 4

---

4 The boycott was in protest against Japanese actions during the so-called "Jinan Incident" (May 1928).

Crime and Punishment 273

There was a sequel to the recent shooting incident this morning. When three Chinese were charged on the following account: inveigling Dr. Ang Kee Eng to a boarding house and with threats demanding money from him, shooting him at his dispensary on August 6; and shooting at Special Police Officers during their arrest on August 13. One of the accused admitted the inveigling and extortion, and also the shooting on August 6. The other men admitted being accomplices of the first accused on August 6 but denied shooting at the police during the arrest. They repeated the full story of the plot against the doctor "for dealing in Japanese goods". The case is proceeding.

Singapore Free Press, 21 August 1928, p. 9

Nat Yit Süe and two other Chinese gunmen who were previously convicted and sentenced to heavy terms of imprisonment for seriously wounding Dr. Ang Kee Eng in August last, were brought up in the Bangkok Criminal Court for judgment on the fresh charge of murder, following upon the death of the victim. All three were found guilty and sentenced to death.

The Bangkok Times, 13 February 1929, p. 6

Missions

To this list of Foreign Missions in Siam in 1909 should be added the Anglican Society for the Propagation of the Gospel in Foreign Parts (S.P.G.), established in 1903, which came to be known as the St Mary's Mission. The Seventh Day Adventists arrived after the Great War.

Roman Catholic Church, American Presbyterian Mission, American Bible Society, Siamese Baptist Mission, American Baptist Missionary Union, Church of Christ, Great Britain.

Perkins, Travels (1909), p. 262

Though Buddhism may not hold the sole place in the hearts of the Siamese, its influence has proved an insurmountable obstacle to the proselytising efforts of foreign missionaries who have attempted to make converts among the people and who have been present in the country ever since the beginning of the 16th century A.D. From that time down to the present the Roman Catholic religion has maintained a footing in the country but, the only thing of genuine good resulting to the country from 250 years of labour, sacrifice, intrigue and quarrelling, is the secular education which the Mission offers to the young of both sexes in its colleges and convents. Since the early part of the 19th century an American institution known as the American Presbyterian Mission, has been at work in Siam. Its members are widely dispersed over the country and by reason of the medical knowledge which is one of the qualifications for the calling, have done a great deal of good in introducing simple remedies amongst the country people and in promoting the study of medical science by the Siamese generally. Their schools have also been of much value to the country in the past but, like the Roman Catholics, they have failed in the main object of their existence, and after nearly a hundred years of work have very few Siamese Christians amongst their flock.

Graham, Handbook (1912), pp. 549-550

Catholic Missions

The Roman Catholic Missions have and are doing a commendable and grand work for Siam. They have also a good hospital where patients are well cared for and have established the well known Assumption College and numerous schools where children, young men and women are taught Latin, French, English and Siamese and are thus being prepared for the activities of their lives. The good, talented and scholarly Bishop Pallegroix prepared a Siamese Dictionary with Latin, French and English definitions, thus enabling all familiar with either of these languages to acquire a good knowledge of the Siamese language.[1] God bless the Roman Catholic Missions in their noble and uplifting work.

Smith, Brief Sketches (1909), p. 29

There are now two Roman Catholic Bishops in Siam, and the work of the Church is divided between the two Missions of Siam and Laos. Within the bounds of the Catholic Mission of Siam there are 56 Churches, five of which are in Bangkok. In addition to the Bishop there are 44 priests. Generally speaking there is a school attached to each station or church, and the total number of schools now is 61. These schools are attended by 4,060 pupils of both sexes. In addition, the principal educational institutions under the Mission are the Assumption College (say 800 pupils), the Convent Boarding School of St. Joseph (140 pupils), the Assumption Convent day school lately erected (102 pupils), and the Clerical College (College of the Sacred Heart of Jesus) with some 82 students.

Bangkok Directory (1914), p. 211

Conspicuous among the foreign clergy are the Catholic priests, whose black cassocks, full beards and beaver-skin hats are as distinctive in their way, and exactly opposite to, the yellow robes and shaven faces of their Buddhist brothers. But remote as they are in outward appearance both orders have very much in common. The Roman Catholic fasts, tends the sick, goes on foot, educates the young, leads a sober and continent life, and so also does the Buddhist priest.

Forty, Bangkok (1929), p. 30

---

1 Jean-Baptise Pallegoix (1805-1862), Vicar Apostolic. His dictionary appeared in Paris in 1854.

A postcard issued by the Missions-Etrangères de Paris. The Rev. Fr. Colombet is to the right of the priest celebrating his jubilee. The Editor's Collection.

The celebration of the Silver Jubilee of the priesthood of the Right Reverend Bishop Perros was a memorable event and highly successful. After the religious ceremonies in the morning, at which a big congregation attended, a photograph of His Lordship and others was taken by the proprietor of the Talat-Noi Photo Studio in front of the cathedral.

The Bangkok Times, 24 November 1929, p. 5

Gone are the old church of the Assumption, and the College of the French Mission, but not the Reverend Father Colombet, who is perhaps the oldest European resident in the country, whose acquaintance I was, unhappily, unable to renew as he was confined to a sick bed.[2] A new church in ornate Italian style whose ceiling scintillates with gold has risen from the site of the old one; and the new school house is an imposing building capable of accommodating over a thousand pupils – a great improvement on the one I remember by the brink of a large pond of fresh water which the boys were lapping up with their hands. Ponds were dug all over the city to collect rain water – and mosquitos.

Pasqual, A Trip: Through Siam (1925), p. 55

---

2 Rev. Fr. Émile Auguste Colombet (1849-1933) had arrived in Siam in 1872.

CHRIST CHURCH.

Protestant Missions

King Mongkut's generosity provided a chapel for the foreign community, which is in the care of the British and has an English chaplain, but all nationalities and every sect have the use of it if they desire.³

Wheatcroft, Siam and Cambodia (1928), p. 97

Rev. Henry J. Hillyard, "M.A., LL.D., Chaplain of Christ Church, Bangkok'" writes about the new church.

The present church, which was opened for service on Sunday, April 30, 1905, under the name of Christ Church. When the church was being built it was decided to build a chaplaincy beside it, which was accordingly done. The church contains a Willis two-manual organ, and is fitted with electric light. There is a surpliced choir, and the services are fully choral. Neither of the churches was consecrated, as they are not under the jurisdiction of any bishop.

Twentieth Century Impressions of Siam (1908), p. 217

The marriage of Mr. William Dick Brown and Miss Effie Grace Swanson was solemnised at Christ Church yesterday afternoon after the ceremony at the British Legation in the morning. The Rev. Cecil R. Simmons officiated. The bridegroom awaited the bridge dressed in kilts. The bridge was exquisitely dressed in shimmering iridescent sequins, with a train of the palest pink georgette which was carried by Ruth and Jinty Cochrane in pale pink and forget-me-not, and David Simmons, as a white satinned page boy. After the ceremony the largely attended

---

3 A plaque in the church explains: "In the deed of his gift His Majesty stipulated that the land should be used only as a site for a church open to all Protestant Christians without distinction of nationality or sect".

reception was held at the residences of Mr. and Mrs. Swanson in Convent road. Thereafter the bride and bridegroom left for Phya Thai palace. This morning the couple left for Hua Hin where they will spend a few days before leaving for home.[4]

The Bangkok Times, 24 February 1926, p. 7

A Memorial in Christ Church ...

TO THE GLORY OF GOD AND
THE AFFECTIONATE MEMORY OF
HENRY HOOKER
This tablet is erected by his many friends to mark
Their appreciation of his Christian character & liberality
To this Church & other institutions in Bangkok.
He was for 20 years a member of this congregation
For many years Secretary to the Church Committee
& a member of the Choir. A window is also erected
to his memory in the Chancel of this Church.
"REST IN THE LORD"
BORN Sept 23rd 1859. DIED June 12th. 1909

Rev. C. W. Norwood discusses the fortunes of the Society for the Propagation of the Gospel Mission.

In January 1914, the Rev. C. R. Simmons offered himself to the S.P.G. for service overseas and was told of the urgent need that existed in Bangkok. The Society in London, also throughout the war, were unable to send any financial help. However, the work was taken in hand at a house in the New Road, near the present General Post Office, and was slowly built up in spite of set-backs. Pastoral and evangelical work went on, in and through and beside the educational work, and the little chapel continued

---

4 The bride was the daughter of the engineer J. H. Swanson; the bridegroom was an employee of the Chartered Bank in Bangkok. The bridesmaids were presumably related to Isobel and William McNair Cochrane (1883-1945). Cochrane was Manager of the Bangkok Dock Company, later Chieftain of the St Andrew's Society and a Master of the Masonic Lodge "St John, Bangkok, 1072, S.C". He died in August 1945 and is buried in the Protestant Cemetery.

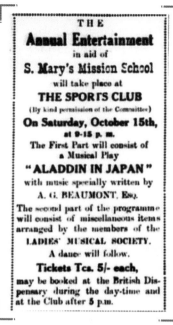

Advertisement in *The Bangkok Times* for a musical play by A. G. Beaumont, 13 October 1927, p. 7.

to be a center of congregational life. In 1922, premises were rented in the Rajadamri Road, which are now well known as the girls' school of the mission, S. Mary's, S.P.G. The boys' school was moved to premises in the Siphya Road in May 1926, and it carried on under the name of S. Peter's, S.P.G.

McFarland (ed.), Historical Sketch (1929), pp. 258-269

Owing to the dearness of rice and the increased cost of living generally, S. Mary's Mission is finding it practically impossible to make ends meet, if it is to continue to carry on the work to which it is committed. That statement will evoke general sympathy. The annual sale of work is to be held early in March and a big effort will be made to ensure a greater success than ever before. Many people can give a little help to that end, and regular subscriptions are suggested. The Mission has in its schools 140 pupils, and is entirely for 12 orphan children.

The Bangkok Times, 6 December 1919, p. 4

The American Presbyterian Mission has four churches in Bangkok. The Mission also conducts a bazaar chapel at Ban Maw, Bangkok. The Mission has started a young men's institute in Bangkok, the Boon Itt Memorial Institute, a work similar to the Y.M.C.A. In Bangkok the Mission has three schools, the Bangkok Christian College with an enrolment of over 250 boys, the Wang Lang Girls' School with an enrolment of nearly 150, and the Boys' School at Samray with about 100 pupils enrolled. An extra year has been added to the curriculum of the Bangkok Christian College, making it an eight year course instead of seven.

Bangkok Directory (1914), pp. 211-212

These agencies and the great heathen city present the field and the forces that need just now to be supplemented by a worthy evangelistic effort, so that the great city may feel in many districts the transforming power of the evangel.

Siam: The Need, the Opportunity (1916), p. 4

Rev. Boon Itt, "the most enlightened Siamese Christian", died of cholera in 1903. A memorial institute was founded in his honour …

Mr. Clarence A. Steel [sic – actually Steele], of the Portland, Oregon, Y.M.C.A, has been chosen as superintendent, and it is expected that he will be able, as soon as he acquires the language, to push the work in a large way for the winning to Christ of many young men in Bangkok. The mistake of the telegraph operator in Portland, Oregon, we believe is prophetic. When he received from New York the following message for Mr. Steel: "The Board of Foreign Missions has appointed you to Boon Itt Institute in Bangkok, Siam," the operator made it read, "Mr. C. A. Steel. You are appointed by the Board of Foreign Missions to boom its institute in Bangkok, Siam."

Bradt, Around the World (1912), p. 142

The Boon Itt Memorial Institute for Young Men, or Bangkok Y.M.C.A, has had its ups and downs, but for the past three years its hold on the young men has greatly increased. An average of 34 men used the building and the Y.M.C.A. privileges every day during the past year, and 273 men have been members at one time in this same period. A good Bible class is the strongest feature in the religious work, though an average of 72 attended the Sunday night meetings and illustrated lectures on the Life of Christ. Educational work was carried on in two English classes, but the attendance was not large, as it is difficult to persuade men in this climate to study much at night.

Presbyterian Church in the USA, Board of Foreign Missions, 81st Annual Report, 1918, p. 322

In this great city we have at present not a missionary giving himself to the evangelistic work. All are engaged in educational or institutional work which it is possible to do without a mastery of the language in many cases. In the long conferences with the Bangkok station the immense difficulties of the task of evangelistic work in Bangkok were recognized. The atmosphere of society, the difficulties of confession of Christ on the part of young men and women, especially from good homes, who had come to believe on Him in our mission schools, the greatness of the city, the secularism of its life, the influence of Buddhism, these things ought not to be allowed to daunt us.

Speer, Report (1916), p. 123

The Rev. Forrest A. Pratt discusses the early years of the Seventh-Day Adventist Mission.

The growth of the Seventh-Day Adventist Mission has been slow but steady.[5] At present we are operating four chapels, two in Bangkok. The standard has been held high and no one is admitted into the church by baptism who has not given up smoking, drinking, and betel-nut chewing. There have been some remarkable cases in which the Lord has given victory over these particular habits. In the year 1927, we published 10,000 copies of the Chu Chart Temperance Magazine and within three weeks, they were all sold.

McFarland (ed.), Historical Sketch (1928), p. 268

---

5 In fact, the first Siamese convert had been made in 1925, some seven years after the Adventists' arrival in Bangkok.

In School

Compared with some countries, education, speaking generally, in Siam is still barely out of the embryonic stage; in fact, the Decree which was issued some time ago, ordaining the introduction of universal education, is only being seriously applied for the first time to-day. The fees charged are very low indeed, in order to bring education within the reach of all. In addition to these State schools of various grades, there is now a university at Bangkok for male students, and there exist also normal colleges for the training of teachers. But besides these State schools, there are a large number of private schools, both Siamese and foreign, in addition to those – again a large number – which are attached to the wats (temples). The whole system has not yet had time for a fair trial, but there seems every prospect of its proving a success.

Macmillan, Seaports of the Far East (1925), p. 487

There seem to be but two classes – the educated and the common people. I understand that there is a well developed system of education, but from my observation it cannot be very extensive or produce visible results. The higher class seems to be highly educated; many of the prominent men, usually those with titles, having been educated abroad.

Hendley, Trifles of Travel (1924), pp. 199-200

They make excellent scholars, for they are very bright and intelligent. Only a mere handful of the population attend any school regularly, but all those who hope to obtain any Government employment must at least learn to read and write. Those that do attend the schools learn to draw accurately and neatly after very little practice. They need no teaching with regard to modelling in clay, their representations of elephants in particular being beyond criticism. All ordinary school subjects are rapidly acquired by them, and they are adepts in the acquisition of a foreign language. They learn to read, write, and speak English in the Anglo-Vernacular schools in about three years, with great ease and fluency. Many boys will speak in English concerning the common events of their daily lives after a few months' tuition. They are helped in this matter by their wonderfully retentive memories which enable them to remember a large number of words and idioms. Inquisitiveness is politeness, and it is rather bewildering to the English teacher new to his work, especially when he is constantly questioned as to his age, the price of his watch, the amount of his salary, or the date when he last had his hair cut.

Young, The Kingdom of the Yellow Robe (1898), pp. 55-56

It is the unanimous opinion of the Educational Authorities, including the European staffs, that the Siamese boy is an excellent scholar. He is docile, intelligent, avid to acquire knowledge and shows commendable application. He responds to kindness and is dejected by blame which, however, he appears seldom to merit.

Harris, East for Pleasure (1929), p. 58

The Siamese boy, though far more naturally lazy and apathetic than his English confrere, takes readily with a little encouragement to outdoor games and pursuits. It is more difficult, however, to impress him with the English sense of honour and esprit de corps, and it is therefore of the greatest importance to train him in these qualities. There is no need to make an English boy of him; let him preserve his Siamese individuality: but the Siamese ideal in the past has been so essentially different from the English, that there is no great danger of his turning out what some Siamese are afraid of, too Anglicised a product.

Campbell, Siam in the XXth Century (1902), pp. 259-260

Bishop René-Marie-Joseph Perros (1870-1952), the Vicar Apostolic of Bangkok, writes about the plan to create a school run by members of the Ursuline Order in Bangkok.

At Bangkok we have four parishes; one of these, called Rosaire, is Chinese and numbers about 2,000 faithful. The sisters would be in charge of the parish school where the teaching is done in both Chinese and Siamese. (At the beginning they could use native teachers while the sisters learn Siamese, which is not very difficult.) There would also be an English class for children just beginning this language and a workroom for manual arts – sewing, cooking, managing a household – everything necessary for the mother of a family. The most important, of course, is the formation of good Christians. For this, there must be both devotion and zeal. As the work progresses, they will also receive pagans who will come to learn English, French, design, embroidery, etc., while at the same time receiving knowledge of the true faith. There will also be some orphans to take care of; and later a dispensary will be added for distributing medicines for the sick who will come to consult the sisters. The good that will be accomplished will be immense, not only through words but above all by example.

Letter dated: 29 January 1924; quoted in Mahoney, Far Country, pp. 4-5

The American nun Sister Marie de Lourdes née Simons (1899-1984), writes to her community on arriving in Bangkok in October 1927 to work in the new school.

The house is much bigger and nicer than I expected. The classrooms are very nice. Our dormitory is quite nice. There are five of us there. We have big beds with a canopy of mosquito netting. The beds have no springs, just boards and a light mattress about two inches thick.

In the same month, she writes to her parents ...

I am writing this letter in a classroom in the presence of 15 children at play, and you should hear them! I love the work here with the poor children; it is always a sacrifice when I have to go back to the "princesses." [This] is a mission after the fashion of the pictures you see in the magazines. Mater Dei is run on the style of Merici School; only the pagans make it impossible to have the warm religious atmosphere we have at home.[1] At first it was hard to get used to this but I have long since realized that words and works count for little in this work in comparison with the power of prayer.

... and again in Spring 1929 ...

Our school is a real Siamese puzzle. To watch the children pass reminds me of Adam in the garden of paradise when Almighty God has all the animals pass before him – two of each kind. In the class of our little ones, first comes a lively little Italian, partner to a mischievous little English boy, followed by four lads from Denmark, a little American from Cleveland, a little Indian with his queer little dark features and bright blue satin trousers

---

1 Merici School: an Ursuline school in New Rochelle, NY.

and white blouse. Besides these we have a little French boy and girl and Chinese, Anamites and Siamese. The big girls come to us some knowing English and no Siamese, others knowing Siamese and little English and we have had Chinese knowing neither Siamese nor English. Can't you picture us trying to grade them!

Quoted in Mahoney, Far Country, pp. 53, 65, 66

Pupils in Bangkok have a delightful habit of *sampling* schools, in fact things had come to such a pass, no leave being taken of the last school before going on to the next, that they were required to bring a certificate from their late headmaster to the newly-favoured, stating their reason for leaving the previous school. A boy high up in his Siamese school might suddenly decide that a little English would be useful to him, and come to St. Peter's, where, for the continuity of his Siamese studies, he would be placed in the top form though not knowing a word of English. This was distinctly hard on the teachers of English subjects, and handicapped the other pupils too. Fortunately the Government standard for English was low.

Wheatcroft, Siam and Cambodia (1928), pp. 206-207

The Presbyterian Mission's Boys' High School was founded in 1852; it was later renamed Bangkok Christian College (BCC). In 1931, it had 328 pupils.

Rev. J. A. Eakin, D.D, has been principal of the High School many years and all the teachers are Christians, two of them elders of the church. The school is in seven grades and includes a large Chinese element. The sixth grade, in Miss Galt's charge, was composed of only four boys. Their English lesson was upon the "complex sentence." The schoolroom is provided with American desks, and blackboards on which a class was doing simple examples. Of thirteen members, five were down with fever; in another class of sixteen, half were down. Another class of twenty under a Chinese teacher were analyzing English sentences with, one might say, over-minuteness, for they went as far into details as would be done in an American town. It is a very interesting school. There was no appearance of stubbornness or suspicion, as is seen occasionally in India or China. There was a pervading air of politeness, good will and excellent attention. Some Western ozone has certainly gone into that school.

Woman's Work, May 1903, pp. 102-103

Bangkok Christian College is the only high grade Protestant school for boys in lower Siam, and occupies a unique position of usefulness. Every effort should be made to increase its equipment and efficiency. The whole spirit and atmosphere of the College is Christian. The educational work is always kept subordinate to the spiritual and evangelistic. There is no stronger missionary agency in Siam than Bangkok Christian College. It is an interesting and encouraging fact that all the higher education in the Siam Mission is practically self-supporting.

Bradt, Around the World (1912), pp. 160-161

In two articles, Kru Leck Taiyong writes about the Mission's plans for BCC.[2]

The purpose of this school is to train Siamese boys for the uplifting of their Nation, mentally, physically and morally. This purpose has been faithfully kept as seen thru the high position held by those boys who have left the school. "The school is indeed very big!" said a boy who left the school seven years ago. It occupies about three acres of land and, after the South Playground was bought for the school it seemed to be very large. But it is now very small for the present number of boys enrolled. We are hoping for a large plant in the future.

The Siam Outlook, April 1925, p. 137

*

Siam is now a progressive country, and by faith, the writer hopes that some day, Siam will become a great nation. This will be through Christian education. Now we are looking forward with great joy to the Greater B.C.C. well out of the city where the boys can have a quiet place for study. At the new place there will be ideal conditions for building Christian character to serve the better Siam, and to serve our Lord and Master. There will be the beautiful Dunlap Chapel, a fitting place kept entirely for the worship of God. We look forward to great recitation rooms, a well equipped science building, a good library, masters' residences and ample

---

2 According to Kenneth Wells, Taiyong left the school after sixteen years in 1935 to work in a government school.

teachers' quarters. There will be better places for exercise, with football fields, and enough tennis courts. It is not far from the tram car line, and young men will be able to come as day students. There will of course be dormitories for the boarders. It is planned to receive only young men of the five highest classes at the new B.C.C. and students below fifth standard are to be taken care of at our present school. Readers, you are welcome to make hearty gifts for this great work.
The Siam Outlook, October 1926, pp. 49-50

Although no direct effort is made to convert the scholars besides caring for their minds and persons, the two schools give their pupils every opportunity of learning Christian doctrine and Anglican Church practice. At St. Mary's all boarders were expected to attend morning and evening chapel. To prayers before school the day girls came too, whether Christians or Buddhists, and all attended the Bible lessons. The sacrament was administered every Sunday and Feast day, and other services were provided both at St. Mary's and at St. Peter's.
Wheatcroft, Siam and Cambodia (1928), p. 212

The chapel was a plain room, painted cream. When it was not in use as a place of worship it served as the first grade classroom. The furnishings were simple wooden benches in two ranks, a piano, and a table on a low dais for the leader of the meeting. The singing had started as India came down the stairs. She could hear the children's voices in their favorite hymn.

> "When He cometh, when He cometh,
> To make up His jewels,
> All His jewels, precious jewels,
> His loved and His own."

Kru Darun was leading the singing, and Kru Suwon was at the piano. Only the front benches were filled, for the day pupils were not due until nine o'clock. This was the school's private devotions. Kru Darun read the morning Scripture lesson. There was a brief prayer, a second hymn, and the service was over. The day's duties were assigned, straightening the dormitory, sweeping, dishwashing, the care of the small children, office duty, practice teaching.

Landon, Never Dies the Dream (1949), pp. 44-46

Frank Exell is first sent to work at Suan Kularb ("Rose Garden School"), an elite institution founded by King Chulalongkorn in 1882 (Headmaster: Norman Sutton, "a blunt Yorkshireman").

My first impressions were favourable. The school was a long, two-storied building which ran rather more than the length of the well-kept football ground. At one end was a teachers' training college and at the other the teachers' club. On the side opposite the school was a small pavilion and drawing rooms. A narrow veranda ran the length of the classrooms, the walls of which were made up of arches to allow the passage of light and air. From the rooms came the low hum of voices. It was all in Siamese and I paled at the thought of ever having to teach in the language. Norman Sutton rose from his chair, his burly form filling his white tunic to capacity. His smile was friendly as he gripped my hand. "You'll be coomin' here, lad," he said, confidently, "I'll tak' you rooned."

But Exell's services are also coveted by the English headmasters of other government schools and he is eventually sent to Pradumaganga, "an inferior school in the Chinese quarter which did not even have a football team" (Headmaster: A. C. Churchill).

As I entered the classroom the head boy or *hua nah* chanted solemnly, "*Nueng, song, sarm*" – one, two, three. The class rose to its feet, nodded a polite little bow and sat down again expectantly. I was as new to them as they were to me. The big question was, would they understand me? I had a horrible feeling that they would not. And yet I had been assured that they had more than a smattering of English. One thing was quite certain, it was no use their speaking to me in Siamese. "Good morning," I said, as a feeler. "Good morning, sir," replied thirty voices in prompt unison, accompanied by thirty pleasant smiles. The ice had been broken.

It was the top class – *madhayom* eight. They ranged in years from sixteen to eighteen. All were dressed alike, neat white tunics buttoned up at the neck, black shorts and, in most cases, bare feet. Very few indeed wore stockings and shoes. Their school uniform would be completed by a straw "boater" on the front of which was the school monogram. At first glance

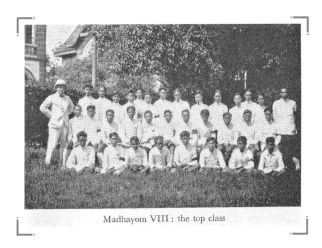
Madhayom VIII : the top class

they all looked alike – except for size. Black hair, almost jet black, wide foreheads, broad nostrils and high cheek bones. Eyes were only slightly slit except for those of obvious Chinese parentage. The school was in the Chinese quarter of the town. Most had a sallow, coppery complexion of an up-country lad whose early life had been spent in the paddy fields. They had one thing in common though, they smiled. It was a natural, friendly smile which gave me confidence. I felt sure I was going to like these boys.

Exell, Siamese Tapestry (1963), pp. 21-22, 25

As the senior mathematics master, I found it very difficult to select problems suited to the boys' everyday life. It was expecting rather much of them to be interested in how long it would take to fill a bath with water if one tap was full on and the other half on, when some fool had left the plug out. They none of them had a modern bath at home anyway and, for that matter, had probably never seen one. Their idea of having a bath was a metal dipper and the nearest *klong*.

Exell, Siamese Tapestry (1963), p. 69

The return journey to St. Mary's and fresh air was specially pleasant. Situated in a fine and treeful compound the main building consisted of two floors, both surrounded by verandahs.[3] On the ground floor on a foundation raised well above the ground was the Chapel, etc., and behind it a small room used as a dining-room by the English staff who lived in that house. The upper floor was divided roughly into five. A large piece of front verandah projecting porchwise over the entrance served as general sitting-room. It was walled with Venetian shutters kept closed against sun and rain or opened to the breeze, as we willed.

Wheatcroft, *Siam and Cambodia* (1928), p. 209

The American missionary teacher Annabel Galt describes a day at the Presbyterian Mission's Harriet House School for girls.

When at half-past five the rising bell rings, eighty curtains are raised and out wriggle eighty dark-eyed girls. In relays or divisions, twenty in each, they go down to the bathroom where river water has been thrown into a large tank by a force pump and is drawn into basins from faucets. Orientals have little privacy and so learn to dress modestly. Our girls come forth as clean and sweet as flowers, in their fresh white waists and bright one-colored *panungs*. All day long, in varied occupations, they are kept so busy as to have no time to get tired of each other and quarrel. From their early light breakfast, their sweeping, dusting, lamp tending and table-setting, they go to the opening school exercises. There is cheerful singing, and prayer, a talk by the leader, Scripture reading, and usually recitation of Scripture by the whole school, by classes or by individuals. Class work follows, till the big breakfast of rice with meat curry, vegetables, fruit or dessert. At 11.30, school resumes for the afternoon with a period of kindergarten games for the younger ones, with music, drawing and

"Siamese Christian Women of Bangkok in Native Costume. Teachers of Harriet House School". The teacher on the left had studied in the United States for four years "and now has charge of the first Kindergarten ever opened in Siam". *The Missionary Review of the World*, June 1918, p. 421.

---

3 A photograph can be found on the back cover of the edition of McFarland (ed), *Historical Sketch* published by White Lotus.

sewing during the last hour. It is then the girls hem the towels, sheets and pillow slips for the school. They learn to make garments for themselves, to knit, crochet, do drawn-work, bead-work and embroidery. In the Bangkok climate, a bath after school is necessary to make the dinner hour enjoyable and recreation in the open air at sunset. Evening prayers and study hour close the day and nine o'clock finds the girls once more behind their mosquito curtains.

Woman's Work, May 1907, pp. 109-110

In estimating community building values, a long column would be necessary if full credit were given to the mission schools. The educational system is headed by the Prince Royal's College and Prarachaya School, Chiengmai; Bangkok Christian College and the Harriet House School in Bangkok, the latter now expanded into the Wattana Wittaya Academy.[4] This school has sent out over one hundred girls who are now teaching, forty-two of whom are in mission or affiliated schools. Miss Edna Cole, who has given more than forty years to the school, recently at the unanimous request of the mission returned to Siam from furlough. She was greeted with a series of receptions and heartfelt tributes such as a monarch might envy.

Presbyterian Church in the USA, Board of Foreign Missions, 86th Annual Report, 1923, pp. 255-256

When mission schools are subject to inspection by representatives of the Board of Foreign Missions from the United States, India Severn finds herself envying the facilities at Wattana Wittaya …

Buildings of brick and stone could be displayed. There was the lovely approach by canal, slow and pleasant along shady waterways. Then there were the broad green lawns leading up to the buildings, clipped shrubs, neat flower beds, shady trees. Everything would be freshly painted and immaculate, big and adequate, businesslike and yet gracious. The men would be impressed by the classrooms with their good lighting and modern furniture, their maps and up-to-date equipment, the well-dressed

---

4 This refers to Presbyterian Mission schools and not to the "education system" as a whole, as readers might have assumed.

'A Girls' School' from Carter, *The Kingdom of Siam* (1904).

and well-cared-for children in the school uniform of dark red *pasin* and white blouse. They had the intelligent appearance of upper-class girls and the special charm of that special class of Siamese child, which was a combination of physical beauty, gracefulness, and punctilious manners. The teachers were alert and well dressed, too, intelligent and able to speak English with the visitors. There were the playgrounds, the big airy dining room, the little hospital, the domestic science kitchen.

Landon, *Never Dies the Dream* (1949), p. 198

Lucie Chandler visits Rajini School which was founded by H.M. Queen Saovabha Phongsri in 1904. The Japanese principal to whom she refers was Tetsu Yasui (1870-1945) who had studied at Cambridge and later became Dean of Tokyo Woman's Christian University. She was succeeded in 1907 by H.S.H Princess Bichitr Devakul (d. 1943), said the have been the first Siamese woman to become a professional teacher.

Apropos of education, it was my privilege to visit the most progressive institution in the country – the Rajini School, the principal of which is a royal princess. It is interesting to note that when the Siamese government decided to establish this school, they sent to Japan for a Japanese teacher, with Western advantages, to get the wheels in motion. One day I was invited to spend a day at the school, to visit all the classes and dormitories and to see the wheels go round, as it were. There were classes in Siamese, in geography, in mathematics, in embroidery, and drawing and English. It amazed one to see how apt the children were and the holiday spirit in which they took their education. They appeared to think everything a

In School   293

game and to enjoy it hugely. It was a yellow day, and during the recreation hour, when the children were flitting about in their gay scarves and *panungs* ranging in color from deep orange to pale cream – the compound was like a field of lovely yellow butterflies in perpetual motion. The most amusing sight of all was the gymnasium class, held in an open pavilion. Orientals do not take kindly to athletics, and this class was the only one which they seemed to regard as serious business. A superannuated piano haltingly ground out "Comin' Thro' the Rye" and the poor little youngsters gyrated like stiff-jointed puppets laboring under the burden of the song.

Travel, November 1916, pp. 29, 46

Discipline was generally easy, but naturally infants did not always respond to a word, and sometimes had to be punished. I peeped round the screen dividing my small classroom from a smaller, one day, to discover that cause of long-continued sobbing, and beheld a little boy made to stand on the table and curtsey! Punishments which do not "fit the crime" can be wonderfully stupid. I am told that this was probably of the teacher's own invention. She was Siamese. Modern educationalists will commend the Siamese in that the slap is barred. A Eurasian teacher once slapped a small delinquent, and there was a terrible descent of indignant parents on the Mission. They acknowledged that punishment was deserved, and even requested that the culprit should be chastised, but to slap with the palm of the hand. … To our idea their choice of a suitable instrument was most strange - a bamboo or a piece of rope! Either would be far more painful than the hand. It is necessary that foreigners walk warily in these matters, lest through ignorance they transgress. With cane, rattan, only criminals are chastised, and tamarind twigs are used to cast out evil spirits from the hysterical. It would seem that manners and superstitions are inextricably mixed.

Wheatcroft, Siam and Cambodia (1928), pp. 204-205

The highest ambition of the Bangkok school-boy is to end his years at school by passing the examinations of Matayom 8 grade. This year (B.E. 2468) 336 youths sat for these examinations last month, and it is now announced that 106 have passed. Of the 106 some 16 had attained the age of 20 years, the oldest being 23 years and 11 months. The youngest was a *dek jai* of 13 years and nine months at Suan Kularb, closely followed by one of 13 years and 11 months at Pradumagonga School.

The Bangkok Times, 21 January 1926, p. 5

I had noticed in *Madhayom* Seven a cheery faced boy who would often be sound asleep and incapable of remaining awake for long. I was surprised to learn from his form master that he was actually the brightest boy in the class. He was obviously highly intelligent and I decided to probe a bit. I found that he was of very humble origin and that his parents operated a boat which ferried people across the river to Dhonburi. Business was brisk last thing at night and the lad was kept up until the early hours of the morning, collecting fares and such like. His father could not afford to employ an assistant. Churchill and I got together and decided to put up the money for an assistant if the boy could be allowed to sleep at nights. It did not amount to a great deal and it seemed worthwhile. Our gesture proved unnecessary. When the parents learned of their son's high promise, he was allowed to sleep. Nai Porn, or to give him his full name, Nai Porn Srijamorn, proved more than highly intelligent. He was brilliant, especially at mathematics. We took him out of the classroom and installed him in our own room where he shared my desk. The fairy tale came true, of course. He won a King's Scholarship, the first ever to come to Pradumaganga. It was the sort of thing which makes the teaching profession worthwhile. Later it gave me quite a thrill to hear from my fiancée that he had taken her out to tea in London and to hear from my parents of his visit to them in Torquay. After six years in England, he returned to Siam to become, later on, the head of all its electricity undertakings.[5]

---

5 Dr Porn Srijamorn PhD, A.G.C.I., D.I.C. (London) also became a special lecturer at Chulalongkorn University in the early 1950s.

Health and Hygiene

On 30 May 1914, "the first Red Cross hospital in Siam was opened with all due ceremony by His Majesty King Rama VI". It was named The King Chulalongkorn Memorial Hospital.

The inaugural address made by the Minister of War clearly stated the object of the Hospital:

"TO EXAMINE AND TREAT ALL SUFFERERS REGARDLESS OF RACIAL DIFFERENCES."

There are now 323 beds, 243 of which have been endowed at from 3,000 to 6,000 per bed. To the Siamese people modern medicine had never been popular. They had always a fear of being "cut up" or something done to them against their will while in hospital at all. But the result of the treatment was so far superior to the old Siamese method that people began to seek admittance, and it needed a great exertion on the part of the Red Cross Society to advertise for funds necessary to the rapid extension of the wards. Perhaps in no other country has the response been so well given, and it stands to-day a credit to the Nation that the Hospital shows up as it does, one of the finest and most up-to-date in the Far East.

Siam: General and Medical Features (1930), pp. 311-314

'The Out-patient Department of the Chulalongkorn Hospital.' From *Siam: General and Medical Features* (1930).

The Hospital General St. Louis is conducted by the Sisters of St. Paul de Chartres, under the control of the French Catholic Mission. A French physician, Dr. Poix, who is also physician to the Siamese Court, is attached to this hospital. Any physician may, however, send his patients to the hospital and attend them there. The hospital is situated in a cool and healthy part of the suburbs. The principal buildings are two stories in height. They are surrounded by deep verandas. The wards are small. There is a separate building for children who are frequently left at the hospital by their parents. The ground floor of the main building is devoted to out-patient service and consultation room. The operation and sterilizing rooms are in a wing of the main building. The total number of beds is 30.

Hospital Management, November 1922, p. 51

We regret to announce the death of Mr. August Baer, which occurred at the St. Louis Hospital last night about midnight. Mr. Baer was a native of Horgen in Switzerland, and was for several years with the Swiss firm of Volkart Brothers of Winterthur, serving them in England and at Karachi. Some seven years ago he came to Bangkok for Messrs. Berli and Co. Mr. Baer had been in ill-health for some time and more recently it was ascertained he was suffering from consumption. In September he went to Koh Lak for a change, but returned considerably worse, and since then he had been very ill. In the course of this week he was removed to the St. Louis Hospital and died as stated above. Mr. Baer planned to go home, but his strength failed so rapidly that the voyage was out of the question. Of a quiet disposition, he had many friends, who will learn of his death at the early age of 38 with regret. The funeral takes place to-morrow morning at the Protestant Cemetery at 8 o'clock.[1]

The Bangkok Times, 24 November 1917, p. 4

The Bangkok Nursing Home, which is situated near the Protestant Church, in the healthiest part of Bangkok, is supported by all the large firms, irrespective of nationality. It is in charge of a matron and three

---

1 Baer's grave is in Block F.

European nurses, and, there being no resident physician, the patients are attended by their respective medical advisers.

Twentieth Century Impressions of Siam (1908), p. 128

The Bangkok Nursing Home as an example of a comfortable and a successfully maintained home, primarily for members of the foreign community, is worthy of interest. In its early years its life was rather precarious and, being entirely dependent upon the voluntary contributions of residents, at times it has been in danger of expiring. As it now stands the Home consists of a new block, containing matron's office, lounge, stores, etc. on the ground floor, with above private wards for six patients, each having a separate verandah, four bathrooms, two specimen and wash up rooms. Pantry with food safe, bedding store room, and duty room. Connected with this wing by passages are an operating block, consisting of Theatre, Sterilizing room, Anaesthetic room, and X-ray room, and a maternity block of three private wards, complete with bathrooms. In return for their contributions, subscribers are entitled to the use of a room with board and nursing.

Siam: General and Medical Features (1930), pp. 325-327

The death has been announced of Dr. Reynold A. Spaeth which took place on June 26 at the Bangkok Nursing Home. Dr. Spaeth's death is keenly felt by his colleagues working under him under the Rockefeller Foundation. Much sympathy is felt with Mrs. Spaeth in her loss. Their only son, aged eleven, recently returned to the States under the care of Dr. Earle Blunt, but Mrs. Spaeth and her young daughter are in Bangkok. Dr. Spaeth was only 38.[2]

Singapore Free Press, 11 July 1925, p. 9

In October he moved his family to Bangkok. He was very happy there; perhaps more happy than he had been anywhere before. He liked the place and the climate. He made friends there, as he always did readily. He felt that the opportunities for research were exceptional and that everything was coming his way at last. During the spring he made three expeditions

---

2 Dr Reynold A. (Albrecht) Spaeth (1886-1925) was buried in the Protestant Cemetery.

into the jungle for the purpose of collecting material for his studies. On all these trips he suffered some hardships – was in fact lost in the jungle without food for thirty hours on one occasion – but felt no ill effects which he could not, in his vigorous way, disregard. Apparently his energy and self-confidence led him to neglect the necessary safeguards of his health and he had become worn down by his activities more than he realized. In June, while in the midst of preparing a report on his research work, he became ill. Septicemia, resulting from the extension of an infection contracted on his first jungle expedition, had developed and in two weeks he was dead. So ended the scientific career of Reynold Spaeth, before the promise of his early years could be fulfilled.

ALFRED C. REDFIELD
Science, 23 October 1925, p. 365

Bangkok Nursing Home: Charges (1926) ...

Usual Charge – Subscriber 6 Ticals 6. – per diem Non-Subscriber Ticals 20. – per diem Minimum Subscription – Tcs. 60 per annum for individuals. Tcs. 80 per annum for families.

Or minimum monthly payment of Tcs. 5, or Tcs. 7, respectively. For further particulars apply to Mr. C. S. Richardson, Hon Secretary, or H. Forrest, Hon. Treasurer.

Advertisement in The Bangkok Times, January 1926

DR. LI WAI FUN, M.D.
Siang Kong, Bangkok.
GRADUATE OF THE HACKETT MEDICAL COLLEGE.
Expert in Midwifery, Diagnosis, Treatment, Injection and Operation. Can be consulted at any hour of the day, either at the above office, or the patient's house.[3]
Siam from Ancient to Present Times (1926)

---

3 The Hackett Medical College for Women was founded by Dr Mary H. Fulton, a Presbyterian missionary, in Canton (Guangzhou) in 1902.

Betel-nut chewing, with its invariable concomitants of lime and a green leaf, so stains the teeth and lips that it is a disgusting habit to a foreigner, but the dark-red color is highly prized by the Siamese, and physicians told me that the habit is not so deleterious to health as the tobacco habit in America.

Speer, Report (1916), p. 6

The most striking thing to a stranger in Bangkok is the chewing habit of the people and their black teeth. The Siamese have turned ruminants and are always moving their jaws and expectorating the resultant red fluid of the chewed betel. What internal injury to the digestive organs is caused by the swallowing of lime and tannic acid in such large quantities is not known, but the blackening of the teeth and mouth has robbed the belles of Siam – and some of them are extremely pretty – of the most kissable mouths in the world, and reduced courting to a tame affair of making glad-eyes and singing songs. Kissing is unknown in Siam and no wonder.

Pasqual, A Trip: Through Siam (1925), p. 57

Lucie Chandler heard that the popularity of betel-chewing had begun to decline around 1910…

They told us in Bangkok that the Coronation of the present King, bringing its influx of foreigners, wrought consternation in the land of betel-nut chewers, and an importation of American dentists was the result. The nut is the fruit of the betel palm and is as popular in Siam as chewing gum is supposed to be in America.

Travel, November 1916, p. 27

In fact, Dr George McFarland had opened the "first American dental office" in Siam in 1891. As his wife explained, "he introduced black false teeth, because in those days no self-respecting Thai had white teeth. All chewed betelnut and its four accessories".[4]

In November 1891, I opened a private dental office at Bak Klong Dalat where I had taken up residence with my parents. Of course there were the variety of dentists who "pull teeth while you wait" but I was the first

---

4 McFarland: Our Garden Was So Fair, p. 43.

American dentist. As soon as buildings were finished I moved my office to Sri Kak Pbya Sri where I kept office hours from 3.00 p.m. onward, until the year 1916 when I gave up my dental work in the pressure of other duties. Many aches were relieved and my own meagre salary was supplemented. I introduced ebony-black false teeth which were exceedingly popular in those days. My practice was extensive and often took me into the palace where the King and palace ladies called me. Dentistry was not so far advanced in those days and it was possible to carry my equipment with me – all but my dental chair. Many a time as I worked over some royal patient comfortably seated on the floor I thought longingly of the empty dental chair in my office.

McFarland, Reminiscences (1936), p. 11

AMERICAN DENTISTRY
G. B. McFarland, M.D., D.D.S.
New Road Circus.
CITY.
All descriptions of fillings, plates and surgical dentistry
on latest approved methods.
THE ONLY DENTAL OFFICE IN BANGKOK WHERE
GAS IS ADMINISTERED
DR. McFARLAND finds it necessary to point out that all appointments must be punctually kept, failing which specific charges will be made for time wasted.

Advertisement in Bangkok Directory (1894)

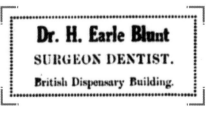

Advertisement in *The Bangkok Times*, February 1925.[5]

---

5   For many years, Blunt's advertisements appeared in The Bangkok Times almost daily.

Health and Hygiene

R. OMODA
First Class Hairdresser. Coiffeur Japonais.
(Corner of Bush Lane.)
Begs to inform the public and foreign residents generally, that he has engaged a competent new assistant who speaks French, so that the owner of this saloon is now able fully to meet the requirements of his patrons, and also to welcome the French community as well as the English speaking residents.

Advertisement in The Bangkok Times, February 1909

R. OMODA. INTERNATIONAL TOILET SALOON.
Ladies' hair bobbed in three styles. Four professional expert assistants.[6]
Customers can now be attended at their private residences at the following charges.
Electrical massage and hand shampoo Tcs. 8. Men's haircutting and shaving Tcs. 3.
Efficiency and Prompt Service Guaranteed.

Advertisement in The Bangkok Times, February 1927

Mrs. M. Pecchioni Beauty Specialist
Her Speciality is Permanent Waving
Agents for Elizabeth Arden's Venetian Toilet Preparations
638, Suriwongse Road.[7]

Advertisement in The Bangkok Times, January 1926

Use Tricofilina. – The only remedy against hair falling out. To be had at Tapan Lek Dispensary, Kiam Hoa Heng & Co., G. Bovo & Co. Sole Agents, BANGKOK TOILET CLUB.

Advertisement in The Bangkok Times, February 1909

---

6 Two years later, Omoda was claiming to have six expert assistants. Before the Great War, he also sold "Japanese bricks and tiles" made in Bangkok.

7 Mrs Pecchioni was presumably the wife of M. Pecchioni, a foreman with Siamese State Railways.

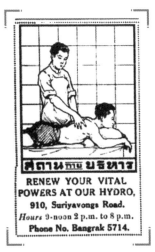

Advertisement in *The Bangkok Times*, September 1931.

MISS J. M. NEWLANDS
(Diploma of the Institute of Beauty [Glasgow])
Is now in attendance at
THE LADIES' HAIRDRESSING
AND BEAUTY SALON
AT THE MASSAGE AND
ELECTRICAL CENTRE
910, SURAWONGSE ROAD,
Where appointments can be made for
the highest service in
Both hairdressing and beauty treatment,
at moderate fees.
Hours: 8 a.m. to noon. 2 p.m. to 4 p.m.
Saturdays 8 a.m. to noon.
Telephone Bangrak 5714.
Advertisement in The Bangkok Times, August 1929

Dispensaries

The British Dispensary, situated in the New Road, right in the heart of the European quarter of the city, cannot fail to attract the notice of the visitor to Bangkok. It is an up-to-date establishment with a large and varied stock of such goods as are naturally to be found in the shops of high-class

The British Dispensary, from *Twentieth Century Impressions of Siam* (1908).

J. J. McBeth in 1908.[8]

chemists and druggists, while, in addition, there is a well-arranged department devoted specially to the sale of cameras and photographic supplies. Besides its large European connection the house does a considerable trade with the natives, among whom it has a very high reputation, and furnishes a good proportion of the drugs, medicines, and other commodities of a like nature to the planters and residents in the interior of Siam.

The dispensary was established some twenty years ago by the late Dr. Gowan, Physician to his Majesty the King, and subsequently passed into the hands of Dr. T. Hayward Hays, the chief medical officer to the Royal Siamese Navy and the medical officer to the Government Railway Department. Shortly after Dr. Hays became the proprietor of the undertaking, a branch, which is still carrying on a flourishing trade, was established in Bangkok city proper. In 1906 Dr. Hays disposed of his interests in the firm to Mr. McBeth, who had been associated with him in the business since 1898. Mr. McBeth is assisted now by Mr. Davies, a qualified chemist, who has had many years' English and Continental experience.

Twentieth Century Impressions of Siam (1908), p. 275

An action brought by Dr. Heyward Hays against Mr. J. J. McBeth was begun in the International Court this morning. Plaintiff claimed Tcs. 50,000 as the purchase price of the British Dispensary. Dr. Hays said that before the contract of June 30th 1906 the defendant had been engaged by him for about five years as assistant. It was agreed defendant should purchase the Dispensary for Tcs. 75,000. He paid the sum of Tcs. 19,529. The balance was to be paid off by defendant in five years. In 1911 he wrote a chit asking for an extension of one year in which to pay. Eventually a new contract was made on August 19th, 1912. Defendant broke the contract.

---

8 John James McBeth (1878-1940).

From witness's knowledge of the business defendant could undoubtedly have paid all the money out of the profits of the business. Witness knew defendant had invested the money in other concerns.

The Bangkok Times, 25 February 1914, p. 5

The decision was in favour of the plaintiff. The judgment of the Court is that the money paid into the court by the defence be paid to the plaintiff and that the defendant immediately pay to the plaintiff the balance of the money due, together with acquired interest. The defendant to pay court fees and counsel's fee Tcs. 1,000.

The Bangkok Times, 28 February 1914, p. 5

Advertisement in *The Bangkok Times*, February 1918.

Trade-Marks Applied for.
Design of a snake pierced by an arrow: for medicinal chemicals (3). By J. J. McBeth, The British Dispensary, New Road, Bangkok, Siam.

The Chemist and Druggist, 31 December 1910, p. 61

"ST. LUKE": for medicinal chemicals (3). By J. J. McBeth, The British Dispensary, New Road, Bangkok, Siam.[9]

The Chemist and Druggist, 29 April 1911, p. 113

"SEKTOLENE": for insect repelling preparations (3). By J. J. McBeth, The British Dispensary, New Road, Bangkok, Siam.

The Chemist and Druggist, 5 April 1924, p. 501

---

9 "St. Luke's Fly Spray (Double Strength)" was later introduced in at Tcs. 1.25 for a 24 ounce bottle. McBeth emphasised that it did "NOT cause headaches" (advertisement in *The Bangkok Times*, October 1930).

Advertisement in *The Bangkok Times*, March 1926. Presumably "Macbeth's Sketolene" was a different product from J. J. McBeth's Sektolene.[10]

EYE SIGHT
Tested by the Latest Methods
Our Optical Department is in charge of a qualified optician
and we can fill all requirements.[11]
British Dispensary,
(Established over 25 years).
Advertisement in The Bangkok Times, December 1919

FOUR MORE REASONS WHY
The British Dispensary
IS THE PRESCRIPTION PHARMACY
(1) The Pharmacy Is Open From 7.30 a.m. Until 6 p.m.
Without Interruption. Except Sundays
(2) All Night Service for Prescriptions.
(3) All Drug Buying from Standard Houses
(4) Constant Telegraphic Singapore Supply for Unusual Drugs.
Advertisement in The Bangkok Times, January 1926

---

10 According to an advertisement in *The Commercial Directory for Siam* (1939), Whiteaway Laidlaw & Co, were then the "sole distributors for Macbeth's Sektonline [sic] the original and only real preventive of mosquito bites. Tcs. 1.75 each".

11 The reference is to A. H. Hale.

A talk on 20 years of his residence in Siam was given before the Bath branch of the Pharmaceutical Society by Mr. A. H. Hale, M.P.S., Bath, at the Information Bureau on Wednesday. Mr Hale went to Siam in 1918 to join the staff of the British Dispensary in Bangkok, and returned to this country in 1937. He said he was surprised that the British Dispensary was quite a modern ferro-concrete building, larger than any pharmacy in Bath. The prescriptions had to be copied in Chinese, Siamese and Malay. His first job was to superintend the making of 1,000 elephant tonic pills about the size of golf balls, and containing four grains of arsenic and a drachm of powdered nux vomica.

Bath Chronicle and Weekly Gazette, 16 February 1946, p. 10

In an article recalling his years in Siam, A. H. Hale describes pharmacies in Bangkok.

What strikes the visitor in the New Road, the main thoroughfare, is the number of shops apparently Chinese-owned. Pharmacies are well to the fore and are nearly all called dispensaries. Some years ago there were British, French, German and Japanese as well as Chinese and Siamese in this thoroughfare. In one stretch the writer once counted no fewer than fourteen dispensaries in less than a mile all dealing in what one might term western medicine. In the same stretch there were a number of Chinese shops dealing in purely Chinese medicine and a few shops selling fresh plants, roots, etc., for use as medicine. Many of these dispensaries have quite large and imposing premises and it is amazing the variety of drugs and medicines obtainable in these pharmacies.

The Chemist and Druggist, 15 March 1941, p. 170

Mr. A. H. Hale, M.P.S., F.B.O.A., F.S.M.C., who is in charge of the Department of Pharmacy, Chulalongkorn University, and also head pharmacist of the Siriraj Hospital, Bangkok, served his apprenticeship with Mr. F. Moss, Kingswood, Bristol. After experience in London and passing the optical examinations, he proceeded in 1918 to Siam for the British Dispensary, Bangkok. In 1921 Mr. Hale joined the Faculty of Arts and Sciences of the Chulalongkorn University as lecturer in materia medica and pharmacy to the medical students. In 1923 he was placed in charge of the newly-formed School of Pharmacy and in 1927 became head pharmacist of the Siriraj Hospital, Bangkok. (The School of Pharmacy, which was made into an independent department in 1936, works in conjunction with the Siriraj Hospital.) Mr. Hale is one of the founders of the Pharmaceutical Society of Siam and its first vice-president.

The Chemist and Druggist, 26 June 1937, p. 756

"Group photograph, second annual meeting of the Siamese Pharmaceutical Society, the president (since deceased) is seated, the author standing behind" (*The Chemist and Druggist*, 15 March 1941, p. 168).

DO YOU NEED GLASSES?

It is possible you can see well yet be seriously straining your eyes. You cannot tell yourself. Only a scientific test, such as we use, will decide this. I shall be pleased to test your sight. Under no circumstances are glasses recommended unless absolutely necessary. A. H. Hale. M.P.S., D.B.O.A, Ophthalmic Optician, over The Jawarad Co. Ltd., 239 New Road. Opposite Chartered Bank.[12]

Advertisement in The Bangkok Times, 30 September 1922, p. 3

Advertisement in Seidenfaden, *Guide* (1927). The Jawarad Company Limited, which was founded in 1911 and is still in existence, were "General Merchants, druggists and opticians, etc.".

308   In Bangkok

Wonderful Cures

"Dr. Williams' Pink Pills for Pale People" was an American patent medicine which was marketed heavily through the foreign-language press in the Far East. The advertisements often took the form of lengthy testimonials by real people which appeared word for word in different newspapers in the region. Many Bangkok residents had obtained the pills from the British Dispensary.

Mr. P. N. Massang, the gentleman whose portrait is here shown, is over 60 years of age, and is well-known and respected in Bangkok, Siam, where he resides.[13] In his youth he travelled much. "It was whilst living in the island of Labuan some thirteen years ago that I first contracted Beri-beri," said Mr. Massang, when relating the remarkable circumstances here recorded. "Two months after my arrival in Labuan," he continued, "I felt numbness in both my legs. When I had been in the hospital two and a half months the doctors told me that if I stopped there for years I could never get cured, and so they discharged me as incurable. Then, thinking my end was near, I sailed for Bangkok to spend my last days among my relations. One day a nephew of mine suggested that I should try Dr. Williams' Pink Pills for the Pale People, he having heard that these Pills had cured cases similar to mine. I bought a bottle of the Pills at the British Dispensary here in Bangkok, and started taking them, carefully following the directions. The first symptom of benefit I noticed was that my bowels began to act regularly. I went on with the Pills, feeling better and better every day. By the time I had finished eight bottles of Williams' Pink Pills I was completely cured."

---

12 In another advertisement in the same period, Hale promoted "Kyptok Invisible Fused Bifocal Lenses".

13 P. N. Massang is listed in the 1889 *Directory & Chronicle* as a "tidewaiter" for the Customs in Bangkok. Apparently, he had relatives living in Penang. The portrait is "from a photo by the Charoen Krung Studio, Bangkok, Siam".

Dr. Williams' Pink Pills for Pale People are obtainable at most shops where medicines are sold, and also direct from the Dr. Williams' Medicine Co., Singapore, who send 6 bottles for $8 or 1 bottle for $1.50, post free.
Overland China Mail, 22 January 1907, p. 16

Charles Cowan is listed in the Bangkok Directory of 1913 as a "Share Broker & Commission Agent" of New Road, Bangkok (and also "Manager, The Auctioneering Mart").[14] *He died in Bangkok in 1934, aged 65, and was buried in the Protestant Cemetery.*

LIKE RED-HOT NEEDLES.

"For about fifteen years I suffered agonies with sciatica, said Mr. Charles Cowan of New Road, Bangkok, Siam. During that time I consulted doctors and took their medicine, but these proved of little use. Finally on a friend's advice I tried Dr. Williams' Pink Pills, and it was with much surprise and delight that after a few bottles I was feeling great relief. I continued taking Dr. Williams' Pink Pills and as I did so my health steadily improved, the pains decreased, my appetite returned, I began to sleep well at night. Since my wonderful cure three years ago", concluded Mr. Cowan, who it may be mentioned carries on business as a broker in Bangkok, "I have recommended Dr. Williams' Pink Pills to many of my friends".
North China Herald, 7 January 1910, p. 54

---

14 The text here is derived from the *North China Herald* of Shanghai. The illustrations of Cowan are from there and also from a Dutch-language newspaper published in Batavia in 1908. Cowan's story also appeared in the Singapore press.

Death of Mr. Charles Cowan. He had been ill a long time, first as an inmate of the Military Hospital at Phya Thai, later being removed to the Chulalongkorn Hospital. The Hospital management did much to make his latter days comfortable, and though Christmas is not a festival officially observed in that institution, its occurrence was not forgotten in his case.
The Straits Times, 19 February 1934, p. 12

In September 1915, advertisements began to appear in The Bangkok Times on behalf of a "Dr. K. S. Aiyar".

DR. K. S. Aiyar, B.A., M.B., C.M., D.P.H. (Lond.)
Specialist in Midwifery and. in Eye Diseases. Expert in lunacy, leprosy, paralysis, consumption, etc. Assistant G. J. Williams.[15] Consultation at Si-Phya Road, Bangkok.
20 August 1915, p. 4

Dr. Aiyar's Ophthalmic Hospital.
SI-PHYA ROAD (Late Residence of Dr. Poix) BANGKOK.[16]
Hospital and consulting hours 7 to 10 a.m. and 4 to 5 30 p.m.
POOR PATIENTS WILL BE TREATED FREE OF CHARGE, PARTICULARLY LEPERS, ETC.
Urgent cases will be attended to at all times. Beds for the in-patients are provided, with all home comforts, at a very reasonable charge.
23 September 1915, p. 5; 1 October 1915, p. 2

"Dr." Aiyar has been arrested by the police.
11 October 1915, p. 4

Dr. Aiyar has resumed practice in Bangkok.
13 October 1915, p. 4

A rather curious situation has arisen in Bangkok, a city where rather curious situations are not altogether rare. A few months ago there came to

---

15 Williams was the manager of Apothecaries Hall, a pharmacy.
16 Dr Poix: Alphonse Poix of St Louis Hospital, formerly a court physician.

the capital of Siam – where by the way there is no registration of medical practitioners – an Indian who called himself Dr. Aiyar and displayed on his card quite an imposing array of qualifications. He set up in practice and, claiming to perform the most wonderful cures, obtained extremely large fees from quite a number of patients. Then he suddenly vanished and the Bangkok papers were full of his disappearance. By this time the police had begun to take an interest in him and managing to apprehend him up-country locked him in gaol. But it does not seem he had done anything to bring him within the clutches of the law so he was released, breathing threats of vengeance and invoking the protection of the German Minister for he claims that, although he is an Indian born and educated in India, he was naturalised in Germany and is a subject of the Kaiser, who in the opinion of most Englishmen in Bangkok, is heartily welcome to such a liege.

Straits Echo, 22 October 1915, p. 5

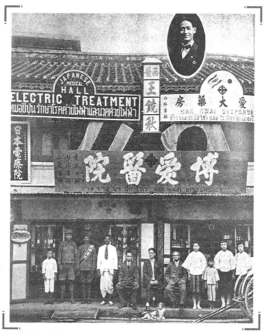

The Hak Kwai Dispensary with its Japanese Medical Hall Electric Treatment, from *Siam from Ancient to Present Times* (1926).

Sports and Games

The foreign resident in Siam has to make his own amusements and as a general thing succeeds pretty well. As in all places in the tropics he usually has plenty of leisure at his disposal, the climate is distinctly against violent out-door exercise except in the early mornings and evenings. Despite these drawbacks, however, the Bangkok *farang* generally manages to get plenty of recreation. Whether it be tennis or shooting, racing or bridge he goes into it with plenty of vim.

Antonio, Guide (1904), p. 23

Hunting is in great favor, for game can be found near Bangkok, and at not a remote distance lurk the rhinoceros, buffalo, tiger, leopard, deer, antelope, hare, and crocodile. Elephants abound, but may not be shot.

Peck, Travels in the Far East (1909), pp. 198

If variety is wanted, and a day's shooting longed for to make a break in sight-seeing, the visitor should go to Sala Ya (Kins. 19) on the Southern Line or Klong Rangsit on the Northern Line. These are two of Bangkok's best snipe shooting grounds and are famous for bags obtained by individual guns. Records of fifty and sixty couple are common and a good shot will always do well in the season.

Seidenfaden, Guide (1932), p. 53

Thirty sportsmen were counted on the Petriu train yesterday. The majority were Siamese, drawn from all ranks of society. It would appear from this that they no longer regard shooting as a somewhat barbarous pastime. A few were after snipe, and one man's efforts were rewarded with 31 couple of these toothsome, and just now none too plentiful morsels. Birds were extraordinarily wild.

The Bangkok Times, 18 January 1926, p. 4

    There's no getting away from a Greener Gun.
    GREENER GUNS FOR DUCK SHOOTING.

> Noted for Hard Hitting. For Killing. Agents for Siam
> The British Dispensary, New Road, Bangkok.
>> *Advertisement in The Bangkok Times, September 1922*

Tastes, opinions, and constitutions of course vary, and every old hand at shooting in Bangkok as elsewhere has his own ideas, evolved by experiment, and enhanced to him in value by habit. But the tyro often turns out in some kit which is unsuitable and likely to cause discomfort, if nothing worse. The following will be found as suitable and serviceable for the work in hand as any other.

1. Comfortable well-ventilated light sun-hat lined with red.
2. Ordinary thin red vest (Aërtex cellular.)
3. Short wide khaki knickers, hanging below the knee.
4. Canvas leggings.
5. Woollen socks.
6. Khaki shooting-coat.

Forty, Bangkok (1929), pp. 93-94

Games, which are held in such high honor in Siam, form part of those Oceanic customs that are perhaps the last reminiscence on earth of a terrestrial paradise. Siamese football, called *takro*, is played without the use of the hands, like soccer. The players send the ball forward with their heads or backward with their feet, and their agility is breath-taking. There are times when the ball never touches the ground at all. Cock-fighting has gone out of fashion. Great fights between wild beasts are no longer to be seen. Quail duels, in which each seeks to tear out the other's tongue, are foresters' pleasures. Combats of crickets that have been stimulated by aphrodisiacs are Chinese. But there is one sport of which I am very fond: it is fish-fighting.

Morand, Nothing but the Earth (1927), pp. 140-141

On the eve of our departure, a member of "The Chummery" volunteered to show us the night life of Bangkok. It was late by the time we had piled ourselves into a two-horse "gharry," and were driving through the crowded bazaar. We stopped at a booth in the Sampeng quarter to watch an exhibition of fighting fish. These small creatures when swimming about in their own glass bowl were not in any way remarkable. But when a bowl containing another fish was placed alongside, an amazing transformation occurred. Crests, bristles, spikes and fins that had previously been invisible rose on end, and the small fish had doubled in size and was positively pulsating with pugnacity as he bumped against the side of the bowl in an effort to get at his hated rival. And when the two little furies were put into the same tank together, there ensued a fight to the death, on the result of which the native audience wagered freely.

Williams, Green Prison (1941), p. 29

Siamese fighting fish are well known. They are most beautiful little creatures, with long, lacy fins, and their scales show all the colours of a sunset sky. Their pugnacity is remarkable; not infrequently both combatants succumb to their injuries, their fins being so torn that they cannot swim. A great deal of money is staked on fish fights, but to Europeans they are rather slow and unexciting performances. Sometimes the two fishes will hold onto one another's mouths for about an hour; the spectators wait in rapt attention, but I must admit that I long to poke the performers with a stick to make them do something more lively. I have often felt the same way at a cricket match.

Wood, Land of Smiles (1935), pp. 85-86

A Portuguese conducted me stealthily to an abode of sin in the suburbs. I say abode of sin because cock-fighting is strictly forbidden and this was a cock-pit, a big shed of palm and bamboo. In the centre was the pit, surrounded by tiers of raised benches. In a bamboo cage an old native squatted, staring at rows of glass jam jars. Other natives sat on benches, also crystal-gazing. War-worn game-cocks, "bloody but unbowed," crowed defiance at each other from rattan coops. But there was no cock-fighting that afternoon. The proprietor of this sanguinary establishment, a plump, benign Malay, simply clad in a sarong and steel spectacles, came forward murmuring apologies. There had been some trouble about stake money, so they were matching fish instead.

Garstin, The Dragon and the Lotus (1928), pp. 308-309

There is the game known amongst the Malays as "main raga," which consists of keeping a ball made of wicker-work in the air as long as possible. To do so for any length of time is an extremely difficult matter, i.e., without letting the ball fall to the ground: yet it is on record that four players in Siam once kept the ball in the air for 55 minutes – an absolutely wonderful performance, as all athletes will admit.

Macmillan, Seaports of the Far East (1925), p. 490

The undersigned, chief teacher of the Art of Japanese "Jujitsu", undertakes to give daily lessons in Jujitsu to ladies, gentlemen and boys, a complete course in 6 months. For further information please apply to F. Watanabe, No. 199 Si Phya Road.

Advertisement in The Bangkok Times, July 1916

The Football Boom

The football "boom" is still continuing in Bangkok, and seems likely to continue. A team representing Siam has twice defeated the Royal Bangkok Sports Club and also the Scots of Bangkok. The Siamese undoubtedly play an excellent, if strenuous, game. They have any amount of speed, and are wonderfully nimble on their feet.

London & China Telegraph, 14 February 1916, p. 4

His Majesty, the present King, introduced Association football on his return from Europe, and the Siamese have already shown by their speed and "nippy-ness" their very considerable aptitude for the game: in fact, a Soccer league already exists.

Macmillan, Seaports of the Far East (1925), p. 489

From an advertisement in *Echo de l'Assomption*, March 1933.

It was not very long before I was mixed up in school football, and "mixed up" are the right words. Inter-school rivalry was bitter and, I am sorry to say, was over encouraged by the staff, including the Europeans. The winning of a match

316   In Bangkok

was given an absurd prestige value. When it came to football, Debsirindr hated the guts of Suan Kularb and both hated even more the guts of the French Roman Catholic Colleges of Assumption and St. Gabriel and the American Christian College. Buddhists might tolerate the free practice of all religions but their toleration did not extend to the winning of football matches. Play was reasonably clean but, all the same, it could be rough. In an important league match I sent a boy off the field. Pandemonium broke out. The spectators invaded the pitch and me in particular. A posse of Siamese police tore to my aid and I was given police protection most of the way home.

Exell, Siamese Tapestry (1963), pp. 43-46

The following team will represent the Sports Club versus the Navy in the match to be played on Wednesday the 2nd instant at Suan Kularb ground commencing at 4:0 p.m. sharp: – Lowden, Lambert, Knight, Williams, McKenzie, Sparrow, Robins, Klingenfuss, Exell, Malcolm and Jamison. Club colours will be worn, and players are particularly requested to be on the ground sharp on time.

The Bangkok Times, 1 February 1927, p. 5

Kite-Flying

Mr. H. G. Q. Wales,[1] formerly of the teaching staff of the Vajiravudh College, writes in *The Field* as follows: – Kite-flying is now a very popular sport for adults. Motorists often take kites with them into the country to indulge in altitude competitions, and a club is being formed to foster the interests of the sport.

In the East the sport has achieved a dignity undreamed of in the West, and the art of manufacture is far in advance of anything known in this country. Kite-flying is the national pastime in Siam; and although in recent years it has suffered a great deal from the introduction of European football, it still holds first place in the hearts of the majority of Siamese people.

The Bangkok Times, 13 February 1929, p. 5

---

1 Horace Geoffrey Quaritch Wales (1900-1981), author of Siamese State Ceremonies (1931).

"National Kite Flying Pastime on the Pramane Ground, Bangkok". From *Siam from Ancient to Present Times* (1926). The "kites" seem to have been etched on the photographic plate.

Kite-fighting is so popular that the southwest wind is called "Lom Wow," or "The kite-flying wind." The Pramane Ground, close to the Palace, is the usual battle-field, but at the time I was there the late king's funeral pyre was being erected on the Pramane and the kite-flyers had shifted outside the city limits, whither, one blustering Sunday, I followed them. There were six pairs of kites in the air, big and little; to each Goliath a David. The small kites were flown by two men only. The big kites had a whole host of attendants: the owner who directed its flight, a heavy-weight who sat on the fair-lead to keep it down, and lastly a pack of men and boys who, were the kite threatened, laid hold of the string and fled, the frantic owner hurling abuse (and his hat) at them.

On the 1914 city map, Sanam Luang/Pramane Ground is marked as the "Kite-Flying Oval".

My Portuguese cicerone got so excited as to become inarticulate in three languages and it was impossible to follow his rendering of the rules, but as far as I could understand the big kite's object was to entangle the little chap and drag it home by sheer weight, while that of the

318 In Bangkok

smaller was to rip up or cut off the bigger. However that may be, it was a pretty sight, the shining white specks manœuvring and swooping, fighting like eagles for the supremacy of the blue.

Garstin, *The Dragon and the Lotus* (1928), p. 308

Nothing could be more perfectly set than kite-flying on the immense *Phra Meru*, look down its length from the Old Palace, a wonderful background of holden spire glittering in the evening sun. Day after day in the windy season, all Bangkok assembles to see kites flown, and to back the favourites. In the shade of the wide avenue, which runs down the west side of the ground, are whole families in hundreds of cars. Under the double row of tamarinds, which surround the great grassed space, are endless little refreshment stalls of sweets, curries, seeds and what not. The sweets are on trays, the curries are cooking in small braziers, and each has its group of patrons. On the ground itself is a huge multitude drawn from every class. Every kind of dress may be seen, and the gayest of colours, red predominating as always in the tropics, though here the yellow of monkish draperies, billowing in the strong breeze, is a keen rival. The game that the crowd has come to see consists in fouling your adversary's flight, or in bringing him or her down, for it is a war of the sexes.

Wheatcroft, *Siam and Cambodia* (1928), pp. 186-189

Rachel Wheatcroft, 'Kite Flying on the Phra Meru', from *Siam and Cambodia* (1928).

Sports and Games 319

Wongkit's Dream

We were next taken to see some Siamese boxing, a traditional sport which allows the use of the feet. There is a lot of posturing and dancing as the combatants circle round each other. Their fists are thinly bound round with cloth, and we expect to see some bloodshed. But we are not prepared for the astonishing agility with which one of them leaps high in the air and delivers an upper-cut to the jaw with his left foot! It seems to be the etiquette that an exchange of blows should be followed by more posturing and dancing. A white-coated official is refereeing at the ringside, and the end of each short round is proclaimed by a gong. One lad's face is now bleeding freely and he tries to keep out of reach. His opponent is shortly pronounced the victor on points, and signalises his triumph by leaping in the air and dancing all round the ring, to the "chaiyohs" (hurrahs) of his supporters.

Williams, Green Prison (1941), pp. 29-230

In Siamese boxing the combatants can do almost anything but bite each other. Hitting in holds, hitting with the flat of the hand, using the

knee or elbow, butting with the head, are all allowed, and even straight-out kicking. Up till recently no padded gloves were used, but now this is necessary, besides the binding of the fists. Imagine oneself in a ringside seat, costing two ticals (about 3s. d.). The "ring" is the same as in Europe. Enter the combatants, stripped except for shorts and an abdominal protector. On their heads is a rope charm, blessed by the gods to give victory. Round the right or left arm are green or red ribbons, a further charm against defeat.

Bong! No bell is used, just an ordinary native drum. The timekeeper is eyeing his watch. The seconds are out, and the two judges on either side of the ring settle with paper and pencil; on the fourth side sits a very old ex-champion boxer, who gives his casting vote if the two judges disagree. Meanwhile a soft swirl of native music is heard, and the combatants are on their knees in the ring kow-towing to some unknown deity who watches over boxers. What happens next is difficult to see from one side of the ring, but the frenzied skirl of the music indicates that the battle rages. Arms are flying, legs kicking in all directions, and knees seeking vulnerable spots. The music has now reached a terrible pitch, but is nearly drowned by the cries of spectators.

Illustrated London News, 16 August 1930, p. 12

I'm going to the fights this afternoon, dad, because Wongkit is fighting.

Wongkit is a boy from the northern hills who is so strong that men even in Bangkok heard about him. They heard that in the games he could throw the teak log farther than any other. Thinking that he might become a champion boxer, they sent for him. Six weeks ago he arrived in Bangkok, bringing his old father.

I first heard about Wongkit from Tom, my guide. "He will make a great boxer," Tom said, "greater than any we have seen." Then he cautioned me not to speak of Wongkit. "Only a few persons know of him and we want to keep him secret; we want to bet our money and get good odds. That's why we brought him."

We drove across town. "Where's Wongkit's place?" I asked. "A little farther on," Tom said, and pointed. We walked over the planks, mud oozing up beside them, until we came to a clearing where stood three frame houses, one of them Wongkit's. "He will be in the back," Tom said. We found him there, totally naked. I have never seen such a body. He was tall for a Siamese, almost six feet, and the upper half of his body was a magnificent triangle; then his hips spread, and his legs rippled down in perfect symmetry. At a glance one could see his tremendous strength, his muscles live as young rattan. Wongkit's features looked less like an Oriental's than those of a Greek from the time of Praxiteles. When Tom introduced me, Wongkit put his hands together and crouched, saluting me as royalty. I took one of his hands and shook it. He didn't understand the custom and looked puzzled until Tom explained; then slowly he shook my hand four times, nodding and smiling as he did. In the corner of the room stood an old man with white hair and wrinkled face. Tom introduced me, and the old man bowed and spoke. "He says," Tom interpreted, "that he is Wongkit's father." In the softest and most musical voice I have ever heard, the father bade me welcome.

We sat down and watched the boy at his training. He shadow-boxed, flexed his legs, slashed backward with his elbows, rammed forward with his head; everything he did was poetry of motion. He worked for an hour and we watched. Afterward we drank tea. Then Tom and I went back to our boat. Wongkit, still naked, came with his father to see us off. "What do you think of him?" Tom asked, as we passed through the canals. "I don't know, Tom. I don't know enough about Siamese boxing, but to me he doesn't seem vicious enough." Tom laughed. "That's because he's not fighting against anyone. Wait until he gets in the ring. He will –" Tom flung out one foot and almost lost his balance, he will win us a lot of money.

Yesterday Wongkit and his father asked me about boxing in America. Wongkit wanted to know about the strange world where boxers never lack rice, and have beds to sleep on. "My father," Wongkit said, "approves of my going to America. He will come with me. He will live as I live. He will have rice whenever he wants." This afternoon Wongkit is fighting for the first time. Tom already has gone, vastly excited: he and his friends have bet all their money. I haven't bet any money, but I, too, am excited, for I have come to be fond of Wongkit, so gentle and tender with his father, and I have learned truly to love the old man. The fight is to begin in forty minutes. I must hurry to get to the ringside; I told them I'd sit in the front row. I'll finish this letter later. …

I promised I'd finish this letter and because of my promise I shall. Wongkit went into the ring at ten minutes after four. He wore red tights. They were a little too short for him. After he had prayed, he turned and looked at his father. The old man nodded and held up his hands, gave his blessing to his boy. It was two minutes later that the other fighter, an experienced fighter, kicked Wongkit in the spleen, ruptured it, and killed him. Wongkit fell to the canvas, trembled, and lay still.

Some day, Dad, I may forget Wongkit, for he was a young man, strong, peering over the horizon, his dream bright within him; and he went out in a flash, before he knew. I may forget him, but I'll never, never forget the look of the old father as he stared at that limp thing they carried away in their arms.

Childers, From Siam to Suez (1932), pp. 31-38

The Press

Bangkok possesses three newspapers printed in English, the *Bangkok Times*, *Siam Observer* and *Siam Free Press*. The first two of these are generally supposed to look after British and Siamese interests whilst the third looks after French interests. Each is issued every evening, Sundays and holidays excepted. There are various papers in the vernacular, the Siamese being great readers.[1]

Antonio, Guide (1904), p. 27

Antonio refers to the printing office of "the Rev. S. (Samuel) J. Smith, of the Baptist Mission, a venerable gentleman who has spent no less than 55 years of his life in Siam". It was located on the east bank of the river "after leaving the tramway terminus". This was where Rev. Smith printed his Brief Sketches of Siam *in 1909.*

The Am. missionaries made several unsuccessful attempts to start newspapers. The "Bangkok Recorder" and the "Siam Times" each existed but a short time. The "Siam Daily and Weekly Advertiser" made their appearance in 1868 and were discontinued in 1878. Since then the "Bangkok Times," the "Siam Free Press" and the "Siam Observer" in English and Siamese, each made their successive appearance and are now the popular and flourishing English journals of Siam. The Chino-Siam Warasap is a daily newspaper printed in Chinese and Siamese.

Smith, Brief Sketches (1909), p. 31

Journalism is at present represented in Siam by three daily papers, *The Bangkok Times*, *The Siam Observer* and *The Bangkok Daily Mail*, all printed in English and Siamese, *The Chino-Siamese Daily News* and *The Kew Sing*

---

1 For the press, see also Van Beek: *Bangkok Then and Now* (2008), pp. 66-70.

Daily News, printed in Chinese and Siamese, and *The Nangsue Pim Thai* and the *Siam Rat*, printed daily, in Siamese. Recently there has been an efflorescence of Siamese evening papers, some daily and others weekly, that are sold by newsboys in the streets, at the railway-stations and in the cinema halls. Individually their career is usually brief, as they are, in most instances, run by ex-officials who, having been discharged for malpractices, are naturally against the Government, and utter criticisms of those in high places that bring about their speedy suppression.

Graham, Siam (1924), vol. 1, pp. 303-304

The Bangkok Times, which is the oldest established newspaper in Bangkok, and may be said to have the largest circulation among the European residents, was founded by Mr. T. Lloyd Williamese in January, 1887. It was first published as a small weekly journal containing six pages and thirty columns of printed matter. It met with a considerable share of success from its inauguration, was subsequently converted into a bi-weekly paper, was afterwards published three times a week, and in the early nineties became a daily evening journal. It has been considerably enlarged, and now comprises eight pages, containing forty-eight columns. The editor of the paper is Mr. W. H. Mundie, M.A., and he has two European assistants, Mr. R. Adey Moore and Mr. E. B. Gatenby.

Twentieth Century Impressions of Siam (1908) p. 295

The Bangkok Times, which had the lion and the unicorn over its leader and was British subsidized, edited by a fine old Scotsman called Mundie, was a little paper, but it was in the tradition of *The Times* of London. It was cautious and unemphatic. "Earthquake in Japan," it would declare, "said to be severe." The only subject on which the Times was apt to let itself go was royalty, Siamese royalty. I liked the *Bangkok Times*. It was snobbish, accurate, faithful, and discreet.

Sparrow, The Golden Orchid (1963), p. 47

I liked Siam, and set out to find employment. There were three daily newspapers printed in English. Considering their limited number of readers, none of them appeared to be very prosperous. All three, being edited by Englishmen, were much alike, with advertisements covering the front page. The contents consisted of a ponderous editorial, a dozen cable dispatches so brief that they merely whetted the curiosity, and a column of personal items such as, "We are indebted to the East Asiatic Company for the gift of a very handsome block calendar which now rests upon the editorial desk." Nevertheless, I decided to try them.

I liked most of them. The Englishman is the acme of national conceit and self-sufficiency, and his manners toward foreigners are not the best in the world, but he is absolutely honest and tells you what he thinks. Furthermore, he is always a sportsman, and respects you if you fight back. Considering that the people at home in New York were paying five dollars a seat to hear America criticized by visiting British lecturers, I figured that I received at least a hundred dollars' worth of abuse every evening. But I found no job with the British concerns.

Foster, A Beachcomber in the Orient (1923), pp. 128-130

Louis and Kosol left me in the "office" with a dozen copies of the *Bangkok Daily Mail*. They were staid British sheets with advertisements on the first page. Except for one column of cables, each paper contained a monotonous array of clipped items from six weeks to three months old. They were set up under lifeless headlines like black clay pigeons waiting to be shot. When I had gone through three of them, I realized that my stay in the Land of the White Elephant was not going to be a holiday. The only thing to do was to throw the old paper into the waste basket and begin again. From across the weed patch came the thumping clangor of flat-bed presses. Two half-naked, grimy Chinese squatted on their haunches outside the pressroom smoking cigarettes. A tall Indian watchman with fierce black mustaches sat on a gasoline can and drowsed. If the job was going to be hard, at least it was going to be colorful.

Freeman, Brown Women and White (1932), pp. 58-59

My visit seems to dominate the newspapers here. One newspaper in the Tei language (Siamese) is called the *Daily Mail*, and is a copy of my *Daily Mail*. The papers have been extremely good to me.

Harmsworth, Voyage Round the World (1923), p. 205

"Daily Mail, Gentlemen, Daily Mail"! This is the cry I heard when arriving at Samyek. It was the anniversary of the birth of His Majesty the King; I took the tram with my younger brother to go for a walk at the Royal Palace. During this short journey, I would take pleasure in the contemplation of the lights and ornaments on both sides of the avenue.

"Daily Mail, Daily Mail"! The cry caused me to look toward where it came from. Beside the tramway office, I observed a boy around thirteen years old, repeating for the third time: "Daily Mail".

He wore a jacket close to blue, since the sun and the rain had their effect; however, it was evidently clean. This boy was obviously poor, but he seemed intelligent. His right hand held the newspaper and he incited the travellers to buy it; on his left shoulder was suspended a bag down to his waist that contained around twenty of the same newspaper; all was well organized and very clean. There was something about this boy that charmed me. I called him and bought one of his papers. His voice and accent indicated that he was not from the capital and came from the north. He spoke little, but politely. I gave him a five satang coin for a newspaper that cost only three and I pretended to forget the extra two. "Sir, here are your satangs", he told me; I saw in him a probity that was rare in those of his profession.

I realized that even among newspaper vendors there were good boys. I had heard that certain great men of Europe and the Americas started their lives in this way; I predicted that this one would be, in the future, if not a great man of the Nation, at least a good citizen. In fact, it is not right to look down on who or what they might be, even the poorest and least fortunate. "Walk on fallen trees, if you wish, but never walk on men below you", a Siamese proverb tells us with reason. These reflections caused me to miss the fact that my tram had departed. And I could still hear the voice of the small newspaper vendor: "Daily Mail! Daily Mail! ...".[2]

Puey Ungbhakrana[3]
VIIIème Classe
Echo de L'Assomption, March 1933, pp. 22-23

---

2 Translated from the French by Rebecca Weldon.
3 Puey Ungphakorn MBE (1916-1999) later studied at Thammasat University and the London School of Economics. He became Governor of the Bank of Thailand, then Rector of Thammasat University, but was forced into exile in 1976 and died in England.

I look into the city room. It is a large room flanked by a porch into which a guava tree pushes its branches. There are two tables. At one are the reporters of the Siamese edition of the *Daily Mail*, a morning paper. Sitting on her haunches on a chair is a wizened little woman chewing betel nut. She spits into a yawning, giant cuspidor as she translates a Chinese fairy story into Siamese for the next morning's installment. At the other table is the staff of the English edition banging away on typewriters. The telephone booth, on the door of which is a sign: "Abandon hope all ye who enter here," separates the two staffs. Soh is in the booth yelling in Siamese to the district man that he's a "lousy reporter." The office boy dozes at the copy shoot, a tin can on a rope through a hole in the floor to the composing room below. I go downstairs to make up. Sixteen semi-naked Siamese, Chinese and Indians are setting type by hand. They are illiterate and recognize the letters of the alphabet only as physical objects. The copy they send upstairs must be proofread several times before it is clean. Columns of type are expertly placed in forms and locked up. The big flatbed press starts to moan and bang. Page proofs are pulled for dropped type. I glance over the saucy little sheet with its pictures and piquant headlines:

SIAMESE DANCER MAY BE CAMBODIA'S QUEEN
MEKLONG RAILWAY UNSAFE DECLARES GOVERNMENT
LONE AMERICAN FLIER SPEEDING ACROSS ATLANTIC
ACCOUNTANT CONFESSES EMBEZZLING 30,000 TICALS

"Okay, let 'er go!"

Freeman, Brown Women and White (1932), pp. 106-107

The *Daily Mail*, which had been bought out by Rama VI, had become a drain on the Privy Purse; and in 1927 the king sold it to his father-in-law, Prince Svasti.[4] In 1928 this anglophobe Prince hired as editor an American-Jewish journalist, A. A. Freeman. Technically well-equipped, Freeman was a crusader, who employed tabloid methods. Photography in the Hearst manner was supplemented by sensational revelations of

---

4 This refers to King Prajadhipok.

police corruption and Bangkok prostitution; and an attack on the Paknam Railroad administration brought the paper's circulation up to about 1,200. Freeman antagonized the European colony in Bangkok, particularly *The Bangkok Times* and its public. Svasti, who was pro-American, was delighted. The King was at first amused by the new editor's energy and reforming zeal, but he had to call a halt when the French Legation protested against articles featuring the king of Cambodia's relations with a Siamese dancing girl.

Thompson, Thailand (1941), p. 793

KEW SING DAILY NEWS.
(Organ of the Chinese Overseas.)

No. 1451-1452 YAWARAJ ROAD, BANGKOK, SIAM.

Publishers and General Job Printers. *The Kew Sing Daily News* is the paper that has the largest circulation in Siam and is widely circulated in the Far East. It is therefore the best medium for advertising. The aim of the paper is to serve the public faithfully, publishing accounts of truth and criticising public acts without fear or favour. The only Paper that every Chinese in Siam reads; so if you want to make your goods better known, send your advertisements to us at once. Both Europeans and Chinese advertise in our columns.

For contract or casual rates, please apply to C. S. THAM, Manager.

Siam from Ancient to Present Times (1926), p. XXXVII

Scholarly Pursuits

Foreigners were closely involved with many of the scholarly and cultural institutions founded during the period, including Chulalankarana (Chulalongkorn) University (founded 1917), the Vajiranana National Library and Archaeological Service, the National Museum, the Siam Society (1904), and the Natural History Society (which merged with the Siam Society in 1925).[1] *In many of these institutions, a leading role was taken by Prince Damrong who is revered today as "the Father of Thai History".*

We all took tea at Prince Damrong's House. The three daughters we met had been schooled to entertain his foreign guests. The house was filled with beautiful Chinese and European furniture. Prince Damrong is a connoisseur of Siamese and Chinese art and is the chairman of the trustees of the Bangkok museum. His conversation would do credit to a gentleman of any nation.

Cravath, Notes on the Cruise of the Warrior (1928), pp. 126-127

In accordance with the agreement between the Rockefeller Foundation and the Government of Siam, the Siamese authorities appointed as Director of Studies and Professor of Pathology in the reorganized medical school of Chulalongkorn University (Royal Medical College) at Bangkok, Dr. A. G. Ellis, formerly of Jefferson Medical College, Philadelphia. The Foundation is planning to co-operate with the Siamese in securing the services of five other foreign professors who will, over a short period of years while Siamese personnel is being trained, organize and initiate medical teaching in the school.[2]

Rockefeller Foundation, Annual Report (1923), p. 292

---

1 In addition, the Alliance Française (established 1912) and the Società Dante Alighieri ran cultural programmes.

2 Dr Aller G. (Gustin) Ellis (1868-1953) had held a previous appointment in Bangkok as head of the Pathology Department at Siriraj Hospital (1919-1921); after his return in 1923, he stayed until his retirement in 1938, becoming Dean of the University's Medical Faculty and serving a year (1935-1936) as Rector of the University. He was also active in the Siam Society and briefly President of the Rotary Club.

In the July number of Asia Mr. F. Y. Thompson writes of his work and the students he met: – "One can only wish the Chulalankarana University well, if only in acknowledgment of the spell it casts over all that teach there. It is no small distinction to have witnessed a real King distributing prizes – and to have listened – albeit uncomprehendingly – when a chapter of yellow-robed monks intoned blessings over the heads of the assembled students, to have watched the yellow candles flare before the bright image of the man who gave the University its name, and to have shared the daily life of the university men from the four corners of the globe. The memories one carries away are not those of an orthodox pedagogue. The professor in Siam cannot pride himself on a daily tally of the young brains he has stuffed his information of debatable value. He learns much more than the students. He learns how little it profits a man to have followed the scholiasts from Aristotle to Spengler and to lack the essential sunniness of a people who, although "backward" and as they themselves say lazy, have conquered secrets of life which the Western World would do well to understand."

The Bangkok Times, 20 July 1935, p. 9

Dr Frankfurter writes about the National Library.[3]

In memory of King Mongkut his direct descendants founded, in 1882, the hundredth anniversary of the establishment of Bangkok as the capital of Siam, a library, which was called by the name the King held whilst in the priesthood, the Vajirana. The library was originally conceived as a general one; and as the libraries of King Mongkut and his brother Phra Pin Klao were incorporated with it, the collection of books in foreign literature, especially English, was for that time a valuable one. With regard to Siamese literature an endeavour was made to collect all books published in Siam, and copies were added of some of the valuable and unique MSS. contained in the Royal Scribe Department. Members were admitted by

---

3 Dr Oskar Frankfurter (1852-1922) was the director of the National Library until his dismissal in 1917. He was succeeded by the French scholar George Cœdès (1886-1969).

vote of the committee. They had to pay an annual subscription of twenty ticals, and the friendly intercourse thus established on neutral ground was one of the great benefits derived from that institution.

Twentieth Century Impressions of Siam (1908), pp. 248-251

A reading room in the Vajiravudh Library

At first the library had its place inside the Grand Palace, but as the collection of books and manuscripts grew bigger the demand for more spacious premises became imperative, and in 1917 it was transferred to the building in front of Wat Mahathad. This building now houses the department of Printed Books which is called the Vajiravudh Library in memory of H.M. King Maha Vajiravudh or Rama VI, whose collection of books was, after His demise, handed over to the National Library. The public have free access to the Vajiravudh Library and can make use of several reading-rooms, one of which is specially reserved for the readers of newspapers and magazines, both Siamese and foreign.

Seidenfaden, Guide (1927), pp. 189-190

During the Presidency of His Majesty the present King, the need for book-cases was strongly felt, but as sufficient funds were not available, it was decided to apply to the Abbots of a number of temples for gifts of some of the cupboards lying useless in their charge, and to keep them

in the Library as national property. When the Abbots saw how beautiful their cupboards looked, when carefully cleaned and properly kept, they became more and more willing to part with them for the benefit of the Library, which now possesses over three hundred of these book-cases forming a most interesting and representative collection of this branch of Siamese art.[4]

Cœdès, The Vajirañāna National Library of Siam (1924), p. 14

BANGKOK LIBRARY
Over Falck & Beidek's Godowns
Open daily (Sundays excepted)
From 4 to 6.30 p.m.
Advertisement in The Bangkok Times, April 1909

Neilson Hays Library
Suriwongse Road
Open Daily, 9. to 12.30 and 4.30 to 7 p.m.
Subscriptions: – 1 month, Tcs. 5, with 5/. deposit on each book.
Subscriptions include use of reading-rooms, reference-books, and British and American periodicals.
Apply at the Library or to Mrs. E. E. Groundwater, Hon. Treasurer.
Advertisement in The Bangkok Times, January 1926

Bertha McFarland writes about the Neilson Hays Library...

For over thirty years I have been a member of the committee of women managing the Neilson Hays Library, a private subscription library that has

---

4 See above (The King's Birthday) for Wheatcroft's suggestion that Siamese music had "much analogy with the beautiful designs on the lacquered bookcases in the National Library".

Scholarly Pursuits 333

served the English-speaking community since 1869. There were very few Western women in Thailand in those days, but they were dauntless; they had almost no funds, but they wanted a library. They began with very few volumes – and a name, "Ladies' Library." For twenty-five years Mrs. T. Heyward Hays was the president.[5] For it she organized bazaars and gave the untiring devotion that raised the library to greater efficiency year by year. On her death her husband contributed her whole estate to paying off the few debentures still outstanding, and in erecting a beautiful and commodious library building on the site of the former building. At that time the name was changed to "Neilson Hays Library" in her honour. I became the president of the committee and have continued in that office ever since. Dr. Hays survived his wife by only a few years. He left to the library a very considerable bequest, which made it possible for it to branch out into wider usefulness. We then began employing a library clerk and kept the library open daily for five to six hours. We culled outdated books, added many new ones, started a reference section, bought current magazines. Monthly book lists were ordered from London and New York. Property adjacent to the library was bought and a free library was opened for those unable to pay the annual subscription fee of the main library. The Library Committee was limited to twelve women; all had definite duties to perform, and incidentally read book reviews with avidity. The result was one of the best small libraries of the Far East.

McFarland, Our Garden Was So Fair (1943), pp. 111-113

Books or Magazines after perusal may be "Exchanged" for others of the same price by paying a fee of 20 cents, provided they are in no way damaged, and are returned to him within a week after being purchased. E. M. Pereira & Co. Wholesale & Retail Stationers.

Advertisement in The Bangkok Times, November 1923

To the traveller, inexperienced in Siamese art, the National Museum is a revelation.

Harris, East for Pleasure (1929), p. 77

---

5 Jennie Neilson, Mrs Heyward Hays, died of cholera in 1920.

The Neilson Hays Library, opened 26 June 1922. Architect: Mario Tamagno.

When in 1882 a national exhibition was held to celebrate the hundredth anniversary of Bangkok as the capital of Siam the exhibits then made were collected in the museum, and thus the foundation of the National Museum was laid. The museum was removed in 1890 to an old palace building, which is a good specimen of Siamese architecture, and now contains specimens of the arts, manufactures, household goods, antiquities, and coins of Siam and neighbouring countries, as well as specimens of natural history. The intention exists to collect and make a permanent exhibition of the antiquities scattered throughout the country. The museum is open daily, except on Saturdays and Sundays, from 10 to 5, and the public are admitted in the afternoon from 2 to 5.

Twentieth Century Impressions of Siam (1908), pp. 251-252

The Royal Museum is of great value to the ethnologist and the antiquarian interested in the past of this section of the world. Some of its relics, though badly assorted, are really beyond price. The museum is open to the public free of charge on certain days each week, from 11 a.m. to 5 p.m.

Perkins, Travels (1909), p. 265

The royal museum, Wang Nah, is near the royal palace. It is full to repletion with objects of interest, especially to the ethnologist and to the archaeologist. Some of the treasures are almost beyond price in value, but they are not very well displayed. The galleries are open to the public, free of charge, and the visitors' book is quite interesting, as it contains the signatures of a number of royalties and celebrities. Several of the attendants spoke excellent English and were most courteous in their explanations.

Peck, Travels in the Far East (1909), p. 181

The Economic Museum is situated under the viaduct approaching Phra Buddha Yod Fa Bridge on Bangkok side. The Museum is under the Department of Commerce, Ministry of Agriculture and Commerce and is devoted entirely to the exhibits of Economic Products of Siam. It is open free to the public from 10 to 17 o'clock on week-days except Wednesdays and from 11 to 17 o'clock on Sundays and holidays.

Among the products of Siam exhibited in the Museum are bamboo, basket-work, beans, bulbs, cereals, condiments, cottons, dyes, fibres, firewood, fodder, food, fruits, gums, hides, horns, ivory, lac, lacquer work, medicinal products, minerals, metal works, oils, paper, peas, pottery, rattans, resins, rice, rubber, roofing materials, scented wood, silk, spices, stimulants, tans, timber, tubers, etc. There are many drawings, executed in water colours portraying the various agricultural products of Siam, on exhibit, and in addition to this there is a series of interesting photographs showing the different aspects of modern farming in Siam. Many species of timber are being exhibited in the Economic Museum.

Seidenfaden, Guide (1932), p. 283

'The Economic Museum', from *Siam: General and Medical Features* (1930).

Bertha McFarland recalls her husband's long association with the Siam Society ...

George was a member of the Siam Society, a learned society devoted to research, organized in 1903. For many years it had published a journal containing lectures given at the Society headquarters together with other historical material. This journal is now one of the richest sources of information available on many subjects connected with Siam. In the course of the years the Siam Society absorbed the Natural History Society, the results of its research being included in the Siam Society Journal. These publications were among those constantly consulted during the compiling of the *McFarland Thai-English Dictionary*. In the early years the working members of the Siam Society were all foreigners, but later educated Siamese joined and many articles both in English and Siamese came from their pens. For some years George was a member of the Council of the Siam Society which met monthly. The meetings were lengthy and wordy but wild horses could not have kept him from them. The association met his need for stimulating companionship of like minds.

McFarland, McFarland of Siam (1958), p. 250

THE SIAM SOCIETY
Agriculture, Travel and Transport Section.

The Section is proposing to make a trip to Nakon Pathom on Saturday 18th November to see the Temple and surroundings. Provided a sufficient number of members express their intention of visiting this place, special arrangements will be made for the journey and for meals. Members and their friends wishing to make the trip are requested to send in their names to the undersigned on or before 10th November. E. Wyon Smith, 1774 Sathorn Road, Hon. Secretary of the Section.

The Bangkok Times, 1 November 1923, p. 8

The year 1927 has been one of importance in the history of the Society, and of more than usual activity. On two occasions His Majesty the King, the Patron, with Her Majesty the Queen, honoured the Society by being present at meetings: at one held in June in the Council Room of the Royal Institute under the auspices of the Natural History Section, and at another in December. The latter took place in the Isaravinichaya Hall of the National Museum, and was arranged by the History, Archaeology, Philology and Literature Section. The thanks of the Society are again due to H.R.H. Prince Damrong, the Vice-Patron, for allowing the Society to meet in the Royal Institute.

Journal of the Siam Society, vol. 22 (1928), pp. 59, 62

On his retirement not long after the Revolution of 1932, members of the Siam Society entertained Reginald Le May, a long-standing and active member and a Vice-President, to lunch at the Trocadero Hotel. Le May spoke in reply to a toast to his health.

I very much regret that I shall not be here to see the Society's new home opened, but it is a matter of great satisfaction that it is now nearing completion and I do not think that members present realise the satisfaction they will derive from sitting in the Society's new home in the cool of the evening, with nothing but *padi* fields and an invigorating breezes between them and Paknam. This brings me to my next point, that of membership. Hitherto we have been slow in attracting the young Siamese to our fold. This is chiefly because the whole idea of scientific and artistic research and enjoyment is new to them. But I see signs on all hands that the Siamese are beginning to awaken to the value and need of a scientific and artistic training. Very few Siamese know their country well, but many have naturally local and special knowledge which no European, however gifted, can ever attain. The European, on the other hand, brings a trained mind to the task, and if both are imbued with the true spirit of research and scholarship, then together they can combine with the most fruitful results, if they have a mutual respect for each other.

The Bangkok Times, 28 November 1932, p. 7

The Siam Society's new building, 1933. Architect: Edward Healey of Siam Architects.

The Visual Arts

"His Majesty King Prajadiphok" from *Siam: General and Medical Features* (1930).

Photography is a particular hobby with King Prajadhipok, who, besides directing affairs of State of nearly 12,000,000 people, finds time to operate several American-made, amateur motion-picture cameras with almost professional skill. Every year at its exhibition of paintings and photographs, the Siam Art Club, which enjoys the patronage of the King, usually has a number of entries in superb monochrome and color work produced by one of the King's half-brothers.

Siam is one of the best fields in the world for persons with the hobby of making pictures. The architectural features and the wealth of color in Bangkok's several hundred temples present inexhaustible opportunities for the artist, whatever his medium of expression may be. The many canals teeming with boat traffic and venders of rare tropical fruits, the fields where the country grows rice that places her third among rice-exporting nations, and the northern hills in which the valuable teak trees are cut and then hauled by elephants to streams to be floated to Bangkok, are fascinating subjects for a camera lens. Siam's religious ceremonies, with hundreds of monks in yellow robes, and State processions are many and varied, revealing all the chromatic splendor of rich oriental pageantry.

Geographic News Bulletin (National Geographic Society), 7 May 1934

I think one day an artist will arise and discover Bangkok, and surely he will have pictures to give us not easily found elsewhere. The glittering pagodas and the deep gold and green slope of the double or treble roofs of the wats, their quaintly beautiful gateways opening on to the rank tropical vegetation of the enclosing garden, where a yellow-robed "Phra" gives a note of colour – these form ready-made pictures. But perhaps even the "New Road," that terrible attempt at the "progrit" of the farang (foreigner), may tempt his brush; for here, in a background of little shops, Chinese joss-houses and modern buildings, the most curious specimens of humanity jolt and jostle.

Landon, 'Mid Pleasures and Palaces (1907), pp. 56-57

Advertisement for an exhibition of work by Rachel Wheatcroft from *The Bangkok Times*, August 1925.

A few pictures by local artists, some of merit, others of none, are to be seen on the walls of private houses, and recently the desire for mural decoration has increased, and to supply this want, works, usually of a religious character, have been sent to Europe and lithographed. The crude results of this enterprise are now exposed for sale in the shops of the capital and are hawked about the interior by pedlars. Whether or not they should find a place in a disquisition on Art is doubtful.

Graham, Siam (1924), vol. 2, p. 169

Siam Art Club. Chairman – F. S. Harrop. Committee: – Mrs. R. S. Le May, E. Healey, C. Rigoli, J. J. McBeth.[1] Hon. Sec. and Treas. – Miss M. Ayer.

Bangkok Directory (1925), p. 257

The Siam Art Club is holding its annual exhibition this week, and the quality of the picture exhibited is up to the standard of previous years. The number of Siamese artists is steadily increasing and the riot of colour in buildings and the dress of the people makes Bangkok a paradise for the water colour artist. Their Majesties honoured the exhibition with a visit, and the King spent nearly an hour wandering around with the Queen

---

[1] Carlo Rigoli (1883-1962) had originally come to Bangkok to work with Galileo Chini (1873-1956) and other Italian artists on the decoration of the Throne Hall. In 1925, he was still in the employment of the Fine Arts Department.

commenting on the different pictures, eventually choosing three water colours by Miss Margaret Ayer.[2]

Singapore Free Press, 17 December 1926, p. 3

The members of the Siam Art Club gathered together during the week for a private view of the work of many of the members. The annual exhibition takes place later. There are many Siamese artists of promise including members of the Royal family. The photographic section is always a strong feature of the exhibition, and promises to be exceptionally strong this year.

F. S. Harrop, 'Courtyard, Wat Poh', from *Siam: General and Medical Features* (1930).

The Minister of Commerce has been studying colour photography while in Europe, and several studies in colour of his family are expected to be hung. As is generally known, the King is a most enthusiastic photographer, especially in the realm of cine-photography.

Singapore Free Press, 17 October 1929, p. 7

Photographers

Messrs. Robert Lenz & Co., "Photographers to the Court of Siam," has a most comprehensive collection of photographs both descriptive and characteristic of the people of Siam. This firm also has up-to-date photographs of the Royal family of Siam. The traveler will here find all

---

2 Margaret Ayer (1894-1981) is probably best remembered today as a book illustrator, her work including line drawings in Phyllis Ayer Sower's children's novels *The Lotus Mark* (1935) and *Elephant Boy of the Teak Forest* (1949), and in Margaret Landon's *Anna and the King of Siam* (1944). Her father, Dr Ira Ayer, was an adviser to the Siamese government in the field of public health.

the necessary photographic materials, including plates, films, etc. Also developing done. Address New Road near Royal Palace. Branch Store, New Road near Oriental Hotel.

Mr. J. Antonio, "Charoen Krung Photographic Studio," also has a very extensive collection of views characteristic of Siam's people and scenery, also of the ancient ruins in all parts of Siam.

Two of Antonio's "pictorial post-cards characteristic of Siam". The Editor's Collection.

Here may be found a very elaborate collection of pictorial post-cards characteristic of Siam. Mr. J. Antonio was awarded a silver medal by the St. Louis Exposition in 1904 for the best collection of views of Siam and surrounding country. The traveler will be able to get developing done here.

Perkins, Travels (1909), p. 262

Antonio's premises were taken over by the Japanese photographer Y. Ebata who named his shop "Prom Photo Studio" in honour of his Siamese wife.[3] Wikimedia Commons.

---

3 The shop survives today, though considerably altered, as a stationer's. It formed part of the original Central Department Store, opened in 1950.

ROBT. LENZ & CO.
PHOTOGRAPHERS TO THE COURT OF SIAM.
BY SPECIAL APPOINTMENT.
Studio open from 7 a.m. to 5 pm., Sundays excepted.
TYPES AND VIEWS OF SIAM.
Ansichtspostkarten (Postal Cards with View of Siam.)
TERMS STRICTLY MODERATE.
LARGE STOCK OF FRAME MOULDINGS
ALBUMS WITH INSCRIPTION "SIAM."
From 35. Tcls. to 100 Tcls. each, complete.

Bangkok Directory (1900)[4]

BEFORE GOING ON LEAVE.
You should inspect our collection of
Views & Types of Siam.
Complete albums with 24 different views
According to your own choice TICALS 12 only.
Fine presentation albums made to order.
Moderate prices. Always Novelties.
ROBERT LENZ & CO.,
COURT PHOTOGRAPHERS.

Advertisements in The Bangkok Times, February 1911.[5]

Robt. Lenz & Co.
Photographers to the Court of Siam.
E. Groote, C. Pruss – Partners
O. Pruss – assistant
Mann Cheen – book-keeper.
Som Boon, Ah Lock – collectors.

Bangkok Directory (1914), p. 319.

---

4 Reproduced by Bautze (*Unseen Siam*, p. 292). Bautze calls Robert Lenz (1864-1939) "the most productive and most influential" photographer then working in Bangkok. He sold his business to Emil Groote and Carl Pruss in 1907. They continued the business under the name "R. Lenz & Co.".

5 Lenz advertised "albums of Siam" as "suitable X'mas presents" in 1898.

Photographics. – The British Dispensary, New Road and Seekak, Bangkok, Siam, publish a nicely produced illustrated list of photographic apparatus and sundries. The list contains ninety-six pages, and is equal to any retail list published at home. The use of films is not recommended in the tropics, "the various operations being a source of worry rather than a pleasure," so runs a prefatory note.

The Chemist and Druggist, 30 March 1907, p. 475

Advertisement in *The Bangkok Times*, March 1917.

The Talat Noi Photo Studio, COURT PHOTOGRAPHERS
No. 327/329 New Road, Studio and Work Rooms.
No. 434/436/438 New Road,
Special Electrical Studio and Arms and Ammunition Department.
Orders received and executed at both premises. See our Signboards on both sides of the Road.
Telephone No. 208 Telegrams "Enterprise"
Managing Proprietor – Nai Sut Chamlong.

Advertisement in Seidenfaden, Guide (1927)

Tourists

To the professional tourist and globe-trotter, who goes about with a well-worn Baedeker in his hand and visits all the places marked with a star, Bangkok offers little of interest, for it has no ancient and world-renowned monuments, nor has Baedeker yet reached this remote corner of the earth. And if he had, the stars would certainly be both few and small.
Prince William, In the Lands of the Sun, (1915), pp. 81-82

There are no licensed guides, so it is best to have the hotel management procure for you the services of a reliable native to conduct you about the city. The usual price paid is 292 Ticals per day.
Perkins, Travels (1909), p. 262

The guides in Siam are not very competent, and could give us only ordinary information, so there was little for us to do but to speculate on certain points. We were hampered before reaching this country by the lack of a guide-book (as we had been in Java), Murray's enlightening knowledge having extended only through India, Burma, and Ceylon; but after our arrival in Bangkok we found some local guide-books.[1]
Peck, Travels in the Far East (1909), pp. 189-190

"A. R. M." contributes to the Field of October 4th, an article entitled "Modern Bangkok," from which we take the following: –

"Taken as a whole, Bangkok is not a show place, though there are some fine avenues and vistas in the neighbourhood of the royal palaces. The place is too flat, and its roads are too straight, to be beautiful, though the foliage is luxuriant. There are many fine Buddhist temples, but most of them are partially spoilt by their surroundings; only a few can be admired except at quite close quarters. Still, the visitor to Bangkok, if he goes about it intelligently, can spend a very interesting and instructive week "doing" the town.

---

[1] Peck is presumably referring to Antonio's Guide (1904).

The less said about Bangkok's hotels the better; the accommodation available is quite inadequate for a place of its size and importance. Bangkok has sometimes been called the dirtiest town in Asia - and possibly deserves the title. Of roadways out of Bangkok there are none."[2]

The Bangkok Times, 4 April 1923, p. 6

Mr. Walker, of Messrs. Thomas Cook and Sons, is at present in Bangkok looking over the ground. Bangkok hitherto has been sadly neglected by the tourists, although it is one of the most interesting countries in the East. The life is entirely different to anything else in the East, while days can be profitably spent "doing" the temples and palaces. Siam has a fascination all its own and the attachment of old residents is a wonderful thing, not at first easily understood.

The Straits Times, 17 October 1923, p. 10

What has Siam to offer comparable with other lands? Well, it all depends on what one is seeking. The average modern traveller wants, as a rule, a great deal of comfort, luxurious trains, palatial hotels, perfect cuisine and services, beautiful cars and roads for motoring; and if he does not find all these, he is apt to grumble. Yet, even so, Siam has now reached a reasonably high standard of material comfort, and visitors will find mail trains from Penang smooth-running and well-appointed, and the hotels in Bangkok are as satisfactory as in most other ports in the East.

You will say that I am prejudiced by long association. It may be so, but come and see for yourself and I will guarantee that you will soon fall victim to the charm of the setting, the blending of the colour scheme, and above all to the grace of the buildings themselves.

Le May, Siam as a Tourist Resort (1928), pp. 5-7

The preface to Seidenfaden's Guide (1927, 3rd edit., 1932) is signed by the Administration of Royal State Railways.

A certain amount of courage is needed to bring out a guide book, lest the reader may not be satisfied with the information given therein.

---

2 "A. R. M.": very possibly A. R. Malcolm of the Borneo Company.

From *The American Mercury*, June 1927.

Nevertheless we feel that short and concise information is very much needed for the growing number of tourists who visit the City of Bangkok; hence we have asked Major Erik Seidenfaden, a resident in this country for a long time past and a real lover of Siam and things Siamese, to guide you through the most fascinating City of Palaces and Temples of Oriental splendour in this hitherto little known corner of Asia.

Seidenfaden, Guide (1927)

The Siamese encourage visitors, and have provided ample accommodation for them; also, there is none of that anti-foreign feeling, or red influence, which has gone so far towards wiping China out of the peaceful sightseer's map.

Forty, Bangkok (1929), p. 15

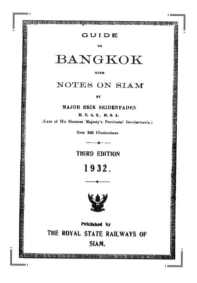

It is a remarkable fact that up till now tourist traffic to Bangkok has not been very important, although I hasten to state that personally I am not sorry for it. However, of late more interest has been shown abroad for Siam and Bangkok, also as a tourist country, and this especially in the United States, and France. Of course, this cannot be avoided, but I truly hope that an influx of tourists will not cause an alteration in the general very sympathetic attitude of the common people towards the unobtrusive sightseer. At present one can go in Bangkok anywhere without in a too shameful manner being overcharged, or bothered by beggars and the like, neither is one troubled by over-officious guides. Even the ricksha coolies are civilized when compared with those of some other places out East.

The Mid-Pacific Magazine, July 1926, p. 137

Advertisement in *The Bangkok Times*, June 1925.

348 In Bangkok

The Passenger & Information Bureau of the Royal State Railways of Siam is a government organization having as its main object the encouragement of tourist traffic to Siam. The Bureau supplies travel information free to all tourists; introduces them to the famous sights, scenes and resorts of Siam; assists them in planning itineraries, securing trustworthy guides or interpreters, and renders them all possible assistance during their sojourn in Siam. Tourists are welcome to call at the Bureau, at the Bangkok Railway Terminus, at any time during office hours:

Week days from 9 to 17 o'clock.
Sundays & Holidays from 12 to 17 o'clock.
Telegrams: "Railbureau, Bangkok".
Telephone: Railway 549.

Seidenfaden, Guide (1932), p. 284

Wherever one sees the name of Royal State Railways of Siam, that means the able and energetic Prince Purachatr of Kumbeng Besjra who is of the royal family. From his offices in the building at the railway head are issued the permits for various pleasures, such as public parts of the Royal Palace and Throne Hall. Bangkok is full of things one wants to see, a constant pageant, and the way to many of them is through the bureau of this able young man. Incidentally it is he who supplies the inspiring photographs of his country that make magazine readers eager to come and see it.

Candee, New Journeys in Old Asia (1927), p. 169

Prince Purachatra, ca. 1920, from *Royal State Railways of Siam. Fiftieth Anniversary* (1947).

Tourists

We were furnished first-rate motor cars and intelligent guides by the Siamese official travel bureau. For five days we devoted ourselves industriously to seeing the sights. Bangkok is at once a surprising and a disappointing city in its lack of picturesqueness that comes with antiquity.
Cravath, Notes on the Cruise of the Warrior (1928), pp. 120-121

We got up early next morning for a trip through the klongs. The Bureau of Tourist Information's handy booklet, This Week in Bangkok, contained a list of Siamese phrases. With this in hand, we were able to hire a motor boat (for one tical per hour) to take us around. We kept the boat for several hours and succeeded quite well in directing it to go where we wanted. Traveling is no fun unless you plunge right into the life of the country and experiment with the language. Smiles, gestures, and drawing pictures will always work.
Rickover, Pepper, Rice, and Elephants (1975), p. 159

To the Editor of "The Bangkok Times."
Dear Sir,
I have always had the impression that tourists were welcomed in a country for the money they spent and, in some cases, for improving contact with the outside world. In Siam, however, the reception given to the tourist by her immigration formalities leads one to infer that a great favour in being conferred upon one in being allowed the privilege of a few days' stay in Siam. Why should there be an Information Bureau and why should Siam be advertised to the tourist? These are questions which I asked myself on entering the country. I would like to emphasize that the Siamese officials I had to deal with were most polite and courteous. I have nothing but the greatest praise for them. It is the laws they were enforcing that I write against.
Yours faithfully, H. C. Lall.
The Bangkok Times, 26 November 1935, p. 5

Hotels

Bangkok is veritably a city of hotels, that is to judge by the number of signboards which meet the eye everywhere, but few of these can be recommended. Bangkok hospitality is proverbial and the "he is a stranger;

Royal State Railways postcard: "Phia Thai Palace for Comfort". The Editor's Collection.

take him in;" maxim is generally found to be in full working order in this city by the Menam. Parenthetically it may be remarked that occasionally the stranger has taken in his host, but that sort of thing generally carries little weight with the latter.

Antonio, Guide (1904), p. 15

Accommodation: *Oriental Hotel*, on the banks of the river, average, not cheap, sends a motor boat to the steamer; *Hotel de l'Europe*, very average; *Bristol Hotel and Restaurant* (German, C. Prüfer), well regarded, clean, reasonable prices, German keg beer, Pens. 6, monthly 150 Ticals; gathering place of German sea-captains. Pension per night 8-12 Ticals (Breakfast 8 o'clock, Tiffin 12, Dinner 7).

Meyers Reisebücher, Weltreise. Part 1, 2nd edit., Leipzig and Vienna (1912), p. 171

The principal hotels in Bangkok are:

The Phya Thai Palace (5 miles from the town).
The Oriental Hotel (centre of the town).
The Trocadero Hotel

The Royal Hotel
The Rajdhani Hotel (at the railway station).
The average charges for inclusive board are Ticals 12.00 (£1 2s. 6d.) per diem.
United Kingdom, Department of Overseas Trade, Report on the Commercial Situation in Siam (1931), p. 7

I was to be Beaumont's guest until I found a suitable mess. It was as well. As he had predicted, there was no one to meet me. In a dilemma, I might have booked in at the "Oriental", the "Grand", or the "Trocadero" whose runners pounced on me with eager outstretched hands. Any one of them would have broken me financially in a couple of weeks. In my ignorance, I might even have attempted Spenser's Hotel which was a low dive where misguided Scandinavian ships' officers would buy ginger ale for Russian girls at champagne prices – a sort of honky tonk where suicides were not unknown. My gratitude to Beaumont knew no bounds.
Exell, Siamese Tapestry (1963), pp. 17-18

We come to the fashionable Phya Thai Palace, one of the biggest and grandest hotels of the Orient, standing in the midst of a park. It is a hotel that offers every kind of comfort; it is new and modern, splendid, but in good taste.[3]
Kornerup, Friendly Siam (1930), p. 240

At the Phai [sic] Tai Palace we found ourselves at the most pretentious hotel we had encountered in the East. One of our rooms had its own swimming pool.
Cravath, Notes on the Cruise of the Warrior (1928), p. 120

The Phya Tai Palace, which had once belonged to the Royal Family, was now a hotel, cool, spacious and reasonably comfortable, although I must admit that I once woke up from my after-lunch siesta to find a majestic procession of red ants making a forced march from one side of the mattress to the other, by way of my stomach.
Coward, Present Indicative (1937), p. 382

---

3 The former palace was formally opened as a hotel in February 1926.

```
┌─────────────────────────────────────────┐
│  PHYA THAI PALACE                       │
│    A CORONATION DINNER AND DANCE        │
│       will be held on the evening of    │
│       Thursday the 25th February.       │
│  Champagne will be Served free during Dinner. │
│       Subscription    Tcs. 10.00        │
│       Booking at the Phya Thai Palace   │
│         Telephone No. 1685-1688 (4 lines) │
│         or at the Railway Information Bureau │
│         Telephone No. 874-5 (2 lines).  │
└─────────────────────────────────────────┘
```

Advertisement in *The Bangkok Times*, February 1926.

Opinions about the Oriental Hotel seem to have changed quite radically over time.

I must admit that, at first, the Siamese capital got a little "on my nerves". The Oriental Hotel, the only one that decent Europeans can use at present, was hardly up to my expectations. Originally, it had been an elegant and well-run house, but was now – under the proprietorship of a penny-pinching coloured lawyer – very run-down, both the building itself and in other ways. Frequently, geckos (a kind of lizard of respectable size) could be found sticking to the walls and ceilings of the rooms. As they are excellent catchers of mosquitoes and flies, they enjoy the right to live there.

Wilda, Reise auf S.M.S. "Möwe" (1903), pp. 275, 279

In comparison with its exorbitant charge, the accommodations are abominable.

Perkins, Travels (1909), p. 261

The proprietor of the Oriental Hotel from 1910 was the Swiss J. A. (Jules Auguste) Maire (1880-1934). After he had been declared "of unsound mind" in 1920, the hotel was managed by his German-born wife Maria Maire, née Faller (1882-1961). This brochure entitled The Fascination of Siam was printed in England about 1922.[4]

This is – without question – the only hotel for the traveller in Bangkok, whether he be on business or pleasure. Every room is fitted with electric light and fans, and specially constructed mosquito rooms can be constructed if requested. The hotel launch meets all boats and trains and the traveller will receive every attention, arriving at the hotel in a few minutes, to find he is in easy distance of the wharfs, railway stations, banks and business quarters. The hotel garage is a recent and most useful

---

4 See *The Bangkok Times*, 18 June 1920, p. 4; 1 July 1920, p. 3.

addition – private cars can be stored and private cars can be hired, at a minute's notice, on application at the office.

Oriental Hotel, The Fascination of Siam (ca 1922), p. 3

THE ORIENTAL HOTEL

Close to all the Banks, the Legations, and Clubs, right in the heart of the business quarter, and at the same time it is quiet and comfortable. 40 large airy comfortable rooms with electric fans and light; each room with private bathroom attached, and all MODERN SANITARY conveniences. Everything under the personal supervision of Mrs. A. J. Maire, special attentions being given to the cuisine.

Siam from Ancient to Present Times (1926), p. 29

Somerset Maugham's first experience of the Oriental Hotel was less than happy …

I felt very unwell, but I was not sure whether my trouble was bodily or spiritual, so to settle the matter I took my temperature. I was startled to see that it was a hundred and five. I went to bed and sent for a doctor. He told me that I had probably got malaria and took some of my blood to test; when he came back it was to say that there was no doubt about it and to give me quinine. One morning I heard the manageress of the hotel, an amiable creature but a good woman of business, in her guttural German voice say to the doctor: "I can't have him die here, you know. You must take him to the hospital." And the doctor replied: "All right. But we'll wait a day or two yet." "Well, don't leave it too long," she replied.

Maugham, The Gentleman in the Parlour (1930), p. 168

Major Foran had a more positive experience of the manageress, the celebrated Mme Maria Maire.

Madame Maire, the genial and charming proprietress, makes a hobby of seeing that her guests are comfortable. In addition, she has lived many years in Bangkok and knows it like a book. Her store of knowledge is always readily placed at the disposal of visitors; and her kindly assistance saved me much time, avoided much waste of effort, and contributed considerably to my enjoyment during my stay in Bangkok.

The Straits Times, 5 March 1925, p. 9

This week Madame Maria Maire has said good-bye to Bangkok. She is striking proof that hard work for a Mem in Bangkok is perhaps the best passport to a healthy life. The unofficial club which met in the bar daily, Sundays excepted, drew its membership almost exclusively from the mercantile houses on Oriental Avenue and Chartered Bank Lane. Madame had a smile and a jest for her regulars, and the hotel prospered. In 1924, Madame being anxious to share her responsibilities, offered to form the business into a limited liability company. But the scheme was not proceeded with, and Madame carried on until she was able to hand over the business to Lt.-Col. Sylow and Mrs Sylow, who are adapting the business to the modern needs of a capital which is rapidly becoming a link in the international travel system.[5]

The Bangkok Times, 31 March 1932, p. 7

Rudolf Bode was a German naval "Captain-Lieutenant (Ret.)" who entered Siam through the Shan States early in 1904 after several years' travel on horseback through central Asia.

Already on the second day, the Oriental Hotel turned out to be rather unpleasant. The mosquito net was torn, the pillows and bed-linen threadbare. The amount of food provided hardly justified the 8-10 ticals a night. On Thursday April the 21st, I was given almost nothing to eat for breakfast, so I resolved to move to the Hotel de l'Europe that very afternoon. This hotel is principally a watering-hole for German ships' captains who, since there is no official closing time, turn up here when all the other hostelries have shut for the night. The resultant hubbub plus hammering on the piano is indescribable. It only ends early in the morning with a mighty brawl, though even that is not enough for the consular authorities to take action to force the place to close at midnight.[6]

Bode, Reise-Erinnerungen an und Erlebnisse in Siam (1906), pp. 82-83, 94

---

5 Carl Valdemar Sylow (1880-1945) had served with the Provincial Gendarmerie in the north until 1926 and had then become Secretary of the United Club in Bangkok.

6 When, in 1904, Bode told some other Germans of his intention of moving to the hotel, they objected that it was "dirty and bad and besides they are Russian Jews" (Reise-Erinnerungen, p. 92). Nevertheless, he found the food rather good. He names the proprietress at the time as "Madame Elianoff".

WANTED

A lady pianist. European or Eurasian for the Astor House, Bangkok.[7] For terms and particulars, apply to the CHIEF STEWARD, S.S. Nuen Tung.

Singapore Free Press, 18 October 1911, p. 3

On arriving in Bangkok, Harry Foster proceeds to the Oriental Hotel where he expects to find Enrico, an Italian poet, to whom he has entrusted his belongings. Enrico, however, is nowhere to be found. Having pawned his camera, Foster finds a cheaper hotel.

My lodging house was a small establishment, which needed a coat of paint, but which was prominently situated upon the main street in the European business district. Its lower floor consisted mostly of a bar whose few bottles were spread across the shelves at wide intervals in an attempt to make a better display. In one corner stood a piano. Its loud pedal was permanently stuck. In the evenings an English lady of broken fortunes would play upon it for the entertainment of the mates or sea-captains who drifted in from the little cargo boats in the river. When my landlady discovered that I also could play the instrument, and that my ragtime found more favor with the seafaring patrons than did the classical pieces performed by the English lady, my credit at the establishment became more secure.

Foster, A Beachcomber in the Orient (1923), pp. 120-122

The Royal Hotel (or Hotel Royal) on Sathorn Road. Left: from Seidenfaden, Guide (1932); right: in its present state, restored as part of the W Hotel (Wikimedia Commons). The "Sathorn Mansion" was originally built as a residence (1888). The building later served as the embassy of the Soviet Union/Russian Federation.

Maurice P. Dunlap stayed at the Royal Hotel on his arrival in Bangkok in 1922.

The Royal Hotel is an institution in Bangkok. At the gate a tall Sikh watchman in uniform salutes each car as it enters. The hotel, I am told, was formerly the palace of some Chinese merchant-prince, built for a bevy of fascinating wives, but he was murdered in one of the rooms (the guests still speculate as to who has the "ghost room") and now an Italian lady – a clever and capable woman – has made such a good hotel out of it that royal permission has allowed her to call it the "Royal" and over the doorway shines a golden Garuda, the fabulous bird which has displaced the elephant as the national Siamese emblem.[8]

American Consular Bulletin, January 1923, p. 4

The airy dining-room is gay, all the tables are taken, and it is not pure chance that makes the place so full, for the Hotel Royal is known to have the very best kitchen in Bangkok.

Kornerup, Friendly Siam (1926), p. 239

Joshua Bartlett Palmer (1882-1961) was President of the Palmer School of Chiropractic.
In our bath room at the Royal Hotel in Bangkok hung a sign "ring the bell, call the coolie and have him empty at once." A bath room consisted of a commode, a box of sawdust, and a large earthen barrel-like tub filled with water. A tin dipper was handy. To take a bath, you splash water over yourself. It is surprising how cooling this was in a hot climate. Pompeii had more sanitation and plumbing, two thousand years ago, than they have here right now. There are open drains in the rooms and hallways. In our bath room were scorpions, centipedes, and one-minute snakes. We had to watch for them, particularly around the seats of the commodes. The Hotel Royal is "out in the woods" sure enough.

Palmer, Round the World (1926), pp. 272, 299

Advertisement in *The Bangkok Times*, July 1935.

7 Proprietor: Adolphe Landau.
8 The Italian lady was Adele Staro, who left Bangkok in 1925.

We entered the Royal Hotel. None but the head-boy, clad in black to distinguish him from the other white-clad boys, would do for Jack. We reached our table and took our seats. The scene in the big dining-room was brilliant. Wealthy Siamese in blue and yellow and scarlet *panungs* and white high-necked tunics dined with their women-folk, lovely creatures with jewels in their jet-black hair and beautiful soft brown eyes and skins. Between their tables were scattered Europeans in the more conventional evening dress. Huge fans droned softly, sending perpetual streams of cool air unobtrusively through the room, Chinese boys, slit-eyed, attentive, moved with the unhurried concentration of cats. From a hidden corner there came the soft strains of a string Hawaiian band. And only a few months gone by I'd been a typist in the employ of Messrs. Stiggins & Stiggins, brokers, of Mincing Lane, London.

Campbell, *The Bangkok Murders (1939), pp. 15-16*

The agent of the Europe Hotel who met us at the station insisted that we go there. The proprietors of this little hotel welcomed us with lugubrious faces, acting as if a major catastrophe had occurred in our lives when they could not give us a room. Diffidently, they suggested that we engage a room at the Rajdhani Hotel and, if the food there was too bad, come and take our meals with them. As it turned out the Rajdhani was one of the nicest places we ever stayed and treated us with such courtesy and personal concern in our welfare that then and there we fell in love with the Siamese. It was a big, well-run hotel, operated by the Royal State Railways of Siam and built above the station. For just eleven ticals they gave us a huge, high-ceilinged room with private bath – of the dimensions of a ballroom – plus five delicious meals, while at the Europe the cheapest

The Hotel Rajdhani opened in 1927 and closed in 1969. The building has been preserved as part of Hualampong Station. From *Royal State Railways of Siam*. Fiftieth Anniversary (1947).

cubbyhole of a room without bath was fourteen ticals. This was a good example of the curious sense of superiority that afflicted Europeans in the Orient. The Europe was owned by Danes, the Rajdhani run by Siamese; hence, it was taken for granted that the former must be better than the latter, and apparently nobody except us took the trouble to investigate the truth of the matter.

Rickover, Pepper, Rice, and Elephants (1975), p. 182

The Pension-Botha was a rooming house in the Sathorn District, run by an enormous Boer-woman, so fat she was chair-bound, and it catered for Indian travelling salesmen and needy Europeans. Socially it was somewhere between a house of joy and a hostel for embarrassed wayfarers.

Thompson, Water-Lily (1952), p. 13

Excursions

From an advertisement for Capstan cigarettes in Seidenfaden, *Guide* (1932), p. XXI.

A great drawback to Bangkok is the fact that there is no place for the jaded European to go to for a few days' change. There are no hill stations up country.

Campbell, Siam in the XXth Century (1902), p. 57

There are several interesting towns which are within a few hours' railway communication with Bangkok, but we could only read of them, as none of them had hotels or even rest houses for the convenience of tourists. This state of things will be remedied as soon as it is realized that the outside world is interested in this far away kingdom, the first tourist party having visited Siam only two years ago.

Peck, Travels in the Far East (1909), p. 189

> EXCURSIONS TRIPS TO CHANTABOON AND KRAT.
> Beautiful Scenery and Splendid Weather.
> The commodious and comfortable passenger Steamer "Krat", Capt. Schmith, leaves every Saturday at noon.
> Price for First Class Ticals 45.
> For particulars etc apply to
> The Siam Steam Navigation Co. Ltd.
> THE EAST ASIATIC COMPANY LTD.
> *Managing Agents.*
> *Advertisement in The Bangkok Times, February 1911*

> Six bungalows now available by the sea-shore at Cha-Am, provided with every comfort, with rooms completely furnished containing 28 beds in all. Charges for accommodation
> Tcs. 1.50 per day.
> EXCELLENT SIAMESE AND EUROPEAN CUISINE.
> Table d'hôte and à la Carte. Moderate Charges.
> *Advertisement in The Bangkok Times, May 1923*

When school closed for the first term on September 10, Angela was strong enough to go with India to Nong Khae.[9] This was a seaside resort five hours by train south of Bangkok, where the Mission had several cottages. India felt sure that salt air and a change would complete the cure. India bought second-class tickets for herself and Angela, third-class tickets for the children and servants. The third-class benches were too crowded and hard for Angela after her illness. There were dozens of frail baskets called *chalom* filled with fruit, boxes, bales, and packages to be

---

9   Now an area of modern Hua Hin.

stacked around them in the train, even a few suitcases. When it was all in, no one could move more than a few inches. The train was a local, stopping at many country stations where the children bargained for rice baked in lengths of bamboo, fruit, and sweetmeats.

Landon, Never Dies the Dream, (1949), pp. 169-170

At Ayudhya, km. 72 of the Northern Line, the old capital, are many fine ruins. More modern tastes are catered for by the Railway Hotel at Hua Hin-on-Sea, km. 212 on the Southern Line. The Hotel, situated close to the sea, is extremely comfortable and the cuisine excellent. The Royal Hua Hin Golf Course, 18 holes, one of the finest courses in the East, is available for visitors at a moderate charge. First class sea bathing is obtainable at all states of the tide. Tennis and billiards are catered for, and some rough shooting is obtainable at nearly all seasons.

Siam: Nature and Industry (1930), p. 279

Hua Hin, the seaside resort, is soon reached. The sea is some ten minutes quiet walk from the station, and situated right on the beach are bungalows which can be rented by applying to the Traffic Superintendent of the Siam State Railways at Bangkok. Here in addition to excellent sea bathing, one may shoot leopards, deer, hares and rabbits.

Oriental Hotel, Fascination of Siam (ca 1922), p. 21

Souvenirs

The legal currency of Siam is the silver Tical, divided in half, quarter and eights, composed of 64 Atts. The Tical January, 1909, is worth about 38 Cents U.S. Currency, or about 13 ticals to $5.00 U.S. Currency, or £1, Sterling.

Perkins, Travels (1909), p. 267

All the days the tourist has allotted for Siam, all the traveller's checks he has allotted for the East might profitably be spent in the Bangkok district of Sam-Peng. Every foreigner in Bangkok becomes a collector. Each house has its vases, its pottery and porcelain, its ivory and bronze, its fabrics, and to each home is thereby given a mystic interest.

Candee, New Journeys in Old Asia (1927), p. 155

"Sellers of Buddha Images in Sampeng" from *Twentieth Century Impressions of Siam* (1908).

There are shops with dried fish; the smoked roes of fishes; dealers in rude wooden-ware, scoops, bowls, plates, spoons, etc.; oil dealers, their casks in rows set into the earthen walls; traders in brass bowls, vases, and basins, also cylindric spittoons, and boxes for the areca, or betel-nut. Mercenary sellers of Buddhas of all dimensions, even smaller than an almond; also covered cups in which to offer tea to Buddha. Weavers' shops with primitive, diminutive looms; women at work, slowly, patiently passing the shuttles back and forth, stopping every moment to avoid either knot or blemish. Sarongs of two and a half metres in length; some with intricate designs throughout the centre in several colors, others with a plain centre of one and a half metres, and at either end ornamented stripes fifty centimetres in breadth, in red, yellow, green, and blue. Makers of red, blue, and green morocco shoes and slippers; candy, confections, mostly fruit pastes or sweetened gums, pink, white, red, pale green, etc.; itinerant pedlers [sic] of sweets suspended in front of them on a tray, carrying a sun-umbrella with bells on its tips to attract attention; others striking a drum held aloft. Flag-makers,

Two Street-Sellers from Lindenberg, *Kurt Nettelbeck* (1903).

362 In Bangkok

the favorite design being the symbolic flag of Siam, with red field, and bearing the white elephant in its centre; some carefully woven in silk, many only printed on fine muslin. Kite-makers, with a score of boy customers on any day; the making of kites their only means of subsistence. High temperature plenty; fan manufacturers plenty.

Sommerville, Siam on the Meinam (1897), pp 37-39

Sommerville with a souvenir.

In the shops of the Sampeng quarter I did not see one single thing to induce me to loosen my purse-strings. I found great difficulty in persuading any shopkeepers to produce specimens for inspection; and still more difficulty getting them to accept what I believed to be a fair price to offer. If I had been in less unpleasant surroundings, perhaps I may have bargained at leisure. Then the story might have ended otherwise.

Foran, Malayan Symphony (1935), p. 122

The law forbids the export of statues of Buddha or other objects belonging to the Buddhist cult without a special license issued by the archaeological service of the Royal Institute. But besides these there are many other highly valuable and interesting things which are well worth getting, such as old Siamese porcelain, nielloware, silverware, silk, carved things of wood or ivory, bronze statuettes, gongs and objects of Chinese manufacture.

Seidenfaden, Guide (1927), p. 131

Perhaps the most interesting of the curios to be obtained in Siam, is the carved ivory. The original ivory is obtained from the wild elephants in the Northern jungles of the country, and then worked in wonderful manner by the people. Siamese silver-work, beautifully carved in designs entirely different from those of any other country, is also well worth obtaining. In addition the silks are of fine quality and many of the brocaded designs are worthy of the notice of the most fastidious.

Oriental Hotel, The Fascination of Siam (ca 1922), p. 7

Should the visitor to Siam desire to make "a deal" by taking animals home he can readily do so by investing in a few gibbon or *wah-wah*, Schomburgk's deer (*cervus Schomburgki*), or binturong. The latter is known as the bear-cat and is a very interesting animal as a household pet. Siamese cats – that is the true variety without a kink in the tail – are now becoming comparatively scarce in and around Bangkok, but readily fetch high prices in Europe. They are somewhat difficult to get home safely, however, as they are prone to die after passing Suez.

Antonio, Guide (1904), p. 80

I haggled over a sepia-coated Siamese cat, which had a quaint and perky expression. The Chinaman who owned this creature would not deal, much to my regret.

Foran, Malayan Symphony (1935), pp. 123-124

Schomburgk's Deer, from Whitney, *Jungle Trails and Jungle People* (1905). The antlers were much collected; it was reported that Lt.-Gen. E. W. Trotter "had probably the largest private collection in Bangkok" (*The Bangkok Times*, 9 October 1935, p. 6). Perhaps inevitably, it became extinct around 1938.

The Aerodrome

Aeroplanes fly over the Throne Hall and the equestrian statue of King Chulalongkorn. A silhouette in *Siam: Nature and Industry* (1930), p. 298.

The Australian government offered a prize of £10,000 for the first all-Australian crew to complete the journey from London to Australia.

Information was received here this morning that Captain Ross Smith and Lieut. Smith, on their great flight to Australia, were to leave Rangoon at 7 o'clock this morning and were due at Don Muang aerodrome at noon. Just before one o'clock the big Vickers-Vimy 'bus was sighted, sailing speedily along, a splendid sight.[1]

The Bangkok Times, 1 December 1919, pp. 4-5

Following downstream, we landed at Don Muang aerodrome, twelve miles north of Bangkok, after a flight that will live long in my memory. Don Muang is the headquarters of the Siamese Flying Corps. They have several hangars, a number of machines, and up-to-date workshops. We were met by the British Consul General, Mr. T. H. Lyle, with whom I had stayed on my previous visit and who now rendered us valuable and appreciated assistance. The Siamese also displayed the warmest hospitality, and the Commandant very kindly placed his own bungalow at our disposal. It was found necessary to regrind the valves on two of the

---

[1] The Smiths reached Darwin on 10 December 1919. Their plane is preserved in Adelaide.

cylinders of the starboard engine. An electric lamp was rigged up over the engine, and all the flying ants and insects in Siam collected around it, which greatly added to the discomfort and hindrance of the work.

Smith, 14,000 Miles Through the Air (1922), pp. 97-98

SEE OUR LATEST FROM WONDER-LAND.
Sensational flights from Don Muang
In wind-proof aviation kit.
But you are not like yourself a bit!
Some "snaps" would surely win a prize
In aerial competition show –
But, come and satisfy your eyes
AT The Talat Noi Photo Studio.

Advertisement in The Bangkok Times, December 1919

Saturday, December 24th, 1921

Yesterday I went with Prince Purachatra to the aerodrome at Don Muang, which has a staff of 650, and 115 aeroplanes mostly French Breguets and Nieuports. They gave me a great display, not only of flying, but of jujitsu and queer Siamese boxing. They fly extremely well. They can make every part of the aeroplane except the motor and the rubber tyres. I wonder how much initiative they would have in organizing an air fight.

Harmsworth, Voyage Round the World (1923), p. 206

DON MUEANG – FLYING OVER BANGKOK – BACK TO DON MUEANG
In Latest Model All-metal Junkers Passenger Airplane. Six Seater.

366 In Bangkok

During 1925 some 85,000 people flew over Europe in Junkers 'Planes without injury or mishap. Flights now take place from Don Mueang Aerodrome from 8 a.m. to 5 p.m. daily. Refreshments may be taken at Don Mueang. There is a convenient service of trains and trams to and from Don Mueang.[2]
PRICE TCS. 24 PER SEAT PER FLIGHT.
For all particulars apply to Windsor & Co.
Advertisement in The Bangkok Times, February, March 1926

Another way of spending Sunday seems to have caught on. The big Junkers plane made six flights yesterday and carried thirty passengers.
The Bangkok Times, 15 March 1926, p. 4

The Dutch air mail is this year again making a series of experimental flights from Amsterdam to Batavia calling at Don Muang, the aerodrome for Bangkok. The service is a fortnightly one and mail is accepted on both outward and homeward trips. The charge for letters to Europe is one Tical for the first 20 grammes. The time taken is about nine days as compared with 23 by railway and steamer.
United Kingdom, Department of Overseas Trade, Report on the Commercial Situation in Siam (1931), p. 22

Tragic disaster befell the Dutch air liner, carrying an exceptionally heavy Christmas mail for Europe. When it attempted to take off for Rangoon from the Don Mueang aerodrome, near Bangkok, early on Sunday morning, the machine failed to rise, plunging its nose into a paddy field and turned upside down. The force of the impact caused the engine to shoot forward, right through the cabin, pinning down those inside. Two passengers, the second pilot and a mechanic were killed on the spot.[3] The

---

2 In fact, passengers were obliged to take a train or tram to Don Mueang there being no road at the time.
3 Among those killed: "M. Charles Baudart, City Engineer at Bangkok". The wireless operator who survived the crash at Don Mueang was killed in a subsequent KLM crash in Iraq in December 1934.

mails have all been recovered, though some of the bags have been damaged, and a plane is to be sent from Batavia on Friday to carry them to Europe.

The Straits Times, 7 December 1931, p. 11

When this aerodrome has been adequately protected from flooding Bangkok will be the great air junction of the East. As it is she boasts three air services a week (British, French and Dutch) to Europe. More or less equidistant from Calcutta, Singapore and Hongkong she forms the essential link between them, and when (as can only be a question of time) the air service is extended via French Indo-China to China itself, Bangkok will hold a key position among the air stations of the world.

Balfour, Grand Tour (1935), p. 271

Bangkok is easily accessible by sea, by land and by air. By air there are, at present, excellent services of the K.L.M., the Imperial Airways, and the Air France.

Kawata, Glimpses of the East (1939), 'Siam', p. 5

What Price Progress?

Bangkok is taking on the motley appearance of an Oriental city turned topsy-turvy by electric lights and trolley cars penetrating quarters of such squalor, one marvels that life can exist there at all. It is a strange, half-floating city, this Bangkok, overrun by pariah dogs and crows; Oriental despite its improvements, and one of the most interesting places in the Far East. Yet a sad city for the visitor with mind apart from "margins" and time saving machinery. At every turning are evidences of the decay of native art, and in their stead commonplace things bearing the legend "Made in Germany." When we behold a people discouraging and losing their splendid ancient arts, and giving instead a ready market to the cheap trash which comes out of the West, we may hardly look for native industrial development.

Whitney, Jungle Trails and Jungle People (1905), p. 39

The first noises to be noticed in the capital were the clang and rattle of electric trams, which, I learned with surprise, were running in Bangkok before they had appeared in the streets of Birmingham. This is typical of the inverse progress of Thailand, where the obvious is always struggling to catch up with the unexpected. Telegraphs preceded railways, and railways preceded roads. In later days, peasants in the more remote provinces who had never seen a railway train or a motor-car were quite accustomed to the sight of 'planes employed on a regular commercial air service! Furthermore, this triumph of modernity caused them no surprise whatever. The reactions of the most primitive jungle villagers to such inventions as the gramophone, the wireless set or the cinema were always the same – pleasure and amusement, but never amazement or curiosity. There was something in their way of living which made such toys superfluous. How often during my time in Thailand was I to wonder if civilisation were worthwhile!

Williams, Green Prison (1941), pp. 13-14

D. R. S. Bourke-Borrowes writes about the role of Bangkok in Siamese society …

The amenities and attractions of Bangkok have had, and still have, rather a bad influence on the Siamese official classes, in that they tempt numbers of the younger men to spend lives of comparative ease in the city rather than to go out and serve under the rougher conditions prevailing outside in the districts.

Journal of the Royal Central Asian Society, vol. 15 (1928), pp. 306, 315-316

What Bangkok says to-day, the rest of the country will say next year! No other country is so dwarfed and dominated by its capital. Bangkok is the brains as well as the backbone of Thailand.

Williams, Green Prison (1941), p. 225

Bangkok is so far in advance – in the Western sense – of the rest of the country that provincial Siamese dream of nothing but going there; and once in the city, they can almost never be persuaded to return home.

Thompson, Thailand (1941), p. 325

At five o'clock on the morning of June 24th, 1932, the revolution began. Machine guns, tanks, and other military equipment raced through the streets to various palaces. H.R.H. Prince of Nagor Svarga was the first to be visited. A half-brother to the king, he was also Minister of the Interior. By one o'clock in the afternoon about forty important persons were held prisoners in the Throne Hall. The following ultimatum was sent to the king: "The People's Party consisting of civil and military officials have now taken over the administration of the country. Their principal aim is to have a constitutional monarchy." A few hours after the coup d'etat a printed leaflet was scattered throughout Bangkok, announcing what had been done and the reasons for doing it. The purpose of the leaflet was to inflame the people and so to guarantee the success of the revolution. Within two days the leaflet was recalled. By the first of July the People's Party announced that King Prajadhipok was favourable to their venture and inflammatory publications and statements were decreased. The first official act of the king was to grant pardon to all of the revolutionists.

On the 27th of June, King Prajadhipok announced his acceptance of a provisional constitution. It provided that the country should be governed by a king, an assembly, a state council, and the law courts. The first meeting of the People's Assembly was held on June 28th, 1932.

On December 7th, 1932, the leaders of the People's Party had an audience with King Prajadhipok, the purpose of which was to ask his pardon formally for any lack of respect accorded him during the excitement of the revolutionary period.

Landon, Thailand in Transition (1939), pp. 9-20

In October 1933, Prince Bovoradej, a former Minister of Defence, launched a counter-coup ...[1]

Bangkok, Jan. 14.

Under the patronage of the Siamese Government cinemas are commencing showing to-day a film entitled "Crushing Bovoradej's Rebellion." The prices of admission have been raised and cinema fans are urged to see with their own eyes "what happened at the front when all Siam was menaced by the recent bloody rebellion" and the unforgettable incidents leading to the victory of the Government troops.

Singapore Free Press, 15 January 1934, p. 1

For the people of Thailand the years between 1932 and 1935 were a time of upheaval and social change. Absolute monarchy under the rule of King Prajadhipok, who later abdicated, was already coming to an end at the start of my first period of work in the Bangkok convent. There was in fact gunfire and shooting on the day I entrained for Chieng Mai. It was another salvo in the several coups which were leading to the formation of a new system of government, a form of democracy after a fashion, a brand-new constitution – and a new set of growing pains for the whole nation.

Lightwood, Teresa of Siam (1960), p. 47

SIAM: THE OVER-WESTERNIZED

---

[1] For Prince Bovoradej's earlier role as High Commissioner in Monthon Payap, see *Enchanted Land*.

Siam is suffering from political indigestion. Always fond of novelty, she has been put by her present rulers on a diet of Western progress and democratic ideals which she is assimilating so rapidly as to preclude sufficient mastication. Hence the body politic has suffered no less than three attacks of "malaise" – bloodless but significant revolutions - within the last three years. It is difficult as yet to gauge whether government by the people will prove as efficient as the former "government by the princes." Many European advisers still remain in Government service, but their numbers and functions are dwindling. Whatever changes the next few months or years may bring forth, no anxiety need be felt for the safety of the European population of Siam. Hospitality to and good treatment of foreigners have ever been the custom of the country. Siam has already attained a civilization which makes it unnecessary that any further steps forward should be taken without due deliberation.

The Sphere, 10 November 1934, p. 22

Looking back on the past I conclude that, all things considered, it was more fun to be living in Siam when I was a young man than it came to be in later days, and in that feeling, which I do not ascribe merely to the fact that I have grown older, I think we may find the measure of the difference between the old and the new Siam. Conditions of life in Siam at that time had about them more of a special, unique flavour of their own. We were comparatively secluded from the rest of the world and what we saw going on around us was for that reason of a more individual nature and more racy of the soil. Romance, in fact, has flown out at the window as modern progress has come in at the door.

Crosby, Siam (1945), pp. 43-45

Bangkok is not an old abode of mankind. Yet it has gathered round its outlines the peculiar atmosphere of things artistic and venerable, which remain notwithstanding the many modern innovations. Notwithstanding electric streetcars, and electric light, waterworks, amongst the finest in the East, modern office buildings and stores, and all the other paraphernalia of a large Westernized city, Bangkok has remained itself.

The Mid-Pacific Magazine, July 1926, p. 135

The Protestant Cemetery

It was not a long drive to the cemetery. At the gate we got out of our machines and went in to walk along the paths, and to put flowers on the graves of such of our countrymen as had come to their long rest in far Siam. There were not many: a few missionaries of the old days; a few travellers and business people who had succumbed to cholera; a few sailors. Especially to an inveterate rover, there is something profoundly moving in the sight of a grave of one who has died far from his home country. These lonely resting places touched me deeply, and I was very glad to have taken my part in this small ceremony of remembrance.

Norden, From Golden Gate to Golden Sun (1923), pp. 131-132

> SACRED TO THE MEMORY OF EDGAR BONDS A.I.M.M.
> AGED 34 YEARS.
> THE DEARLY BELOVED HUSBAND OF
> MARJORIE ERNESTINE BONDS
> OF PLYMOUTH, ENGLAND.
> ACCIDENTALLY DROWNED WHILE BATHING
> AT NONG KHAE, APRIL 7TH 1923.
> REST IN PEACE.
> THIS CROSS WAS ERECTED BY
> HIS FRIENDS AS A TOKEN OF
> THEIR AFFECTION AND ESTEEM.

A distressing fatality occurred at Hua Hin on Saturday afternoon when Mr. Edgar Bonds lost his life. With Dr. and Mrs. Tilika, Mr. Bonds went to Hua Hin on Saturday, and in the afternoon about five o'clock the party went to bathe. With them were Mrs. Griffin and Mr. Harrop. They were not in deep water, when Mrs. Tilika saw a big wave coming and called to the others to look out and hasten ashore proceeding to do the same herself. Mr. Bonds was also out of his depth and, being unable to swim, he tried to keep afloat till Mr. Harrop could get to him. Just as Mr. Harrop was about to reach him, Mr. Bonds fell over and sank. His body was recovered at once and carried on shore. The whole occurrence lasted only a few minutes. Artificial respiration was tried for nearly three hours and everything possible was done for Mr. Bonds but the action of his heart could not be restarted. H.S.H. Prince Valapakorn, Dr. Tilika and Rev. M. B. Palmer did all that they could, and ladies provided hot water bottles, but all was to no avail. The late Mr. Bonds, came out to Bangkok in July last accompanied by his bride whom he married in April. Previous to coming here Mr. Bonds was engaged in mining. The body was brought to Bangkok and the funeral took place this morning at the Protestant Cemetery, Rev. R. J. Hitchcock officiating.[1]

The Bangkok Times, 9 April 1923, p. 7

DEM ANDENKEN MEINER UNVERGESSLICHEN FRAU
WAH SANDRECZKI GEWIDMET CARL SANDRECZKI.[2]
*
CARL SANDRECZKI
GEB. 9 MAI 1847 † JULI 1929

---

1 Bonds is buried in Block G. On 12 December 1923, the British Minister, R. H. Greg, presented F. S. Harrop with a Testimonial of the Royal Humane Society for rescuing Dr Tilika. Bonds' wife remarried in 1927 and lived until 1988.

2 "Dedicated to the Memory of My Wife, Wah Sandreczki, Never to be Forgotten, by Carl Sandreczki". Wah Sandreczki was buried in September 1915.

> SACRED TO THE MEMORY OF MAY (MA LAT)
> THE BELOVED WIFE OF E. W. TROTTER
> DEPUTY COMMISSIONER OF POLICE
> WHO DEPARTED THIS LIFE ON THE
> 3ᴿᴰ DECEMBER 1904
> REQUIESCAT IN PACE.
> Also Little Wallace Trotter
> † 27/IX 1905
> Aged 2 Years

*

> SACRED TO THE MEMORY OF MY BELOVED HUSBAND
> LIEUTENANT GENERAL
> ERNEST WOODBURN TROTTER
> (PHYA VASUDEB)
> SIAMESE GENDARMERIE AND POLICE
> BORN 21 OCTOBER 1871
> DIED 8 OCTOBER 1935

The death has occurred of General Ernest Woodburn Trotter who joined the Bangkok police from Burma in 1901 and was adviser to the police gendarmerie when he was pensioned and continued to live in Bangkok.[3]

Singapore Free Press, 12 October 1935, p. 11

Like a number of other men at the retiring age, Mr. Trotter decided to remain in the country where he had put in the best years of his life and where he felt happiest. He had built himself a residence at Klong Teui then very much less a suburb of Bangkok than now, and here he settled down to follow his hobbies.[4]

The Bangkok Times, 9 October 1935, p. 6

---

3 Trotter was born in India.
4 *The Bangkok Times* obituary makes no special mention of Trotter's wives, but does refer to his daughter Winifred who "married [in 1914] Mr. S. H. Cole, formerly of the Ministry of Justice".

SIAM STONE WORKS

Building stone, sculpture, head stones, monuments, crosses. And stone work of every description. For Specifications apply to the Office, opposite Paknam Railway Station, Hua Lampong.

Advertisement in The Bangkok Times, September 1905

Quarries at Pak Preo, and Hinlap. E. Bock – managing director, E. Brande – secretary and accountant.[5]

Bangkok Directory (1914), p. 342

**Ed. Bock Geb. 21. Januar 1865. Gest. 13 April 1935
RUHE IM FRIEDEN**[6]

The Siam Casket, 117, New Road (opposite Bush Lane)
PROMPT SERVICE
Prices are in accordance with the Protestant Cemetery Committee
List to suit the public taste and pocket.

Advertisement in The Bangkok Times, July 1935

---

5 Eduard Bock, an Austrian, was interned in July 1917, but was able to re-establish himself with an import/export business after the war.
6 "Born 21 January 1865, died 13 April 1935. Rest in Peace."

Going Home

"The South Express leaving Bangkok Station", from *Siam: Nature and Industry* (1930).

MIDNIGHT ON THE MENAM.
The stars have spread
A silver thread
Through the great dome
Above my head;
My soul is led
To thoughts of home.
Reid, Chequered Leaves (1913), p. 235

TO LADIES GOING HOME
Harry A. Badman & Co. ARE MAKING
A Speciality of Ladies' Tailor Made COATS AND SKIRTS
For Landing in or for Steamer Use.
Our new cutter has had extensive experience in high-class work in London, we can therefore guaranteed satisfaction of FIT & STYLE.
A fine blue serge coat, lined with silk, Tcs. 110. A Selection of Patterns sent on Application.

*

ARE YOU GOING HOME?
WHITEAWAY'S HAVE A FINE RANGE OF TRUNKS,
SUIT-CASES AND ALL TRAVELLING GOODS AT MOST
MODERATE PRICES.
THE "TOURIST" CABIN TRUNK.
3 Ply Foundation, covered Green Canvas, Light in Weight, but exceedingly strong.

Advertisement in The Bangkok Times, February 1926

From an advertisement for the Straits Steamship Co. in *The Bangkok Times*, August 1935. A train left Bangkok at 4 p.m. on Saturdays to connect with T.S.S. Kedah leaving Penang at 5 p.m. on Mondays. It was due at Singapore around 1.30 p.m. the following day.

In Frankau's novel, Rosaleen and Derry have very different feelings about going home.

The day of their departure seemed to be upon them before Rosaleen had fully realized that she must uproot herself. It seemed years since the day they had first crossed the mud-bar, with the dim lighthouse on Kaw Chuen facing them beyond the brown and ugly waters. Now she could hardly bear to look at the mangroves, and the white buildings with their flat roofs, the pagoda in the river, and the betel and cocoanut palms, the riverside cottages, the yellowing *padi*, the floating houses on the rafts, the mud-banks, and rice-mills, the lorchas, the steam-launches, the crowded rows of native rice-boats, empty now, and the tall-masted junk-rigged lighters.[1] She saw them all through a mist of tears. What had she not found here? Peace and home at first, love and happiness afterward. What was she going back to, save unrest and doubt? But she did not want him to see her depression; his whole mood was so different.

---

1 Lorcha: small cargo boat.

"I thought we should never get off. Up to the last moment I was afraid something would occur to prevent us starting. It seems too good to be true," he said to her. I'm tired of the palaces, and the pagodas, and all the brown faces. I've been feeling it all these months in Bangkok; at times it's been little but a prison to me."

Frankau, Let the Roof Fall In (1910), pp. 235-236

Llassa Camber reflects on leaving Siam …

As the boat carried her out upon the gulf she gazed across the glassy purple at the island of Koh Si Chang, bulking somberly above the sea-line. In the dusk it resembled a dark mausoleum, and was, to her, symbolical. Behind, buried in the Heavenly-Royal City, was a key to the secret that had drawn her to Asia, but from the old quest had arisen a new purpose, just as a soul rises from the discarded husk.

Hervey, The Black Parrot (1923), p. 93

It will be learnt with regret that the Borneo Company are this afternoon in receipt of a telegram from their Head Office advising the death of Mr. Chester-Master on Wednesday on board the s/s *Ixion*, by which steamer he was travelling home from Singapore. No further details are so far at hand. Mr. John William Chester-Master, who was born on 18th June 1901, arrived in Bangkok for the Borneo Company in July 1922, but on account of continual ill-health was compelled to resign from their service, and left Bangkok at the end of June last. He was suffering from chronic malaria.[2]

Advertisement in *The Bangkok Times*, September 1931.

The Bangkok Times, 8 August 1925, p. 6

---

2 Chester-Master had played for the Bangkok side in the celebrated rugby match against Saigon in October 1923.

Going Home 379

The Borneo Company are this morning in receipt of a further telegram advising that Mr. Chester-Master's death was due to heart failure. He caught a chill on the voyage and had a temperature of 103. He died in his sleep.

The Bangkok Times, 13 August 1925, p. 4

Dusk was already thick over the harbor as they took the launch out to the ship. The lights were on in the cabins. Five or six Siamese students were leaving for Europe, and their relatives and friends were everywhere. The necks of the students were ringed with garlands. India felt a stab of annoyance with herself. She should have ordered a garland for Angela. It would have been the one perfect thing to do. Kurt had filled the cabin with fruit and flowers and books, but India wished that she had thought of the garland. The launch moved away from the ship, which rocked easily on the river swell, with all its lights glittering across the darkness.

Landon, Never Dies the Dream (1949), pp. 302-303

BLUE FUNNEL LINE

	Leaves Singapore	Due Marseilles	Due London
"Agamemnon"	21 August	13 September	19 September

PASSAGE RATES. Bangkok/UK.

"A" Class Steamer – £70 Single, £139 Return
"B" Class Steamer – £63 Single, £111 Return
"C" Class Steamer – £59 Single, £104 Return

A permanent allotment of accommodation is at the disposal of this Agency.

THE BORNEO COMPANY LIMITED, – Agents

Advertisement in The Bangkok Times, 20 August 1935, p. 1

KLM BI-WEEKLY AND ACCELERATED SERVICE.

On the 12th June next the K.L.M. air liner Amsterdam-Batavia will be doubled and at the same time accelerate. Each THURSDAY and SUNDAY at about noon an aeroplane will leave BANGKOK AND ARRIVE AMSTERDAM respectively each MONDAY and THURSDAY with through connections to London, Paris and Hamburg.
FARE BANGKOK-LONDON £140.

Advertisement for K.L.M. in The Bangkok Times, June 1935

Advertisement for Imperial Airways in *The Bangkok Times*, July 1934.

WEEKLY NEWS FOR HOME. THE BANGKOK TIMES WEEKLY MAIL.

This edition is of handy size and contains all the literary matter that has appeared in English in the Bangkok Times for six days previously. The object of the publication is to meet the demand for a cheap, handy and reliable summary of Siam news for residents in Europe, the interior, and elsewhere outside Bangkok. Subscription – per Annum including Postage … Tcs. 30.

2 and 5 Satang Rama VI stamps (1910-1925). The Editor's Collection.

Going Home 381

Sources

Newspapers and Periodicals Most Frequently Quoted in the Text

The Bangkok Times; The Siam Observer; The Bangkok Daily Mail.

The Straits Times; Singapore Free Press.

The London & China Telegraph; The London & China Express.

The Illustrated London News; The Sphere (London).

The Siam Outlook; Woman's Work for Woman; Women and Missions; The Missionary Review of the World.

Collier's The National Weekly; Geographic News Bulletin; Asia and the Americas; The Mid-Pacific Magazine; Travel (New York).

Directories

Bangkok Directory: The Directory for Bangkok and Siam. The Bangkok Times Press (annual).

Commercial Directory for Siam. 4th edit. Bangkok: Department of Commerce 1939.

Single Published Works

António, Joaquím Apolinário: Guide to Bangkok. Revised by W. W. Fegen. Bangkok: Siam Observer Press 1904.

Balfour, Patrick: Grand Tour. Diary of an Eastward Journey. London: John Long 1935.

Bent, George Payne: Tales of Travel, Life and Love. Los Angeles: Times-Mirror Press 1924.

Bartlett, Melissa: Female Medical Missionaries: Using Traditional Roles to Transcend the Status Quo. University of Wisconsin Eau Claire 2009.

Besso, Salvatore: Siam and China, trans. by C. Mathews. London: Simkin, Marshall, Hamilton, Kent 1914.

Blunt, Harry Earle: An American Dentist's Unique Experiences in Foreign Lands. New York: Vantage Press [1963].

Bode, Rudolf: Reise-Erinnerungen an und Erlebnisse in Siam 1904. Vienna, Leipzig: Wiener Verlag 1906.

The Borneo Company Limited: Seventy Years Trade in Bangkok. 1856-1926 [Bangkok 1926].

Bradt, Charles Edwin et al.: Around the World; Studies and Stories of Presbyterian Foreign Missions. Wichita: Mission Press 1912.

Braley, Berton: Pegasus Pulls a Hack. Memoirs of a Modern Minstrel. New York: Minton, Balch 1934.

Bristowe, William Syer: Louis and the King of Siam. London: Chatto & Windus 1976.

Campbell, John Gordon Drummond: Siam in the XXth Century. London: Edward Arnold 1902.

Campbell, Reginald Wilfrid: The Bangkok Murders. London: Cassell 1939.

Campbell, Reginald Wilfrid: The Haunting of Kathleen Saunders. A Novel of the East. London: Cassell 1938.

Candee, Helen Churchill: New Journeys in Old Asia. New York: Frederick A. Stokes 1927.

Carpenter, Frank George: From Bangkok to Bombay. Siam, French

Indo-China, Burma, Hindustan. (Carpenter's World Travels.) New York: Doubleday, Page & Company 1924.

Carter, Arthur Cecil (ed.): The Kingdom of Siam. Ministry of Agriculture. Louisiana Purchase Exposition St. Louis, U.S.A. 1904. Siamese Section. New York, London: G. P. Putnam's Sons 1904.

Cartwright, Basil Osborn: An Elementary Hand-Book of the Siamese Language. Bangkok: Printed at the American Presbyterian Mission Press. Luzac & Co., London 1906.

Childers, James Saxon: From Siam to Suez. New York, London: Appleton 1932.

Cœdès, George: The Vajiranāna National Library of Siam. Bangkok: Bangkok Times Press 1924.

Cravath, Paul Drennan: Notes on the Cruise of the *Warrior* in the Far East [New York 1928].

Coward, Noël: Present Indicative. London: Heinemann 1937.

Crocheron, Bertram Hanford and W. J. Norton: Fruit Markets in Eastern Asia. (University of California, Agricultural Research Station. Bulletin 493.) Berkeley: University of California Printing Office 1930.

Crosby, Sir Josiah: Siam: The Crossroads. London: Hollis & Carter 1945.

Dedication to Prince Damrong of Siam 1947, edit. by Poon Pismai. [Bangkok 1962].

Exell, Frank Kingsley: Siamese Tapestry. London: Hale 1963.

Foran, William Robert: Malayan Symphony. Being the Impressions Gathered During a Six Months' Journey through the Straits Settlements, Federated Malay States, Siam, Sumatra, Java and Bali. London: Hutchinson 1935.

Forty, Charles Heber: Bangkok: Its Life and Sport. London: H. F. & G. Witherby 1929.

Foster, Harry La Tourette: A Beachcomber in the Orient. New York: Dodd, Mead & Co. 1923.

Frankau, Julia [writing as Frank Danby]: Let the Roof Fall In. London: Hutchinson 1910.

Freeman, Andrew Aaron: Brown Women and White. New York: J. Day [1932].

Garstin, Crosbie: The Dragon and the Lotus. London: Heinemann 1928

Gerini, Gerolamo Emilio: Siam and its Productions, Arts, and Manufactures. A Descriptive Catalogue of the Siamese Section at the International Exhibition of Industry and Labour Held in Turin. English edit., revised. Hertford: Stephen Austin and Sons 1912.

Graham, Walter Armstrong: Siam: A Handbook of Practical, Commercial, and Political Information. London: Alexander Moring 1912; 3rd edit. 1924.

Harmsworth, Alfred Charles William, Viscount Northcliffe: My Journey Round the World (16 July 1921-26 Feb. 1922). London: John Lane The Bodley Head 1923.

Harris, Walter Burton: East for Pleasure: The Narrative of Eight Months' Travel in Burma, Siam, the Netherlands East Indies and French Indo-China. London: Arnold 1929.

Heiser, Victor George: An American Doctor's Odyssey. New York: W. W. Norton & Co. 1936.

Hendley, Charles M.: Trifles of Travel. Washington, DC 1924.

Hervey, Harry: The Black Parrot: A Tale of the Golden Chersonese. New York, London: Century 1923.

Kawata, Tomoyuki (ed.): Glimpses of the East. The Principal Ports of the World. (Nippon Yusen Kaisha Official Guide). 21st edit., 1938-1939. Tokyo 1939.

Kirtland, Lucian Swift: Finding the Worthwhile in the Orient. New York: Robert M. McBride 1926.

Kornerup, Ebbe Erland: Friendly Siam, trans. by M. Guiterman. London, New York: G. P. Putnam's Son [1928].

Landon, Kenneth Perry: Thailand in Transition: A Brief Survey of Cultural Trends in the Five Years since the Revolution of 1932. Chicago: University of Chicago Press 1939.

Landon, Margaret Dorothea: Never Dies the Dream. Garden City, NY: Doubleday 1949.

Landon, Mary: 'Mid Pleasures and Palaces. London: Unwin 1907.

Le May, Reginald Stuart: An Asian Arcady: The Land and Peoples of Northern Siam. Cambridge: Heffers 1926.

Le May, Reginald Stuart: Siam as a Tourist Resort [1928].

Lightwood, Teresa: Teresa of Siam. London: Cassell 1960.

Lindenberg, Paul: Kurt Nettelbeck. Abenteuer eines jungen Deutschen in Siam. Berlin: Ferdinand Dümmlers Verlagsbuchhandlung 1903.

Macmillan, Allister: Seaports of the Far East. 2nd edit. London: W. H. & L. Collingridge 1925.

McFarland, Bertha Blount: McFarland of Siam. The Life of George Bradley McFarland M.D., D.D.S., edit. by George McCracken. New York: Vantage Press 1958.

McFarland., George Bradley (ed.) Historical Sketch of Protestant Missions in Siam, 1828-1928. Bangkok: Bangkok Times Press 1928.

McFarland, George Bradley: Reminiscences of Twelve Decades of Service to Siam, 1860-1938. Bangkok: Bangkok Times Press 1936.

MacKirdy, Olive Christian Malvery and W. N. Willis: The White Slave Marke. London: Stanley Paul 1912.

Mahoney, Irene: A Far Country: The Ursulines in Thailand 1924-1945. Bangkok: Udom Suksa 1999.

Maugham, William Somerset: The Gentleman in the Parlour. London: Heinemann 1930.

Miller, Celeste J.: The Newest Way Round the World. New York: Calkins 1908.

Morand, Paul: Nothing but the Earth, trans. by Lewis Galantière. New York: McBride 1927.

Morgan, Ted: Maugham. A Biography. New York: Simon & Schuster 1980.

Norden, Hermann: From Golden Gate to Golden Sun. A Record of Travel, Sport and Observation in Siam and Malaya. London: H. F. & G. Witherby 1923.

Norman, Sir Henry, Bt.: The Peoples and Politics of the Far East. London: Fisher Unwin 1895.

Oriental Hotel (Bangkok): The Fascination of Siam.[ca 1922].

Palmer, Bartlett Joshua: 'Round the World with B. J. Davenport, Iowa 1926.

Parlette, Ralph: A Globegadder's Diary. Chicago: Parlette-Padget Company 1927

Pasqual, Joseph Christopher: A Trip: Through Siam. Penang Gazette Press [1925].

Peck, Mary Ellen Hayes: Travels in the Far East. New York: Crowell 1909.

Perkins, Charlton Bristol: Travels from the Grandeurs of the West to Mysteries of the East, or from Occident to Orient and Around the World. San Francisco 1909.

Powell, Edward Alexander: Where the Strange Trails Go Down. New York: Charles Scribner's Sons 1921.

Reid, Donald Eric: Chequered Leaves from Siam. Bangkok: Bangkok Times Press 1913.

Reid, Donald Eric: Spears of Deliverance. London: Stanley Paul 1920.

Rickover, Ruth Master: Pepper, Rice, and Elephants. A Southeast Asian Journey from Celebes to Siam. Annapolis: Naval Institute Press 1975.

Royal State Railways of Siam. Fiftieth Anniversary. [Bangkok]: Udom Panpipatana 1947.

Sayre, Francis Bowes: Glad Adventure, New York: Macmillan 1957.

Scott, John Hutchinson MacCallum: Eastern Journey. London: Travel Book Club 1939.

Seidenfaden, Erik: Guide to Bangkok with Notes on Siam. Bangkok: Royal State Railways, Passenger and Information Bureau 1927; 3rd edition 1932.

Shriver, Joseph Alexis: Canned-Goods Trade in the Far East. Washington, DC: Department of Commerce and Labor 1915.

Shriver, Joseph Alexis: Pineapple-Canning Industry of the World. Washington, DC: Department of Commerce and Labor 1915.

Siam from Ancient to Present Times. The Souvenir of the Siamese Kingdom Exhibition at Lumbini Park B.E. 2468 [Bangkok 1926].

Siam. Ministry of Commerce and Communications: Siam: General and Medical Features [Bangkok 1930].

Siam. Ministry of Commerce and Communications: Siam: Nature and Industry [Bangkok 1930].

Smith, Samuel J.: Brief Sketches of Siam from 1833 to 1909. Bangkok: Bangkolem Press 1909.

Sommerville, Maxwell: Siam on the Meinam from the Gulf to Ayuthia. Philadelphia, London: Lippincott 1897.

Sparrow, Gerald: The Golden Orchid. London: The Adventurers Club 1963.

Speer, Robert E. et al.: Report of Deputation Sent by the Board of Foreign Missions of the Presbyterian Church in the U.S.A. in the Summer of 1915 to Visit the Missions in Siam and the Philippine Islands. New York 1916.

Thailand. Office of the Prime Minister. Foreign Records of the Bangkok Period up to A.D. 1932. Published on the Occasion of the Rattanakosin Bicentennial. Bangkok 1982.

Thompson, Francis Younghusband: Engagement in Bangkok. London: Jonathan Cape 1951.

Thompson, Francis Younghusband: Water-Lily. London: Jonathan Cape 1952.

Thompson, Peter Anthony: Lotus Land: Being an Account of the Country and People of Southern Siam. London: T. Werner Laurie 1906.

Thompson, Virginia: Thailand the New Siam. New York: Macmillan 1941.

Twentieth Century Impressions of Siam, edit. by Arnold Wright, Oliver T. Breakspear. London, Bangkok: Lloyd's Greater Britain Publishing 1908.

United Kingdom, Department of Overseas Trade: Report on the Commercial Situation in Siam. London: H.M.S.O 1921, 1929, 1931.

United States, Department of Commerce: Commercial Travelers' Guide to the Far East. Washington, DC 1926.

United States, Department of Commerce: Economic Development of Siam. Washington, DC 1929.

Wheatcroft, Rachel: Siam and Cambodia in Pen and Pastel. London: Constable 1928.

Whitney, Caspar William: Jungle Trails and Jungle People: Travel, Adventure and Observation in the Far East. New York: Charles Scribner's Sons 1905.

Wilda, Johannes: Reise auf S.M.S. "*Möwe*". Streifzüge in Südseekolonien und Ostasien. Berlin: Allgemeiner Verein für Deutsche Litteratur 1903.

William, H.R.H. Prince [i.e. Carl Wilhelm Ludvig, Duke of Södermanland]: In the Lands of the Sun: Notes and Memories of a Tour in the East. London: Eveleigh Nash 1915.

Williams, Walter Leigh: Green Prison. London: Herbert Jenkins 1941; rev. 2nd edit.: Jungle Prison. London: Andrew Melrose 1954.

Wood, William Alfred Rae: Land of Smiles. Bangkok: Krungdebarnagar Press 1935.

Wynyard, Noel [i.e. Nancy Everilda Delacherois Davidson]: Durian: A Siamese Interlude. London: Oxford University Press 1939.

Young, Ernest James: From Russia to Siam. Sketches of Travel in Many Lands. London: Max Goschen 1914.

Young, Ernest James: The Kingdom of the Yellow Robe. London: Archibald Constable 1898; 3rd edit. 1907.

Young, Ernest James: Siam. (Peeps at Many Lands.) London: Adam and Charles Black 1908.

Stamp for Harry A. Badman & Co.'s book store on the fly-leaf of a novel by Reginald Campbell published in London in 1930. The Thai text transliterates the name of the store phonetically; the logo is to be read "H A [Bee]". Editor's Collection.

Some Suggestions for Further Reading and Visits

In a sense, the present book follows on from Steve Van Beek's *Bangkok Then and Now*, an anthology of reports published in *The Bangkok Times* in the years 1900-1901. This contains useful background information, illustrations and maps. In 2018, Van Beek published *News From the 90s* covering the previous decade. Chris Burslem's entertaining "scrapbook" *Tales of Old Bangkok* comprises short texts and anecdotes from a much longer period. Excerpts from some of the texts included in the present book were printed in *Foreign Records of the Bangkok Period* (1982), where a useful bibliography can also be found (p. 282). For a more scholarly analysis of western texts about Asia, reference might usefully be made to studies such as Jerry Hopkins' *Romancing the East* or Caron Eastgate Dann's *Imagining Siam*.

Barrett, Kenneth: 22 Walks in Bangkok. Exploring the City's Back Lanes and Byways. North Clarendon, VT; Tokyo; Singapore: Tuttle 2013.

Burslem, Chris: Tales of Old Bangkok. 3rd edit. Hong Kong: Earnshaw 2016.

Bracken, G. Byrne: A Walking Tour of Bangkok. Sketches of the City's Architectural Treasures … Journey through Bangkok's Urban Landscape. Singapore: Marshall Cavendish 2010.

Chakrabongse, Narisa: Exploring Old Bangkok. Royal Palaces – Temples – Streetlife. Bangkok; London: River Books 2020.

Cornwel-Smith, Philip: Very Bangkok. In the City of the Senses. River Books 2020.

Dann, Caron Eastgate: Imagining Siam. A Traveller's Literary Guide to Thailand. Melbourne: Monash University Press 2008.

Davies, Ben: Vanishing Bangkok. The Changing Face of the City. River Books 2020.

Hopkins, Jerry: Romancing the East. A Literary Odyssey from the Heart of Darkness to the River Kwai. North Clarendon, VT; Tokyo; Singapore: Tuttle 2013.

Jablon, Philip: Thailand's Movie Theatres: Relics, Ruins and the Romance of Escape. Bangkok; London: River Books, 2019.

Jefcoate, Graham (ed.): Enchanted Land. Foreign Writings about Chiang Mai in the Early 20th Century. Bangkok; London: River Books 2023.

Kakizaki, Ichiro: Trams, Buses and Rails. The History of Urban Transport in Bangkok, 1886-2010. Chiang Mai: Silkworm Books 2014.

King, Ross: Reading Bangkok. Singapore: NUS Press 2011.

Loos, Tamara: Subject Siam. Family, Law, and Colonial Modernity in Thailand. Chiang Mai: Silkworm Books 2002.

O'Neill, Maryvelma: Bangkok. A Cultural History. Oxford: Oxford University Press 2008.

Saunders, Graham (ed.): Tropical Interludes. European Life and Society in South-East Asia. Kuala Lumpur: Oxford University Press 1998.

Smithies, Michael (ed.): Descriptions of Old Siam. Kuala Lumpur: Oxford University Press 1995.

Sketcher, Louis: Bangkok Shophouses. Bangkok 2022.

Sng, Jeffery and Pimpraphai Bisalputra: A History of the Thai-Chinese. Singapore: Dider Millet 2015.

Suksri, Naengnoi and Narisa Chakrabongse, Thanit Limpabandhu: The Grand Place and Old Bangkok. Bangkok; London: River Books 2014.

Van Beek, Steve: Bangkok Then and Now. 3rd edit. Hong Kong: Wind & Water 2008.

Van Beek, Steve: News From the 90s. Bangkok 1890-1899. Bangkok: Nonart 2018.

Van Roy, Edward: Siamese Melting Pot. Ethnic Minorities in the Making of Bangkok. Singapore: ISEAS Publishing 2017.

Ward, Robin: Exploring Bangkok. An Architectural and Historical Guidebook. Bangkok: Zenn 2014.

Visits

The guide books listed above cover the major historical and architectural sites. We have much enjoyed walks along and around Charoen Krung Road and Yaowarat Road where something of the atmosphere of Chinatown has been kept and a surprising number of historic buildings in various states of (dis)repair can be still found. Among major museums, Museum Siam (Sanam Chai Road) and the King Prajadhipok Museum (Lan Luang Road) are recommended. Both are housed in historic buildings. The former Hotel Royal has been preserved as the "House on Sathorn" at the W Bangkok; the Phya Thai Palace Museum gives a good impression of its former role as a luxury hotel. Among community museums, the Bangkokian Museum (Soi Saphan Yao, Si Phraya, Bangrak), the Yaowarat Chinatown Heritage Center (Wat Traimit), and the Baan Kudichin Museum (Thonburi) are highly recommended. Visits to Christ Church and Assumption Cathedral (both in Bangrak) and to the Protestant Cemetery (Charoen Krung Road, Soi 72) are probably essential, as is a visit to Hualampong Station with its historic trains and small Thailand Railway Museum.

Museum Siam is housed in the former building of the Ministry of Commerce and Communications. Design: Mario Tamagno; construction: 1921-1922. From *Siam: Nature and Industry* (1930), p. 301.

Index[1]

advertising 146, 169, 329
air travel 365-8, 380-1
Ainslie, C. B. 11, 24
Ainslie, G. R. 11, 154
Aiyar, "Dr" K. S. 311-2
American consulate 163-164
American Presbyterian Mission 9, 275, 280-2, 286-8
Americans, British attitudes to 168
Ang Kee Eng, Dr 272-4
Anglo-Swiss Condensed Milk Co. 146
Antonio, J. 30, 67, 342, 345, 382
ants 218-20, 352
Apcar, T. S. 179-80
Arts and Crafts School 23, 268
Assumption Cathedral 277, 388
Assumption College 133, 276-7, 316-7, 327
Astor House Hotel 140, 356
Atkinson, Reginald Douglas 79
Austin Twenty (car) 12
Australia, flight to 365-6
Ayer, Margaret 240-241
Ayudhya, Sri *see* Vajiravudh

B. Grimm & Co. 112-113
B. B. Gaudart & Co. 238
Baan Kudichin Museum 388
Baer, August 297
Balharry, J. R. 90-91
Bangkok Canning Co. 147
Bangkok Christian College 280, 286-8, 292
Bangkok Dock Company 32, 86, 110

Bangkok House Furnishing Co. 178
Bangkok Manufacturing Co. 53-6
Bangkok Nursing Home 224, 298-9
Bangkok Outfitting Co. 181
The Bangkok Times 9, 324-5
Bangkok-Noi (station) 31-2
Bangkokian Museum 136, 388
Bangrak district 17-8, 155, 264, 303, 388
Barland, Agnes 38-39
Beaumont, A. G. 41, 124, 204, 221, 246-7, 352
beer 142, 194-195, 259, 351
Bent, George Payne 26
Besso, Salvatore 244, 382
betel-nut chewing 7, 44, 47, 59, 116, 117, 263, 282, 300, 328, 362
Blue Funnel Line 23, 380
Blunt, Harry Earle 30, 177-8, 223, 298, 301, 282
Bode, Rudolf 355, 382
Bombay Burmah Trading Corporation 27, 110, 190
Bonds, Edgar 373-4
Boon Rawd Brewery Co. 195
Borispah Court (Police Court) 81, 266, 268
Borneo Company Ltd. (BCL) 11, 98-100, 189, 232, 346, 379-80
Bourke-Borrowes, D. R. S. 161
Bovo, Goffredo 85, 206
Bovoradej, Prince 371
Bowring Treaty (1855) 9
"boys" *see* servants
Braley, Berton 7-8, 382

---

1 Please note: anthologised authors are indexed only selectively, focusing on biographical and bibliographical information.

389

Brighouse, Samuel 79
Bristol Hotel 108, 351
Bristowe, William Syer 382
Britain
    journey to Bangkok from 23
    trade with Siam 167
British Club 229-32
British Dispensary 303-7, 309, 344
British Legation 34, 163-7
brothels 254-7
Buddhism 221-2, 275, 282
Buddhist monks 7, 66, 68-9, 82, 116, 148-9, 331, 339
Bulpitt, Charles Edward 89
burglary 212, 266-7

Café Norasingh 140-1
cafés and bars 140-2, 256, 265, 355
Campbell, John Gordon Drummond 46, 382
Campbell, Reginald 158-9, 382
Campbell, Katherine 241
canals *see* klongs
Candee, Helen Churchill 71, 382
Carpenter, Frank G. 74, 382
cars 86-8
    car accidents 88-91
Carter, A. (Arthur) Cecil 9, 58, 383
Cartwright, Basil Osborn 201-2, 383
Catholic Mission
cats 364
celebrations *see* festivals and celebrations
Census (1909) 144
Chakri dynasty 9, 399
Chandler, Lucie 47
Chao Praya river 10, 16-7, 32, 37, 43, 46, 70, 75, 198, 253, 377
Chester-Master, John William 379-80
Childers, James Saxon 70, 321-3, 383
children 49, 73, 74, 90, 118, 121, 124, 148-9, 200, 283-95

Chinese people 10, 125-30
    intermarriage with Siamese 128-9
Chinese quarter *see* Sampeng
Chinese secret societies 130, 272
Chini, Galileo 340
Chino-Siamese Daily News 324
Christ Church 278-9, 388
Christian, Dr Francis 136
Christianity 275-82
Christmas celebrations 197-200, 311
Chulalongkorn, King (Rama V) 8, 59, 85, 152, 331
Chulalongkorn University 33, 283, 330-1
Churchill, A. C. 289, 295
cinemas 227-30, 248-52, 270, 371
climate 14, 33-6
clothing 40-2, 118-20
    colour of 119
clubs 227-38, 256
Cochrane, William McNair 279
cock-fighting 314-5
Cœdès, George 331-3, 383
Cole, Edna S. (Sarah) 150, 292
Colombet, Reverend Émile Auguste 277
Commerce and Communications, Ministry of 25, 385, 388
Convent Boarding School of St. Joseph 276
cooks 63, 125, 159, 176, 178, 192-3, 201, 209, 213
Cort, Mabel 57
coup d'état (1932) 370-1
Cowan, Charles 310-1
Coward, Noel 33-4, 352, 383
Cranmer, C. G. 12
Cravath, Paul Drennan 29, 383
crime 252, 266-74
Crosby, Sir Josiah 38, 78, 167, 372, 383

Decorative initial from Lindenberg's novel *Kurt Nettelbeck* (1903).[2]

Cruiser Fund 245
curries 122-3, 139, 319, 142, 201, 291
Curry, Marian Gilhooly 51
customs duties 30, 169
Customs House 30-1

Dailly, Loulou 236-8
Damrong, Prince 59, 124, 136, 150, 330, 338, 383
dancing 227-8, 233-4
Danby, Frank *see* Frankau, Julia
Davidson, Nancy Everilda Delacherois *see* Wynyard, Noel
De Jesus, F. V. 197
Dean, F. 81
death customs 40, 151-3, 376
  see also funerals
Denmark, commercial links with Siam 101-2, 194
dentistry 30, 300-1
Department of Overseas Trade (United Kingdom) 23, 386

Dering, Sir Herbert 165
Deutsche Klub, Der 106-7, 229
dispensaries (pharmacies) 303-7
Dixie (dancer) 239
dogs 34, 126, 127, 220
  pariah dogs 51, 151, 173, 221-2, 369
Don Mueang aerodrome 365-8
Dorman Long & Co. 399
Douglas, Lucille Sinclair 71
Dr J. Collis Browne's Chlorodyne (patent medicine) 37
Dr Williams' Pink Pills for Pale People (patent medicine) 309-10
drink *see* food and drink
Dunlap, Maurice P. 164, 233, 356
Dunlap Chapel 287
durian (fruit) 24, 147
Dusit Park 85, 140-1, 244-6
Dutch airline disaster (1931) 367-8
Dutch wife (bolster) 218

E. M. Pereira & Co. 57, 122, 180, 215, 334
Eakin, Althea Lyman 173-4, 184-5
Eakin, Reverend John A. 184-5, 286
East Asiatic Co. 23-4, 101-2, 181, 360
Economic Museum 336
Education 283-95
see also schools
Eisenhofer, Emil 113
electric power 149, 154, 163, 177, 216, 258, 278, 353, 366, 369, 372
elephants
  as national symbol 61
  white elephants 60-1
Encyclopædia Britannica 13-5

---

2 The illustrations are by Martin Ränicke (b. 1863) "and others". This depiction of the god Hanuman from the Ramayana epic is presumably by one of the latter.

English language 26, 28-9, 33, 60, 66, 205, 250, 276, 281, 283-6, 289, 293, 324, 331
English people 154, 156, 166, 168, 236, 258
ethnic groups 82, 96, 255-6
Eurasians 130-4, 231
European advisers to government 48, 159-62, 232, 372
European quarter 16-7, 154-5, 303
Europeans intermarriage with Siamese people 231
excursions 359-61
Exell, Frank Kingsley 41, 157, 172-3, 204, 221, 289-90, 316-7, 383
Exhibition of Agriculture and Commerce (1911) 103-4

Falck & Beidek Co. 105, 109-10, 181-3, 333
Fegen, W. W. 10
Feit, Peter *see* Phra Chen Duriyang
Feroci, Corrado (Silpa Bhirasri) 399
festivals 148-50
firearms 30-1, 268, 272, 313-4
"flappers" (girls) 120
Flit insect killer (advertisement) 219
flowers 31, 63, 68-70, 177, 181, 214-6, 380
food and drink 28, 33, 50, 55, 121-3, 145-7
    alcoholic drink 28-9, 50, 157, 194-5, 234, 259-60
    canned foods 146-7
    street food 50, 139-40, 144
    see also specific foods
football 246, 288-9, 316-7
    Rugby football 90-1, 233, 379
Foran, Major W. R. (William Robert) 28, 31, 383
Forty, Lt.-Col. C. H. (Cecil Heber) 40, 264-5, 383
Foster, Harry L. 10, 44, 356, 383

Frankau, Julia ('Frank Danby') 115, 383
Frankfurter, Dr Oskar 331
Fraser & Neave Co. 210
Freeman, Andrew A. (Aaron) 28-9, 176-177, 211-2, 328-9, 383
French Legation 163, 264, 329
Froiman, D. (furniture dealer) 179-80
fruit and vegetables 35, 40, 52, 70, 123, 142, 181, 212, 214, 291
    canned fruit 146-7
funerals 56, 148, 152, 297, 374
furniture and household effects 57, 101, 109, 164, 172, 176-80, 184, 187, 292, 330
Fyshe, Julia Corisande ('Zulu') 197-8

Galt, Annabel 286, 291-2
gambling halls 253, 261-2, 264
Garstin, Crosbie 52, 65, 383
Gerini, Gerolamo Emilio 14, 383
Germany, commercial links with Siam 105-6, 112-3
Gordon, Hilda May 65
Graehlert & Co. 181
Graham, Walter Armstrong 13-6, 161, 383
gramophones and records 179-80, 207, 238, 257, 369
Grand Palace 45, 58-60, 149-51, 332
The Great War (World War I) 109-12
Greg, R. H. 374
Groves, Captain S. P. 269
Grut, William Lennart 102

H. Swee Ho Co. 53, 96
hair 116, 120
    hairdressers 302-3
Hak Kwai Dispensary 312
Hale, A. H. 306-8
Halliburton, Richard 164
Harmsworth, Alfred Charles William,

1st Viscount Northcliffe 62-3, 64-5, 366, 383
Harriet House School for Girls 291-2
Harris, Walter B. (Burton) 74, 383
Harrop, Frederick Samuel 45, 340-1, 373-4
Harry A. Badman & Co. (department store) 14, 181, 184, 386
hat-snatching 270
Haxton, Gerald 254-5
Hays, Dr T. Heyward 304
Hays, Mrs T. *see* Neilson, Jennie
Healey, Edward 100, 268, 338, 340
healthy living 40-2
　see also hygiene, illness and disease
Heiser, Dr Victor G. 62, 217, 383
Hendley, Charles M. 60-1, 383
Hervey, Harry 18, 43, 383-4
Highet, Dr Hugh Campbell 34, 39, 174-5
Hillyard, Reverend Henry J. 165, 278
Hooker, Henry 279
hospitals 39, 296-9
Hotel Royal *see* Royal Hotel
Hotel de l'Europe 351, 355
hotels 50, 199, 256, 346, 350-9
houseboats 72-3
Hua Hin 279, 360-1, 373-4
Hualampong station 31-2, 358, 388
Hunt, George W. P. 271-2
hygiene 37-40, 209, 300-3

ice 53
ice cream 53, 141, 144, 200, 252
Ice Cream Soda Street 144
Iljinsky, Mr. 236-7
illness and disease
　cholera 37-9, 42, 120, 227, 281, 334, 373
　malaria 217, 354, 379
　sunstroke 49, 246
　see also lepers and leprosy
Imperial Airways 368, 381
Indian (South Asian) people 114-5, 116, 118, 134-8, 178, 181, 183, 209, 257, 259, 266, 311-2, 328, 359
Indian watchmen 103, 173, 176, 190, 210, 212, 326, 356
insects 198, 217-9, 366
Irving National Bank 168
Italian people 153, 160, 206-7, 240-1, 340, 356-7
ivory 336, 361, 364

J. Sampson & Son (store) 181
James, Dr Eldon 161
Japanese people 115, 160, 167, 196, 273-4, 293, 302, 316, 342
Jawarad Company Limited 136, 308
Johns, John F. 268-9
Johnson, Jack 249

Karachi Store 183
Kawata, Tomoyuki 17
Kew Sing Daily News 324-5
Khun (pantomime) 242
Kiam Hoa Heng & Co. (store) 181, 184, 198, 302
King Chulalongkorn Memorial Hospital 189, 90, 296
Kirtland, Lucian Swift 148, 384
kissing 31, 300
kite-flying 58, 317-9, 363
K.L.M. (Dutch airline) 367-8, 380
klongs 7, 13, 74-75, 214, 232, 253, 350
Kornerup, Ebbe 49, 384
Kramer, Christian 105, 110, 183
Krung Thep Cinematographic Co. 248

L. G. Riganti & Co. (jewellers) 187-8
Ladies' Musical Society 234, 240

Index　393

*lakhon (*opera ballet) 242
Landau, Adolphe 108, 140, 147, 357
Landau's Restaurant 140
Landon, Kenneth Perry 11, 384
Landon, Margaret Dorothea 11, 33-4, 384
Landon, Mary 66, 384
Le May, Reginald 25, 98, 165, 338, 384
Leang Chai Chaninan Niti 145
legations and consulates 154, 163-9, 265
Lenz, Robert (photographer) 199, 343
Leonowens, Anna 197
Leonowens, Louis T. 197-8
lepers and leprosy 56-7, 311
Lert, Nai 53, 77
Li Wai Fun, Dr 299
libraries 150, 229, 287, 331-4
Lightwood, Ada (Teresa) 35, 48, 203, 371, 384
Lindenberg, Paul 105-7, 384
lizards 220-1
Longway, Reverend E. L. 266
Louis T. Leonowens Ltd. (L.T.L.) 198
Luang Chit Chamnong *see* Tom Yah
Lyle, T. H. 165, 365

M. T. S. Marican Co. 134-5
Macmillan, Allister 16, 52, 384
Maire, Auguste Jules 353
Maire, Marie 353-5
Malay people 114-6, 178, 196, 231, 307, 315-6
Marican, Moona Thabisauboo 134-5
Marie de Lourdes, Sister 49, 285
Masao, Tokichi 160
massages 254-5, 302-3
Massang, P. N. 309-10
Maugham, W. Somerset 16, 36, 254-5, 354, 384

McBeth, J. J. 223, 304-306, 340
McClure, Mrs W. G. 158
McFarland, Bertha 174-5, 240, 333-4, 384
McFarland, Ed 204
McFarland, George 79, 204-5, 300-1, 337, 384
McFarland Typewriter Co. 204-5
Meehan, Florence Burgess 250
Menam River *see* Chao Phraya river
Menard, Wilmon 255
menus 63, 142-3, 209-10
mias 206-8
Miller, Celeste J. 45, 384
missions 275-82
mixed-race people *see* Eurasians
Mongkut, King (Rama IV) 166, 278, 331
Morand, Paul 46, 384
mosquitoes 127, 159, 177, 179-80, 198, 211, 217, 218-9, 221, 234, 285, 292, 306, 353, 355
motorcycles 89, 109
Mundie, W. H. 325
Museum Siam 388
museums 59, 335-6, 388
music 126, 150-1, 229, 233-4, 238-41, 333

Nagor Svarga, Prince of 370
Nana, A. E. 136-7
names 117
Nangsue Pim Thai (newspaper) 325
National Library 59, 330-3
National Museum 59, 330, 334-6
Neilson Hays Library 333-4
Neilson, Jennie 334
New Road (Charoen Krung) 7-8, 18, 38, 88, 95-7, 307, 340
Newlands, Miss J. M. 303
newspapers 9, 324-9, 332

night life 227-9
Nong Khae (Hua Hin) 360-1
Norddeutscher Lloyd Orient line 26, 107, 109
Norden, Hermann 60, 143, 257-8, 384
Norman, Sir Henry 47, 384
Norwood, Reverend C. W. 279-80

Omoda, R. 302
opium dens 258-9
opticians 306, 308
Oriental Bakery 197
Oriental Hotel 65, 102, 142, 351, 353-5, 364, 384
Oriental Stores 101

Pallegroix, Bishop Jean-Baptiste 276
Palmer, B. J. 357, 384
Palmer, Robert 49
panung (garment) 59, 64, 76, 82, 116, 118-9, 129, 149, 211, 263
Parlette, Ralph 309, 384
pasin (garment) 132, 149, 293
Pasqual, J. C. 32-3, 384
Patriotic League of Britons Overseas 110
Paul Pickenpack & Co. 113
pawnshops 262-4
Peck, Mary Ellen Hayes 214, 385
Pedang Besar 28
Penang 23-4, 27, 32-3, 57, 93, 136, 237-8, 239, 241, 309, 346, 378
Peninsula and Oriental Line (P&O) 23-4
People's Party 370-1
Pereira & Co. (auctioneer) *see* E. M. Pereira
Periera, Benjamin A. (auctioneer) 57, 110
Perkins, Charlton B. (Bristol) 43, 163, 385

Perros, Bishop René-Marie Joseph 203, 277, 284-5
Pestonji, D. A. 137
pharmacies *see* dispensaries
Phathanakorn Cinematograph 250-1
photographers and photography 115, 126-7, 199, 304, 328-9
Phra Chen Duriyang 239-40
Phra Meru Ground *see* Pramane/Premane Ground
Phya Anudhutvadhi 147
Phya Thai Palace Hotel 137-8, 227, 279, 351-3, 388
pineapples 146-7
Plion-Bernier, Raymond Clément 264
Poix, Dr Alphonse 297, 311
police force 130, 160, 210, 236-8, 258-9, 262, 264, 266-70, 273-4, 311-2, 317, 375
The Popular Café 142
population of Bangkok 114-5
  Westerners 114, 154-5
  see also ethnic groups
polygamy 206
postal service 92-4
Powell, E. (Edward) 47-8, 385
Pradumaganga School 289-90, 295
Prajadhipok, King (Rama VII) 8, 11, 328, 339, 370-1, 388
Pramane/Premane Ground (Sanam Luang) 58-9, 84, 318-9
Pratt, Reverend Forrest A. 266, 282
Presbyterian High School 286
Price, Hamilton 110
prisons 271-2
prostitution 254-7
Protestant Cemetery 56-7, 108, 279, 297, 298, 373-6, 388
Prüfer, C. 108, 351
Purachatra, Prince 25, 100, 349, 366

Index 395

rabam (dance) 242
raga-raga (shuttle-ball) 271, 316
Rajini School 293-4
Redfield, Alfred C. 298-9
refrigerators 54-5
Reid, Donald Eric 37-8, 230-1, 385
Remington Co. 205
restaurants 64, 139-44, 199, 253
rice 39, 49, 116, 121-3, 133, 139, 145, 169, 206, 220, 233, 280, 291, 322, 339, 361
    rice-milling 12, 47, 73, 98, 145, 147, 378
    rice-planting ceremony 153
Rickover, Ruth 200, 385
rickshaws 7-8, 33, 36, 49-50, 77, 79, 82, 87, 95, 149, 202, 258, 268, 348
Rigoli, Carlo 340
river traffic 72-4
Robert Lenz & Co. *see* Lenz, Robert
Room of the Moon restaurant 143
Rosenberg, "Max" 108
Royal Bangkok Sports Club 62, 89, 91, 111, 227-8, 230-5, 248, 316-7
Royal Hotel 352, 356-8
Royal Institute 59, 337-8, 363
Royal Japanese Cinematograph 248
Royal Ministry of Entertainments 140, 244
Royal Orchestra 239-40
Royal Palace *see* Grand Palace
Royal State Railways 27-8, 72, 83, 159-60, 180, 302, 346-7, 349, 351, 358, 361
    Information Bureau 349, 385
Royal Theatre 240, 242, 246
Rüdt von Collenberg-Bödigheim, Heinrich 107
Russian prostitutes 232, 255-7, 352

S. A. B. *see* Société Anonyme Belge
St Andrew's Society 235-6, 279
St Louis General Hospital 297, 311
St Mary's Mission 59, 173, 275, 280
St Peter's School 280, 286, 288
Sampeng district 17-8, 47, 125-7, 255, 260-2, 314, 362-3
Sanam Luang *see* Pramane/Premane Ground
Santa Cruz Church 134
Saovabha Institute (The Snake Farm) 224-6
Saovabha Phonsri, Queen 293
Sandreczki, Carl 374
Sanuks, The 248
Sathorn district 155, 175, 356, 388
Sayre, Francis B. (Bowes) 34, 385
schools 14, 41, 47, 260, 275-6, 280, 282, 283-95
    discipline in 294
Scott, John H. M. 44, 385
Scottish people 235-6
Seidenfaden, Erik 24, 346-7, 385
servants 113, 117, 157, 159, 176, 190, 192, 209-13, 217, 222
Seventh Day Adventist Mission 266, 275, 282
Siam Art Club 339-41
Siam Electricity Co. 24, 35, 37, 55, 80-1, 92, 100, 102-4, 249
Siam Free Press 324
Siam Observer 37, 42, 56, 169, 180, 236-8, 324
Siam Pineapple Factory 146-7
Siam Rat (newspaper) 325
Siam Society 330, 337-8
Siamese language 201-4
Siamese people 114-25
    facial characteristics of 116-7
    manners and politeness 123-5
Signboards Act (1939) 130
Silom district 17-8, 176
Simmons, Reverend C. R. 278-9

Singapore Free Press 133, 218
Smart, Leslie S. 235
Smith, C. Wilson 67
Smith, Captain Ross 365-6
Smith, E. Wyon 337
Smith, Reverend S. (Samuel J.) 324
Smith Premier Typewriters 205
smoking 120-1
  opium smoking 238-9
snakes 201, 219, 223-4
  see also Saovabha Institute (The Snake Farm)
Société Anonyme Belge (S.A.B.) 110, 189-9, 215
Society for the Propagation of the Gospel (S.P.G.) 56-7, 275, 279-80
Sommerville, Maxwell 8, 152, 217, 363, 385
souvenirs and souvenir shops 272, 361-4
Spaeth, Dr Reynold A. 288-99
Speer, Robert 282, 385
Srijamon, Dr Porn 295
Staro, Adele 357
Steele, Clarence A. 281
stengah (drink) 28, 55
Stiven, A. E. 145, 232
student interpreters 107, 165-6, 264
Suan Kularb College 289, 295, 317
Sun Yat Sen 128
Sutton and Sons (The Royal Seed Establishment) 215
Sutton, Norman 282
Sykora, Bogumil 241

Tagore, Rabindranath 136-8
Talaat Plu market 181, 258
Talat Noi Photographic Studio 198, 277, 344, 366
Tamagno, Mario 32, 335, 388
Tate, Josephine Albert 251

tattoos 117-8
taxis 33, 51, 87
teeth 7, 116, 211, 300-1
telephone service 36, 93
temples *see* wats
Teresa, Sister *see* Lightwood, Ada
theatre 64-5, 141, 167, 242-8, 252
Thomas Cook & Sons 346-7
Thompson, Benita Eugénie (née Aria) 115
Thompson, Francis Younghusband 33, 331, 385
Thompson, Harry Alec 115
Thompson, P. A. (Peter Anthony) 25, 385
Thompson, Virginia 259, 385
Thonburi 31, 70, 34, 295, 388
tical (currency) 49, 361
Tilika, Dr 373-4
Tillleke, William Alfred Goone 79, 81
Tisseman & Co. 181
Tom Yah 145, 147
top-knot cutting ceremony 148-9
topees 40-1, 159
tourism and tourists 25, 183, 242, 345-64
tourist guides 345-8, 360-1, 367, 382, 385
trains 23, 27-9, 32, 44, 83, 107-8, 313, 346, 369, 388
trams 7, 16, 37, 51, 77, 80-3, 85, 94, 224, 367, 369
transport
  regulation of 76, 78, 87-8
  see also cars, rickshaws, taxis, trams, etc.
trees 14, 16-7, 36, 59, 67, 70, 76, 84-5, 170, 177, 214-6
Trocadero Hotel 264, 338, 351-2
Twentieth Century Impressions of Siam (1908) 34, 386
typewriters 166, 204-5

Index 397

Ungphakorn, Puey 327
United Club 38, 355, 229-30
United States
    commercial links with Siam 86, 168-9
    cultural influence on Siam 48, 251

Vajiravudh, King (Rama VI) 8, 62, 64-5, 150, 246, 322
    image on postage stamps 381
Vajiravudh College 317
van Cuylenberg, W. E. M. 56
van Cuylenberg, Mrs 56-7
vegetables *see* fruit and vegetables

Wales, H. G. Q. 317
Wat Arun 45, 70-1
Wat Benchamabophit 87
Wat Po 67, 70, 341
Wat Pra Keo 70
Wat Sutat 68
Watanabe, F. 316
watches 187-8
water supply 29
water-hyacinths 75
wats 51, 66-71, 283
    see also individual wats
Watson, C. L. (Cecil Lilliott) 40, 89, 238
Wattana Wittaya Academy 206, 292
Weber, W. 107-8
Wells, Kenneth 287
western powers, extra-territorial rights of 15, 107
Wheatcroft, Rachel 59, 150, 333, 340, 386
Willis organ 278
Whiteaway Laidlaw & Co. (department store) 41, 96, 185-7, 306, 378
Whitney, Caspar William 122, 386
Wild Tiger movement 64

Wilda, Johannes 37, 386
William, Prince (Carl Wilhelm Ludwig), Duke of Södermanland 62, 386
Williamese, T. Lloyd 325
Williams, Walter Leigh 16, 27, 386
Windsor, Louis 133-5
Windsor & Co. 105, 367
women 47, 72-3, 117, 119, 120-3, 128, 206-8, 211, 249-50, 255-7, 362
Wongkit (boxer) 321-3
Wood, W. A. R. 38, 386
World War I *see* The Great War
Worts, George F. 177
Wynyard, Noel 16, 24, 386

Yambo (dancer) 239
Yaowarat Chinatown Heritage Center 388
Young, Ernest James 69, 386

Zimmerman, Walter A. 200
Zobel, Karl 107, 112

The opening of the Memorial Bridge across the Chao Phra by King Prajadhipok on 6 April 1932 was the last grand ceremony to be held before the People's Party's coup in June that year. The construction by Dorman Long & Co., Middlesborough, had begun in 1929. At the time, it was the world's longest bascule bridge (lifting- or drawbridge). The company also built the Sydney Harbour Bridge (1932). The Memorial Bridge commemorated the 150th anniversary of the founding of the Chakri dynasty and of Bangkok. The colossal statue of King Rama I at the approach to the bridge was by Corrado Feroci (Silpa Bhirasri, 1892-1962), the Italian sculptor and educator, who had arrived in Siam in 1924. It had been cast in Milan. Wikipedia Commons.

Siam Electricity Company, Bangkok map with tramways, ca 1920.